Book Depository 07-20
£23-

CW01494755

SPECIMEN OF BUSHMAN ART.

Exact copy of a picture on the side of a cave on the farm of J. P. Versfeld, Esq., Mouton 'sValley, Piketberg, Cape Colony.

The rock on which the picture is painted is of a d[illegible] [illegible]e; and the figures are coloured exac[illegible]

HISTORY

OF

SOUTH AFRICA

[1691—1795]

BY

GEORGE McCALL THEAL

OF THE COLONIAL CIVIL SERVICE
MEMBER OF THE MAATSCHAPPIJ DER NEDERLANDSCHE LETTERKUNDE TE LEIDEN
MEMBRE CORRESPONDANT DE LA COMMISSION POUR L'HISTOIRE DES ÉGLISES WALLONNES
FORMERLY KEEPER OF THE ARCHIVES OF THE CAPE COLONY

WITH TWO CHARTS

LONDON
SWAN SONNENSCHEIN & CO.
PATERNOSTER SQUARE
1888

PREFACE.

The contents of this volume have been drawn chiefly from the official records of the Dutch East India Company's administration, though the published works of authors of the time have also been consulted. The manuscript records are so voluminous that an ordinary life-time would be too short to read all those relating to the period 1691 to 1795. I cannot profess to have examined them all; but I have carefully gone through the most important of them, and I can venture to assert that, although it will be easy for any author of the future greatly to enlarge upon what I have written, the general tenor of events as recorded in this volume must remain undisturbed.

The time expended by me in gathering from original and hitherto unused sources the materials for this period of our history, if condensed, would amount to at least two years of ten hours a day. The debates and resolutions of the council of policy, the outgoing and incoming despatches, the correspondence with district officials, the journal of important events, reports of commissioners, and diaries of exploring parties have been thoroughly examined. To get a list of shipping alone, I was obliged to read every word of the journal and to make a note of each vessel that arrived.

The church books, proceedings of the high court of justice, declarations, instructions, land grants, district records, and multifarious other documents have been examined, but not so minutely as the more important volumes. Native traditions collected by me in years long gone by have been made use of in chapter XXIII. A list of the printed books consulted will be found at the end of this volume.

I have taken up much space with statistics, which to many people will prove uninteresting. My object has not been to write a pleasant book, but to place before the reader reliable information upon a period of South African history of which little or nothing has previously been known. For this reason I have entered somewhat fully into the public revenue and expenditure, the record of good and bad seasons, the prices of produce at various times, the quantity of grain exported, the number of foreign as compared with Dutch ships that called, and other subjects of a statistical nature.

Money has been reduced to English coinage at the rate of twelve gulden of Holland to the pound sterling, the present rate of exchange. The rixdollar of the records has been computed at 50*d.* before 1770 and at 48*d.* after that date; the Cape gulden at 1/4 and 1/4⅔, according to circumstances. Explanations will be found in the body of the work. Weights have been reduced to English pounds, at the rate of 918 Amsterdam pounds to 1000 pounds avoirdupois. The muid of grain, as used in the records and in this book, weighs 190⅜ pounds avoirdupois. The legger of wine contains 4 aams or 126$\frac{1}{10}$ Imperial gallons. The morgen of ground is equal to rather more than 2$\frac{1}{10}$ English acres. The muid, legger, and morgen, being still in use in South Africa, I have retained, but Dutch money and weights having been replaced by English, I have reduced these to the terms now generally employed.

In the statistics of shipping I have not included vessels employed as coasters or packets kept for the use of the Cape government.

Where the number of those who show an interest in the publication of a book is as large as has been the case in this instance, it is difficult for an author to express his thanks except in general terms. I shall only say that if the members of the Ministry of the Cape Colony had not placed in my way special facilities for research in the colonial archives, this book could not have been written at all; and therefore an acknowledgment of thanks is due to them. To the daughters of the late Advocate De Wet I am deeply indebted for placing at my service a large quantity of ancient documents collected by their venerable father, whose death was a loss to South Africa, inasmuch as it prevented the completion of the historical work to which he had devoted a large portion of his life. From the Rev. Mr. Leibbrandt, Keeper of the Colonial Archives, I have received all the assistance that it was in his power to give, and through his courtesy I have been spared much labour that otherwise I must have undertaken.

While this volume has been in preparation, an esteemed friend and fellow-worker in historical research—the late Mr. Christoffel Coetsee de Villiers—has been removed from South Africa by death. For the preceding six years his time had been devoted to preparing a history of the oldest colonial families, and he had made exhaustive researches in the registry of deeds, baptismal and marriage registers, wills, family records preserved in bibles, and other documents. His notes and memoranda cover many hundred sheets, and he was about to arrange them for publication when he was suddenly taken ill. By his desire, after his death these papers were confided to my care, and I have no doubt that from them more complete lists of family names than are given in this volume might be prepared. But under the circumstances, I do not feel at liberty to use them. I have some hope, with the assistance of others interested in the work, of being able to arrange them for publication, though my time out of office hours must be chiefly occupied with a continuation of the history now in the reader's hands, for which a large amount of material is in readiness.

GEO. M. THEAL.

CAPE TOWN.

CONTENTS.

CHAPTER XVI.

SIMON VAN DER STEL, PROMOTED FROM COMMANDER TO GOVERNOR OF THE CAPE COLONY, 1 JUNE 1691; HELD OFFICE UNTIL 11 FEBRUARY 1699.

CHAPTER XVII.

WILHEM ADRIAAN VAN DER STEL, GOVERNOR, INSTALLED 11 FEBRUARY 1699; HELD OFFICE UNTIL 3 JUNE 1707.

PAGE

in the church at Drakenstein—Proceedings of a marauding party—Wreck of the *Meresteyn*—Expedition to Natal—An English resident at Natal—Fruitless efforts of the directors and the Cape government to make South Africa a wool-producing country—Experiment in silk culture—Placing of partridges and pheasants on Robben Island—Long drought—Increase of population—Want of sympathy between the government and the colonists—Extensive farming operations by the governor and other officials—Complaints of the colonists to the supreme authorities—Violent action of the governor—Arrest of various burghers and their committal to prison—Banishment of a burgher to Batavia and of four others to Europe—Defiance of the government by the country people—Action of the directors in the Netherlands—Recall of the governor and other officials—Arrival of the newly appointed secunde Johan Cornelis d'Ableing and transfer of the administration to him—Views of the colonists and of the directors as to the rights of burghers 16

CHAPTER XVIII.

JOHAN CORNELIS D'ABLEING, SECUNDE, ACTING HEAD OF THE GOVERNMENT, 3 JUNE 1707 TO 1 FEBRUARY 1708.

LOUIS VAN ASSENBURGH, GOVERNOR, INSTALLED 1 FEBRUARY 1708, DIED 27 DECEMBER 1711.

WILLEM HELOT, SECUNDE, ACTING HEAD OF THE GOVERNMENT, 28 DECEMBER 1711 TO 28 MARCH 1714.

Violent conduct of the Rev. Mr. Le Boucq—Church matters at the Cape, Stellenbosch, and Drakenstein—Scene in the Cape church—Deportation of the Rev. Mr. Le Boucq—Arrival of Governor Van Assenburgh—Departure of the recalled officials—Further proceedings against the late officials in Amsterdam—Division and sale of Vergelegen—Visit of the Commissioner Simons—Regulations concerning the manumission of slaves—Series of good seasons—Exportation of wheat to Batavia—Abandonment of the island of Mauritius by the Dutch—Visit of the retired governor-general Van Hoorn—Instructions concerning the tithes of grain—Partial destruction of the village of Stellenbosch by fire—Placaat against destruction of trees—Neglect of tree planting—Definition of a boundary between the Cape and Stellenbosch districts—Death of Governor Van Assenburgh—Election of the secunde Willem Helot to act as head of the government—Enlargement of the colony—False alarm concerning an inroad of the Great Namaquas—Wreck of the *Bennebroek* on the coast of Natal—Sufferings of the sailors who got to land—Friendly treatment of some of them by a native tribe—First appearance of small pox in South Africa—Great loss of life—Effects upon the Hottentot tribes in the neighbourhood of the Cape—Some bad seasons—Appointment of

CHAPTER XIX.

MAURITS PASQUES DE CHAVONNES, GOVERNOR, INSTALLED 28 MARCH 1714; DIED 8 SEPTEMBER 1724.

CHAPTER XX.

JAN DE LA FONTAINE, SECUNDE, ACTING HEAD OF THE GOVERNMENT, 8 SEPTEMBER 1724 TO 25 FEBRUARY 1727.

PIETER GYSBERT NOODT, GOVERNOR, INSTALLED 25 FEBRUARY 1727, DIED 23 APRIL 1729.

JAN DE LA FONTAINE, SECUNDE, ACTING HEAD OF THE GOVERNMENT, 24 APRIL 1729 TO 8 MARCH 1730; GOVERNOR, INSTALLED 8 MARCH 1730, RETIRED 31 AUGUST 1737.

CHAPTER XXI.

ADRIAAN VAN KERVEL, GOVERNOR, INSTALLED 31 AUGUST 1737, DIED 19 SEPTEMBER 1737.

DANIEL VAN DEN HENGHEL, FISCAL, ACTING HEAD OF THE GOVERNMENT, 20 SEPTEMBER 1737 TO 14 APRIL 1739.

HENDRIK SWELLENGREBEL, GOVERNOR, INSTALLED 14 APRIL 1739, RETIRED 27 FEBRUARY 1751.

CHAPTER XXIII.

DESCRIPTION OF THE NATIVE RACES OF SOUTH AFRICA.

CHAPTER XXIV.

JOACHIM VAN PLETTENBERG, FISCAL AND SECUNDE, ACTING HEAD OF THE GOVERNMENT, 12 AUGUST 1771 TO 18 MAY 1774; GOVERNOR, INSTALLED 18 MAY 1774, RETIRED 14 FEBRUARY 1785.

PAGE

dition under Commodore Johnstone sent from England to seize the colony—Expedition under Admiral Suffren sent from France to oppose the English—Naval battle at Porto Praya—Arrival of the French fleet and troops at the Cape—Seizure by Commodore Johnstone of the Dutch ships in Saldanha Bay—Issue of paper money—Composition of the garrison at the Cape—Resignation of the fiscal Boers—Decision of the directors regarding the complaints of the colonists—Appeal of the colonists to the States General of the Netherlands—Changes in the administration—Great damage sustained by the Company in the war with England—Increase of foreign shipping at the Cape—Distinguished visitors—Wrecks on the South African coast—Succession of clergymen in the various churches—Permission obtained by the Lutherans to establish a church—Succession of officers in the country districts 220

CHAPTER XXV.

CORNELIS JACOB VAN DE GRAAFF, GOVERNOR, INSTALLED 14 FEBRUARY 1785; LEFT SOUTH AFRICA 24 JUNE 1791.

JOHAN ISAAC RHENIUS, SECUNDE, ACTING HEAD OF THE GOVERNMENT, 24 JUNE 1791 TO 3 JULY 1792.

Character of the new governor—Decision of the directors concerning the complaints of the colonists—Changes in the administration at the Cape—Long drought—Mossel Bay opened to trade—Timber shipped at Plettenberg's Bay—Erection of fortifications in Table Valley—Troops in garrison at the Cape—Formation of the district of Graaff Reinet—Site of the drostdy—Pursuits of the frontier farmers—Struggle with Bushmen—Dealings with Kaffirs—Condition of the Kosa tribe—Invasion of the colony by Kosa clans—Measures of defence adopted by the colonists—Humiliating arrangement made by the government—Grievances of the frontier colonists—Condition of the people in the districts of Graaff Reinet, Swellendam, Stellenbosch and Drakenstein, and in Cape Town—Reckless waste of the Company's effects by the governor—Public expenditure—The colonial revenue—Insolvency of the East India Company—Reduction of the garrison at the Cape—Very extensive retrenchment—Quarrels among the principal officers of government—Petty conduct of the governor—Political changes in the Netherlands—Recall of Governor Van de Graaff—Flight of the fiscal Van Lynden through fear of incensed burghers—Condition of the fortifications in Table Valley—Cost of the new hospital—Census returns of 1791—Commerce in European wares thrown open to private individuals—Belief in the existence of gold in Great Namaqualand—Journey of exploration undertaken by Mr. Willem van Reenen—First authentic information concerning the

HISTORY OF SOUTH AFRICA.

1691—1795

CHAPTER XVI.

SIMON VAN DER STEL, PROMOTED FROM COMMANDER TO GOVERNOR OF THE CAPE COLONY, 1 JUNE 1691; HELD OFFICE UNTIL 11 FEBRUARY 1699.

Rapacity of the East India Company's servants—Creation of the office of independent fiscal—Condition of the Hottentot clans near the Cape—Account of the captains Klaas and Koopman—Improvements in the town—Experiments in the cultivation of various plants—Damage caused by wild animals—Shocks of earthquake in Table Valley—Particulars concerning ships that put into Table Bay—Changes in the staff of officials—Revenue and expenditure of the colony—Erection of a large hospital—Instances of dreadful ravages of scurvy—Various shipwrecks—Danger from pirates—Seizure of the brigantine *Amy* in Saldanha Bay—Contemplated abandonment of farming operations by the Company—Names of new colonists—Gradual alienation of sympathy between Governor Simon van der Stel and the colonists—High opinion of the governor held by the directors—Resignation of his office by Simon van der Stel—Appointment by the directors of his eldest son as his successor—His retirement to Constantia and subsequent career.

The simplicity of manners and honesty of purpose which were characteristic of the early Dutch traders in Southern Asia disappeared with the establishment of the great power which they built up, and before the close of the seventeenth century corruption in the administration of affairs had become widespread throughout the possessions of the East India Company. There were many men of sterling honesty and of great ability in its service, but the majority of the higher officers were unscrupulous in their pursuit of wealth. In some of the dependencies private trading was practised to such an extent as to destroy the whole of the Company's profits. Worse still, many officials used the power entrusted to them to make money in ways that were decidedly criminal. The remedy would seem to be in making the service attractive by offering liberal salaries to men of talent, while prohibiting every description of private trade and making it penal to take bribes under the name of fees or presents. But in those days of experiments in governing dependencies, this remedy did not occur to the directors, or if any one made such a suggestion it was not acted upon. The old system of small salaries, with permission to receive fees for various services and to trade to a moderate extent, continued in favour.

The directors tried to check the evil by a kind of dual government. In March 1688 they created the new office of independent fiscal, differing greatly from that of the guardians of the law in former times. Before 1690 the fiscals at the Cape were only junior merchants in rank, and the most important duty which they performed was to conduct prosecutions in criminal cases. They were subject to the head of the government just as much as ordinary clerks were. The independent fiscals were responsible to the supreme directory alone, and were free of all local control. To them was confided the regulation of justice. By right of their office, they had a seat in the council of policy next to the secunde, and had access to records, registers, and state papers of every kind. They had entire control of all accounts connected with ships' cargoes, supplies of food for the garrison, and other expenditure. Such were the duties assigned to those appointed to the possessions of the Company in India, and the system at the Cape was made uniform with that elsewhere.

It was hoped that with these extensive powers the independent fiscals would be a check upon corrupt governors, commanders, and subordinate officers of every grade. But no care was taken to put them in a position where they would be unexposed to temptation themselves. Their salaries were inadequate, and they were permitted to charge various fees. They had summary jurisdiction in petty criminal cases, and were allowed to retain for their own benefit one third of the fines which they inflicted. The first fiscal independent at the Cape, Mr. Cornelis Joan Simons, who was appointed in 1689, had a salary from the Company of only 100*l.* a year.

The system of government thus established in this colony remained unchanged during the next century.

Quarrels between the various Hottentot clans within the limits of the European settlement were frequently occurring. The kraals of these people were thinly scattered over the country, and were moved from place to place just as in olden times, except that they could not be erected on ground occupied by white men. The Hottentots were subject to Dutch laws only in cases where Europeans also were concerned. They had become poor in cattle, owing partly to the waste caused by their perpetual feuds, partly to depredations by Bushmen, and partly to their willingness to exchange oxen for brandy and tobacco. The burghers were forbidden to trade with the Hottentots, under severe penalties, but in defiance of the placaats and of the punishment which invariably followed conviction, some of the least respectable among them carried on an extensive barter.

Captain Klaas, once so faithful and so trusted, had now fallen into disfavour. A savage is incapable of continuing long in any pursuit that demands much exertion, and Klaas got weary of travelling about the country purchasing cattle for the Company, whose wants must have seemed to him insatiable. It became necessary again to send out trading parties of Europeans, and these so excited his jealousy that he did his utmost to put obstacles in their way. This conduct led rapidly to something more unfriendly, and in 1692 he used most threatening language towards Ensign Schryver, the head of a bartering party.

Koopman, Klaas's rival in the same tribe, was not slow to take advantage of the new condition of things. He came to the castle with an accusation against Klaas of being in league with those burghers who were carrying on an illicit trade, and he professed to have so great a regard for the Company's interests as to be willing to place his services entirely at the governor's disposal. In the minute details of these events entered in the records of the time, there is found an exact counterpart of numerous well-known transactions of native chiefs of the present day. The result was that Koopman became an ally of the Honourable Company, and Klaas was regarded as an ill-affected mischief-maker. Thus the government completely changed sides with the rival branches of the Chainouqua tribe. Klaas had as wife a daughter of Goukou, paramount chief of the Hessequas, who was commonly called the 'oude heer' by the colonists. His people and the Hessequas were living in close friendship.

On the 20th of April 1693 an urgent request for help was received at the castle from Koopman, who represented that he was about to be attacked by Klaas and the Hessequas. It was therefore resolved to send Captain Willem Padt with a hundred soldiers and a hundred burghers to Koopman's assistance, with instructions to endeavour to capture Klaas.

The commando, aided by Koopman's adherents, surrounded Klaas's kraal in the night, took possession of his cattle, and arrested him and two of his leading men. Some of his followers who attempted to escape were killed by Koopman's people. The cattle were driven to the Kuilen, where they were counted and divided between Koopman and the Honourable Company.

On the 8th of August the three prisoners were brought before the council of policy. Klaas admitted some of the charges against him, but endeavoured to give a satisfactory explanation of his conduct. He denied having ever had hostile designs against the Company. The council admitted that he had not been guilty of any overt act of war, and, on the 17th of August, resolved that as no Christian blood had been shed, further proceedings against the prisoners should be dropped, but to secure tranquillity Klaas should be detained on Robben Island.

The fate of the unfortunate Hottentot, who had once been regarded as the most trustworthy of his race, and who had befriended many Europeans in distress, called forth a large amount of sympathy. Intercession was made to the government on his behalf, and in January 1694 he was released from confinement and permitted to live near Muizenburg with some of his retainers. He had previously been ill, and had been brought to the mainland for medical treatment, but upon recovery had been sent back to the island. When he was allowed to reside at Muizenburg, his wife, the daughter of Goukou, was sent for. She had lived with him about ten years, but when he was arrested by Captain Padt, Koopman had taken her with other spoil. Her father had never visited the Cape, but as a partisan of Klaas he came to the castle on this occasion. The woman was asked by the governor if she desired to live with her husband, and replied that she preferred to remain with Koopman.

A little later Klaas was allowed to return to his old kraal, upon giving a promise to live quietly and peaceably. But he and Koopman at once resumed their quarrel. In February 1697 both were summoned to the Cape, and an apparent reconciliation was effected by the governor. Goukou, whose friendship was valued, as he was considered the most wealthy and powerful of all the Hottentot chiefs in the neighbourhood of the colony, appeared again on this occasion as the friend of Klaas.

The captains had hardly returned to their kraals when fighting between them was renewed. Goukou's daughter changed her mind and attempted to return to Klaas, upon which Koopman put her to death. Klaas and the Hessequas then attacked Koopman, and took his cattle together with some belonging to the Company which were in his charge. A sergeant and twelve men were then sent from the castle to request Klaas to restore the Company's property, but he could not comply, as the oxen had already been killed and eaten. This matter brought him into disfavour again, and thenceforth he was regarded as the principal mischief-maker in the country. Occasionally he visited the Cape in company with Goukou, and promised to live in peace with Koopman, but the promise was soon disregarded. The feud between the two captains was kept up until in a skirmish between them in June 1701 Klaas was killed. The story, as written in minute detail nearly two hundred years ago, might be copied as a faithful description of a quarrel between native clans to-day.

Other Hottentot communities were engaged in the same way destroying each other. Thus in March 1693 four Hessequa kraals were pillaged by the Attaquas. All were exposed to plunder by Bushmen. In April 1694 a large party of these robbers made a descent upon Koopman's kraals, and drove off fully half of his cattle. The Hottentot captain applied for assistance to the governor, and ten soldiers under a sergeant were sent to his aid. The Bushmen were followed up, most of the cattle were recovered, and sixteen or seventeen of the marauders were shot.

The clans of the Goringhaiquas and Gorachouquas were completely impoverished. In 1696 the governor supplied them with some cattle to tend on shares, but the effort to restore them to their former condition was fruitless. Of their own accord they referred their most weighty disputes to the European authorities for settlement, and upon the death of a captain they always applied to the governor to confirm his successor. A staff with a copper head, upon which was engraved on one side the Company's arms and on the other the name given by the governor to the new captain, was considered indispensable to the exercise of authority.

The Grigriqua tribe, then usually living on the borders of the Elephant river, was giving offence by harbouring runaway slaves. In December 1696 Ensign Schryver was sent with thirty soldiers and twenty burghers to endeavour to obtain the fugitives in friendly barter. If the Grigriquas would not restore them, the ensign was instructed to seize some individuals, male or female, and bring them to the castle as hostages. The expedition was not successful in finding the tribe. Some friendly Hottentots, however, secured two Grigriquas, who were detained at the castle for a couple of months. One of them was then sent to his people with a friendly message asking for the slaves. He did not return, and the other was shortly afterwards released.

In the town several improvements were made at this

time. In January 1693 the botanist Oldenland, who was superintendent of the Company's garden and land surveyor for the government, received the additional appointment of town engineer, with an annual salary of 6*l*. 18*s*. 10*d*., partly paid by the burgher council. He died four years later. In October 1695 the Keizersgracht, the present Darling street, was laid out between the Heerengracht, now Adderley street, and the back of the castle. The road to the country at that time ran between the castle and the shore of the bay. In October 1697 the work of levelling the ground between the new street and the shore, since termed the great parade, was commenced. It was previously intersected by several deep gullies, and some knolls of considerable size were standing on it. The Company furnished a party of slaves, and the burghers contributed the remainder of the labour. The work was completed in 1699. In April 1696 the streets began to be patrolled at night by a burgher watch. Constables were not yet employed in the town, though at Stellenbosch and Drakenstein two of those useful officials, there termed veldwachters, were engaged in seeing that the placaats were observed. They were paid at the rate of 1*l*. 2*s*. 3*d*. a month.

In February 1693 a waggon road was completed over the neck beyond Wynberg to Hout Bay. In 1698 the church at Stellenbosch was enlarged, as the original building was too small to contain the congregation. In the same year an abortive attempt was made to form a safe harbour for boats by cutting a passage through the sand from Table Bay to a reach of the Salt river.

Efforts to produce olives were continued, though in all instances resulting in failure. Experiments in the culture of the hop were also being made. The planting out of young oaks in different parts of the Cape peninsula was assiduously attended to.

Wild animals were still giving trouble. In May 1694 a burgher at Drakenstein was killed by a leopard, and another at Stellenbosch was nearly torn to pieces by a lion. On one day in the following month nine cows were killed by lions in sight of the castle. The premium for killing a lion in the Cape peninsula was 5*l.* 4*s.* 2*d.* As late as 1702 an elephant was killed just beyond the Cape flats.

In the morning of the 4th of September 1695 the first recorded shock of earthquake was felt at the Cape. The weather was perfectly calm and clear, when suddenly a noise like a clap of thunder was heard, and a trembling of the earth was felt as if something was rolling beneath the foundations of the buildings. In a few seconds it ceased, and was not repeated. No damage was occasioned by the shock. In the afternoon of the 11th of January 1696 another slight trembling was felt in the town, but unaccompanied by noise.

During the eight years 1692–9 four hundred and thirty-five ships put into Table Bay, or on an average fifty-four yearly. Of these, two hundred and ninety-three belonged to the Company, one hundred and thirteen were English, nineteen were Danish, and ten were French. Since the middle of the century many improvements had been made in the construction of ships. They carried now more sails, but each one smaller, so that they needed fewer hands than formerly. The average number of men in a Dutch Indiaman at the close of the century was one hundred and seventy. The English ships that put into Table Bay were as a rule much smaller, and did not carry on an average more than one hundred men. Many of them were engaged in the slave trade between the West Indies and Madagascar. Others were private traders, or interlopers as they were called. Others again belonged to the new English East India Company. A few were men-of-war sent out to convoy fleets. The old English East India Company's ships usually passed by Table Bay, as they had a refreshing station of their own at St. Helena.

Several changes had taken place in the official staff. On the 22nd of June 1694 Mr. J. W. Grevenbroek resigned his situation as secretary to the council of policy, and became a burgher at Stellenbosch. In November 1694 the independent fiscal Cornelis Joan Simons transferred his duties to

Johan Blesius, and proceeded to Batavia to fill a post of greater importance. In April 1697 Mr. Samuel Elsevier arrived from the Netherlands with the appointment of secunde, Andries de Man having died some time before.

In August 1693 the Rev. Leonardus Terwold was transferred to Batavia. Services were held occasionally by chaplains of ships and by the Rev. Mr. Simond until the 22nd of September 1694, when the Rev. Hercules van Loon, chaplain of the *Nederland*, was detained here, and was appointed provisionally clergyman of the Cape. The directors, however, sent out the Rev. Petrus Kalden, who was inducted on the 4th of December 1695, and Mr. Van Loon was obliged to return to Europe. He left reluctantly, and with the good wishes of the congregation.

The revenue of the colony during the last years of the seventeenth century was derived chiefly from the sale of privileges to sell wines and spirituous liquors, which amounted to about 2,200*l.* yearly. Other sources yielded about 800*l.* more. The average profits on the sale of goods were about 2,000*l.* a year. The expenditure is set down in the Company's accounts at about 12,000*l.* yearly, but this sum includes supplies to ships and other items not fairly chargeable against the Cape, amounting in round numbers to 4,000*l.* The revenue to the Company may thus be set down at 5,000*l.*, and the expenditure at 8,000*l.* a year.

The hospital, built by Commander Van Riebeek close to the beach in front of the earthen fort Good Hope, was at this time in a dilapidated condition. Its site was not good, as it was exposed to the full force of gales. Upon the governor's representations, the directors authorised him to build a larger hospital in a more suitable place. He selected the ground now occupied by the Cape of Good Hope Bank, between the present Adderley and St. George's streets, then termed the Heerengracht and Berg straat. In December 1694 the foundation was commenced, but it was not until July 1697 that the building was taken properly in hand. It was designed to accommodate five hundred patients without crowding, or seven hundred and fifty on an emergency.

A building of this size was none too large for the requirements of the Company's fleets at the close of the seventeenth century. Owing to improvements in the construction of ships, passages were now often made in ninety days between Europe and the Cape, but scurvy still caused terrible havoc among seamen.

On the 8th of February 1693 a boat reached Saldanha Bay with a feeble crew and a sick officer, who reported that they had left their ship, the *Bantam*, anchored off Paternoster Point. On the passage out, two hundred and twenty-one men had died of scurvy, and those left alive were too weak to work. They had therefore dropped anchor, and some of them left in a boat to look for assistance. The boat was swamped, and of her crew only two men got to land. It was believed that one of these died of hunger, and that the other was killed by wild animals. A second boat then left for Saldanha Bay, and fortunately found a large Indiaman at anchor there. A party of men was sent to the *Bantam*, and she was brought safely to Table Bay.

On the 4th of May 1693 the *Goude Buys* sailed from Enkhuizen with one hundred and ninety souls on board, and on the 19th of October dropped anchor off the coast about fifteen miles north of St. Helena Bay, when there were not a dozen of her crew capable of working. On the 11th of November seven men left the ship to seek assistance inland. Of these, five perished of hunger, one wandered along the banks of the Berg river until he was found by some Hottentots and taken to the Company's post at Saldanha Bay, and the other, after roaming about for seven weeks, was rescued. When intelligence of the state of the ship reached the Cape, a yacht was sent to her assistance. Only one living person was found on board, and he died soon afterwards. The *Goude Buys* had drifted ashore, and could not be got off. Most of her cargo was saved, and all the small vessels at the Cape were for some time employed in transporting it to Table Bay.

On the 23rd of November 1693 the *Schoondyk* arrived from Texel with her whole remaining crew of one hundred and twenty men sick. One hundred and thirty-four had died on the passage out. On the 23rd of December 1694 the *Pampus* arrived from Rotterdam with only sixteen healthy men on board. Sixty had died on the passage out, and eighty-three were down with scurvy. On the 11th of November 1695 a fleet of eleven ships arrived from the Netherlands, with six hundred and seventy-eight men unable to walk, some of whom were so far gone that they died while being conveyed to the hospital. A great many others were ill, but were able to go about. Two hundred and twenty-eight had perished on the passage. On the 17th of October 1696 the *Vosmaar* arrived from Flushing with only four sound men on board. One hundred and thirty-nine were ill, and ninety-three had died. Of ten Huguenot passengers for the Cape, five had died.

Several wrecks took place at this time.

During the night of the 4th of June 1692 a heavy gale set in from the north-west, and before daylight of the 5th the Company's ships *Goede Hoop* and *Hoogergeest* and the English ship *Orange* were driven ashore near the mouth of Salt River. There was a large fleet in Table Bay at the time, but the other vessels held to their anchors. The *Goede Hoop* was the same ship that had been taken from the French in April 1689, when she was named the *Normande*. She was now homeward bound from Ceylon. She held together, and most of her cargo, though damaged, was recovered. The *Hoogergeest*, from Batavia, and the *Orange*, from Madras, broke up quickly, but only a few of their people were lost. The men of the *Hoogergeest* were rescued by a quartermaster of an Indiaman, who happened to be on shore at the time. This brave seaman, Jochem Willems by name, fastened a line to his body, and made his way through the surf to the wreck. A hawser was then pulled ashore, and by its means most of the crew escaped before the ship broke up.

Early in the morning of the 20th of January 1694 the yacht *Dageraad*, laden with cargo—including a quantity of specie—from the *Goude Buys*, ran ashore on the western side of Robben Island, and broke up immediately. Sixteen lives were lost. Some of the specie was recovered, but not all.

In the afternoon of the 24th of May 1697 the Company's homeward bound ships *Waddingsveen* and *Oosterland*, with valuable cargoes on board, were driven ashore at Salt River mouth in a great gale, and were dashed to pieces at once. Two other ships out of a large fleet that was lying in the bay narrowly escaped the same fate. Only seventeen men in all were saved from the two wrecks.

On the 27th of May 1698 the *Huis te Crayenstein*, from Middelburg bound to Batavia, anchored in a calm off Camp's Bay. During the night a thick mist set in, and before daylight of the 28th the ship was found to have parted her cable and to be adrift. She was already in the breakers, and before anything could be done she struck on the rocks behind the Lion's Head, and became a complete wreck. No lives were lost.

Scurvy and wreck were not the only perils of the sea. Towards the close of the seventeenth century the Indian Ocean began to be frequented by pirates, who were ready when opportunities offered to pillage the coasts as well as to seize defenceless ships. Among them was the famous Captain Kidd.

On the 2nd of May 1693 a small armed brigantine under English colours, with her main mast gone, put into Saldanha Bay. There was a ship belonging to the English East India Company lying in Table Bay, and her officers assured the governor that the stranger was a pirate, urging him at the same time to take her in custody. An armed vessel was thereupon sent to Saldanha Bay to ascertain particulars. The brigantine was found to have two conflicting sets of papers, and to bear traces of having been in an engagement. Her master, George Dew by name, stated that he was from the Bermudas, bound to Madagascar for a cargo of slaves, and that his crew consisted of twenty-four men. The vessel was called the *Amy*. The Dutch officers considered that they were justified in seizing her, and they brought her to Table Bay. Twenty-four hours after she was in their possession some men were found concealed on board, when her crew reached a total of thirty-five.

There was no doubt as to her true character, so she was condemned, and was kept for use by the Cape government. Captain Dew and his men were sent prisoners to Europe. But it was found impossible to prove legally that Dew was a pirate, and he then put in a claim for damages against the Company and caused the directors much trouble and expense.

In 1695 the directors issued instructions that as soon as possible farming and cattle dealing should be given up by the Cape government. They were disposed to call for tenders to supply the garrison and fleets with beef and mutton, and to allow the colonists to purchase cattle from the Hottentots and fatten them for sale to the contractors. But no steps towards carrying these instructions into effect were taken until some years later.

Between the years 1691 and 1700 the following names of burghers are first found in the records of the colony:

Bakhuizen	de Haas	Odendaal
Bisseaux	Heems	Oertman
Bloem	Helm	Pleunis
de Boer	Heyning	van Rensburg
Brink	Hoffman	le Riche
Coenradie	Hubner	Rotterdam
Couvret	van Jaarsveld	van de Sande
Cronjé	Kerver	Scheffer
Delport	de Kock	Schryver
van Deventer	Kruisman	Slabbart
Diemer	Lutters	Swanepoel
Donker	Maritz	Syfer
Dumont	van Meerland	de Vos
Faber	Menssinck	Wiederhold
Fleuris	Mouton	Willemse
Gardiol	Mouy	Wynoch
Haak	Niel	Zevenhoven

Before the year 1692 Simon van der Stel enjoyed the esteem and affection of nearly every European in South Africa except the French immigrants, but about this date a different feeling began slowly to develop. He was now a disappointed man, for his dream of earlier years, to form here a purely Dutch settlement, had been thwarted. The love of wealth had grown upon him, and his farm Constantia, already beautified with vineyards and avenues of young oaks, year by year occupied more of his attention. The strong personal interest which he had taken in the welfare of the colonists seemed to them to be dying out. And a comparison of the records of the first twelve years of his administration with those of the last seven shows that a change in his feelings had really taken place, for the enthusiastic language of the first period gives way to cold official expressions in the last. Still there were no open complaints, and to strangers and others who could not see beneath the surface everything appeared to be working smoothly.

The directors continued to hold a very high opinion of the governor. In 1692 they conferred upon him the rank and title of councillor extraordinary of Netherlands India, and when in 1696 he requested permission to resign, so as to spend the evening of his life in comparative freedom from care, they named his eldest son as his successor. The newly appointed governor could not immediately leave the Netherlands, however, and it was not until the 23rd of January 1699 that he and his family reached South Africa.

After handing over the administration on the 11th of February 1699, Simon van der Stel retired to his farm Constantia, where he had built a large and handsome residence. There during the next thirteen years strangers of note were always sure of a hearty reception, and the hospitality of the late governor was so great that his house was seldom or never without visitors. He devoted his remaining years chiefly to agriculture and cattle rearing. On the 11th of March 1699 he obtained from the commissioner Daniel Heins a grant in freehold of Zeekoe Vlei with the ground surrounding it an hour's walk in diameter, and on the 1st of February 1700 the commissioner Wouter Valckenier granted him the use of the Steenbergen for the term of his life. Practically therefore he had the whole peninsula beyond his property as a cattle run. The wine which he made was the best in the colony. The burghers believed that he possessed some secret for manufacturing it, and strangers attributed its quality to the care which he took in pressing and fermenting, but it is now known that it owed its flavour to the soil.

The late governor did not confine his attention wholly to these pursuits, and was always ready to embark in any undertaking that promised large returns. In June 1711, when he was nearly seventy-two years of age, in company with the burgher Johannes Phyffer he entered into a contract with the council of policy to supply for five years dried and salted fish, in which the partners secured a monopoly of fishing and seal hunting at Saldanha Bay, on condition of an annual payment of twenty-five leggers of train oil.

Simon van der Stel died on the 24th of June 1712. His remains were buried beneath the pavement of the church in Table Valley. A monument to his memory was erected behind the pulpit, but when during the present century the church was enlarged, it with everything else of its kind was removed and never restored.

CHAPTER XVII.

WILHEM ADRIAAN VAN DER STEL, GOVERNOR, INSTALLED 11 FEBRUARY 1699; HELD OFFICE UNTIL 3 JUNE 1707.

Appointment of Wilhem Adriaan van der Stel as governor—Search for islands with forests on them—Tree planting—Visit of a pirate to Saldanha Bay—Seizure of a pirate vessel in Table Bay—Completion of the new hospital—Tour of the governor—Inspection of the Tulbagh basin—Naming of the Witsenberg—Occupation by graziers of the country about Riebeek's Kasteel and the Tulbagh basin—Formation of a small military outpost in the Tulbagh basin—Permission to the burghers to purchase cattle from the Hottentots—Contract for supply of meat—Cattle breeding henceforth a favourite pursuit of colonists—Troubles with Bushmen—Dealings with Hottentots—Church matters—Discontinuance of the use of the French language in the church at Drakenstein—Proceedings of a marauding party—Wreck of the *Meresteyn*—Expedition to Natal—An English resident at Natal—Fruitless efforts of the directors and the Cape government to make South Africa a wool-producing country—Experiment in silk culture—Placing of partridges and pheasants on Robben Island—Long drought—Increase of population—Want of sympathy between the government and the colonists—Extensive farming operations by the governor and other officials—Complaints of the colonists to the supreme authorities—Violent action of the governor—Arrest of various burghers and their committal to prison—Banishment of a burgher to Batavia and of four others to Europe—Defiance of the government by the country people—Action of the directors in the Netherlands—Recall of the governor and other officials—Arrival of the newly appointed secunde Johan Cornelis d'Ableing and transfer of the administration to him—Views of the colonists and of the directors as to the rights of burghers.

WILHEM ADRIAAN VAN DER STEL had for ten years been filling various offices in the city of Amsterdam, among others that of judge, when the Assembly of Seventeen, in recognition of his father's services, offered him the appointment of councillor extraordinary of India and governor of the Cape Colony and its dependency the island of Mauritius. He had once resided here for a short time, and was well acquainted with the circumstances of the country. There is nothing in the records or contemporary publications to indicate what manner of man he was in personal appearance, though the details of his administration are given very minutely.

Notwithstanding the pains taken by the late governor to promote tree planting, there was a scarcity of timber and fuel at the Cape. It was a difficult matter to supply the ships with firewood. Some skippers reported that in passing by two islands, named Dina and Marseveen, in latitude 41° or 42° south and about four hundred sea miles from the Cape, they had observed fine forests, which they suggested should be examined. The master of the galiot *Wesel* was therefore instructed to proceed to the locality indicated, to inspect the forests closely, and ascertain what quantity of timber was to be had. The *Wesel* sailed from Table Bay on the 31st of March 1699, but returned on the 13th of May with a report that the search for the islands had been fruitless.

The governor, like his father, regarded the cultivation of trees as a matter of great importance. During the first winter after his arrival twenty thousand young oaks were planted in the kloofs at Stellenbosch and Drakenstein where the native forests had been exhausted, and over ten thousand were set out in the Cape peninsula. In the winter of 1701 a further supply was sent to Stellenbosch from the nursery in Table Valley, and the landdrost was instructed to have them planted along the streets.

On the 10th of May 1699 intelligence was received at the castle that a pirate vessel with an English crew had put into Saldanha Bay and taken possession of some galiots and decked boats belonging to the Company and to private individuals, there being nothing else to plunder within reach. Two ships were at once sent to try and capture her, but before they could reach the bay she had sailed. She had taken the little vessels outside, but had then abandoned them, after her master had generously presented four negroes to the owner of one, in return for his stores. A few weeks after this a squadron of English men-of-war touched here on their way to the Mozambique Channel, where they were about to cruize in search of pirates.

On the 28th of December an English vessel named the

Margate put into Table Bay. Her master stated that he was from Madagascar, bound to the Bermudas with one hundred and twenty slaves. Another English vessel, named the *Loyal Merchant*, was lying at anchor in the bay. Captain Lowth, who commanded her, had a commission from King William, authorising him to search for rovers and seize them. He examined the *Margate*, and then took possession of that vessel on the ground that she had been engaged in piracy. The governor protested against this violation of a Dutch port, but to no effect, for Captain Lowth kept his prize and took her away with him. He also examined another English vessel which put in before he left, but released her after two days detention.

In this year, 1699, the new hospital was completed. On the 24th of October it was opened for use, when the sick were moved into it from the old building on the beach.

On the 23rd of November the governor with a party of attendants set out on a tour of inspection of the settlement. He visited Stellenbosch, Drakenstein, and the farms about the Tigerberg, where he found some persons to whom no ground had yet been allotted. The country was inhabited by Europeans, though thinly, nearly as far as the present village of Hermon. Small Hottentot kraals were scattered about, but their occupants were found to be very poor and very lazy.

Keeping down the Berg river, the range of mountains on the right was reported to be tenanted by Bushmen, who were in the habit of descending from their fastnesses and plundering the burghers and Hottentots below. The range was on this account known as the Obiqua mountains. The governor crossed over at a place since termed the Roodezand pass, just beyond the gorge through which the Little Berg river flows, and entered the valley now called the Tulbagh basin.

Though not greatly elevated, this basin is in the second of the steps by which the mainland of South Africa rises from the ocean to the range of mountains enclosing the central plain. If a cane with a large round head be laid upon soft ground, the mark will give an idea of its form.

The hollow caused by the head of the cane will represent the basin, the long narrow groove will indicate the valley between the Obiqua mountains and a parallel range six or seven miles further inland. The Breede river has its source in the third terrace, and, rushing down a gorge in the interior range, now called Michell's pass, flows south-eastward through the valley. Close to Michell's pass the mountain retires, but shortly sweeps round and joins the Obiqua range, the keystone of the arch thus formed being the Great Winterhoek, six thousand eight hundred and forty feet in height, the loftiest peak visible from the Cape.

It was the basin thus enclosed that the governor and his party entered. It was found to be drained by the Little Berg river and its numerous tributary rills, whose waters escape through a gorge in the Obiqua mountains, and flow northwestward. The watershed between the Breede and Little Berg rivers is merely a gentle swell in the surface of the ground. At the foot of Michell's pass, at the present day, a mill race is led out of the Breede and turned into the Little Berg, and thus a few shovels full of earth can divert water from the Indian to the Atlantic ocean.

The basin excels all other parts of South Africa in the variety and splendour of its wild flowers, which in early spring almost conceal the ground. It was too late in the season for the governor's party to see it at its best, still the visitors were charmed with its appearance. Very few Hottentots were found. In the recesses of the mountains were forests of magnificent trees, and although the timber could not be removed to the Cape, it would be of great use to residents. Immigrants were arriving in every fleet from the Netherlands, so the governor resolved to form a settlement in the valley, where cattle breeding could be carried on to advantage. Agriculture, except to supply the wants of residents, could not be pursued with profit, owing to the difficulty of transport. The governor named the basin the Land of Waveren, in honour of a family of position in Amsterdam. The range of mountains enclosing the valley on the inland side and stretching away as far as the eye could reach, as yet without a name, he called the Witsenberg, after the justly esteemed burgomaster Nicholas Witsen of Amsterdam. The Land of Waveren has long since become the Tulbagh Basin, but one may be allowed to hope that the Witsenberg will always be known by the honoured name it has borne since 1699.

Several burghers who had been living at Drakenstein were now permitted to graze their cattle at Riebeek's Kasteel, and on the 31st of July 1700 some recent immigrants from Europe were sent to occupy the Land of Waveren. As it was the rainy season, the families of the immigrants remained at the Cape until rough cottages could be put up for their accommodation. At the same time a corporal and six soldiers were sent to form a military post in the valley for the protection of the colonists. This post was termed the Waveren outstation, and was maintained for many years. On the 16th of October several additional families were forwarded to the new district to obtain a living as graziers.

Ever since 1658 trade between the burghers and the Hottentots was strictly forbidden. The chief object was to prevent any act that might bring on a collision with the natives. In opposition to the law, however, parties of deserters and other persons of loose character carried on a cattle trade, and were often guilty of conduct that cannot be distinguished from robbery. Governor Simon van der Stel thought to check this by threatening more severe punishment, and on the 19th of October 1697 he issued a placaat in which the barter of cattle from Hottentots was prohibited, under penalty of whipping, branding, banishment, and confiscation of property.

The directors disapproved of this. They were disposed to allow the colonists to purchase cattle from the Hottentots and fatten them for sale to such persons as would contract to supply the garrison and fleets with beef and mutton. They therefore annulled the placaat, and on the 27th of July 1699 issued instructions that the cattle trade should be thrown open, on condition that the burghers should supply draught oxen to the government whenever required, at fourteen shillings each.

The council of policy had then no option, but was under the necessity of obeying orders. Tenders were called for, and in February 1700 the burgher Henning Huising entered into a contract to supply the garrison, hospital, and Company's fleets with beef and mutton at twopence halfpenny a pound, he to have the use of the Company's slaughter-houses and as a cattle run the whole of the district of Groen Kloof that was not occupied by Hottentots. The contract was signed provisionally for ten years, but the directors reduced it to five. With this transaction the Company designed to relinquish sending expeditions into the interior to purchase cattle, as had been the custom for nearly half a century; and henceforth it was only when draught oxen were needed that military bartering parties went inland. By a placaat of the council of policy presided over by the commissioner Wouter Valckenier, on the 28th of February 1700 the trade was thrown open to the burghers, with such restrictions as were considered necessary to prevent its abuse.

From this date cattle breeding became a favourite pursuit with yearly increasing numbers of colonists. There was as much to be made by it as by agriculture, and it was attended with less expense and less anxiety. The government gave permission to applicants to use land for grazing purposes at some defined locality, but if the pasture failed or did not prove as good as was anticipated, the occupiers did not hesitate to seek other and better places.

With the enlargement of the settlement in this manner, fresh troubles arose with the Bushmen. In March 1701 a band of these robbers drove off forty head of cattle from Gerrit Cloete's farm at Riebeek's Kasteel. A commando of ten soldiers and thirty burghers was sent after the depredators, but was unable to find them. A temporary military post was then established at Vogel Vlei, at the foot of the Obiqua mountains.

This protection soon proved to be insufficient. In April Gerrit Cloete was again robbed, and eleven head of cattle were lifted from the Waveren post. A commando of twelve soldiers and fifty burghers was then organised to clear the country of Bushmen, but did not succeed in effecting its object. It was hardly disbanded when one hundred and thirty-seven head of cattle were lifted within sight of the Vogel Vlei post. Upon this a reinforcement of six mounted soldiers was sent to each of the two posts, and twelve men were stationed at Riebeek's Kasteel.

The Goringhaiqua and Cochoqua Hottentots now tendered their services to assist the Europeans against the Bushmen, and requested that the captain Kees, who was then living at Groen Kloof, might be recognised as their leader in the expedition. But it was discovered that Kees, who had suffered severely from the Bushmen, had already joined a commando of Gerrit Cloete's friends, and that the joint force was scouring the Obiqua mountains. On receipt of this information, the governor sent instructions to the landdrost of Stellenbosch to have Cloete arrested and brought to trial for waging war without leave, and to ascertain and send in the names of those who had joined him in the expedition.

The prosecution fell through, and the governor thought it best after this to send out only parties of soldiers against the robbers. In September one of these parties recovered one hundred and twenty head of cattle belonging partly to burghers and partly to Hottentots; but in the following month more than two hundred head belonging to the contractor Henning Huising were lifted at Groen Kloof, and a patrol of thirty-five soldiers was obliged to fall back from Piketberg, where the Bushmen made a resolute stand.

In November a sergeant and ten men were sent to form a permanent military post at Groen Kloof. In the Land of Waveren forty head of cattle, mostly belonging to Etienne Terreblanche, were seized by Bushmen, and one of the soldiers who tried to recover them was killed. Two hundred and seventy-four head belonging to Hottentot kraals at Riebeek's Kasteel were driven off, but a party of soldiers followed the robbers to Twenty-four Rivers, and retook most of the spoil. In trying to afford protection, no distinction was made by the government between burghers and Hottentots, the officers at the outposts being instructed to do their utmost to recover cattle stolen by Bushmen and deliver them to their proper owners whoever these might be.

In 1702 the military patrols were kept busy on behalf of the Hottentots, for no complaints of depredations were made by burghers. A large number of cattle were recovered and restored to various kraals, and so many Bushmen were shot that the robbers seem to have been terrified. At any rate they gave less trouble during the next few years, though occasionally it was necessary to chastise them. The sergeants and corporals in command of the outposts were directed to endeavour to induce the Bushmen to keep the peace. When those wild people committed depredations they were to be followed up and punished, but under no circumstances were they to be attacked without provocation. The ruthless nature of the warfare pursued by the Bushmen was evidenced in February 1702, when a Hottentot captain came to the castle and reported that they had killed five of his wives and every one of his children.

There is little else on record concerning the Hottentots at this period. Some of them made such complaints of the rapacity and violence of burgher trading parties that the council of policy provisionally suspended the liberty of free barter, and, owing to the governor's representations, in 1703 the Assembly of Seventeen withdrew the privilege. Commercial intercourse between the two races was again made illegal, and the European graziers were chiefly depended upon to provide as many cattle as were needed.

In September 1704 several Namaqua captains visited the Cape, when an agreement of friendship was made with them. This tribe, like the others with which the Europeans had come in contact, at once accepted as a matter of course the position of vassals. This was shown in October 1705, when three Namaqua captains came to the castle for the purpose of requesting the governor to confirm their authority. They were kindly treated, their request was complied with, and they left carrying with them presents of beads and other trifles and copper-headed canes upon which the new names given to them—Plato, Jason, and Vulcan—were inscribed.

Thenceforth they were termed allies of the Honourable Company. The number of captains mentioned as having applied for staffs is an indication that the tribes were now more broken up than formerly. Sometimes a clan requested the appointment of a regent, as its hereditary captain was a minor. There are instances of clans applying for a brother of a deceased captain to be appointed in his stead, but in such cases they always gave as a reason that the dead chief had left no children. Feuds between clans of the same tribe caused frequent disturbances, though these same clans usually acted together against the adjoining tribe.

After the removal in 1691 of the Rev. Pierre Simond to Drakenstein, there was no resident clergyman at Stellenbosch for nearly nine years. Once in three months the clergyman of the Cape visited the vacant church and administered the sacraments, and occasionally the Rev. Mr. Simond attended for the same purpose. On the remaining Sundays the sick comforter conducted the services. At length the Assembly of Seventeen appointed the Rev. Hercules van Loon, who had once been acting clergyman of the Cape, resident clergyman of Stellenbosch. He arrived from the Netherlands on the 11th of April 1700.

In April 1678 the foundation of a church in Table Valley had been laid, but with that the work had ceased. For another quarter of a century services were conducted in a large hall within the castle. But in course of time the poor funds accumulated to a considerable amount, and the consistory then consented to apply a sum equal to 2,200*l.* of our money to the erection of the building. As the original plan was now considered too small, it was enlarged, and a new foundation stone was laid by the governor on the 28th of December 1700. By the close of the year 1703 the edifice was finished, except the tower. The first service in it was held on the 6th of January 1704, the Rev. Petrus Kalden being the preacher. Of the building then constructed the tower and end walls still remain, these forming part of the side walls of the present church.

At Drakenstein service was conducted sometimes in the front room of a farmer's house, sometimes in a large barn, there being as yet no church building. There was a French clergyman, who was assisted by a French sick comforter. In April 1700 a sick comforter and schoolmaster was first appointed for the Dutch portion of the congregation, that had previously been neglected. An able and zealous man named Jacobus de Groot, who was returning from India to Europe, was detained here for the purpose.

The Rev. Mr. Simond had prepared a new version in metre of the psalms of David, which he was desirous of submitting to a synod of the French churches, as great interest had been taken in the work by the Huguenots in Europe. He therefore tendered his resignation, to the regret of the Drakenstein people, and requested permission to return to the Netherlands. The Assembly of Seventeen consented to his request, on condition of his remaining until the arrival of the Rev. Hendrik Bek, whom they appointed to succeed him. Mr. Bek reached the Cape in April 1702, and was installed at Drakenstein a few weeks later.

There was a desire on the part of the directors that in the families of the Huguenot immigrants the French language should be superseded by the Dutch as speedily as possible. It was only a question of time, for the proportion of French speaking people was too small compared with those of Dutch and German descent for their language to remain long in use in the mixed community. The new clergyman understood French, but at the direction of the Assembly of Seventeen conducted public worship in Dutch. The sick comforter, Paul Roux, continued ministrations to the Huguenots in their own language.

This arrangement created much dissatisfaction. The French immigrants sent in a memorial requesting that the Rev. Mr. Bek should be instructed to preach in their language once a fortnight. They stated that they comprised over a hundred adults, not more than twenty-five of whom understood sufficient Dutch to gather the meaning of a sermon. There was also even a larger number of children of their nationality. The council of policy recommended the memorial to the favourable consideration of the Assembly of Seventeen; but before action could be taken upon it, the Rev. Mr. Bek requested to be removed to Stellenbosch as successor to Mr. Van Loon, who died by his own hand on the 27th of June 1704. The directors then appointed the Rev. Engelbertus Franciscus le Boucq clergyman of Drakenstein, and gave instructions that upon his arrival from Batavia Mr. Bek should be transferred to Stellenbosch. They gave the council of policy permission to allow the French language to be used alternately with the Dutch in the church services at Drakenstein, if it should seem advisable to do so.

The newly appointed minister did not reach the Cape until the 30th of March 1707. Mr. Bek then took charge of the Stellenbosch congregation, which had been for nearly three years without a clergyman, except once in three months when he had preached and administered the sacraments. Mr. Le Boucq should have taken up the duties in the parish to which he had been appointed, but instead of doing so, he got into difficulties at the Cape, as will be related in the next chapter, and Drakenstein was for several years without a resident clergyman.

In the evening of the 3rd of April 1702 the outward bound ship *Meresteyn*, an Indiaman of the first class, ran ashore on Jutten Island, and in less than an hour broke into little pieces. Her skipper was endeavouring to reach Saldanha Bay, and the ship was in a heavy surf before any one on board suspected danger. The majority of her crew were lost, as also were two women and five children passengers for the Cape. Ninety-nine persons managed to reach the shore.

In March 1702 a marauding party consisting of forty-five white men and the same number of Hottentots, whose deeds were afterwards prominently brought to light, left Stellenbosch, and remained away seven months. They travelled eastward until they reached the neighbourhood of the Fish river, where at daylight one morning they were attacked unexpectedly and without provocation by a band of

Kosa warriors who were fugitives from their own country and were living in friendship with the Hottentots. The assailants were beaten off, followed up, and when they turned and made another stand, were defeated again, losing many men. One European was killed. The party then commenced a career of robbery, excusing their acts to themselves under the plea that they were undertaken in retaliation. They fell upon the Gonaquas and other Hottentot hordes, shot many of them, and drove off their cattle.

The perpetrators of these scandalous acts were not brought to justice. In after years when the governor and the colonists were at variance, and each party was endeavouring to blacken the reputation of the other, the governor stated that they were in league with the colonists and were too numerous to be punished without ruining half the settlement. This statement was, however, indignantly contradicted by the most respectable burghers, who asserted that the marauding Europeans were miscreants without families or homes, being chiefly fugitives from justice and men of loose character who had been imprudently discharged from the Company's service. The burghers maintained that they ought to have been punished. The names of the forty-five white men who formed the robber band are given. Forty of them are quite unknown in South Africa at the present day, and the remaining five are of that class that cannot be distinguished with certainty, so that the assertions of the burghers are strongly borne out.

Owing chiefly to the scarcity of timber and fuel, in 1705 it was resolved to send an expedition to Natal and the adjoining coast, to make an inspection of the country, and particularly of the forests which were known to be there. The schooner *Centaurus*, which had been built at Natal in 1686–7, principally from timber growing on the shore of the lagoon, was a proof that the wood was valuable, for she had been in use nearly fourteen years before needing repair. The galiot *Postlooper* was made ready for the expedition. Her master, Theunis van der Schelling, had visited Natal when he was mate of the *Noord* in 1689 and 1690, and therefore knew the harbour. He was instructed to make a thorough exploration of the forests, and to frame a chart of the coast. A sailor who was expert in drawing pictures was sent to take sketches of the scenery.

The *Postlooper* sailed on the 20th of November 1705. She reached Natal on the 29th of December, and found the bar so silted up that she could only cross at high water. There were not so many cattle in the neighbourhood as there had been sixteen years before. Wood still remained in considerable quantities.

In December 1689 a purchase of the lagoon and surrounding land had been made from the chief then living at Port Natal, and had been recorded in a formal contract, two copies of which had been drawn up. The one kept by the Dutch officers had been lost when the *Noord* was wrecked in January 1690, and the master of the *Postlooper* had therefore received instructions to endeavour to procure the other, that had been left with the chief, in order that a notarial copy might be made. The chief who sold the ground was dead, and his son was now the head of the tribe or clan, whichever it may have been. Upon Skipper Van der Schelling making inquiry of him concerning the document, the chief stated that he knew nothing about it, and supposed it had been buried with his father's other personal effects. It was evident that he did not recognise the sale as binding upon him or his people.

At Natal an Englishman was found who gave his name as Vaughan Goodwin, and who stated that he was a native of London. He had two wives and several children. His story was that he had arrived there in February 1699 in a vessel named the *Fidele*, and with two others had been left behind by Captain Stadis, who purposed to form a settlement. They were to keep possession of the place until Captain Stadis should return, which he promised them would certainly be within three years; but he had not yet appeared. In 1700 the natives had killed the other white men.

The life which Goodwin was leading seemed so attractive

to two of the *Postlooper's* crew that they ran away from the vessel. When crossing the bar in leaving Natal the galiot lurched, and the tiller struck the skipper in the chest and hurt him so badly that he became unfit for duty. There was no one on board who could take his place, so the vessel returned to the Cape without any further attempt at exploration being made by her crew. She dropped anchor again in Table Bay on the 8th of March 1706.

The directors were desirous of procuring sheep's wool from South Africa, as some samples sent to Europe were pronounced of excellent quality. They were of opinion that if it could be produced at eight pence a pound, they would be able to make a good profit from it, and the colonists would have another reliable source of income. Instructions were sent to the government to have this industry taken in hand by the burghers. But it was not a pursuit that commended itself to South African farmers at that time. Although a good many European sheep had been imported in former years, there were very few of pure breed left, nearly all having been crossed with the large tailed native animal. It was commonly believed that woolled sheep were more subject to scab than others, and the havoc created by that disease was often so great that the farmers were in constant dread of it. Then there was the expense of separate herds. Further the carcase of the woolled sheep was not so valuable as that of the other, so that the graziers who bred for slaughter could not be induced even to make experiments.

In 1700 the government sent home two hundred and eighty-five pounds of wool shorn from sheep belonging to the Company. This was received with favour, but instead of increasing, the quantity fell off in succeeding years. In 1703 one small bale was all that could be obtained. It realised about fifteen pence English money a pound on the market in Amsterdam. In 1704 a very small quantity was procured, in 1705 none at all, and in 1706 one hundred and fourteen pounds. In the mean time the governor took the matter in hand as a private speculation. He collected all the wool-bearing sheep in the settlement at a farm of his own, wrote to Europe for rams and ewes of good breed and to Java for some Persian sheep, and was about to give the industry a fair trial when he was recalled.

The governor had previously endeavoured to introduce the culture of silk. He made experiments with the white mulberry, which was found to grow and thrive well, but the silkworms which he obtained from imported eggs all died. He then gave up the trial, being of opinion that the mulberry was in leaf at the wrong season of the year for worms from the south of Europe.

A less important but more successful experiment made by this governor was placing partridges and pheasants on Robben Island to breed.

From 1698 to 1705 the seasons were very unfavourable for farming, and no wheat could be exported. In 1700 it became necessary to import rice from Java, as there was not sufficient grain in the country for the consumption of the people and the supply of fresh bread to the crews of ships. In 1705 the long drought broke up, and the crops were very good; but as the wheat was being reaped heavy rain set in and greatly damaged it. There was, however, a surplus above the requirements of the country, and in 1706 exportation was resumed and fourteen hundred muids were sent to Batavia.

The population of the colony was at this time increasing rapidly. The families of the burghers were generally large, they married at an early age, and no young women remained single. From Europe every year a few settlers were received. A custom had come into vogue of allowing soldiers and convalescent sailors to engage for short periods as servants to burghers, their wages and cost of maintenance being thus saved to the Company, while they were at hand in case of need. From a hundred to a hundred and fifty of the garrison and seamen were commonly out at service. A great many slaves were being introduced from Madagascar and Mozambique.

The bad seasons tended to produce a spirit of restlessness among the farming population, which was increased by the conduct of the principal officers of the government. Between Wilhem Adriaan van der Stel and the colonists of South Africa there was not the slightest feeling of sympathy. In all the official documents of the period during which he was at the head of affairs, and the quantity is great, there is not a single expression like 'our own Netherlanders' of his father. He requested the directors indeed to send out industrious Zealand farmers and no more French cadets, but the sentence displays as little affection for the one class as for the other.

The governor was engaged in farming for his own benefit on a very large scale as things were estimated in those days. He could not take ground for himself, but in February 1700 a commissioner, Wouter Valckenier by name, holding authority from the governor-general and council of India, had visited the Cape, and at his request granted him in freehold four hundred morgen of land at Hottentots Holland. To this he afterwards added by granting a tract of the adjoining ground to a subordinate official, and then purchasing it from that individual at a nominal rate. The estate he named Vergelegen.

Upon it he built a commodious dwelling house, with a flour mill, a leather tannery, a workshop for making wooden water pipes, wine and grain stores, an overseer's cottage, a slave lodge, and very extensive outbuildings. He was in the habit of frequently residing there for ten days or a fortnight at a time, when public business was partly suspended. This was concealed from the directors, for there is no mention of Vergelegen or of the governor's absence from the castle in the official journal of occurrences or the correspondence of the period, copies of which were sent to Holland. On the estate were planted nearly half a million vines, or fully one fourth of the whole number in the colony in 1706. Groves, orchards, and cornlands were laid out to a corresponding extent. Beyond the mountains at various places the governor had six or eight hundred large cattle and eight or ten thousand sheep.

The secunde, Samuel Elsevier, obtained a grant of the farm Elsenburg, near Klapmuts. The Rev. Petrus Kalden, clergyman of the Cape, in like manner obtained the farm Zandvliet, between Stellenbosch and the head of False Bay. These officials engaged in farming on a much smaller scale than the governor; but, in the case of the clergyman especially, neglected their public duties to attend to their private properties. The governor's brother, Frans van der Stel, was a farmer at Hottentots Holland. His father was a farmer at Constantia. The market for produce was small, and all of these persons had an entry to it before the burghers could dispose of anything.

There has never been a people less inclined to submit to grievances, real or imaginary, than the colonists of South Africa. Some of the farmers determined to complain to the supreme authorities, and in 1705 privately forwarded to the governor-general and council of India a list of charges. At Batavia no action was taken in the matter. While the complainants were awaiting a reply, one of their number, Adam Tas by name, a native of Amsterdam and now a burgher of Stellenbosch, drew up a memorial to the directors in the Fatherland. This document contained thirty-eight paragraphs, some of great length, in which the governor and the others were accused of acting as has been stated, and the governor was further charged with corruption, extortion, and oppression.

It was affirmed that he employed the Company's servants and slaves at his farm; that he used the Company's materials for building; that his agents when sent to barter cattle from the Hottentots had taken them by violence; that he bought wine at very low rates from those who could find no market for it, and disposed of it at very high rates to strangers; that instead of licensing by auction four dealers in wine, to each of whom the farmers could sell without restriction, he caused the privilege of dealing in that article by retail to be sold as a monopoly to a man who would buy his at a good price; and that he would make no grant of land without a bribe. Some other offences of an equally serious nature were complained of. The memorial was signed by sixty-three individuals, thirty-one of whom were Frenchmen. Their intention was to send it to the directors with the return fleet in the early months of 1706.

The official records of the early years of Wilhem Adriaan van der Stel's administration, to which the burghers had no access, prove that some of the most serious of the charges against him were without foundation. One of his principal opponents—Jacob van der Heiden—was at a later date strongly suspected of having been guilty of dishonest practices himself, and there is good ground for believing that the opposition of another—Henning Huising—arose from his loss at the end of 1705 of the lucrative contract he had held for five years. At the instance of the governor, tenders were called for, and four butchers were licensed, the price of meat being fixed at a penny three farthings a pound to the Company and two pence to burghers. Huising resented this, and as the contract had made him the richest man in the community, he could make his resentment felt.

But after taking these circumstances into consideration, the charges that were unquestionably true make a formidable indictment, and the majority of the governor's opponents were the most godfearing and respectable men in the country. Among them was J. W. Grevenbroek, recently an elder at Stellenbosch, who took an active part in the movement, though his name was not attached to the memorial.

With the arrival of the homeward bound fleet on the 4th of February 1706 it came to the governor's knowledge that a document in which he was accused of malpractices had been sent to Batavia in the previous year. He immediately concluded that similar charges would be forwarded to the Netherlands, and that a memorial embodying them must be in existence; but he was unable to learn where it was, or who were parties to it. The danger of his position now drove him to acts of extreme folly as well as of tyranny. He caused a certificate to be drawn up, in which he was credited with the highest virtues, and the utmost satisfaction was expressed with his administration. The burgher residents of the peninsula were invited to the castle, and were then requested to sign this certificate. The landdrost of Stellenbosch, Johannes Starrenburg by name, a base sycophant who had held office since July 1705, was directed to proceed with an armed party from house to house in the country, and get the residents there to sign it also. By these means two hundred and forty names in all were obtained, including those of a few Asiatics and free blacks.[1] Many, however, refused to affix their signatures, even under the landdrost's threats that they would be marked men if they did not.

The governor suspected that Adam Tas was the writer of the memorial, so the landdrost was directed to have him arrested. Early in the morning of Sunday the 28th of February 1706 his house was surrounded by an armed party, he was seized and sent as a prisoner to the castle, his premises were searched, and his writing desk was carried away. There could be no truce after this between the governor and his opponents, for if a burgher could be treated in this manner, upon mere suspicion of having drawn up a memorial to the high authorities, no man's liberty would be safe. Bail was immediately offered for the appearance of Tas before a court of justice, but was refused. He was committed to prison, where he was kept nearly fourteen months.

In his desk was found the draft from which the memorial to the directors had been copied. It was unsigned, but a list containing a number of names and various letters which were with it indicated several of those who had taken part in the compilation. The completed memorial was at the time in the house of a burgher in Table Valley, where it was intended to be kept until it could be sent away with the return fleet.

The governor thus became acquainted with the nature and terms of the charges against him. Some of the accusations were so overdrawn that he felt confident the directors upon reading them would acquit him of all, and in this belief

[1] This document is in as good a state of preservation as if it had been drawn up yesterday.

he did not hesitate to request that a competent and impartial person might be sent out with the first opportunity to examine matters.

On the 4th of March a number of ships' officers were invited to assist in the deliberations of the council of policy, and the retired and acting burgher councillors were summoned to give evidence. These answered a few questions put to them by the governor, in a manner favourable to him. The broad council then consented to the issue of a placaat, in which all persons were forbidden to take part in any conspiracy or to sign any malicious or slanderous document against the authorities of the country, under pain of severe punishment. The ringleaders in such acts were threatened with death or corporal chastisement. The fiscal and the landdrost were authorised to seize persons suspected of such offences, and to commit them to prison. This placaat was on the following Sunday affixed to the door of the Stellenbosch church.

Within the next few days the governor caused the burghers Wessel Pretorius and Jacob van der Heiden to be arrested and committed to prison, Jan Rotterdam to be sent to Batavia, and Pieter van der Byl, Henning Huising, Ferdinandus Appel, and Jan van Meerland to be put on board a ship bound to Amsterdam. The burghers deported were informed that they must answer before the supreme authorities at the places of their destination to the charges of sedition and conspiracy that would be forwarded by the Cape council, and if they had any complaints they might make them there also.

By these highhanded proceedings the governor hoped to terrify his opponents into signing the certificate in his favour and denying the truth of the charges made against him. But not one of those who were confined on board the ships in the bay faltered for a moment. Their wives petitioned that the prisoners might be brought to trial at once before a proper court of justice, and when it was hinted that if they would induce their husbands to do what was desired, release would follow, these truehearted women indignantly refused.

The arrest and committal to prison of Nicholas van der

Westhuizen, Christiaan Wynoch, Hans Jacob Konterman, and Nicholas Meyboom followed shortly. In the mean time the memorial had been committed to the care of Abraham Bogaert, a physician in the return fleet, who was refreshing himself on shore, and who had a very warm sympathy with the burghers. On the 4th of April the fleet sailed, and when at sea and all fear of search was over Bogaert delivered the document to Henning Huising.

The anchors of the ships were being raised and the topsails being sheeted home when the governor must have reflected that he was making a great mistake in sending four of the burghers to Europe. In great haste he embarked in a galiot and followed the fleet as far as Robben Island. In the official records it is stated that he did this to show respect to the admiral, but no such method of showing respect was practised here before or since, and his opponents were probably right when they asserted that his object was to overtake the ship in which the burghers were, and release them. He did not succeed in doing this, however.

Within a week or two further arrests were made, when the burghers Jacob de Savoye, Pierre Meyer, Jacob Louw, Jacob Cloete, and one or two others were placed in detention. The health of some of the prisoners broke down under the rigorous treatment to which they were subjected: one—Van der Heiden—was confined for twenty-seven days in a foul dungeon, with a black criminal as his companion. Most of these then, to obtain their liberty, disowned the truth of the assertions in the memorial, and expressed contrition for having signed it. They excused themselves afterwards for so doing by arguing that it could not affect the charges against the officials, as these would be brought before the directors by those who were then on their way to Europe. And so after an imprisonment varying in duration from a few days to a few weeks, all were released except Adam Tas and Jacob Louw.

For a short time matters were now quiet, but on the governor coming to learn the names of some more of his opponents, Willem van Zyl, François du Toit, Guillaume du Toit, Hercules du Pré, Cornelis van Niekerk, Martin van Staden, Jacobus van Brakel, Jan Elberts, and Nicholas Elberts were cited to appear before the court of justice. These came to a resolution not to obey the summons before the decision of the directors should be known, and so they failed to attend. They were cited by placaat, but in vain. In consequence, on the 9th of August, by a majority of the court of justice sitting with closed doors each of them was sentenced for contumacy to be banished to Mauritius for five years and to pay a fine of 41*l.* 13*s.* 4*d.*, half for the landdrost as prosecutor and half for the court. They were at the same time declared incapable of ever holding any political or military office in the colony.

This sentence was made public on the 23rd of August, and it tended to increase the hostility to the government. The military outposts, excepting those at Waveren, Klapmuts, Groen Vlei, and Saldanha Bay, at which twenty-four men in all were stationed, had been broken up before this date, so the burghers felt free to act.

In the early morning of the 18th of September the farmers of Waveren, Riebeek's Kasteel, and Drakenstein rode armed into the village of Stellenbosch, and at beat of drum drew up near the landdrost's office. Starrenburg went out to them, and requested the drummer to be still; but that individual, who was a Frenchman, kept on beating, only observing that he did not understand Dutch. Some persons, to show their contempt for the landdrost, began to dance round the drum. Others inquired why there was to be no fair this year, such as there had always been since 1686. Starrenburg replied that the Indian authorities had prohibited it; but they would not believe him, and laid the blame upon the Cape government. Yet it was correct that the Indian authorities were solely responsible in this matter, as with a view to save expense, on the 29th of November 1705 they had instructed the council of policy not to contribute longer towards the prizes or to furnish wine and ale at the cost of the Company. There was thus no kermis or fair in 1706 and later.

After this the women expressed their views. The wives of Pieter van der Byl and Wessel Pretorius, speaking for all, informed the landdrost that they had no intention of submitting to his tyranny, but were resolved to maintain their rights. The spirit of the women of the country districts was thoroughly roused, and their opposition was as formidable as that of their husbands.[1] Starrenburg was obliged to return to his house in humiliation. The burghers remained in the village the whole day, setting him at defiance, but otherwise preserving perfect order.

A few days later two of the persons sentenced to banishment appeared in Stellenbosch without any support, and jeered at the landdrost, who dared not attempt to arrest them, as he could not even depend upon his subordinates. All respect for the government was gone.

It was now arranged between the governor and the landdrost that during the night of the 28th September, after the closing of the castle gate, a party of soldiers should march secretly to the Kuilen. At two o'clock in the morning of the 29th the landdrost was to meet them there, and was then before daylight to arrest those who were believed to be the leaders of the defiant party. But a constable at the Kuilen, who sympathised with the burghers, managed to detain the party for a time, and when they at length left to try and seize Cornelis van Niekerk in his bed, the alarm had been given.

Daylight broke, no one had been captured, and there was nothing left for the landdrost and the soldiers but to retire to the village of Stellenbosch. No one there would give any information or sell a particle of food to the troops, and the landdrost was obliged to kill his own goats for their use until provisions could be sent from the Cape. Starrenburg having now soldiers at his back, the burghers sentenced to exile fled to Twenty-four Rivers, where they concealed themselves. The landdrost did his best to capture them,

[1] 'Maar Edele Gestrenge Heer, de wyven zyn alsoo gevaarlyk als de mans, en zyn niet stil.' Extract from letter of the landdrost Starrenburg to the governor Wilhem Adriaan van der Stel, 18th September 1706.

and on the 4th of February 1707 succeeded in arresting Hercules du Pré and Jacobus van Brakel, who were sent on board the Mauritius packet. A month later Guillaume du Toit was also arrested. During this time the governor dismissed the heemraden and other officers who had been elected in the legitimate manner, and arbitrarily appointed creatures of his own to the vacant places.

At this juncture the homeward bound fleet arrived from Batavia, and in one of the ships was Jan Rotterdam, who returned to the colony in triumph. The governor-general and council of India had taken no notice whatever of the charges made against him by the authorities here, but had treated him with exceptional kindness and given him a free passage back. A ship also arrived from Europe, and brought letters to some of the burghers, informing them that their case had been decided favourably by the directors. As yet no official despatches had been received, but on the 16th of April 1707 the *Kattendyk* from Texel cast anchor in Table Bay, and her skipper, in presence of witnesses as he had been instructed to do, delivered to the governor a letter from the Assembly of Seventeen dated the 30th of October 1706.

Of the four burghers sent to Europe, one, Jan van Meerland, died on the passage home. The others, on arriving at Amsterdam, presented to the directors the memorial which Tas had drawn up. The charges made by the authorities at the Cape had already been received, as had been the governor's denial of some of the statements made by the burghers, and explanation of others. In a matter of this kind it was necessary to act with promptitude as well as with justice. The Company had numerous and powerful enemies always watching for an opportunity to arraign it before the States General, and a charge of oppression of free Netherlanders in one of its colonies would be a formidable weapon for them to use. A commission of investigation was therefore appointed without delay, and the documents were laid before it.

The commission sent in a report condemning the govern

and those who acted with him, in consequence of which the letter brought by the *Kattendyk* was written. It announced that the governor Wilhem Adriaan van der Stel, the secunde Samuel Elsevier, the clergyman Petrus Kalden, and the landdrost Johannes Starrenburg were removed from office and ordered to proceed to Europe with the first opportunity. The governor's brother, Frans van der Stel, was to betake himself to some place outside of the Company's possessions. The burghers were acquitted of conspiracy, the three sent to Europe were restored to their homes at the Company's expense, and orders were given that if any were in prison in the colony they should be immediately released. It was announced that Louis van Assenburgh, who had previously been an officer in the army of the German Emperor, had been appointed governor, and Johan Cornelis d'Ableing, recently commander at Palembang, secunde. In case neither of these should arrive in the colony at an early date, the administration was to be assumed by the independent fiscal Johan Blesius and the other members of the council of policy acting as a commission.

The Mauritius packet had not sailed when this letter arrived, and the fiscal, who was directed by the Assembly of Seventeen to carry out their instructions, at once set at liberty the five burghers Adam Tas, Jacob Louw, Jacobus van Brakel, Hercules du Pré, and Guillaume du Toit. The first named henceforth called his farm Libertas, to signify that freedom had been won, or, as he wittily explained to inquirers as to the meaning of the term, to denote that Tas was free. The place is still so called.

Next morning the council of policy met. It was resolved that the administration should be transferred to the fiscal and others on the 15th of May, if the newly appointed secunde, who was on his way out, should not arrive before that date. It was Sunday, and the Rev. Mr. Kalden preached twice in the church.

During the week an arrangement was made by which the Rev. Messrs. Le Boucq and Bek should conduct the services on alternate Sundays at the Cape, and Mr. Kalden ceased to officiate. Starrenburg, whose last report was that the mutineers were constantly reviling him and that only a Masauiello was wanting to produce an open outbreak, was sent by the fiscal on board a ship returning to Europe. An officer named Samuel Martin de Meurs was appointed to act provisionally as landdrost.

Johan Cornelis d'Ableing, the newly appointed secunde, arrived on the 6th of May 1707. He was a nephew of the recalled governor Van der Stel, and, under pretence that the books required to be balanced, postponed taking over the administration until the 3rd of June. The recalled officials could not then leave for Europe before the arrival of the homeward bound fleet of the following year.

From the vast quantity of contemporaneous printed and manuscript matter relating to the complaints against Wilhem Adriaan van der Stel, the views of the directors and of the colonists concerning the government of the country and the rights of its people can be gathered with great precision. In the Netherlands at that period representative institutions, such as are now believed to be indispensable to liberty, were unknown. Yet the people were free in reality as well as in name. There is not a word expressing a wish on the part of the burghers for an alteration in the form of government, what they desired being merely that the administration should be placed in honest hands, and that their rights should be respected.

The directors desired to have here a large body of freemen in comfortable circumstances, loyal to the Fatherland, ready and willing to assist in the defence of the colony if attacked, enjoying the same rights as their peers in Europe, and without much diversity of rank or position. They stated clearly and distinctly that the closer the equality between the burghers could be preserved the more satisfactory it would be to them. Positive orders were issued that large tracts of land, upon which several families could obtain a living, were not to be granted to any individual.

In giving directions concerning Vergelegen, they stated that as its grant by the commissioner Valckenier to the governor had never been reported to them, they resumed possession of the ground. The large dwelling house upon it, being adapted for ostentation and not for the use of a farmer, must be broken down. The late governor could sell the material for his own benefit. The other buildings and improvements could be fairly valued, and the amount be paid to Mr. Van der Stel, or he could break them down and dispose of the materials if he preferred to do so. The ground must then be divided into four farms, and each be sold separately by auction.

An estate such as Vergelegen would by many people to-day be considered useful as a model. Van der Stel had imported the choicest vines, plants, and trees from foreign countries, and was making extensive experiments there. The ground was the most skilfully tilled in the whole country. But the directors held that such a farm as this, owned by one individual and cultivated chiefly by slave labour, could not be of the same advantage to the infant colony as a number of smaller ones, each in possession of a sturdy European proprietor.

For this reason Frans van der Stel was required to sell his property, and remove to some country not included in the Company's charter. The former governor Simon van der Stel was left in possession of his farm Constantia, but directions were given that upon his death the other land which he held should revert to the Company.

Emphatic instructions were issued that for the future no servant of the Company, from the highest to the lowest, was to own or lease land in the colony, or to trade directly or indirectly in corn, wine, or cattle. Those who had landed property could sell it, but if they should not do so within a reasonable period, it would be confiscated. The burghers were not to be molested in their right to dispose of their cattle or the produce of their ground in any way that suited them. They were to be governed in accordance with law and justice.

On their part, the colonists claimed exactly the same rights as if they were still living in the Fatherland. They held that any restrictions to which the early burghers had agreed were of a temporary nature, and affected only those who consented to them. In their opinion they had forfeited nothing by removal to a dependency, and the violence displayed by the governor towards Adam Tas and his associates was as outrageous as if it had taken place in the city of Amsterdam. They asserted their undoubted right to personal liberty, to exemption from arrest unless under reasonable suspicion of crime, to admission to bail, to speedy trial before a proper court of justice, to freedom to sell to any one, burgher or foreigner, except under special circumstances when restriction was needed for the good of the community, whatever their land produced, after the tithes had been paid and the Company's needs had been supplied. And these claims, made in as explicit terms as they could be to-day by an Englishman living in a crown colony, were not challenged by the directors or even the partisans of the late governor, but were accepted by every one as unquestioned.

The directors were fully aware that a colony of free Netherlanders was to be ruled in a different manner from a dependency inhabited by Asiatics.

CHAPTER XVIII.

JOHAN CORNELIS D'ABLEING, SECUNDE, ACTING HEAD OF THE GOVERNMENT, 8 JUNE 1707 TO 1 FEBRUARY 1708.

LOUIS VAN ASSENBURGH, GOVERNOR, INSTALLED 1 FEBRUARY 1708, DIED 27 DECEMBER 1711.

WILLEM HELOT, SECUNDE, ACTING HEAD OF THE GOVERNMENT, 28 DECEMBER 1711 TO 28 MARCH 1714.

Violent conduct of the Rev. Mr. Le Boucq—Church matters at the Cape, Stellenbosch, and Drakenstein—Scene in the Cape church—Deportation of the Rev. Mr. Le Boucq—Arrival of Governor Van Assenburgh—Departure of the recalled officials—Further proceedings against the late officials in Amsterdam—Division and sale of Vergelegen—Visit of the commissioner Simons—Regulations concerning the manumission of slaves—Series of good seasons—Exportation of wheat to Batavia—Abandonment of the island of Mauritius by the Dutch—Visit of the retired governor-general Van Hoorn—Instructions concerning the tithes of grain—Partial destruction of the village of Stellenbosch by fire—Placaat against destruction of trees—Neglect of tree planting—Definition of a boundary between the Cape and Stellenbosch districts—Death of Governor Van Assenburgh—Election of the secunde Willem Helot to act as head of the government—Enlargement of the colony—False alarm concerning an inroad of the Great Namaquas—Wreck of the *Bennebroek* on the coast of Natal—Sufferings of the sailors who got to land—Friendly treatment of some of them by a native tribe—First appearance of small pox in South Africa—Great loss of life—Effects upon the Hottentot tribes in the neighbourhood of the Cape—Some bad seasons—Appointment of Colonel Maurits Pasques de Chavonnes as governor of the Cape Colony and councillor extraordinary of Netherlands India—Names of new colonists.

THE only circumstance deserving note during the few months that the secunde D'Ableing was at the head of the government was the violent conduct of the Rev. Mr. Le Boucq, which caused much disquiet in the community. That clergyman had arrived at the Cape at a time of clamour and strife, and instead of preaching peace, at once became a promoter of further discord. He took side with the colonists, though there was no good object to be gained by his entering into the question of party politics, since all that the burghers had contended for was secured. He was conversant with the Portuguese language, and could therefore have been of greater service in India than here, but as he was of quarrelsome disposition the authorities at Batavia were glad to get rid of him.

Upon Mr. Le Boucq's arrival at the Cape, the Rev. Mr. Bek removed to Stellenbosch, that the new clergyman might enter upon his duties; but as soon as he ascertained that there was neither church nor parsonage at Drakenstein, he declined to take up the work. Before any pressure could be put upon him, the Rev. Mr. Kalden was suspended, and the government then decided that Messrs. Bek and Le Boucq should conduct the services at the Cape on alternate Sundays. After a little, the two ministers arranged between themselves that Le Boucq should take all the services at the Cape, Mr. Bek going occasionally to Drakenstein; and to this the government made no objection.

The Dutch sick comforter of Drakenstein had some time previously been transferred to the Cape, and the council now resolved to send some one else there. On the 8th of June 1707 Mr. Hermanus Bosman, sick comforter of the ship *Overryp*, was selected for the post. Thereafter he conducted service in Dutch, and Mr. Paul Roux in French, at the houses of farmers at Drakenstein, except when the Rev. Mr. Bek went over from Stellenbosch.

In the morning of Sunday the 28th of August 1707 the congregation of the Cape assembled in the church and listened to an exciting sermon prepared and read by the Rev. Mr. Le Boucq. He had chosen as text the first verse of the 29th chapter of Proverbs, and had previously given out the last two verses of the 149th psalm to be sung. According to his exposition, the saints were the burghers who had recently made a stand for freedom, the noble who hardened his neck and was in consequence destroyed was the recalled governor Van der Stel. At the last election of church officers, Abraham Poulle, who was in the government service, had been chosen elder, and the burgher Jan Oberholster, who submitted quietly to the ruling of the authorities, had been appointed deacon. When the service was ended, the clergyman announced that these persons were deprived of their offices, and exhorted the congregation not to acknowledge them any longer.

This proceeding took most of the congregation by surprise, and caused great excitement to many individuals. One woman fainted, and was carried out of the church to the hospital. No member of the government or of the consistory anticipated anything of the kind, though they were accustomed to very eccentric acts of the clergyman. The members of the council of policy at once retired and held a consultation, after which they sent a request to Mr. Le Boucq not to conduct service in the afternoon, a request which he construed into an order.

Next morning he sent a letter to the council, in which he asserted his right as a clergyman to depose elders and deacons without assigning any reason for doing so, and protested against interference by lay officials in spiritual matters. He followed this up by a letter on the 6th of September, in which he stated that he did not intend to perform service again until the council admitted his views to be correct. Thereupon the council suspended payment of his salary, and instructed Mr. Bek to assume duty at the Cape. Mr. Kalden was requested to assist in the emergency, and showed himself very willing to do so, by holding service occasionally so as to allow Mr. Bek to visit Stellenbosch and Drakenstein.

By the more violent members of the party which he had espoused Mr. Le Boucq was now regarded as a martyr. He went about declaiming against the government, and stirring up people's passions until it was considered necessary to bring him to task. Certain language of his was reported to the government, upon which it was intended to bring a charge. The principal witness was Maria Lindenhof, daughter of a clergyman in Overyssel, wife of Henning Huising, and aunt of Adam Tas. Upon being questioned, she asserted that she had forgotten what he had said. The court of justice then decided to confine hor for eight days to her own house, and then to place her under civil arrest if she did not in the mean time give correct evidence. She remained obdurate, and after eight days was confined in a suite of rooms in the castle. A petition for her release, signed by Tas, Grevenbroek, Van der Byl, and twenty-four others, men and women, was sent in, and after nine days detention in the castle the government thought it best to liberate her.

Mr. Le Boucq next appeared before the court of justice as a litigant in a case with the Rev. Mr. Kalden, and, upon judgment being recorded against him, appealed to Batavia. There also the decision was against him. In the mean time the council of policy, in the belief that concord could not be expected at the Cape as long as this quarrelsome clergyman was here, resolved, 17th of January 1708, to send him back to Batavia with the first outward bound ship; but it was not until the 13th of the following September that this resolution could be carried into effect.

On the 25th of January 1708 Governor Louis van Assenburgh arrived in Table Bay, and next morning he presided at a meeting of the council of policy, though he did not at once assume the direction of affairs. He had been eight months on the passage from Holland, and had been obliged to put into a port on the coast of Brazil. In the same ship with the governor was the Rev. Johannes Godfried d'Ailly, who had been appointed clergyman of the Cape, and who preached here for the first time on the 5th of February. Henning Huising, one of the deported burghers, was also on board. He had entered into a contract with the directors for the supply of half the meat required by the Company at the Cape during the next three years, the object of dividing the contract being to secure competition. Pieter van der Byl and Ferdinandus Appel had reached the colony seven months before.

When the arrival of the governor was known at Vergelegen, Mr. Van der Stel sent a petition to the council of policy requesting that he might be allowed to retain the estate for a few months longer, as he had hopes that by the next fleet from Europe intelligence would be received that the directors had mitigated their decision. The council refused to comply, and the utmost that he could obtain was permission to press the grapes then ripening and dispose of half the wine on his own account, the other half to be for the Company. The quantity pressed was fifty-six leggers.

On the 23rd of February Henning Huising summoned Mr. Van der Stel before the court of justice for 3,056*l.* in addition to the value of nine thousand sheep. The late governor then requested the council of policy to allow him to remain in South Africa for another year, in order to get evidence to defend himself in this case; but upon Huising stating that he preferred bringing the action in the Fatherland to being the means of keeping Van der Stel longer in the colony, the council declined to accede to his request.

On the 23rd of April the return fleet sailed, taking to Europe the late governor, secunde, and clergyman of the Cape, with their families. Nineteen of the burghers empowered Adam Tas and Jacob van der Heiden to continue pressing their charges against the recalled officials, for these, though deprived of authority, were still servants of the Company and in receipt of their salaries. Tas and Van der Heiden therefore left in the same fleet. Another investigation took place in Amsterdam, which resulted in the absolute dismissal of Van der Stel, Elsevier, and Kalden from the Company's service. They left agents in the colony to dispose of their estates and transmit the proceeds.

Vergelegen was divided into four farms, which were sold by auction in October 1709. It was found on measurement to contain six hundred and thirteen morgen. The large dwelling house was broken down, and the material sold for Van der Stel's benefit. The other buildings were taken over by the Company for 625*l.*, though the materials of which they were constructed were appraised at a much higher sum. The four farms brought 1,695*l.* at public sale, the purchasers being Barend Gildenhuis, Jacob van der Heiden, Jacob Malan, and the widow of Gerrit Cloete.

Frans van der Stel returned to Europe in the same fleet with his brother, and took up his residence in Amsterdam.

His wife, Johanna Wessels, was a daughter of one of the leading burghers of the colony. She remained behind with her parents to dispose of the property to the best advantage, and did not leave to rejoin her husband in Amsterdam until April 1717.

On the 1st of February 1708 Governor Louis van Assenburgh was installed in office. He had been a brave and skilful military officer, but in this country he speedily developed a fondness for the pleasures of the table, which caused him to be described as a winebibber. He carried out the instructions of the directors, however, in letter and in spirit, so that he won the regard of the burghers.

The return fleet of 1708 was under command of Cornelis Joan Simons, who had been the first independent fiscal at the Cape, and had resided here in that capacity from 1690 to 1694. He had recently been governor of Ceylon, and was now empowered by the governor-general and council of India to act as commissioner during his stay in South Africa. He issued a number of regulations, but the only one which needs to be mentioned here is that referring to the emancipation of slaves.

During the period that had elapsed since the first appearance of the Dutch in India and Africa, the views of Europeans with regard to African slavery had been gradually changing. At first blacks were enslaved on the plea that they were heathens, but a profession of Christianity sufficed to free them and to place them on a level in civil rights with their former masters. As time wore on, it became apparent that in most instances emancipation meant the conversion of a useful individual into an indolent pauper and a pest to society. Habits of industry, which in Europeans are the result of pressure of circumstances operating upon the race through hundreds of generations, were found to be altogether opposed to the disposition of Africans. Experience showed that a freed slave usually chose to live in a filthy hovel upon coarse and scanty food rather than toil for something better. Decent clothing was not a necessity of life to him, neither did he need other furniture in his hovel than a few cooking utensils. He put nothing by, and when sickness came he was a burden upon the public. Such in general was the negro when left to himself in a country where sufficient food to keep life in his body was to be had without much exertion. Emancipation then became less common, and the view began to be held and asserted that slavery was the proper condition of the black race.

The commissioner Simons, in his instructions to the Cape government, dated 19th of April 1708, directed that no slave was to be emancipated without security being given by the owner that the freed person should not become a charge upon the poor funds within ten years, according to the statutes of India. This was henceforth the law in South Africa.

There was, however, one notable exception to this law. It frequently happened that ladies returning from India to Europe took slave girls with them as waiting maids, and sometimes gentlemen were in the same way accompanied by their valets. These slaves were almost invariably sent back again, as they could be of no service in the Netherlands. The directors issued instructions that such persons were to be treated as free people, proof of their having been on the soil of the republic to be equivalent to letters of manumission.

This was the last year in which nominations from the Drakenstein consistory were sent in the French language. Upon the receipt of the usual documents, written in French, the council of policy directed that in future the nominations of church officers and letters to the government must be in Dutch.

In 1705 a series of good seasons had set in, and now every year a considerable quantity of wheat was sent to Batavia. From 1706 to 1711, both years included, the average export was rather over four thousand muids. The Company paid a little less than twelve shillings of our money a muid for it at the magazines. Rye, barley, beans, and peas were also grown in quantities sufficient to supply the wants of the shipping and of the Indian government. There was, however, a very limited market for these products in India. In 1708 the quantity of rye and beans grown was so greatly in excess of the demand that a notice was issued discouraging their cultivation, and stating that the Company would not purchase any more of either.

The island of Mauritius, hitherto a dependency of the Cape Colony, was at this time abandoned by the East India Company. It was of hardly any use as a station for refreshment, and beyond a little ebony and ambergris it contributed nothing to commerce. The directors came to the conclusion that it was not worth the cost of maintaining a large garrison, and that with a small garrison it was not secure.

Of late years the Company had sustained severe losses there. During the night of the 9th of February 1695 the residency and magazines were destroyed by a violent hurricane. In 1701 a pirate ship was wrecked on the coast close to the settlement, when two hundred armed men got safely to shore, together with twelve English and thirty Indian prisoners out of captured vessels. The master of the buccaneers was an old acquaintance of the Dutch Company, having been in the *Amy* when she was seized in 1693 in Saldanha Bay. The colonists thought it prudent to take refuge in the fort. The commander of the island, Roelof Diodati, to get rid of the unwelcome visitors, was obliged to sell them at half price the Company's packet, for which they paid him 167*l.* out of money saved from the wreck. On the 15th of November 1707 the Company's premises on the island were totally destroyed by fire, the books, records, and goods in the magazine being burned with everything else.

In February 1707 instructions were received at the Cape to withdraw the garrison. The colonists were to have the choice of removal to Java or the Cape. When this intelligence reached the island, the burghers were found to be very averse to break up their homes, but as a matter of necessity nine heads of families elected to come to the Cape, the remainder preferring Batavia. In September 1708 two vessels, the *Carthago* and *Mercurius*, were sent to commence transporting the people and their effects. The *Carthago* went on to Batavia, the *Mercurius* returned to the Cape, and landed her passengers here on the 26th of January 1709. Among them were Daniel Zaaiman, Gerrit Romond, and Hendrik de Vries, with their families. The names of the others are not given.

The *Beverwaart* was then sent to remove the garrison, and on the 25th of January 1710, Abraham Momber, the last Dutch commander, with the subordinate officers and the troops embarked in her and set sail for Batavia. Previous to going on board, the garrison destroyed everything within reach that could not be taken away. Even the forests were damaged as much as possible. All the hounds were left behind, that they might become wild and exterminate the game. The object of this wanton waste was to prevent the abandoned station being of service to any one else.

On the 10th of January 1710 the retired governor-general Joan van Hoorn, accompanied by his wife and daughter, arrived in Table Bay on his passage back to the Netherlands. He remained several weeks in the colony, where he acted as commissioner, presiding in the council and on all occasions taking precedence of the governor. On the 26th of February the three burgher councillors appeared before him, and on behalf of the whole body of freemen preferred a complaint. Instructions had recently been received from the supreme authorities to demand tithes of the whole uantity of corn gathered, and not of that portion only which was brought for sale, as had previously been the custom. The burgher councillors requested that the farmers might be relieved from payment of tithes of such grain as they required for their own consumption and for seed. The commissioner considered their request reasonable, and suspended the levy upon the whole until further instructions could be received.

The directors took another view, and in despatches received here in February 1711 the farmers were required to pay tithes upon all grain harvested, as those in Europe had to pay. In vain they represented to the council of policy that in the Fatherland the tithe was collected upon the ground, whereas here it was delivered at the Company's magazines. They were informed that the council had no power to make concessions in opposition to commands of the supreme authorities. An effort was made in 1712 to farm out the tithes by public auction, the purchaser to collect upon the ground; but no one would make an offer of any kind. The Company still maintained its claim, but the condition of the country settled the question in the farmers' favour, for it was soon found impracticable to collect a tithe upon all that was grown, and after a time a fixed amount was deducted from the price of grain brought for sale.

The writing desk of Adam Tas had been all this time in possession of the government. A council, presided over by Mr. Van Hoorn, appointed a committee to examine its contents. A report was brought up that some of the papers were seditious, when it was resolved that they should be destroyed and the others be returned to Tas.

On the 15th of March 1710 a young man named Jan de la Fontaine arrived in Table Bay as bookkeeper of the ship *Horstendaal*. The commissioner Van Hoorn took a liking to him, and gave him the appointment of master of the warehouses, thus introducing him to a career of official life in this colony which ended many years later in his occupying the post of governor.

On the 30th of April 1710 the secretary to the council of policy, Willem Helot by name, who had been sixteen years in service at the Cape, was by order of the directors raised to the rank of senior merchant and took over the duties of secunde, Mr. D'Ableing having been instructed to proceed to India to fill an office of greater importance. The late secunde left South Africa on the 10th of July following.

On the 17th of December 1710, at ten o'clock in the morning, a fire broke out in the village of Stellenbosch. There was a high wind, and a slave who was carrying a lighted fagot allowed some sparks to be blown into the thatch with which the landdrost's office was covered. In a minute the roof was in flames. The fire spread to the adjoining buildings, which were all covered with thatch, and in a short time the church, the whole of the Company's property, and twelve dwelling houses were burned down. Fortunately the church books and district records were saved.

There was not so much attention paid now to the cultivation of trees as there had been in the time of the governors Van der Stel, still this useful work was not altogether neglected by the authorities. In the winter of 1709 a number of young oaks were sent to Stellenbosch to be planted along the streets. Some of those previously planted in the same places had been wantonly or thoughtlessly destroyed. In consequence, on the 8th of August of this year a placaat was issued, in which damaging trees on public property was prohibited under penalty of a sound flogging at the foot of the gallows, and a reward of 2*l.* 1*s.* 8*d.* was promised to any one bringing offenders to justice.

There was a regulation under which any one felling a tree on his own ground was to plant an oak in its stead, but it was generally neglected. The farmers of Stellenbosch and Drakenstein assigned as a reason for not carrying it out that as they had only sixty morgen of land they had not sufficient space, because trees in the neighbourhood of vineyards and cornfields attracted and harboured birds. The forests in the mountain kloofs near the Cape were by this time exhausted, but a commission which was sent to examine the Land of Waveren reported that there was still a considerable quantity of timber suitable for waggon making and house building to be found there.

On the 13th of April 1711, the council, presided over by the commissioner Pieter de Vos, admiral of a return fleet, decided to press upon the landdrost and heemraden of Stellenbosch and Drakenstein the necessity of planting trees along the roads and of selecting suitable places for laying out groves. A commission, consisting of the acting fiscal Willem van Putten and the master gardener Jan Hertog, was appointed to examine the mountainous country along the left bank of the river Zonder End, and report upon the forests there. The commission found a supply of timber sufficient for existing needs, which set the question at rest for a while.

In consequence of an attempt of the landdrost of Stellenbosch to press for the public service some waggons belonging to residents of the Cape peninsula, the burgher councillors appealed to the council of policy to define the bounds of that officer's jurisdiction, and on the 15th of December 1711 it was decided that he had no authority on the Cape side of the Mosselbank and Kuils rivers. Beyond those streams his jurisdiction extended as far as Europeans were settled.

Governor Van Assenburgh was taken seriously ill early in the year 1711. He had never interfered with the pursuits of the farmers, and had given the colonists that protection to which they were entitled, so that he stood fairly well in their regard. He had not indeed mixed with them and interested himself in their personal affairs, as Simon van der Stel in his earlier years had done, so there was not that affection for him that there had once been for the other. He seldom left the castle. On new year's day and on his birthday it was the custom for the principal burghers with their wives to call at the castle between ten and eleven in the morning, and present their compliments. They were then invited to remain to dinner, and did not usually leave until nine in the evening. Also on the yearly muster of the militia of the Cape district, when the company of cavalry and two companies of infantry had gone through their exercises and been inspected, the officers were entertained at the castle. At these receptions the governor was very friendly, and he was at all times easy of access, but he did not court society. There was only one instance of departure from his usual habits, and that somewhat startled the steady burghers of the Cape. When the afternoon service was concluded on Sunday the 11th of November 1708, the governor invited the principal townspeople to the castle, and made an effort to entertain them with a fight between bulls and dogs.

When he was taken ill, the burghers suspected that he had been poisoned, and one writer of the period does not hesitate to affirm that the poison had been administered to him in a glass of wine when on a visit at Constantia. The dates of the visit and of his illness, however, overthrow this statement. He was confined to his room for about eight months, and died on the afternoon of Sunday the 27th of December 1711, five days after he had completed his fifty-first year.

Next morning the council of policy met, when the secunde Willem Helot was elected to act as head of the government until the pleasure of the directors could be signified. The election was a matter of form, for there was no one else eligible. On the 2nd of January 1712 the body of the late governor was buried beneath the pavement of the church, with a great deal of state. His administration had not been an eventful one, and his name was soon forgotten.

Some years before this date immigration from Europe had practically ceased. Occasionally a family from abroad was added to the burgher population, or a servant of the Company was discharged in South Africa, but the increase of the colonists was now due chiefly to the excess of births over deaths. Cattle farmers were pushing their way from the Land of Waveren down the valley of the Breede river and from Hottentots Holland eastward along the course of the Zonder End.

The town in Table Valley was growing also. It had not yet become the custom to call it Cape Town, it being usually termed the Cape, or sometimes the town at the Cape. Official letters were addressed from and to the Castle of Good Hope. At the date of Governor Van Assenburgh's death the town contained about two hundred and fifty private houses, besides the buildings belonging to the Company.

In October 1712 a report reached the castle that four or five thousand Hottentots of the Great Namaqua tribe had made an inroad upon the natives living along the Elephant river, and had threatened to plunder some graziers at Piketberg, who had in consequence been obliged to retire from their farms. The government thereupon instructed Johannes Mulder, who was again landdrost of Stellenbosch, to call out twenty-five burghers from Drakenstein and twenty-five from Stellenbosch. The same number were called out in the Cape district, and with twenty-five soldiers were sent on to meet the country contingents at the farm of François du Toit. Lieutenant Slotsboo was in command of the expedition. His instructions were to endeavour to come to an amicable understanding with the Namaquas, if possible to induce them to return to their own country, and not to attack them unless they had done some harm to the burghers. The commando returned to the castle on the 22nd of November, and reported that there were no Namaquas at Piketberg and no burgher had been molested.

On the 16th of February 1713 the ship *Bennebroek*, homeward bound from Ceylon, after being disabled in a storm ran ashore in broad daylight on the coast of Natal, at some point which was never exactly ascertained. She commenced to break up immediately. Fifty-seven Europeans and twenty Malabar slaves intended for the Cape got to land on pieces of the wreck, the remainder of the crew perished. Those who were saved collected some food which washed up, and then set out to travel to the Cape. But they could not cross a deep river which was in their way, and after a few days some of them turned back to the neighbourhood of the wreck. There they remained until June, subsisting upon milk, meat, and millet which they obtained from the natives for pieces of iron and copper. At last the metal in the wreckage was exhausted, and they then made another attempt to reach the Cape by going far inland to avoid the lower courses of the rivers. But they did not succeed, and, after wandering about for some weeks, hunger and fatigue compelled the Europeans who still survived—seven in number—to take refuge with a tribe of natives, who treated them with great kindness. Here they found a Frenchman who had been wrecked thirty years before.

The natives with whom they thenceforth lived were carrying on a perpetual war with Bushmen. Their residence was near the coast, on the bank of a river with a navigable mouth. The food of the tribe consisted chiefly of milk, varieties of pumpkin, and bread made by rubbing millet between stones, then mixing the pulp with water, and baking it in ashes.

Of those who did not turn back to the wreck, all perished except one Malabar slave. He pushed on westward for a whole year, overcoming every difficulty in his way. At length a burgher found him near the mouth of the Breede river, and sent him on to the castle, which he reached on the 26th of February 1714.

In 1713 a terrible calamity fell upon the country. In March of this year the small pox made its first appearance in South Africa. It was introduced by means of some clothing belonging to ships' people who had been ill on the passage from India, but who had recovered before they reached Table Bay. This clothing was sent to be washed at the Company's slave lodge, and the women who handled it were the first to be smitten. The Company had at the time about five hundred and seventy slaves of both sexes and all ages, nearly two hundred of whom were carried off within the next six months.

From the slaves the disease spread to the Europeans and the natives. In May and June there was hardly a family in the town that had not some one sick or dead. Traffic in the streets was suspended, and even the children ceased to play their usual games in the squares and open places. At last it was impossible to obtain nurses, though slave women were being paid at the rate of four and five shillings a day. All the planks in the stores were used, and in July it became necessary to bury the dead without coffins.

For two months there was no meeting of the court of justice, for debts and quarrels were forgotten in presence of the terrible scourge. The minds of the people were so depressed that anything unusual inspired them with terror. Thus on the 10th of May two doves were observed to fall to the ground from the parapet of the governor's house in the castle, and after fluttering about a little were found to be dead, without any injury being perceptible. This was regarded by many as an omen of disaster. The very clouds and the darkness of winter storms seemed to be threatening death and woe. During that dreadful winter nearly one fourth of the European inhabitants of the town perished, and only when the hot weather set in did the plague cease.

The disease spread into the country, but there, though the death rate among the white people was very high, the proportion that perished was not so large as in the town. It was easier to keep from contact with sick persons. Some families living in secluded places were practically isolated, and the farmers in general avoided moving about.

The burgher rolls are not to be regarded in any year as more than approximately correct, but, in common with all other contemporary documents, they bear witness to the great loss of life. According to them, in 1712 the number of colonists—men, women, and children—was one thousand nine hundred and thirty-nine, and in 1716, three years after the cessation of the plague, notwithstanding the natural increase, only one thousand six hundred and ninety-seven.

Among the Hottentots the disease created the greatest havoc. Of the Europeans who were smitten, more recovered than died; but with the Hottentots, to be ill and to die were synonymous. The state of filth in which they lived caused the plague to spread among them with fearful rapidity. When the kraals were first infected, and the number of deaths became startling, the Hottentots of the Cape fled across the mountains, declaring that the Europeans had bewitched them. But as soon as they got beyond the settlement they were attacked by tribes of their own race, and all who could not get back again were killed. The probable object of this slaughter was to prevent the spread of the disease, but if so, it failed. Then the wretched creatures sat down in despair, and made no attempt to help themselves. They did not even remove their dead from the huts. In Table Valley it became necessary to send a party of slaves to put the corpses under ground, as the air was becoming foul. Whole kraals absolutely disappeared, leaving not an individual alive.

The very names of the tribes for a great distance inland

were blotted out by the fell disease. They no longer appear in the records as organised communities, with feuds and rivalries and internal wars, but as the broken-spirited remnant of a race, all whose feelings of nationality and clanship had been crushed out by the great calamity. The farmers who had been accustomed to employ many hundreds of them in harvest time complained that none were now to be had. Strangers who had visited the colony before 1713, and who saw it afterwards, noticed that the Hottentot population had almost disappeared. From this date until other tribes were reached by the expansion of the settlement, the only difficulty with the natives was occasioned by the Bushmen. Owing to the isolation of these people, they escaped the disaster which overtook the higher races.

The crop of 1710–11 was a poor one, but there was a quantity of grain in store which enabled the government to keep up the supply to Batavia. But in the two following seasons also insufficient rain fell, and the yield of the harvest was so small that only one thousand and twenty muids in 1712 and nineteen hundred and fifty-six muids in 1713 could be exported. In 1713 the fall of rain was ample, but the small pox prevented extensive cultivation. The returns for seed sown were, however, exceptionally large, and in 1714 the quantity of wheat exported amounted to four thousand three hundred and seventy-five muids.

Upon intelligence of the death of Governor Van Assenburgh reaching the Netherlands, the directors appointed as his successor Lieutenant-Colonel Maurits Pasques de Chavonnes, a native of the Hague, who had commanded an infantry regiment in the army of the States, but had been thrown out of employment by the reduction of the troops at the peace of Utrecht. He had the rank, title, and salary of a councillor extraordinary of the Indies given to him. The new governor arrived at the Cape on the 24th of March 1714, and was formally installed on the 28th of the same month.

Between the commencement of the eighteenth century and the arrival of Governor De Chavonnes the following names, now well known throughout South Africa, are found in the colonial records :

van Aardt	van Heerden	Oelofse
Badenhorst	Herbst	Paassen
Bek	Holland	Pottier
Bernard	Holm	van Reenen
Best	Human	Richter
Beukes	Kleinveld	Robberts
Blankenberg	Knoetsen	Roos
Bok	Kotzé	Scholtz
Bosman	Langeberg	Steenekamp
Bronkhorst	Lens	Stols
du Buisson	Ley	Sweetman
Buys	van der Linde	Sweris
Cilliers *vel* Sellier	Loré	Terreblanche
Ditmaar	Lourens	Uys
Eksteen	Maasdorp	Verron
van Emmenes	Maré	Vlodman
Faure	Meyboom	Voogt
Fick	Moolman	de Vries
le Grand	Munnik	van der Walt
Grobbelaar	Niemand	de Wet
Hasselaar	Oberholster	Zaaiman

CHAPTER XIX.

MAURITS PASQUES DE CHAVONNES, GOVERNOR, INSTALLED 28 MARCH 1714; DIED 8 SEPTEMBER 1724.

Efforts to equalise revenue and expenditure—New taxes—An English trader on the coast of Kaffirland—Basis of colonial law—Dismissal of the secunde Helot—Hostilities with the Bushmen—The first colonial commando—Trouble caused by fugitive slaves—Struggle for place and rank—Difficulty of finding a market for farm produce in good seasons—Important questions submitted by the directors to the council of policy—Experiments in the production of wool, indigo, tobacco, and olives—Efforts to find a market for Cape wine—Bad seasons—New diseases among horned cattle and sheep—Scarcity of butcher's meat—Prohibition of sale of meat and vegetables to foreigners—Ruin of the Namaqua tribe—Outbreak of horse sickness—Expansion of the Company's trade after the peace of Utrecht—Sailing of fleets from Table Bay—Refusal of supplies to private traders—Establishment of a Dutch factory at Delagoa Bay—Disasters at Delagoa Bay—The great gale of June 1722—Heavy loss of life and property by shipwrecks in Table Bay—Wreck of the *Schoonberg* at Agulhas, and of the *Meteren* near the mouth of the Elephant river—Church matters—Erection of church buildings at Drakenstein and Stellenbosch—Death of the secunde Cranendonk, and appointment of Jan de la Fontaine as his successor—Promotion of the governor to the rank of ordinary councillor of Netherlands India—Death of the governor—Election by the council of Jan de la Fontaine to act as head of the government—Names of new colonists.

THE first object to which the new governor turned his attention was an attempt to make the revenue of the colony more nearly meet the expenditure than had previously been the case. Though the returns were made out yearly to fractions of a farthing, it is impossible to say exactly what was the expenditure of the colony. This is owing to the accounts of the Cape being kept as of a branch business. Every penny received from every source was entered on one side, and every penny paid out, no matter for what purpose, was entered on the other.

Thus, in the charges against the Cape are included all sums paid for refreshment of the crews of ships, wages paid to sailors in such ships, the expenses of the hospital, and other items which should not fairly be placed against the colonial revenue. But these items cannot be wholly struck off. The hospital, for instance, afforded accommodation for the sick of the garrison, and thus a portion of its cost was a proper charge against the colony. Then again, sums paid in the Netherlands and in India for strictly colonial purposes do not appear in the accounts. The most that can be done is to state the expenditure approximately, and probably no two persons examining the records would do this in exactly the same figures.

The principal source of revenue was the money paid for the exclusive right to sell wines and spirituous liquors by retail, and this was determined by public auction on the last day of August. During the first quarter of the eighteenth century it averaged 3,167*l.* Besides this, there were the tithes of grain, transfer dues on sales of ground, and profits on sales of goods. On an average, these together amounted at this date to 4,739*l.* yearly. The colonial revenue was thus about 8,000*l.* a year. In converting the money of that day into British coinage, the heavy gulden generally used in accounts transmitted to the Netherlands is valued at one shilling and eight pence, and the light gulden used in transactions in the colony and in India at sixteen pence and two-thirds of a penny. Before 1743 it is often doubtful which was meant. In that year an order was given that the heavy gulden should be exclusively used in accounts prepared for the directors.

The expenditure, after deducting all expenses connected with shipping, cannot be estimated at less than 14,500*l.* a year. It was kept at the lowest possible sum by the payment of very small salaries and allowing privileges of different kinds to the officers, by permitting from one hundred and fifty to two hundred out of a garrison of about five hundred and fifty men to take temporary service with farmers, and by employing slave labour in building and gardening. The cost of transport, ammunition, building materials sent from the Netherlands, and various other items are not considered in this calculation, because it cannot be even approximately given.

There was thus a large excess of expenditure over revenue, though it is not possible to state the exact amount in figures. The directors instructed the governor to try and devise means of meeting it, in part if not wholly.

No revenue had yet been derived from leases of land used for cattle runs. After the 3rd of July 1714 a rental of twenty-five shillings for six months, or fifty shillings a year, was charged, in addition to the tithe of grain produced. Old residents in the Land of Waveren and elsewhere were permitted, however, to take out freehold titles on application to the governor, in order to encourage them to improve the land. All building sites given out in the town were to revert to the Company if houses were not put up on them within twelve months.

After the 20th of July 1714 it was required that stamps should be affixed to different kinds of documents to make them legal. These documents included deeds of transfer of land and slaves, wills, contracts of marriage, certificates of inheritance, licenses to trade, powers of attorney, and generally all notarial acts and papers passing through courts of law. The stamps required ranged in value from six pence to twelve shillings and six pence.

On the 12th of March 1715 a tax of four shillings and two pence was laid upon every legger of wine pressed in the colony. This article had not been subject to tithe or any tax whatever before this date.

On the 4th of September 1714 a decked boat twenty-eight feet long by nine feet beam arrived in Table Bay under English colours. Her master reported that she had been built in England purposely for trading on the south-eastern coast of Africa, and had been taken to Delagoa Bay in pieces in a vessel named the *Clapham Galley*. She had been put together there, had since been trading on the coast, and had now come to Table Bay according to arrangement to wait for the return of the *Clapham Galley* from India. She had entered a river, the name of which is not given, and had there found the seven surviving sailors of the *Bennebroek,* four of whom she brought to the Cape. The most interesting part of the narrative of the master of the boat is that at various places at which he had touched below Delagoa Bay he had obtained a large quantity of ivory in exchange for beads and copper rings that had been expressly manufactured in England for trade with the Kaffirs.

In November the galiot *Postlooper* was sent to search along the coast of Natal for the wreck of the *Bennebroek,* and if possible to recover her cannon and anchors as well as the three surviving sailors; but after an absence of nearly six months she returned with a report that neither men nor wreck could be found.

As the high court of justice was desirous of having the laws according to which they were to decide cases properly defined, the council of policy on the 12th of February 1715 directed that the statutes of India were to be strictly followed, except when they were modified by placaats issued by competent authority at the Cape. In the following year the summary jurisdiction of the court of landdrost and heemraden was extended in civil cases to 10*l.* 8*s.* 4*d.*

In May 1714 the secunde Helot, who had recently been acting head of the government, was suspended for appropriating to his own use property belonging to the Company, and upon the circumstances being reported to the directors, the council was instructed to send him to the Netherlands without rank or salary. Abraham Cranendonk, recently fiscal of the establishment on the Hoogly, who was named as his successor, arrived at the Cape and took over the duty on the 4th of March 1715.

For some time back the Bushmen had not been giving much trouble, but in 1715 their depredations were renewed. These people would not change their mode of living, and, as the game was being destroyed, a conflict between them and the farmers was inevitable. At that time no one questioned the right of civilised men to take possession of land occupied by such a race as the Bushmen, and to the present day no one has devised a plan by which this can be done without violence.

In August 1715 the wife of a Drakenstein farmer appeared at the castle and informed the governor that the Bushmen had driven off over seven hundred sheep belonging to her husband, after murdering the shepherd. Thereupon, the governor gave a general permission in writing to the neighbours of the man who had been robbed to follow the plunderers and retake the spoil. A notification to this effect was also sent to the landdrost.

With this permission the first purely colonial commando took the field. It consisted of thirty mounted burghers, who chose as their commandant a farmer named Hermanus Potgieter. They did their utmost to trace the robbers, but without success.

The Bushmen then commenced plundering generally the farmers along the Berg river and in the Land of Waveren. They murdered some herdsmen, set fire to several houses, and drove off a large number of cattle. It was feared that they would burn the ripening corn. Some of the most exposed farmers abandoned their homes, and a few families were quite ruined. Several commandos in succession were raised and sent to expel the marauders, the government supplying ammunition. The instructions under which they took the field were emphatic that bloodshed was to be avoided if possible, and women and children were not to be molested. But this was a kind of warfare in which men's hearts were apt to become hardened.

It was easy to resolve to drive the marauders from a stated tract of country, but very difficult to carry the resolution into effect. The keen-sighted Bushman, when he observed the approach of an enemy, concealed himself and his family; and as soon as his pursuers retired, worn out in looking for him, his depredations were resumed. None of the commandos sent out in this year effected their object, though some of them believed they had done so until they learned that as soon as they were disbanded the marauders were busy again.

Early in 1716 one of the commandos lost a man killed with a poisoned arrow, and had another wounded. A sergeant and twenty soldiers were then directed to guard the most exposed positions, and a strong party of the Company's servants and burghers was sent with some arrack, tobacco, and beads to try and make peace. This party succeeded in obtaining a meeting with a company of Bushmen, and returned to the castle with a report that an agreement of friendship had been entered into. And it certainly was the case that robberies ceased for a time.

In August the newly-formed military posts were withdrawn at the request of the burghers, who had a lively dread of tyranny being established by means of troops. The old outposts at Waveren, Saldanha Bay, Groen Kloof, and Klapmuts were still maintained; but there were never more than seven men at each.

Until January 1719 no fresh charge of depredations by Bushmen was made, and then the complaint came from another direction. Seven hundred head of cattle were driven away from Jacob van der Heiden's farm on the river Zonder End. The Bushmen asserted that this raid was in retaliation for injuries inflicted upon them by people who gave out that they were sent to barter cattle for the Company. The records do not supply sufficient evidence in this instance to enable it to be said whether they had, or had not, received such provocation as they complained of. At Van der Heiden's request, permission was given for a commando to assemble; but the cattle could not be recovered.

At this date fugitive slaves were giving a great deal of trouble to the colonists. These wretched beings formed themselves into bands, and plundered the farmers whenever necessity impelled and opportunity offered. Though they usually selected a retreat in some place difficult of discovery and access, they were much more easily found than Bushmen.

A subject that occupied a good deal of attention during the whole of the eighteenth century was the relative rank of the different individuals in the community, and, as the church was the place where all met, the position which each should occupy in that building. The directors desired that the burghers should be as nearly as possible of the same station, but when civil and military offices of various kinds were created, some distinctions were inevitable. There was, however, a general feeling of respect for legitimate authority properly exercised, so that with the burgher population each one's place was recognised without much difficulty. In the country the landdrost ranked first, as the representative of the Honourable Company. He had the front seat in the church, which was slightly elevated and distinguished by a canopy. Next to him in rank came the clergyman. The heemraden followed, and had a special seat in church just behind the landdrost. The elders and deacons had seats on each side of the pulpit, and the military officers had recognised places in the body of the building, according to their grade. The wives of all these notables sat on chairs placed in the order mentioned above, it being one of the duties of a church officer called the koster to see that the seats were in their proper positions.

Among the servants of the Company the struggle for place was constant. In the army and navy it was easy to define the grades, but outside of these branches of the service complicated questions were constantly arising. There were the grades senior merchant, merchant, and junior merchant, yet these did not meet the difficulty. The following instance will show how important such matters were considered.

The supreme authorities having decided to erect additional fortifications in Table Valley, on the 20th of February 1715 the governor laid the foundation stone of a battery which he named Mauritius, near the sea shore at the foot of the Lion's Rump. But the Assembly of Seventeen then thought that before proceeding further, plans and specifications should be drawn up by an engineer and submitted to them, and Mr. Pieter Gysbert Noodt, director of fortifications in Netherlands India, was instructed to visit the Cape for that purpose. He arrived on the 6th of May 1718, and remained until the 18th of April in the following year. He was a surly quarrelsome man, who would not so much as show the governor the plans he was making, though repeatedly requested to do so. He had not been here long when a quarrel arose between him and the secunde Abraham Cranendonk upon the question of precedence. They disputed as to which should receive the highest military salute, whose wife should occupy the foremost seat in church, whose carriage was to keep the crown of the street when they met, and other similar matters. They came before the council of policy, each with a long written statement of his claims. The council took the matter into serious consideration, and after some discussion decided in favour of Mr. Noodt.

The crops of 1714 to 1716 were so good that fifteen thousand four hundred muids of wheat were sent to Batavia, or more than five thousand muids on an average yearly. But in the Company's possessions in India, the demand for wheat was limited, and it could be obtained elsewhere at a lower rate than twelve shillings a muid, which was the price paid at the Cape. The governor-general and council of India were of opinion that the Company could be supplied from Bengal and Surat to greater advantage. They were satisfied with the quality of Cape wheat; but it was too dear, and the quantity produced fluctuated so greatly from season to season that a constant supply could not be depended upon. They proposed to allow the Cape farmers to send wheat to any part of India, and sell it there at whatever price could be obtained. But to this the burghers objected, as they asserted that they were not in a position to carry on a trade of this kind, and could not afford to wait long after harvest without any return. The colony would be ruined if the Company ceased to purchase their grain.

The directors decided that it would be better to support the burghers than natives of Hindostan, but the price of wheat at the Cape was reduced to ten shillings and eight pence a muid. As it was asserted that they must purchase all that was grown, or ruin would follow, they wrote that no more ground was to be given out for the production of wheat and wine, without their approval being obtained in each instance. To encourage the colonists to grow other produce, they gave directions that ships from India were to be supplied at the Cape with peas, beans, and husked barley sufficient for the passage home, though peas were then bringing the high price of twenty-nine shillings, and beans twenty-five shillings a muid.

On the 24th of June 1716 the directors submitted a series of questions, upon which they required the opinions of the members of the council of policy.

The principal queries were whether the country could maintain a larger number of colonists; whether it would not be more advantageous to employ European labourers than slaves; whether such articles as coffee, sugar, cotton, indigo, olive oil, tobacco, flax, silk, and hops could not be produced, so as to enable a larger number of people to gain a living; and whether a tax could not be imposed on provisions supplied to foreign ships.

Each member of the council was required to take these questions into consideration and to bring up a report. Probably no subject of equal importance to South Africa has ever since engaged the attention of the authorities, for upon these reports was to depend whether the country should be occupied solely by Europeans, or whether there was to be a mixture of races in it. As yet slavery had not taken deep root, and could easily have been done away with. The number of slaves was small, and nearly five-sixths of them were adult males. Without further importations, the system would have rapidly perished.

It must ever be deplored that of the men who sat in the council in February 1717 there was but one who could look beyond the gains of the present hour. The governor, Maurits Pasques de Chavonnes, the secunde, Abraham Cranendonk, the fiscal independent, Cornelis van Beaumont, and the junior members, J. Cruse, J. de la Fontaine, K. Slotsboo, and H. van der Meer, were all in favour of slave labour. They stated that a slave cost less than 3*l.* a year for maintenance, whereas a white labourer would cost at least as much as a soldier, whose pay and rations amounted to more than 12*l.* a year. The slave was tractable, whereas the European was prone to be rebellious. White men often became addicted to drunkenness, and none could be obtained who would be willing to perform the severer kinds of labour in this climate.

The commander of the garrison, Captain Dominique Pasques de Chavonnes, was alone in advocating the introduction of European workmen only. Slaves in this country, he observed, were like a malignant sore in the human frame. They kept the colonists in a state of unrest, and notwithstanding the terrible punishments inflicted upon them, they were not deterred from running away and committing atrocious crimes. If the cost of purchasing them—about 4*l.* each, bringing them to this country, providing for them, and guarding them, were taken into consideration, their labour would not be found much cheaper than that of white men, especially as they required supervision, and did neither so much nor such good work. On the other hand, Europeans would give security to the country, and would help to increase the revenue.

There is little doubt that if these views had been held by the other members of the council, and had been pressed upon the directors, the many evils which slavery produced in South Africa would have been prevented. Nothing was said of the bearing of the question upon the African: it was almost a century too early in the world's history for his interests to be taken into consideration.

Whether coffee and the other plants named would thrive at the Cape was regarded as doubtful by all the members. Some of these plants, such as the olive and indigo, had already been fruitlessly experimented with. In any case, men having special knowledge would be needed to test them, for no one in the colony understood their culture. Whether a larger number of Europeans could exist here without being a burden upon the Company or the poor funds would depend upon the result of such experiments.

All were agreed that it would not be advisable to levy a tax upon provisions supplied to foreigners, as it would not amount to much, and might drive away strangers who brought ready money into the country. None of the members thought that any profit could be made from an alleged discovery of coal on Pierre Rousseau's farm at French Hoek. Nor were any of them of opinion that manufactures could be introduced. Isaac Taillefer, it was stated, had made good hats from Cape wool; but when he died that industry ceased. Others had knitted socks and gloves of woollen yarn made by themselves, but that also had been discontinued.

Upon receipt of these reports, the directors resolved, 17th of April 1718, that experiments should be repeated with all diligence in the cultivation of tobacco, silk, indigo, and olives; and that a person having special knowledge in the production of each should be sent out to superintend the work.

Sheep's wool was not referred to, as all attempts to encourage the growth of a marketable article had hitherto failed. In 1714 six hundred and fifty pounds were sent to Europe, but the quality was so bad that it did not produce at public sale as much as it had cost. Another experiment was made in 1716, when three thousand pounds were purchased at seven pence a pound and sent to Amsterdam. The quality of this shipment was likewise so inferior that it was unsaleable for spinning purposes. It was then resolved to let this industry remain in abeyance until another breed of animals could be introduced, and as the greatest difficulty was now being experienced in getting as much meat as was needed, wool, which was of less importance, was not spoken of.

A large quantity of indigo seed was sent with an expert from Batavia in 1719, and for many years experiments were made with it. There was no difficulty in getting the plant to grow well in sheltered positions and in rich soil; but it was found that it would not answer as a general crop.

Silkworm eggs from Persia and Bengal were sent at the same time, but were found to be bad on their arrival. The white mulberry trees which were planted throve as well as could be desired. The chief experiment in the production of silk was not, however, made until a few years later, and will be noticed in another chapter.

An expert in the cultivation and manufacture of tobacco, Cors Hendriks by name, was sent from Amsterdam in 1719. He made a tour through the colony, and upon his return to the castle pronounced very unfavourably upon the appearance of the soil. The most suitable place for an experiment that he had found was a plot of land about two morgen in extent, adjoining Rustenburg at Rondebosch. There and in the Company's garden in Table Valley a large number of tobacco plants were set out by slaves under direction of the expert. At first they throve well, but after a time some were destroyed by violent winds, and others by the heat of the sun. The seed had been carefully selected, but the leaves which reached maturity were so bad in flavour that Hendriks, who attributed the quality to the soil, despaired of success, and advised that the experiment be given up. The members of the council of policy were of the same opinion, and in 1722 the tobacco expert became a burgher.

The experiments with the olive had the same result as on every previous occasion. The trees grew most luxuriantly, but many of them suddenly died without any accountable cause. From others the fruit dropped when still young, and the few olives that ripened in exceptionally good seasons were of very inferior quality.

The directors were of opinion that if the flavour of Cape wine were improved, a large market could be found both in Europe and in India, to the advantage of the colonists as well as of the Company. They were then paying 6*l.* a legger for ordinary wine for the use of the fleets, and 8*l.* for old wine for use in the hospital. On the 27th of June 1719 they wrote for some selected samples, and with the next return fleet six half aams were sent. When it reached Amsterdam it was found unfit for use. It was the same with six half aams sent to Batavia. The directors supposed that the reason might be the small size of the casks, and therefore directed another trial to be made with half leggers instead of half aams. In 1722 ten half leggers were sent to Amsterdam and Middelburg, but the result was the same as before. An experiment was then made with bottles, a thousand of which were sent out to be filled with wine and returned. It succeeded no better than the others.

The wine made at Constantia had, however, a good reputation in Europe. Johannes Colyn, the owner of the farm at that time, produced yearly from ten to twelve leggers of red wine, for which he received 16*l.* 13*s.* 4*d.* a legger, and about twenty leggers of white wine, which he sold readily at 10*l.* 8*s.* 4*d.*

Arrangements had hardly been made for the supply of wheat to India, and beans, peas, and husked barley to the return ships, when a series of dry seasons set in. In 1718 the harvest was poor, but a small quantity of wheat was exported. It was the same in 1719. In 1720 less than a hundred muids were sent out of the country. In 1721 it was not possible to supply the ships with beans, peas, and barley, and rice was served out to the garrison instead of bread; but fifty-one muids of wheat were sent to Batavia to keep up the name of exportation. In the winter of 1721 the seasons changed for the better, and in 1722 nearly three thousand five hundred muids of wheat were exported, followed in 1723 by over four thousand muids.

In 1714 a calamity worse even than loss of crops fell upon the country. Horned cattle and sheep were attacked by a disease unknown before, and great numbers died. By 1718 it was so difficult to obtain animals for slaughter that when the contract to supply the Company with meat was offered for sale by auction there was not a single bidder. The sheep in possession of the burghers had decreased by nearly fifty-six thousand. It was necessary to make a private arrangement with Jacob van der Heiden, by which he undertook to supply meat at three pence a pound and live sheep at twelve shillings and sixpence each. On the 2nd of July 1720 the sale of live animals to foreigners was prohibited by placaat, and henceforth no sheep were sent on board the Company's ships. Meat had now risen to 3¼*d.* a pound.

English captains had been in the habit of purchasing cattle in considerable numbers, slaughtering them, and salting the meat. They had also generally taken away a number of sheep. Upon the prohibition being applied to them, they made loud complaints in Europe, and the directors issued instructions that they should be treated as well as possible.

After a time Van der Heiden informed the council that he could not continue to supply meat unless permission was given him to procure cattle from the Hottentots in the distant interior. Leave was therefore granted, but in February 1723 it was withdrawn upon the Drakenstein consistory complaining that the trading parties sent out by him had used violence towards the natives, and had even murdered some Hottentots. The matter was investigated by the fiscal and the landdrost, but sufficient evidence could not be procured to secure the conviction of the offenders, though there was no doubt that very atrocious crimes had been committed.

The price of sheep sold at public auction at this time was from 11*s*. 1*d*. to 13*s*. 11*d*. taking one with another in a flock, and of draught oxen 4*l*. 3*s*. 4*d*. each. The scarcity was increased by the tongue and hoof sickness making its first appearance in 1723.

By order of the directors, a placaat was then issued, 24th of February 1723, prohibiting the sale of fresh meat or vegetables to strangers, under penalty of deportation to Europe and a fine of nearly 70*l*. This was construed to mean that permission must first be obtained from the council, for upon English captains requesting to be allowed to purchase supplies of fresh provisions for their sick, leave was invariably granted. On the 6th of April of the same year another placaat was issued requiring the farmers to provide the Company with meat at two pence a pound and sheep at ten shillings each, under penalty of a tithe of all animals reared being required. But legislation such as this was fruitless.

An attempt had previously been made to procure cattle from the Hottentots of the interior, and even from the Kaffirs, by licensing a certain burgher to carry on the trade under surveillance; but the great distance caused the scheme to fail. Ensign Rhenius was then sent with a trading party to the Namaquas. In November 1724 he returned unsuccessful. He reported that the Namaqua tribe had been fearfully reduced in number by a disease resembling small pox, that the Bushmen had taken advantage of their weakness to rob them of most of their cattle, and that in reckless despair they had slaughtered and consumed the remainder.

The Company was then compelled to submit to circumstances, and to pay the high prices determined by public tender.

The troubles of the community were increased by the horse sickness making its appearance in a very severe form in 1719. There is no mention of it in the records before that date, and it is described as a new plague. It has never left South Africa since.

On the 11th of April 1713 the peace of Utrecht concluded a war with France of twelve years duration. The Company then resolved to enlarge its commerce, and a number of ships of the first class, carrying from two hundred and eighty to three hundred and fifty men each, were speedily built. After 1715 the number of persons visiting the Cape every year was much greater than before. During the fifteen years from 1st January 1700 to 31st December 1714 one thousand and seven ships put into Table Bay, or on an average sixty-seven yearly. Of these, 683 were Dutch, 280 English, 36 Danish, 6 French, and 2 Portuguese. During the ten years from 1st January 1715 to 31st December 1724 the number that called was eight hundred and seventy-one, or on an average eighty-seven yearly. Of these, 645 were Dutch, 192 English, 17 French, 10 Danish, 4 Portuguese, and 3 Flemish.

The Company's ships assembled in Table Bay to return to Europe in a fleet. The slowest sailers were despatched first from Batavia, and usually arrived here in January. Then came the Ceylon squadron, and last the late ships from Batavia. They endeavoured to leave Table Bay about the end of March or beginning of April, and it must have been something worth seeing when twenty to thirty large ships set their sails and stood away together. This was called the summer fleet, and it usually carried to Europe merchandise which had cost from five to seven hundred thousand pounds sterling. Sometimes a number of English vessels sailed in its company. The winter fleet was much smaller, often consisting of only three or four ships. At a date somewhat later than the period to which we have now arrived, it became usual for the summer ships also to sail in small squadrons, as they could be got ready.

The English Government had protested against the assistance formerly given to private traders at the Cape, and an arrangement had been made between the Assembly of Seventeen and the directors of the English Company that neither would permit interlopers to obtain anything whatever in their ports. In consequence, when an English vessel arrived, unless her master could produce a royal commission or proper credentials from the East India Company, she was warned to make sail at once, and no intercourse was allowed with the shore. The Flemish ships which put in for supplies were treated in the same manner.

The Portuguese having abandoned Delagoa Bay in 1692, in 1720 the Dutch East India Company resolved to take possession of that port and establish a factory there. It was intended that the station should be a dependency of the Cape government, just as Mauritius had been. Thus important cases were to be sent for trial to the Cape, and in all cases except the most trivial there was to be a right of appeal to the high court of justice at the castle of Good Hope.

Towards the close of the year the advance party sent from the Netherlands to form the station, consisting of forty-four soldiers and a few mechanics, arrived in Table Bay in two small vessels, the *Kaap* and *Gouda*. The officer who had been appointed head of the expedition died soon after reaching South Africa, when the council of policy selected a clerk on the Cape establishment, Willem van Taak by name, as his successor. A council was chosen to assist him, and a petty court of justice was constituted.

On the 14th of February 1721 the expedition, accompanied by a small vessel named the *Zeelandia*, sailed from Table Bay, and on the 29th of March reached its destination. A site on the left bank of English river near its mouth was selected for the fort, but before much building was done fever attacked the party, and within six weeks two-thirds of them died, including the commander and the engineer. At length, with the assistance of some natives, a small fort was constructed, and then the *Zeelandia* was sent back to the Cape with letters and a little ivory and wax obtained in barter. She returned in August, together with the yacht *Uno*, taking provisions and eighty soldiers to strengthen the garrison.

Upon learning what had occurred, the council of policy appointed Casparus Swertner successor to Mr. Van Taak, with the rank of junior merchant and a salary of 2*l.* 15*s.* 6*d.* a month. He was then at Delagoa Bay, but he died before the news of his appointment reached the station. A subaltern, named Jan Michel, was then chosen to be head of the party of occupation. The council hoped that by this time the survivors from the fever were seasoned to the climate, and that henceforth all would go well. But the outpost was destined to further trouble.

Time passed in trading, exploring, and gathering information, until the 19th of April 1722, when a report was brought by some blacks that three ships had entered the bay. These proved to be manned by buccaneers, who attacked Fort Lagoa, took possession of it after a short cannonade, and plundered the store. They did not, however, otherwise illtreat the garrison, eighteen of whom joined them. When they were ready for sea they compelled one of the officials, named De Bucquoi, to pilot them out, as he had surveyed the bay and made a chart of its soundings. They also took with them the vessel which was employed as a packet, to be able, as they said, to send the pilot back when they got outside. They failed to keep their word, however, and De Bucquoi and the crew of the *Kaap* were obliged to remain with the buccaneers until they reached another port, from which they made their way to India.

The garrison at the station was by this disaster cut off from communication with the outer world. But in course of time relief came, and the exploration of the country around the bay for a few miles inland was then completed. A little gold was brought by blacks from the interior to exchange for beads, and though the whole quantity was less than two ounces, it was sufficient to excite hope. The natives who brought it asserted that they had travelled three moons and a half, but this statement was not credited. The first who came had a little scale, with pebbles of different sizes for weights, from which it was known that he had dealt before with white men, probably Portuguese. Over two tons of ivory and four hundred and ninety pounds of copper were procured. The locality in which the copper mines were situated could not be ascertained, as the natives either could not or would not give information concerning it.

A report of an iron mountain some distance inland lured a party of nineteen men, under the secunde Jan Christoffel Stefler, to go in search of it. They left Fort Lagoa on the 9th of August 1723, with three pack oxen to carry provisions. At the end of a week they were in a charming country. In mountain kloofs were magnificent forests, the soil was rich and covered with long grass, streams of fresh water were numerous, and different kinds of game, particularly elephants, were seen in great abundance. When crossing a river, the leading division of the exploring party was attacked and destroyed by a band of natives, and as no one capable of giving directions was then left, the survivors returned to the bay.

In May 1724 an active junior officer, named Jan van de Capelle, was appointed provisional commandant of Fort Lagoa, as Jan Michel had requested to be relieved. It was not a place to which people went willingly, for the climate had the reputation of being in the summer season one of the most deadly in the world.

The year 1722 was the most disastrous one yet known for the Company's fleets in these seas. On the 17th of January the richly-laden ships *Sampson* and *Amstelveen*, belonging to a large return fleet, encountered a great gale off the southern coast, and went down in the open ocean. Two men belonging to the first and one belonging to the last were found by other ships of the fleet some hours later floating on pieces of wreckage. The remainder of their crews perished.

On Sunday the 14th of June a gale from the north-west set into Table Bay. There were lying at anchor, belonging to the Company, two second class outward-bound ships, the *Standvastigheid* and *Rotterdam*, together carrying 453 men, two third class outward-bound ships, the *Zoetigheid* and *Lakeman*, together carrying 283 men, a small outward-bound vessel, the *Schotsche Lorrendraayer*, carrying 52 men, the packet boat *Gouda*, ready to sail to Delagoa Bay with supplies, and the brigantine *Amy*, which had been in use at the Cape ever since her seizure in Saldanha Bay in 1693. There were also lying in the bay three English East Indiamen, the *Nightingale*, bound to Madras, with a crew of 140 men, and the *Addison* and *Chandos*, with crews respectively of 80 and 70 men, homeward bound from Bengal. The last named had put in a fortnight before in distress, having been dismasted in a gale at sea.

All that day the danger to the shipping was great, but no accident worse than parting cables and swamping boats occurred. On Monday the gale lulled, but during the night the wind shifted to north-north-west, and on Tuesday morning the bay seemed to be covered with breakers. Still up to dusk the ships held to their anchors.

As darkness set in the gale increased. At seven o'clock minute guns were heard between the gusts, and the firing continued until midnight. The sea was breaking on the beach with such violence that it was dangerous to pass along the road between the castle and the shore.

At dawn in the morning of the 17th it was seen that not a single vessel was afloat in the bay. The *Amy* was under the castle, and had broken up, but her crew had got safely ashore. The *Chandos* was next, close to the castle. She had partly broken up, but only two of her crew had been drowned. Then came fragments of the *Zoetigheid*, nearly half of whose crew had perished. The *Lakeman* was high on the land a little further on, with only one man missing. Just beyond were the crushed fragments of the *Standvastigheid*, *Rotterdam*, and *Schotsche Lorrendraayer*, all together, and of their crews only forty-five men were living. The *Gouda* and the *Nightingale* were some distance off, both high on the land and not much broken. The *Nightingale* had lost one man, the other none. The *Addison* had struck in the mouth of Salt River, and had overturned and broken up. Only ten of her crew had got to land. In all six hundred and sixty men perished in that dreadful gale, and property valued at nearly a quarter of a million sterling was lost.

On the 20th of November of this disastrous year the *Schoonberg*, homeward bound with a valuable cargo, was run ashore near Cape Agulhas in broad daylight and in fine weather, through the culpable negligence of her officers. The ship broke up, but all on board got safely to shore.

The next wreck that occurred on the coast was on the 7th of November 1723, when a little vessel named the *Meteren*, which was on her passage out to be employed as a packet between the Cape and Delagoa Bay, was lost on the coast a little to the north of the mouth of the Elephant river. She had left Texel with a crew of twenty-nine souls. Scurvy made its appearance, and six died on the passage; while of the others, only ten were at length able to work. In a calm her anchor was dropped close to the coast, but a swell set in, when she dragged, and was cast ashore a complete wreck. Five men were drowned. The remaining eighteen got to land, where nine of them, who could walk, wandered about for twenty-five days before they were found. The others were believed to have died of want.

In the church, matters had assumed a very satisfactory aspect. The Rev. Mr. D'Ailly remained as first or chief minister of the Cape. The rector of the school, the Rev. Lambertus Slicher, was an ordained clergyman, but had been engaged as a teacher only. In that capacity he had been some years in service here, when at the request of the council of policy and with the consent of the directors he began to assist in the church. His first service was held on the 15th of June 1721. He still continued to perform the duty of rector of the school, though in February 1723 he was formally inducted as second or assistant clergyman of the Cape congregation. In 1720 some persons subscribed the necessary funds for the purchase of an organ for use in the church.

The Rev. Petrus van Aken, who had been appointed by the directors clergyman of Drakenstein, arrived in August 1714, and took over the duty at once. In 1717 a commencement was made with building a church at Drakenstein. The funds were derived from a legacy of 208*l.* 6*s.* 8*d.* bequeathed for the purpose by Henning Huising, 314*l.* 8*s.* 6*d.* left with the government here for charitable purposes by individuals in the fleet under the governor-general Van Hoorn, 698*l.* 12*s.* 2*d.* lent by the consistory of the Cape, and 715*l.* 12*s.* 6*d.* raised partly by special collections and partly by making use of the poor fund. The building was completed in 1720. When Paul Roux died, the consistory requested the council of policy to appoint another French sick comforter in his stead, as there were still some twenty-five or twenty-six old people living who did not understand Dutch. The council, 23rd of February 1723, declined to do so until the pleasure of the directors could be made known, and their decision was unfavourable.

At Stellenbosch, where the Rev. Mr. Bek was clergyman, a commencement was also made in 1717 with building a church in place of the one that had been destroyed by fire. The cost was borne by applying the poor fund, by special collections, a loan from the Cape consistory which had then over 9,300*l.* to the good, and by a lottery for which permission was obtained from the directors.

On the 8th of October 1721 Abraham Cranendonk died, when Jan de la Fontaine, who had been working his way upwards during the eleven years of his residence in South Africa, was chosen by the council of policy to act as secunde until the pleasure of the directors could be known. In 1724 the appointment was confirmed by the Assembly of Seventeen.

On the 14th of June 1724 the fiscal independent, Cornelis

van Beaumont, died. The council selected Adriaan van Kervel, who had been sixteen years in service at the Cape, to act until a new appointment could be made by the directors. He also was confirmed in his office.

Governor De Chavonnes managed to preserve the good will both of the directors and the colonists. He embarked in no costly undertakings, did his utmost to keep down expense, and preserved concord in the settlement. He was a quiet, religious man, who might have taken for motto a verse which closes the journal for one of the years when he was at the head of affairs:

'Geluckigh is hy die syn tyd
In stille rust en weldoen slyt,
Die al hetgeen den Hemel geeft
Nooyt in syn hert mispreesen heeft.'

The directors were so well satisfied with his administration that they raised him to the rank of ordinary councillor of India, a dignity enjoyed by none of his predecessors. The letter containing the announcement of his elevation reached the Cape on the 1st of June 1721.

The governor was suddenly taken ill on the 7th of September 1724, and died early on the following morning. A few hours later the council of policy met and decided that Jan de la Fontaine should act as head of the government until an appointment could be made by the Assembly of Seventeen. His nomination as secunde had not yet been confirmed by the directors, and he was only in rank a merchant; but there was no other officer at the Cape in a better position. Within a few months despatches were received in which he was promoted to be a senior merchant, and was approved of as secunde.

On the 14th of September the body of the late governor was buried under the pavement of the church, with all the state that was possible, nearly the whole of the colonists of Stellenbosch and Drakenstein as well as those of the Cape district attending the funeral. His widow and daughters returned to Europe with the next fleet from India.

G 2

During the period 1714 to 1724 the names of but few new colonists are found in the records. The following are all that need to be mentioned: Christiaan Ackerman, Pieter van Breda, Hermanus Combrinck, Jan Hop, Hendrik Klopper, Hermanus Kriel, Daniel Krynouw, Abraham Peltser, Melt van der Spuy, Jan de Waal, Pieter Wion, and Jan de Wit.

CHAPTER XX.

JAN DE LA FONTAINE, SECUNDE, ACTING HEAD OF THE GOVERNMENT, 8 SEPTEMBER 1724 TO 25 FEBRUARY 1727.

PIETER GYSBERT NOODT, GOVERNOR, INSTALLED 25 FEBRUARY 1727, DIED 23 APRIL 1729.

JAN DE LA FONTAINE, SECUNDE, ACTING HEAD OF THE GOVERNMENT, 24 APRIL 1729 TO 8 MARCH 1730; GOVERNOR, INSTALLED 8 MARCH 1730, RETIRED 31 AUGUST 1737.

Falling off in foreign shipping visiting the Cape—Statistics of ships that put into Table Bay—Exportation of grain—Attempt to plant the Cape flats—Experiment in silk culture—Efforts to produce kirman hair at the Cape—Establishment of an outpost on the river Zonder End—Arrival of Governor Noodt—Character of the new governor—Attempt to recover treasure from wrecks in Table Bay—Wreck of ships in Table Bay in July and December 1728—Loss of the *Saxenburg* off Cape Agulhas—Examination of various bays—Treatment of Bushman marauders—Sudden death of Governor Noodt—Particulars of the trial of some soldiers, and of their execution on the day of the governor's death—Election of Jan de la Fontaine to act as head of the government—Appointment by the directors of Jan de la Fontaine as governor, Adriaan van Kervel as secunde, and Daniel van den Henghel as fiscal independent—Decline in prosperity of the Netherlands East India Company—Events at Delagoa Bay—Abandonment of Delagoa Bay by the Company—Efforts to explore the south-eastern coast of Africa—Introduction of a new system of land tenure in the colony—Project of trade between the colony and the east coast and the islands—Visit of the governor to Mossel Bay—Establishment of an outpost on the Buffeljagts river—Wreck of a packet in Table Bay in 1736—The great gale of May 1737—Wreck of nine ships, with loss of over two hundred lives and a large amount of property—Summary punishment of thieves—Succession of clergymen at the Cape, Stellenbosch, and Drakenstein—Wanderings of elephant hunters—Massacre by Kaffirs of a party of elephant hunters—Names of new colonists—Retirement of Governor De la Fontaine, who is succeeded by Adriaan van Kervel.

In consequence of foreign ships being prevented from obtaining supplies at the Cape during the period of scarcity, very few vessels not under the Dutch flag now put into Table Bay. The burghers felt the loss severely, for foreigners had brought ready money into the country; but it was hoped that with better times they would return again. This hope was not, however, realised. The plague among the cattle after a few years decreased in virulence, and beef and mutton were obtainable at a penny halfpenny to two pence a pound; but the Cape had lost its reputation of affording cheap supplies of fresh provisions, and it was a long time in regaining it. During the thirteen years, 1725–1737, embraced in this chapter, one thousand and seven ships put into Table Bay, or on an average seventy-seven yearly. Of these, 868 belonged to the Company, 91 were English, 27 Danish, 19 French, 1 was Portuguese, and 1 was Flemish.

The harvests during this period fluctuated considerably. The directors, having gained experience of the uncertainty of the seasons in South Africa, issued instructions that a year's supply of wheat should always be put by as a reserve before any was sent to India. In 1724 and again in 1725 over five thousand muids were exported. In 1726 none could be spared, owing to drought. In 1727 there was not sufficient for home consumption, owing to rust, which had attacked rye before, but not wheat. From 1728 to 1737 there was a constant export, sometimes of as much as seven thousand muids, though the crops were not uniformly good.

The isthmus connecting the Cape peninsula with the continent was at this time a barren waste of sand. With difficulty laden waggons traversed it, for there was no road, and nothing but a line of poles indicated the best course across. From reports of skippers, the directors were led to believe that Table Bay would at no very distant date be filled with the sand which violent south-east gales swept into it during the summer months. To prevent this, they issued instructions that attempts should be made to fix the sand by planting it with grass and trees, and in the winter of 1724 the work was commenced. Seventy slaves and a gang of convicts were employed in planting knot-grass and seeds of the wild olive, and, when these failed, in ensuing rainy seasons the experiment was repeated with belts of sods.

The valuable properties of the mesembryanthemum for

binding surface sand were then unknown. For eleven years, with one short interval, the effort to plant the flats was continued, every winter much labour being expended upon it; but in 1735 it was abandoned in despair. The directors, however, were by this time satisfied that Table Bay was in no danger of silting up. A commission of nautical men that was appointed to examine it carefully sent in a report that within the preceding half century, so far from its filling up with sand, the water had become deeper.

To superintend the experiments in silk culture, which the directors resolved should be made, the services of a competent man, named François Guillaumet, were secured. In October 1726 he and his family arrived at the Cape. Attempts had previously been made to bring silkworm eggs from India, but in no instance had they been successful. Some had been received in good condition from Europe, however, and the worms when hatched had been carefully attended to in the houses of Messrs. Jan de la Fontaine and Nicholas Heyning. They were now handed over to Guillaumet. There were plenty of healthy mulberry trees, and the expert was furnished with whatever slave labour he asked for. Everything was thus in favour of the experiment.

In the first year eight pounds weight of good silk was obtained, which was sent to the Netherlands, and was an object of considerable interest at Amsterdam and Middelburg. Anticipations arose of another manufacturing industry in the mother country, with an article produced in a Dutch colony. The members of the council of policy at the Cape were equally enthusiastic. A large building was immediately erected close to the Company's garden, and was placed at Guillaumet's disposal for keeping the worms in. The children in the slave lodge close by were all to be employed out of school hours in winding silk. Some thousands of young mulberry trees were planted in selected places. Any burghers who had a fancy to join in the industry, which was now believed to have passed the experimental stage, were supplied with a few eggs and the necessary instructions.

Yet in no subsequent year did the production of silk exceed ten pounds in weight. The great majority of the worms always died before making cocoons, and in one particular season they would have become extinct altogether if it had not been that a few were preserved by some burghers. It was soon ascertained that the returns were so trifling as to forbid the industry being attractive to people who could make a living in any other way. For eight years, however, the experiment was continued by the government. In 1735 every one admitted that it could not be made to succeed, and by order of the directors it was then given up.

Another industry which the Company at this time attempted to establish in South Africa was the production of kirman hair. Shawls made of this hair were then considered second only in value to those of Cashmere. The goat which produces it is reared in Persia, and in that country twenty-four young animals were obtained, which were sent to Ceylon to be forwarded to the Cape. In February 1725 eight of these reached South Africa, the others having died on the way. Of the eight, only one was a she-goat, and that died shortly after being landed. From ordinary she-goats cross-breeds were obtained, and from these and the pure animals, now reduced by death to two, goats with tolerably long and fine hair were bred. Some burghers were then induced to make experiments with the animals. After a few years trial they informed the council that unless the Company would pay forty pence a pound for the hair, it would not be worth their while to keep separate flocks. That price could not be given even for a superior article. But instead of improving the quality, the owners of the goats allowed the hair to deteriorate by mixture with native animals until a quantity sent to Europe in 1735 was quite unsaleable. The experiment was then abandoned.

In November 1726 a corporal and six men were sent over the Hottentots Holland mountains to form an outpost at a place called the Ziekenhuis, on the river Zonder End. The few Hottentots left in that part of the country had complained to the government that they were not able to hold their own against the Bushmen, and that they were also exposed to depredations from vagrant Europeans, who professed to visit them for purposes of trade, but in reality robbed them of cattle. Owing to these complaints the outpost was formed, in order that acts of violence might be prevented. The directors were so dissatisfied that the Europeans of Van der Heiden's party, of whom the Drakenstein consistory had complained, had not been brought to justice for their conduct towards the Hottentots, that they issued instructions to prohibit all dealing by private persons with natives under heavier penalties than before. In consequence, on the 9th of April 1727 a very strict placaat to that effect was issued.

The officer whom the Assembly of Seventeen selected as governor was the director of fortifications, Pieter Gysbert Noodt, who seven years earlier had inspected the shore of Table Bay and prepared plans of defensive works. Intelligence of his appointment reached South Africa in January 1726, and on the 6th of December of that year he left Batavia as admiral of a homeward bound fleet of nine ships. On the 13th of February 1727 he reached the Cape, and on the 25th of the same month was formally installed as governor. His family was small, consisting only of his wife and one son.

Mr. Noodt was a coarse, harsh, ill-tempered man, full of pride and self-conceit, and therefore generally disliked. He took special pleasure in irritating the secunde Jan de la Fontaine, and attempted even to injure that officer's reputation. In consequence, De la Fontaine tendered his resignation ; but the directors, instead of accepting it, increased his salary from 6*l.* 13*s.* 4*d.* to 10*l.* a month.

In 1727 a party of five English divers under a foreman named John Lethbridge, who had been engaged in Europe and sent out by the directors, endeavoured to recover the treasure buried in wrecks in Table Bay. The apparatus which they brought with them is not described, but whatever it was, it enabled them to remain a considerable time under water. They recovered some coin and a quantity of goods, but found that most of the wreckage was deeply covered with sand.

During the summer the forests along the river Zonder-End were examined by the governor in person, with a view of ascertaining whether they could not be made of greater use to the Company. But the mountain range separating them from the Cape was found to be too formidable a barrier to allow the transport of timber with profit.

On Saturday the 3rd of July 1728 there were six ships at anchor in Table Bay, when a gale set in from the north-north-west. At one o'clock in the afternoon the *Stabroek* parted her cables and was driven ashore between the castle and the mouth of Salt River. She was followed two hours later by the *Haarlem,* which grounded nearer the castle. Neither of these vessels was broken, and only two men of each were drowned in endeavouring to get to land. A little after three o'clock the *Middenrak* went ashore just beyond the mouth of Salt River. There were seventy-five men on board, and the ship was in a raging surf, but it was not possible to render any assistance. Night set in, and the hull of the *Middenrak* still held together. But when morning dawned on Sunday the 4th, all that remained of the ship was strewed along the beach, and not one of the seventy-five was saved to tell when she had gone to pieces. The other three vessels rode out the gale.

The *Haarlem* was got afloat again, and was sent to Saldanha Bay to be repaired. This was effected, and she returned to Table Bay on the 4th of December. At that season of the year danger was not suspected, though the day was rainy and the wind was variable from north-west to south-west. At ten o'clock that night the *Haarlem* parted her cables and went ashore close to the mouth of Salt River, where she broke up at once. Of one hundred and seven men on board, only sixteen got to land on pieces of the wreck.

On the morning of the 9th of January 1729 the provision ship *Saxenburg,* bound from Batavia to the Cape with rice and other Indian produce, went down in a gale off Cape

Agulhas. Of eighty-eight souls on board, all perished but seven, who were picked up on pieces of the wreck by other vessels a few hours later.

In consequence of the numerous disasters that had occurred in Table Bay in the winter season, the directors issued instructions that the several harbours in the neighbourhood of the Cape should be carefully examined, and a report be submitted to them. To perform this, a commission was appointed, consisting of two old skippers, one named Jacobus Möller, who was then acting as master of the naval establishment at the Cape, the other named Jan de Heere, who had been for some time living in the colony as a burgher. They sounded Table Bay and made a chart of it, reporting that it was not filling up, that it could be made a perfectly safe harbour by means of a mole, but that the mole would cost a great deal of money. Saldanha Bay they described as secure, but as wanting in everything else that could make a refreshment station valuable. Simon's Bay they thought more highly of. Eight or ten ships could there find shelter in all weathers, and there was plenty of fresh water to be had. Its drawbacks they reported to be no ground in its neighbourhood fit for gardens and difficulty of access by land.

There is at this period hardly any mention of the natives in the records, as they seldom gave the Europeans trouble. An exception occurred in December 1728, when a party of Bushmen drove off the cattle from the farm of Jan Valk near Piketberg. Valk's neighbours assembled and pursued the robbers, who offered resistance when they were overtaken. Two Europeans were wounded, but a volley of slugs put to flight all the Bushmen who were not struck. The cattle were recovered, except two oxen. The government approved of the action of the colonists in following the robbers and firing upon them, but directed the landdrost to be careful that no provocation was given to Bushmen who did not first offend.

The only other instance of the kind that is recorded during the period embraced in this chapter occurred in

March 1731. Some Bushmen drove off a herd of cattle from the farm of Hans Potgieter, but were pursued by twelve of Potgieter's neighbours, who hastily assembled and formed a commando. The robbers were overtaken, when some of them were shot, and the cattle were recovered.

Mr. Noodt was at the head of this colony for a period of two years and two months. He was generally disliked, but as he did not interfere with the burghers, they did not complain of him as they had of the younger Van der Stel. He died suddenly when sitting in the pleasure house in the Company's garden between three and four o'clock in the afternoon of the 23rd of April 1729. A few hours before, when apparently in perfect health, he had signed documents which are still in existence. On the last day of the month his body was buried with state under the pavement of the church, but in the records there is no trace of regret shown by any one for his death. With the first homeward bound fleet of the following year his widow and son returned to Europe.

The character of this governor is usually pictured in the blackest colours. It was so drawn in an account of the Cape written by a German tutor who lived in the colony for several years after 1732, and whose narrative of the trial of some soldiers for conspiring to desert and of their execution on the day of Mr. Noodt's death has not only been copied in many modern books, but was the foundation of a drama which was popular some years ago. Yet that account is almost entirely ideal, being nothing more than a tale by a man who had no other means of obtaining information than gossip upon a past event.

In the records of the high court of justice, which are in perfect preservation, the circumstance is thus related. Fourteen soldiers planned to desert from the garrison and march overland to the Portuguese possessions beyond Delagoa Bay, where they supposed they would find means to get to Europe. In the night of the 2nd of April 1729 two of them were on guard. These deserted with their arms and assisted some of the others to rob the guardhouse of nine muskets with ammunition. One was unable to get away, the remaining thirteen marched towards Stellenbosch. During the next day they visited the farms of Andries Schutte and Izaak Nel, where they obtained food, and then continued on their journey.

The governor, meantime, instructed Pieter Lourens, landdrost of Stellenbosch, to assemble a party of burghers and arrest the fugitives. Early in the morning of the 4th they were overtaken at Hottentots Holland kloof, but only two gave themselves up when the landdrost summoned them to surrender. The others maintained a running fight for three hours, when their leader was shot and eight were captured. Another was made prisoner a few days later, and the remaining three returned of their own accord to the castle and surrendered.

They were brought to trial, and on the 21st of April sentence was passed. Four were condemned to be hanged, and their bodies afterwards to be exposed to perish by the air and the birds. Five were to be flogged, branded, and made to labour fifteen years in chains. Three were to be flogged and made to labour ten years. And the last was to be flogged and made to labour three years. At the foot of this sentence the original signatures may still be seen of the members of the high court of justice: Pieter Gysbert Noodt, Jan de la Fontaine, Johannes Theophilus Rhenius, Nicholas Heyning, Hendrik Swellengrebel, Christoffel Brand, J. P. van Coller, and Ryk Tulbagh.

The sentence was carried into effect on the morning of the 23rd, and the only interference of the governor that is recorded is that he used his power of mitigation to permit the burial of the four who were hanged, instead of allowing them to be exposed. The punishment was in accordance with the spirit of those times, and was not more severe than was inflicted for similar offences in other countries.

At eight in the morning after Mr. Noodt's death the council of policy met, and decided that the secunde Jan de la Fontaine should again act as head of the government until the pleasure of the supreme authorities could be known. With the next homeward bound fleet they sent a request to the directors that he should be permanently appointed governor, and on the 20th of February 1730 despatches were received to the effect that their request had been complied with. The fiscal independent, Adriaan van Kervel, was appointed to succeed him as secuude, and Daniel van den Henghel, who was then in service at Colombo, was appointed fiscal. On the 8th of March 1730 Mr. De la Fontaine took the oath of office and was formally installed as governor. On the 21st of March 1732 he was further promoted to the rank of councillor extraordinary of Netherlands India.

The East India Company, upon whose fortunes this colony greatly depended, had now passed the zenith of its prosperity. Its dividends, which for the ten years ending 31st December 1722 had been at the rate of thirty-seven per cent per annum upon the paid up capital, averaged only twenty-one per cent for the ten years 1723–1732, and never afterwards rose higher than twenty-five per cent. Many of its trading establishments were not returning the expense of maintenance. The commerce of the English and French in the East was making enormous strides, and some branches were completely lost to the Dutch. The coasting trade of Southern Asia, which had once been almost exclusively in possession of the Company, had fallen into other hands.

In Holland matters were quite as bad. The directorate was secured by members of powerful families, who were content to draw a revenue without troubling themselves to correct abuses. Their influence was sufficient to prevent the States General from exercising the right of inspection into the Company's affairs, and of seeing that its transactions were conducted in such a manner as not to be prejudicial to the interests of the republic.

Under these circumstances the corruption, which for a long time had been prevalent in the public service, extended more deeply than before. The appointment of independent fiscals had done nothing to check it. In the Asiatic dependencies, where there were no intelligent freemen to resist oppression,—which indeed at its worst did not equal that of the native princes,—wealth was accumulated by the Company's servants in shameless ways. The ancient simplicity of manners had disappeared. The officers of government lived in a style of ostentation resembling that of Asiatic rulers, and bribery and fraud were commonly practised.

At the Cape there was less opportunity for such malpractices, as the colonists were not the people to submit tamely to wrong of any kind. Further, it may have been accidental, or it may have been owing to their living in a healthier moral atmosphere, but the chief officials in South Africa for many years after the death of Governor Noodt were men held in general esteem, whose probity was never questioned.

The early disasters at Delagoa Bay had not discouraged the Company, and for a long time hopes were entertained of a profitable trade being carried on there. In 1725 a little ambergris, some aloes, three hundred pounds weight of copper, more than two tons of ivory, thirty-four slaves, and a few ounces of gold dust were received from that station. It was impossible to obtain any reliable information concerning the interior of the country from the natives at the bay; but it was observed on one occasion that two of the chief Maphumbo's men went inland and returned with some gold dust within fourteen days. This raised a hope that the gold fields might be easily reached, and on the 27th of June 1725 an expedition left Fort Lagoa in search of them. It consisted of thirty-one men under Sergeant Jan Mona, with a clerk named Frans de Kuyper as journalist. After a toilsome march of twenty days, a party of hostile blacks was encountered, who opposed further advance. In a skirmish several of the natives were shot, but as the pack oxen were killed by the enemy and all the baggage and goods were seized, the expedition was obliged to return.

An attempt to search for the copper mines, made by a party under the mineralogist Jan Hendrik Hoorn, was also a failure.

The directors now issued instructions that attempts to

reach the gold fields and the empire of Monomotapa, which was still believed to be a reality, should be made by means of boats pushing their way up the rivers. An old skipper, named Jan de Koning, was appointed commander, and the garrison was strengthened with a hundred soldiers and sailors.

At the end of May 1726 Commander De Koning arrived at Fort Lagoa. He found the secunde, Jan de la Capelle, who had been acting head of the station, engaged in making experiments in the cultivation of sugar cane and indigo. There were constant feuds between the various clans around the bay, but the Europeans were on good terms with all. The most powerful of the chiefs was named Maphumbo, but another, named Manisa, was almost as strong. The latter had his kraals on the banks of the river Dos Reys of the Portuguese, where Vasco da Gama had landed; and the Dutch called the stream after him, the Manisa.

The natives were credited with a belief that the Europeans purchased slaves to fatten and eat them, and it was supposed that this belief was the cause of their bringing so few for sale. To counteract it, Commander De Koning sent three men of rank with their attendants on a visit to the Cape, that they might see for what purpose slaves were needed. One of those who visited the Cape was a nephew of Maphumbo. He had been to England, and had there received in baptism the name of John; but had been sent back to Delagoa Bay in 1723. He spoke English fluently. The visitors professed to be pleased with the manner in which they saw the slaves were treated; but the traffic did not increase after their return.

As Fort Lagoa was too small for the accommodation of the garrison now stationed there, a larger area was enclosed with earthen walls, to which the name of Lydzaamheid was given. The rivers were ascended as far as they were navigable with boats; but very little information was obtained concerning the country. The Dutch officers were never able to ascertain the exact position and distance of either the copper mines or the gold fields. The gold dust brought by the natives for sale was so mixed with other substances as to cause the assayers in Batavia to assert that every stiver's worth cost the Company a florin.

In December 1726 fever attacked the garrison, as it had done every previous summer, and in a few months thirty-eight men died, among them being Commander De Koning. The secunde Jan de la Capelle then became acting head of the station again. Reinforcements were sent from the Cape, and attempts to explore the interior were renewed, but with no greater success than before. At the beginning of the following summer a party of sixteen soldiers deserted and made their way overland to Inhambane, where most of them perished. A little later sixty-two men at the station entered into a conspiracy to rebel and desert, but the plot was discovered in time to prevent its being put into execution. The garrison was then one hundred and eighty-six strong.

The directors now resolved to leave the abandonment or retention of Fort Lydzaamheid to the discretion of the council of policy at the Cape. The council thereupon resolved, 11th of June 1730, that the sooner it could be abandoned the better. On the 12th of August the little vessels *Snuffelaar*, *Zeepost*, and *Feyenoord*, which were employed as packets at the Cape, left to bring away the garrison and effects. Before their arrival another disaster occurred. Ensign Mona and twenty-nine Europeans were surprised and killed by a party of natives. On the 27th of December 1730 the acting commander Jan de la Capelle and one hundred and thirty-three men, to which number the garrison had been reduced, embarked in the vessels sent for them, and they arrived at the Cape on the 13th of the following January.

Delagoa Bay was abandoned, but the Company had still a strong desire to establish a station somewhere on the south-eastern coast of Africa. In September 1731 the *Snuffelaar* and *Zeepost* were sent to examine the seaboard carefully as far north as Inhambane. Jan de la Capelle accompanied the expedition as journalist. A Portuguese station was visited, but nothing unknown before was discovered. At and near St. Lucia Bay many lives were lost by fever, and the survivors then returned to the Cape with a report that no suitable place for a station could be found. The expedition was absent five months.

In September 1732 the *Zeepost* and *Feyenoord* were sent to make another search. After spending four months examining the coast, they returned to the Cape, when their officers reported that north of Port Natal they could find no place where a station could be established to advantage. The design was then given up by the directors.

Previous to 1732 ground was held by individuals in the colony either under freehold title or annual leases. On the 18th of February of this year, by order of the directors, another system of land tenure was introduced. It was enacted that garden ground in the Cape peninsula and small plots of land adapted for agriculture and bordering on freehold farms could be leased for periods of fifteen years, during which they were to be irreclaimable; and if at the expiration of any term of fifteen years the Company should resume possession, the tenant was to be compensated for all buildings at a fair valuation. The rental first named was eight shillings and fourpence a morgen yearly, but in the following year it was permanently fixed at two shillings and a penny a morgen. At the same time the rental of the large farms or cattle runs held under annual leases was raised from 2*l.* 10*s.* to 5*l.*

As far back as 1719 the burgher councillors, acting on behalf of several colonists who were acquainted with the east coast and the islands of Madagascar and the Mascarenhas group, had requested liberty to trade with those countries upon payment of reasonable import and export duties. They proposed to purchase manufactured goods from the Company, and to exchange these goods and Cape produce for slaves, ivory, gold dust, and anything else of commercial value that should be obtainable. The directors had at first hesitated, but they were now disposed to take the request into favourable consideration, if the colonists would submit their plans in detail. In 1732 a committee of officers of the Cape government, consisting of Messrs. Adriaan van Kervel, Nicholas Heyning, and Ryk Tulbagh, was appointed to meet the acting and retired burgher councillors, and after discussing the question with them, to draw up a report for transmission to the Netherlands. The conference took place; but the burgher councillors stated that circumstances had changed since 1719, those who were then prepared to embark in the trade having died or engaged in other pursuits, and they thought no advantage could now be derived from the project.

In June 1734 a homeward bound Indiaman, named the *Huis te Marquette*, put into Mossel Bay in distress, which led to the governor visiting that port. On the 7th of July he left the Cape, attended by the secretary, Ryk Tulbagh, the master of the naval department, Jacobus Möller, Ensign Rudolph Sigfried Alleman, and the burghers Jan Kruywagen, Jan Hop, Jan Christoffel Bek, Jacobus Botha, and Andries Grove, whose farms were in the neighbourhood of Mossel Bay and who offered the use of their waggons and cattle. The distressed ship was relieved, and the bay was examined; but the governor left with a very poor opinion of its capabilities as a harbour. The party proceeded eastward to the forests in the district once occupied by the Outeniqua tribe, which the governor wished to explore. Heavy rains, however, set in, which necessitated a return before the rivers should become flooded. The party was absent not quite two months. At Mossel Bay the governor caused a stone beacon, with the arms of the republic engraved on one side and those of the East India Company on the other, to be erected as a mark of possession.

A few weeks later, a small military outpost, similar to those at Waveren and the river Zonder End, was established at Riet Vlei, on the Buffeljagts river, between the present villages of Swellendam and Heidelberg. The objects were to prevent illicit cattle dealing with the natives, and to provide protection to the farmers and the Hottentots from the Bushmen. In the same year a corporal and six men were sent to form a temporary outpost at St. Helena Bay, where it was feared that the French had an intention of establishing a refreshment station. After an occupation of a few months, upon receipt of intelligence from Europe, this outpost was broken up.

During the night between the 1st and 2nd of July 1736 the brigantine *Feyenoord* was driven ashore in a gale near Salt River mouth, and became a wreck. Only one life was lost.

The following year was one of the most disastrous ever known to shipping at the Cape. On the 21st of May 1737 a fleet of nine ships, mostly of the third class, was lying at anchor in Table Bay ready to sail for the Fatherland. During the preceding night a heavy gale had set in from the north-west. At daylight the wind veered a little more to the westward, increasing the swell of the sea. Huge waves were rolling in between Robben Island and Green Point, and the bay was like a sheet of foam. As the gale increased, the ships' cables began to part, and between ten and eleven o'clock in the morning minute guns were heard.

In a short time the *Ypenroode* was seen to be drifting. She struck close to the mouth of Salt River, and with the shock her masts fell and she broke into fragments in the surf. Some of her crew managed to get to land. The *Goudriaan* parted next. She struck broadside on, with her stern in the mouth of Salt River, and went to pieces at once. The larger number of those on board perished. At noon the *Flora* struck at the same place as the *Goudriaan*. She, too, went to pieces immediately, and of her crew only six men got to land. The *Paddenburg* followed, but her crew were more fortunate. She was carried in on the crest of a mountain wave, and passed directly over the other wrecks, striking high up on the beach. She went to pieces with the shock, but most of those on board escaped with their lives. At half past two in the afternoon the *Westerwyk* was driven ashore at the same place. She ran high on the beach without breaking up, and only a few of her men were lost. At four o'clock the *Buys* struck close to the *Westerwyk*, but she went to pieces at once, and only five of her crew were saved.

Early in the evening the *Duynbeek* was driven ashore beyond Salt River mouth, and broke up immediately, very few of her men being saved. Later on, the *Roodenrys* struck at the same place, but she held together until all of her crew but six got to land by means of a rope attached to a yard which was washed up. At the same time the brigantine *Victoria*, one of the Cape packets, was carried by a great wave high on the beach, where she lay dry when the gale was spent. Nearly all of her crew were saved.

There were now left in the bay only the *Papenburg*, homeward bound Indiaman, and the *Goede Hoop*, a small vessel built at the Cape in 1733 and used as a packet. These managed to ride out the gale.

In all two hundred and eight men were lost out of seven hundred and thirty-nine that formed the crews of the wrecked Indiamen. The purchase price of the cargo with which the beach was strewn was 160,128*l.*

While the ships were drifting ashore a placaat was issued threatening summary execution to any one found pilfering the wrecked cargo. A military guard was stationed on the beach, and four men who were caught stealing were actually hanged on a gallows erected near the water's edge, where their bodies were left exposed as a warning to others. These executions took place on the same principle as that which permitted the shooting of Bushman cattle-lifters, the principle that it is justifiable to put to death a thief caught redhanded.

In the preceding chapter we left the Rev. Messrs. D'Ailly and Slicher clergymen at the Cape, Mr. Bek at Stellenbosch, and Mr. Van Aken at Drakenstein. In December 1724 Mr. Van Aken died. For some months the pulpit was vacant, but at length the council of policy resolved to send Mr. Slicher to Drakenstein, and leave the Cape to the care of Mr. D'Ailly alone until another clergyman should be provided by the directors. Mr. Slicher accordingly took over the duty on the 15th of July 1725. Early in the following year Mr. D'Ailly was taken seriously ill, and he died in June, when Mr. Bek was removed to the Cape, Mr. Slicher being directed to hold services occasionally at Stellenbosch. So matters remained for more than three years.

The directors sent out as second or assistant clergyman at the Cape the Rev. François le Sueur, who conducted service here for the first time on the 16th of October 1729. In June 1730 Mr. Slicher died, when the council instructed Mr. Le Sueur to act provisionally at Drakenstein and Stellenbosch. He returned to the Cape in April 1731, upon the arrival from Europe of the Rev. Johan Wilhelm Hartzogenrath, who had been appointed by the directors clergyman of Drakenstein. At the same time the council resolved that Mr. Hartzogenrath should act as consulent of Stellenbosch, and permitted Mr. Bek, who was advanced in years and very feeble, to retire on a pension.

In April 1732 the Rev. Hendrik Kock arrived from Europe, having been appointed second clergyman of the Cape, and he was followed in November of the same year by the Rev. Salomon van Echten, who was sent out as clergyman of Stellenbosch. Thus the whole of the churches were again supplied with ministers, after a series of vacancies during eight years. In June 1736 the Rev. Mr. Hartzogenrath died, when Mr. Van Echten was removed to Drakenstein, with instructions to act as consulent for Stellenbosch.

The country at this time must have been explored far inland, for parties of elephant hunters were sometimes absent from the settlement eight or nine months together before returning with their waggons laden with ivory. But these people were very reticent upon the subject of routes and hunting grounds, and information obtained from them was known to be so unreliable that the government did not take the trouble to place it on record.

There was, however, one notable exception.

In May 1736 a party of elephant hunters, headed by a man named Hermanus Hubner, left the settlement, and travelled eastward to Kaffirland. There were eleven white men in the party, with thirteen waggons and a strong band of Hottentots. Passing through the district occupied by the Gonaquas, at whose head was a chief whom they called

Captain Babbelaan, they came to the kraal of a petty Kosa chief, and then to the residence of Palo, paramount ruler of the Kosa tribe. Proceeding still further, they reached the country of the Tembus, where they found four colonists, with six waggons, hunting elephants and trading with the natives for ivory.

The two parties here united, and went on to a district which they believed to be part of Natal, where they found a tribe whom they termed Nomotis. There can hardly be a doubt that the Pondos are the people referred to. Here they met three Englishmen, named Thomas Willer, Henry Clark, and William Bilyert, who had been shipwrecked many years before, and were living in all respects like the natives, having numerous wives and children. From these Englishmen they purchased on credit about five tons of ivory, for which they undertook to deliver at a future date a certain quantity of iron, copper, and beads. They had now sufficient ivory to load ten waggons, each with eighteen or nineteen hundred pounds weight. They therefore commenced the return journey, intending to hunt by the way, the three Englishmen proposing to accompany them as far as Palo's kraals. From the country of the Nomotis, they passed through that of the Tembus, and kept on until they reached the kraal of Palo, where it was their purpose to remain for a week or two to let their cattle rest. So far they had been treated in a friendly manner by the natives with whom they had come in contact, and they had no cause to suspect different conduct at Palo's kraal.

After resting a while, nine of them, with seven waggons, went on ahead, and after a day's journey came to a river which was so swollen that they were obliged to encamp on its bank and wait its fall. The name of this river is not given. The three Englishmen were with this party, but did not intend to proceed further. The river was falling, though slowly, and on the eighth day after leaving Palo's kraal they were still waiting on its bank, when two of the Hottentots whom they had left with their companions appeared and informed them that all the others had been massacred.

The Hottentots stated that Hermanus Hubner was sitting in front of the tent, in which the other Europeans were lying down, when one of the servants reported that he had observed indications of a hostile design on the part of Palo's people. Hubner took no notice of the warning, replying that the people were friendly and there was no cause whatever for alarm. Shortly afterwards some Kaffirs drove up eight oxen, and on behalf of the chief presented them to Hubner. While they were talking, one of them suddenly stabbed Hubner with an assagai. He drew the weapon from his body, and tried to reach his gun, but before he could do so was killed by another stab in the back. The Kaffirs then rushed upon the tent from all sides, and murdered Frederik Hubner, Andries Esterhuis, and Gerrit van Vuuren before they could take any step to protect themselves. Philip Constant and Anthonie Pottier managed to get out of the tent, but were killed close by. The bodies were afterwards mutilated.

The murderers then unloaded the twelve waggons and burnt them, probably to get the iron. Among the stores were three kegs of gunpowder, each containing fifty pounds. The Kaffirs broke these open, and threw the powder on a heap, when suddenly there was a tremendous explosion and a great number of those who were close by were killed and wounded.

Upon learning the fate of their comrades, eight of the Europeans at the river hastened across with the waggons. The three Englishmen, who had no fear of the Kaffirs, remained behind, and one of the hunters, by name Louis Cloete, thought it advisable to place himself under their protection. Soon after crossing the river, the party was overtaken by a great horde of Kaffirs, among whom they recognised some half-breeds. They fired upon the pursuers, and struck down eight or ten; but as they had very little powder left, they took the first opportunity of abandoning the waggons and continuing their flight on foot. For three days and two nights the Kaffirs followed, until they came to the Gonaqua country, where Captain Babbelaan gave them an escort as far as the Fish River. One of their number, by name Christoffel Hoogreefde, became faint on the way, and they left him under the care of the Gonaquas.

The seven who had escaped continued their journey on foot to the Sunday river, where they met another party of elephant hunters, under Gerrit Oosthuizen and Jacob van Deventer, travelling eastward. Four of them—Daniel de Vries, Jan de Bruin, Jan van Vuuren, and Coenraad Scheffer—joined this party. The other three—Hendrik de Vries, Hendrik Scheffer, and Jan de Vries—came on to the Cape, where on the 10th of July 1737 the two first-named gave an account of their journey in the form of an attestation.

During the period embraced in this chapter, or so shortly afterwards as to be practically within it, the following names are found in the records: Jeremiah Auret, Jan Bam, Jan Blignaut, Carel Buitendag, Dirk Craffort, Jan Ditlof, Jan Fleck, Andries Holtshuizen, Hermanus Keeve, Frans Marx, Jacob Naude, Hendrik Nefdt, Adriaan de Nys, Godlieb Opperman, Christiaan Rabe, Pieter Radermacher, Andries Schutte, Frederik Seele, Jan Serrurier, Jan Hendrik Swemmer, Jan Andries Truter, Willem van de Vyver, and Ernest Wepener.

Governor De la Fontaine was now advancing in years, and infirmities were creeping upon him. He was a widower, his wife having died in June 1730. He had children for whom he desired the advantages of a residence in Europe, and from whom he did not wish to be separated. During the twenty-eight years that he had served the Company he had amassed considerable wealth, and it had become a desire with him to spend the evening of his life in repose in the Fatherland. In 1736 he applied to the directors for permission to retire. They heard of his resolution with regret, for he had performed his duties to their satisfaction; but his request was so reasonable that it could not be refused. They therefore appointed the secunde Adriaan van Kervel as his successor, and promoted Mr. Hendrik Swellengrebel to be secunde.

The retiring governor was permitted to hand over the administration whenever it should please him to do so, and to return to Europe with his rank and salary. On the 17th of June 1737 despatches to this effect were received at the Cape, and on the 31st of August Mr. De la Fontaine transferred the duties to Mr. Van Kervel. He remained in the colony until the month of March following, when he sailed for Europe as admiral of a fleet of five ships.

CHAPTER XXI.

ADRIAAN VAN KERVEL, GOVERNOR, INSTALLED 31 AUGUST 1737, DIED 19 SEPTEMBER 1737.

DANIEL VAN DEN HENGHEL, FISCAL, ACTING HEAD OF THE GOVERNMENT, 20 SEPTEMBER 1737 TO 14 APRIL 1739.

HENDRIK SWELLENGREBEL, GOVERNOR, INSTALLED 14 APRIL 1739, RETIRED 27 FEBRUARY 1751.

Death of Governor Van Kervel—Election of the fiscal Van den Henghel to act as head of the government—Appointment by the directors of the secunde Hendrik Swellengrebel as governor—Petty insurrection under Etienne Barbier—Raid by Bushmen—Game laws—Visit of the governor-general Gustaf Willem van Imhof—Establishment of churches at Waveren and Zwartland—Moravian mission to the Hottentots—Account of the missionary George Schmit, and of his work—Opening of Simon's Bay as a port of call in the winter season—Failure of an attempt to construct a mole in Table Bay—Agreement with the burghers concerning the purchase by the Company of wine, peas, and beans—Perquisites allowed to the officers of government—New system of land tenure—Establishment of the district of Swellendam—Price of wheat—Condition of the farmers—Powers and duties of the boards of landdrost and heemraden—Construction of fortifications in Table Valley—Supposed discovery of a silver mine at Drakenstein—Proceedings of a mining association—Succession of clergymen in the different churches—Ships that called—English services in the Dutch Reformed church at the Cape—Wrecks on the coast—The seasons—Exports of the colony—Intercourse between colonists and natives—Extent of the European settlement—Shocks of earthquake—Appointment of the stadtholder to be chief director and governor-general of the East India Company—Rejoicings at the Cape—Retirement of Governor Swellengrebel—Appointment of the secunde Ryk Tulbagh as governor—Departure of Mr. Swellengrebel for Europe—His death at Utrecht.

GOVERNOR VAN KERVEL had passed a great portion of his life in South Africa. From 1719 to 1725 he had been secretary to the council of policy. Then he became fiscal, and afterwards secunde, so that his experience was varied and extensive. He held the highest office in the land less than three weeks, and only presided in the council on one occasion. After a short illness, he died on the 19th of September 1737.

As he had expressed a desire to his daughter that his funeral should be conducted without the usual state, the council respected his dying wish, and his remains were buried in the church between seven and eight o'clock in the evening of the 24th, the officers of government and principal burghers attending without the parade of draped banners, muffled drums, and minute guns. He left a widow and a daughter, who remained in the colony, as most of their near relatives were resident at the Cape.

On the morning after the governor's death the council met for the purpose of electing an acting head. There were six members present, and of these, two put forward claims to the vacant place. The secunde, Mr. Hendrik Swellengrebel, was one. He was by birth a colonist, being a son of Johannes Swellengrebel, who, after holding several less important offices, was dispenser and member of the high court of justice at the beginning of the century. He based his pretensions on precedents, the custom having invariably been that upon the death of a governor the second in command should act until the pleasure of the supreme authorities could be known. It was true he had only been secunde nineteen days, but that did not affect his position, for, as he had been a member of the council of policy for thirteen years, he had ample experience.

The independent fiscal, Mr. Daniel van den Henghel, claimed the appointment, on the ground that he had been a senior merchant longer than Mr. Swellengrebel. He had been in the colony since March 1731.

The question was put to the vote, when Messrs. Nicholas Heyning and Christoffel Brand were found to favour the fiscal's claim, while Captain Johannes Tobias Rhenius and the secretary Ryk Tulbagh supported the secunde.

Hereupon the fiscal objected to Mr. Tulbagh having a voice in the matter, because he was married to Mr. Swellengrebel's sister, and must therefore be held to be prejudiced in his favour.

The secretary replied that the right to vote had never before been disputed on such grounds. He had been a member of the council of policy for nine years. During that time he had always voted according to his conscience, and he would continue to do so.

The others maintained Mr. Tulbagh's right, upon which the master of the warehouses, Mr. Brand, proposed that as the members were equally divided and no decision could be arrived at, the lot should be cast. This was agreed to, when, the result being in favour of the fiscal, he took the vacant chair.

The Assembly of Seventeen did not approve of the appointment of Mr. Van den Henghel, because they considered the secunde the proper person to assume the chief authority upon the death of a governor. They therefore sent out instructions that he should return to his office of independent fiscal, that Mr. Swellengrebel should take the place of governor, and Mr. Ryk Tulbagh that of secunde. These changes took effect on the 14th of April 1739.

Mr. Van den Henghel remained in the colony as fiscal until the 18th of September 1741, when he was relieved by Pieter van Reede van Oudtshoorn, who was sent out by the supreme authorities. A few months later he returned to Europe as commodore of a squadron of four vessels.

In 1739 a petty insurrection took place. Some Hottentot captains having complained that a party of Europeans living along the Elephant river had robbed them of cattle under pretence of barter, these persons were summoned to appear before the landdrost's court at Stellenbosch, and their stock was summarily impounded to prevent concealment. They declined to obey the summons, and raised an outcry that the landdrost's assistant had acted in excess of the law in taking possession of their cattle before it was proved that they had been engaged in the forbidden traffic. The matter was referred to the fiscal, who investigated the case, and found the Hottentots had sufficient cause of complaint. Their property was therefore restored, and they were taken under the Company's protection. At the same time the landdrost's assistant was found to have acted with unnecessary violence, and he was in consequence replaced by a more prudent officer.

A summons was now issued for the Europeans to appear before the court of justice and answer for their conduct in ignoring the constituted authority. But, as on the former occasion, they did not comply. A turbulent individual named Etienne Barbier, by birth a Frenchman, who had been in the Company's military service and had risen to the rank of sergeant but had deserted about a year before, represented to these persons that he possessed great influence in Europe, and induced them to join him. His object was to attain such a position that he could make terms with the government. The malcontents were joined by some other disaffected Europeans, chiefly deserters and Company's servants with passes to seek employment, and on Sunday the 1st of March 1739 the whole rabble, mounted and armed, appeared at Drakenstein. After reading a seditious document to the people, Barbier affixed it to the door of the church. Upon intelligence of this event reaching the castle, instructions were sent to the landdrost to have Barbier seized and brought before the high court of justice, and, if resistance was made, to shoot him.

Just at this time a horde of Bushmen made a raid upon the scattered farmers of Piketberg and the Bokkeveld, murdered two Europeans and several slaves, set fire to some houses, and swept off large herds of cattle. In the preceding year the same maurauders had driven off the stock of a farmer named August Lourens, but had been pursued, and the cattle had been recovered without any bloodshed. By direction of the council, the landdrost and board of militia of Stellenbosch had then requested a discreet farmer to endeavour to enter into a friendly agreement with the Bushmen, and presents were made in hope of inducing them to abstain from robbery. The farmers of the frontier, however, had no confidence in the success of such treatment, and they were now seized with a general panic, fearing that the government would again try to conciliate rather than punish.

Most of them in consequence abandoned their farms and fell back towards the Cape.

The government, however, acted in a different manner. The old burgher councillor Jan Kruywagen was instructed to raise a commando and follow up the marauders, and all who had joined Barbier were offered pardon if they would take part in the expedition. Fifteen of them accepted the offer at once, and the remainder shortly afterwards. Barbier managed to keep in concealment for a few months, but was eventually apprehended. In November he was tried, condemned to death, and executed. After the barbarous manner of that time in Europe as well as in South Africa, his body was divided into portions, which were affixed to posts in different parts of the country.

Some of the farmers who were called out by Kruywagen refused to act under him, and his commando was too weak to accomplish the purpose for which it was raised. In attempting to expel the Bushmen from a mountain, a number of men, including the commandant, were wounded, and one was killed. A stronger force was then raised, and took the field in two divisions, some soldiers having previously been sent to occupy temporary stations in the disturbed districts, where the families of the men on commando could be protected. In August one of the marauding bands was defeated and some cattle were recovered, only one burgher being killed. Reinforcements were then sent to the front, and in October more than sixty Bushmen were killed and upwards of thirty others were wounded. A party of Europeans, who were searching along the coast for a ship that was supposed to have been wrecked, shot from thirty to forty more. The Bushmen then agreed to terms of peace. On the European side during the latest operations three farmers had been wounded in action, and two—Jan Engelbrecht and Philip Meyer—had been surprised and murdered.

In September 1740 the leaders of these Bushmen, to whom the Dutch had given the names Waterboer, Anthonie, Dragonder, and Klein Jantje, with a small following visited the castle, where they were well treated, and acceptable presents were made to them when they left.

From time to time regulations were issued for the preservation of harmless wild animals, and for the destruction of beasts of prey. In November 1739 the reward for killing a lion was reduced from 3*l.* 9*s.* 5*d.* to 2*l.* 1*s.* 8*d.*, for a leopard from 2*l.* 1*s.* 8*d.* to 1*l.* 5*s.* 0*d.*, and for a hyena from 12*s.* 6*d.* to 8*s.* 4*d.* Half of these premiums were paid by the Company, the other half by the burgher council if the animal was destroyed in the Cape district, and by the court of landdrost and heemraden if it was destroyed in the district of Stellenbosch and Drakenstein. In 1745 a regulation was made that in order to obtain the premium the dead animal must be exhibited at the castle or at the office of the landdrost. Previous to that date it had been paid on exhibition of the skin, but at this time it was suspected that some unprincipled persons were bartering furs from the Hottentots of the interior.

The elephant had nearly disappeared from the settled districts, owing to the demand that always existed for ivory. In July 1737 elephant hunting beyond the eastern border was prohibited, owing to the massacre of Hubner's party. The love of gain was, however, so strong that in the following October the prohibition was cancelled, and the only restriction placed upon elephant shooting was that each hunter should pay two shillings and a penny for a license. In the license it was forbidden to molest natives or to trade with them.

In 1742 an order was issued prohibiting the destruction of zebras under a penalty of 10*l.* for each offence. The remarks of the members of the council of policy with regard to the extirpation of this animal show that they could look at the question in a broader light than that of mere profit. Its presence on the hillsides, according to them, was an attractive feature. They thought also that it could be tamed, and with a view of making an experiment, they offered a premium of 20*l.* each for three young ones to be delivered at the castle.

In January 1743, Gustaf Willem van Imhof, governor-general of Netherlands India, called at the Cape on his way to Batavia, and was installed here with much ceremony. He made a short tour of inspection in the country, and instituted an inquiry into the condition of the farmers, the result of which was very unsatisfactory.

The only churches in the colony were at the Cape, Stellenbosch, and Drakenstein. These were at the time all provided with clergymen, the Rev. Willem van Gendt having been sent out by the directors and stationed at Stellenbosch in December 1738. At each of these places there were schools, but everywhere else the education of the children was greatly neglected, being in most instances entrusted to no more competent a teacher than a soldier engaged for a short term. There were over four hundred leasehold farms or cattle runs, some of which were three or four days' journey from the nearest church, so that the attendance on public worship was frequently neglected for long periods. The governor-general consulted the clergymen François le Sueur and Willem van Gendt, who recommended the establishment of more churches and schools. At this date the European population of South Africa consisted of about four thousand colonists and fifteen hundred servants of the Company with their families.

The governor-general called the members of the council of policy together, and issued certain instructions. Two new churches were to be erected in the outlying districts with as little delay as possible, and at each were to be stationed a clergyman and a comforter of the sick, the latter of whom should also act as schoolmaster. The clergymen were to be detained from the first Indiamen calling at the Cape with chaplains on board. A comforter of the sick was also to be sent without delay to labour among the scattered inhabitants beyond the Breede river.

The places selected for the new churches were the sites of the present villages of Tulbagh and Malmesbury.

The first was the most convenient place of meeting for the farmers occupying the country on that side of Riebeek's Kasteel, the Land of Waveren or present Tulbagh Basin, the Warm Bokkeveld, and the valleys of the Upper Breede and Hex rivers. It was beyond the first range of mountains, but was accessible by a road over the Roodezand pass, not far from the ravine through which the Little Berg river flows, and where the railway now enters the Tulbagh Basin. The course of the old road can still be clearly traced, and a formidable rock that nearly blocked up the passage is yet an object of interest to the inhabitants of the neighbourhood. The landdrost and heemraden of Stellenbosch used frequently to spend an hour or two trying to devise some means of getting rid of this rock, but they never succeeded in their object. Some few years after this date the Roodezand pass was abandoned, and a rough waggon road was made through the New Kloof, which is the gateway of the valley at the present day.

A site was selected along a gentle slope, where water could easily be led on, and here the foundations of a church and parsonage were laid without delay. The original buildings are standing yet, the parsonage, which is partly constructed of materials imported from Holland, still serving the purpose for which it was designed. A few weeks after the governor-general's instructions were given, a ship put into Table Bay, having on board as chaplain the Rev. Arnoldus Maurits Meyring, who was detained for duty here. He preached at the Cape for the first time on the 31st of March 1743. The Rev. Hendrik Kock had returned to Europe in February 1742, and Mr. Meyring was therefore kept at the Cape as assistant clergyman until the parsonage at Waveren was fit for occupation. He held the first service there in September 1743, but the regular duty was not begun until some months later. On the 8th of October 1743 a consistory was established, when Jacobus Theron and Pieter Theron were approved by the council of policy as elders, and Jacobus du Pré and Gerrit van der Merwe were selected as deacons from a double nomination. Between the church and the parsonage gradually rose the houses of a little village, which until 1804 had no other name than Roodezands Kerk.

There was a little difficulty in selecting a site for the second church. It was recognised that the situation in which it would be of greatest service was in the centre of the district known as the Zwartland, then as now the best wheat-producing tract of country in South Africa. But upon inspection it was found that there was no suitable place which was not already occupied as a farm. At length the widow of Pieter van der Westhuizen made an offer, which the council of policy accepted on the 16th of June 1744. She received in exchange for her farm another which she had previously selected, and the congregation paid her a sum of money equal to one hundred and seventy-four pounds sterling for the buildings. A sick comforter, Wietse Botes by name, who was serving on board a ship in the bay, was thereupon transferred to the church place, and opened a school at once. On the 9th of May 1745 an agreement was made with the Rev. Rutger Andries Weerman, chaplain of a passing ship, and he became the first pastor of the congregation. A consistory was formed on the 8th of July, when Pieter Venter and Gerrit Olivier were chosen as elders, and Jan Loubser and Floris Smit were appointed deacons. The church place was known as Zwartlands Kerk until 1829, when it received the name of Malmesbury.

Close by is a hot mineral spring, like those which are found in many other parts of South Africa, and which are used by persons troubled with rheumatism and some other diseases. But even with the advantages of a central situation, a church, and a mineral bath, besides having no mountain barrier between it and the Cape, the site was not an attractive one. The ground is very uneven, and the colonists of those days were partial to tolerably level surfaces for building upon. There is no permanent stream of water which can be led out for household purposes and to irrigate gardens, the supply in summer being obtained from wells. Further, the belief was general that the brackish soil, though capable of producing the finest wheat in the world, was unfit for the growth of trees, a matter always of primary importance in a Dutch village. This belief had some slight foundation, but of late years it has been put to the test, and the trees now flourishing in the streets of Malmesbury and on many farms in the district prove that with industry and care the defects of the soil can be overcome.

The boundaries of the several parishes were settled on the 30th of August 1745 by a combined ecclesiastical council, consisting of the clergyman and an elder of each of the five congregations, presided over by a political commissioner. Thereafter such councils met yearly, on the third Monday of every January, to arrange matters of common interest.

While the number of parishes connected with the state religion was thus being increased, dissenters were prohibited from establishing churches in which a different form of worship should be practised. There were many Lutherans at the Cape, and they were anxious to have a resident clergyman, but could not obtain permission from the government. In 1742 a strong petition of theirs was refused. No objection was raised to Lutheran chaplains of Danish ships holding service in a private house, but this was the utmost liberty that was granted.

Another instance of the same kind of treatment occurred in connection with a Moravian missionary who was sent from Germany to attempt the conversion of the Hottentots to christianity, and who established himself for that purpose at Baviaans Kloof, now Genadendal, in the district of Stellenbosch. The first mention of this missionary is found in the proceedings of the council of policy of the 11th July 1737, in which it is stated that 'a certain person named George Schmit had come here in the ship *Huis te Rensburg*, with the object of converting the Hottentots to christianity, if that should be possible; that it was to be hoped such a desirable result would be attained by the blessing of the Lord upon the means to be employed, so that those people might be brought to the true knowledge of God; and therefore all possible assistance was to be given to the said person in the prosecution of that meritorious work.'

It was contemplated that if any Hottentots should be converted to the christian faith the missionary would present them to the clergyman of the parish for baptism, and that he would not attempt to form a separate congregation with rules differing from those of the Dutch Reformed church. He collected a party of Hottentots, with whom he laboured for five years, doing his utmost to teach them the doctrines of christianity and the advantages of a settled industrious life. All this time he met with nothing but kindness from the government, but when in 1742 he baptized five of his converts he was immediately called to account.

On the 4th of September of that year the matter was discussed by the council of policy. Schmit's authority to administer the sacraments was examined and found to be a document signed by the head of a foreign society, which the council ruled could not be held to have any force in South Africa. The missionary was therefore forbidden to baptize any more, but he was advised to continue instructing the Hottentots, in which work his great zeal was admitted. The clergymen of the Cape, Stellenbosch, and Drakenstein were requested by the council to draw up a report of the circumstance and submit it to the classis of Amsterdam for instructions.

This decision seemed to the missionary to make his position, if not quite untenable, at least very unpleasant. In his account, he says that he thought it very absurd that he should teach the Hottentots and send them for baptism to ministers who did not concern themselves about their conversion. But now he had to contend against popular prejudice, for his conduct caused many of the colonists to regard him as a heretic, and it came to be generally believed that the Moravians were fanatics who held wild views of christianity. The people whom he had collected together left him, probably out of love of change, though he believed it to be owing to representations by neighbouring farmers that the religion he was teaching was not that of the bible. He complained of this to the council, and instructions were sent to the sergeant in command of the military post close by to inquire carefully into the matter, in order that any one hindering him in his good work might be brought to account; but the people who had dispersed could not be collected together again.

Under these circumstances Schmit found himself incapable of effecting any good, and he therefore requested permission from his Society to return to Europe. He hoped that upon his representations the Moravian body would be able to obtain from the directors a reversal of the order concerning baptism, and that he might return to South Africa with assistants to carry on the work. The Society acceded to his request, and on the 28th of January 1744 he appeared before the council of policy and asked for a free passage in one of the Company's ships to Holland. This was granted, and he returned to Europe. But the directors refused to permit any other church than the Dutch Reformed to be established in the colony, and therefore the Moravians were compelled to abandon their benevolent enterprise.

Owing to the heavy losses which the Company had sustained by shipwrecks in Table Bay, in 1741 the directors resolved that their fleets should thereafter refresh at Simon's Bay from the 15th of May to the 15th of August, the season when gales from the north-west were common. The time of sailing from the Netherlands and the Indies was so arranged that under ordinary circumstances there would not be many ships in our seas during that period, but storms and unavoidable detentions had to be taken into account. Simon's Bay offered secure shelter during the winter season, but there was a drawback to its use in difficulty of access by land, which made the supplying a ship with fresh provisions very expensive. In 1742 it was first used as a port of call, when it was found that in fine weather boats could ply from the head of Kalk Bay, thus shortening the land carriage considerably.

In February 1743 a site for a station was selected by the governor-general Van Imhof on the southern shore of the bay, and in the following month a commencement was made with the erection of a building to serve as a magazine, a hospital, and quarters for the party in charge. A few soldiers were stationed there under command of Sergeant Justinus Blas, who had the title of postholder. In course of time a small village was built, which was occupied by fishermen and people who depended for a living upon the shipping. It took its name from the bay, being called Simon's Town.

The establishment was at first conducted in the least expensive manner possible, for the directors had resolved to make an experiment with the construction of a mole or breakwater in Table Bay, and should this succeed, the other port would not be needed. The mole was commenced on the 4th of February 1743. As it was considered a work of importance to the colony as well as to the Company, a special tax was levied upon all the Europeans in South Africa, Company's servants and burghers. Those in the Cape district were assessed at the labour of 153 stout slaves for two months in the year, and those in the country at 293*l.* 6*s.* 8*d.* in money or provisions. All the Company's slaves and all the waggons and cattle that could be spared from other work were employed upon the mole. A strong gang of convicts was sent from Batavia to assist in its construction.

The general direction of the undertaking was entrusted to Messrs. Johannes Carolus de Wet and Jacobus Möller, the first a retired burgher councillor and the other the head of the Company's naval establishment at the Cape. They gave the mole a base of one hundred feet in breadth, sloping upwards to twenty-four feet at the top. By the close of 1746 it was three hundred and fifty-one feet in length from the shore; but the work was then suspended, owing to the destruction of vegetation by a plague of locusts. In the mean time, the convicts sent from Java had nearly all died from change of climate and excessive fatigue, and the burghers declared that they could not pay their quota any longer. The expense was found to be beyond the means of the Company, and the completion of the mole was abandoned. As far as could be judged, it promised, if carried out to a sufficient length, to protect the bay without causing it to silt up. The water remained at its original depth on the inner side, while on the outside a bank of sand had formed, which strengthened the work.

The abandoned mole, after being beaten down by storms and waves, and serving as a quarry for buildings in its neighbourhood, is still to be seen like a reef running out from under the present lighthouse, its site having ever since been called on that account Mouille Point.

For a long time past the winefarmers had been making complaints of there being no sale for the produce of their vineyards, then from two to four thousand leggers a year; and to relieve them the directors had resolved, if no other remedy could be devised, to substitute wine for spirits to a large extent in their ships and Indian establishments, provided a moderately good article could be obtained. The burgher councillors, on behalf of the farmers, addressed the governor-general Van Imhof on this question. The governor-general offered them free trade in India, upon payment of 16*s*. 8*d*. freight and 2*l*. 10*s*. 0*d*. duty a legger. The burghers replied that such a privilege would be of no use to them. The governor-general then proposed that the tax on wine should be increased from 4*s*. 2*d*. to 12*s*. 6*d*. a legger; that upon payment of this, a fee of 4*s*. 2*d*. to the fiscal, and a fee of 1*l*. 0*s*. 10*d*. to the licensed dealer, the burghers should be at liberty to sell without let or hindrance to all visitors, Dutch or foreign, at the best price they could obtain; and that the Company should purchase at 5*l*. 5*s*. 10*d*. a legger sufficient for its own needs, which would be on an average about four leggers for each ship leaving the port, in addition to a quantity to be sent to the Netherlands and to Batavia for ships coming to the Cape and for the use of the work-people in India. With this proposal the burgher councillors on behalf of the farmers expressed themselves satisfied.

The question of a market for other produce than corn and wine then came on for discussion. The governor-general proposed to reduce the price of peas to 1*l*. and of beans to 16*s*. a muid, and offered on behalf of the Company to take as much as they chose to grow at those prices. Whatever was not needed for the use of the ships could be sent to Batavia. To this arrangement also the burgher councillors agreed.

Since 1722 the officers of government at the Cape had been permitted to have gardens for their own use, not exceeding two morgen in extent; but they were prohibited from selling anything out of them or of trafficking in any manner whatever with farm produce. Their salaries were insufficient for their decent maintenance, but they had been allowed to trade in various kinds of foreign wares on their own account. The governor-general prohibited further trading, and as compensation allowed the officials certain fixed sums on different transactions. Thus, for every legger of wine purchased by the Company from the farmers, ten rixdollars were to be divided between the governor and the secunde in the proportion of two-thirds to the former and one-third to the latter. In practice it came to this, that a farmer who delivered a legger of wine for exportation or for the use of the Company's ships signed a receipt for 8*l.*, but actually received only 5*l.* 5*s.* 10*d.*, 12*s.* 6*d.* being deducted for the Company, 1*l.* 7*s.* 9*d.* for the governor, and 13*s.* 11*d.* for the secunde. The fiscal had corresponding privileges in issuing licenses to trade, and the minor officers were provided for in a similar manner.

No official document could be drawn up for a burgher without a heavy fee being paid. This was an ever-increasing evil, for the fees were constantly being augmented. Thus, a few years later, a certificate of release from the service of the Company had to be written on a stamp of 12*s.* 6*d.*, and the secretary of the council of policy received 2*l.* 1*s.* 8*d.* for drawing it out and signing it.

The practice of using different money from that of the Netherlands opened a door to what would now be termed fraud, but what was in those days regarded as a legitimate perquisite of the officers of government. In the accounts, two and a half Dutch gulden of twenty stivers each were equal to one rixdollar. But at the Cape and throughout India a fictitious gulden, of which there was no metallic representation, was in use. In receiving money for taxes or goods, three of these were counted as one rixdollar. But in paying out money—for instance to a Cape farmer for grain—the fictitious gulden was reckoned at sixteen stivers, thus giving to the officer in charge of the granaries a perquisite of four per cent upon the value of the transaction. In converting the money of the old records into British coinage, the fictitious gulden must therefore sometimes be taken at one value, sometimes at the other. Before 1770 there was no attempt to rectify this evil. Another perquisite—considered legitimate—was receiving grain at a heavier weight the muid than it was debited to the Company. The last or load, in which the accounts were kept, at this time consisted of seventeen muids, a few years later of eighteen muids and a half. The muid, as charged to the Company, weighed 175 Amsterdam pounds, as delivered by the farmer, weighed from 180 to 190 pounds.

The colonists were constantly taking possession of new tracts of country and laying them out in cattle runs never less than five or six thousand acres in extent, for each of which they paid to the Company a yearly rental of 2*l.* 10*s.* before 1732, and 5*l.* after that date. Upon the slightest fault being discovered in a cattle run, the occupier did not hesitate to abandon it and move to another further in the interior. A vast region, almost untenanted since its desolation by small pox in 1713, lay open before the colonists.

The governor-general Van Imhof regarded this condition of things as boding no good to the future of the European race in South Africa. In his opinion it would tend to unsettle the colonists and turn them into a body of half barbarous nomads. To attempt to fix the people to the soil, he issued instructions that any one who so desired could convert sixty morgen of ground about his homestead into freehold property, upon application to the council of policy and payment of from 10*l.* 8*s.* 4*d.* to 41*l.* 13*s.* 4*d.* according to the value of the land. The remainder of the farm was to be held as before; its use, as long as it was not required by the Company, being allowed upon payment of a yearly rental of 5*l*. This measure, though well intended, had not much effect, as very few farmers availed themselves of it.

Before 1743 there was outside of Cape Town but one seat of magistracy in South Africa. Over all the wanderers who were pushing their way inland the landdrost and heemraden of Stellenbosch legally held jurisdiction, but practically many of them were soon beyond the reach of law. On the 12th of November of this year four heemraden were appointed to form a court of justice for the residents beyond the Lower Breede river. Their names were Cornelis van Rooyen, Jan Loots, Andries Holtshuizen, and Jacobus Botha. They were selected out of a double number nominated by the board of landdrost and heemraden of Stellenbosch and Drakenstein, as it was at first intended that for general purposes they should sit in that court.

In January 1744 Mr. Johannes Theophilus Rhenius, previously a bookkeeper in the Company's service, was appointed assistant landdrost and secretary in subordination to the landdrost of Stellenbosch. Almost immediately a dispute arose concerning the rank of the officials. The heemraden maintained that Mr. Rhenius, being their secretary, was beneath them in dignity, while he on his part contended that as assistant landdrost he was their superior officer.

The question was referred for settlement to Governor Swellengrebel and the council of policy. They decided that when the court sat to hear judicial cases Mr. Rhenius was to preside, but when it sat to arrange district affairs the oldest heemraad present was to occupy the chair. This arrangement did not answer at all. But on the 31st of August 1745 the dispute was ended by the separation of the country beyond the Lower Breede from the district of Stellenbosch, and the elevation of Mr. Rhenius to the full rank of landdrost. The number of heemraden was increased to six, owing to the great size of the new district, the boundaries of which were not otherwise defined than 'where the power of the Honourable Company ends.' Half of the heemraden retired every year, after sending a list of six names to the council of policy, from which list their successors were chosen by that body.

There was as yet no place selected for the seat of the new magistracy, and for a time the court met at the residence of one of the heemraden. The government wisely left this to be arranged by the court itself. Some excellent sites were already occupied as farms, but it was not deemed advisable to eject government tenants. The board of landdrost and heemraden prudently took time, and only after much inspection and discussion was a site agreed upon. Application was then made to the governor and council, by whom on the 25th of October 1746 permission was given to use the ground selected and to put up such buildings as might be needed.

Mr. Rhenius and the district councillors chose a charming locality. From the Langebergen issue at various places little streams of clear fresh water, feeders of a river which drains a valley stretching from the Warm Bokkeveld to the sea. One of these streams which, for want of a more original name, was called the Cornlands river, winds through a dell some miles in length before it unites its waters with those of the Breede. Here, with the mountains close in front and rich soil capable of being irrigated around, a drostdy and other necessary buildings speedily arose. At the present day the village, with its scattered houses and gardens on each side of a single winding street, extends quite three miles along the vale, but in the middle of last century few people could maintain themselves except by farming, and hence many years elapsed before it could fairly be called more than a hamlet. It received a name in 1747, as on the 26th of October of that year the council of policy decided that the district should be called Swellendam, and in conformity with the usage of the time the seat of magistracy took the same name. Building sites for the use of persons not in the government service were first surveyed in 1750.

In 1744 the Indian authorities reduced the price of wheat delivered at the Company's magazines at the Cape to 9*s.* 4*d.* the muid. Thereupon some of the most substantial burghers in the country assembled at Stellenbosch to confer with the landdrost and heemraden, and endeavour through their solicitation to obtain a higher price.

They represented that the ordinary work of the agriculturist was performed by his slaves, but at harvest time he required more labourers. These he obtained by hiring slaves from the townspeople at the rate of from 1*s.* 8*d.* to 2*s.* a day. If he needed the services of a European mason or carpenter, he had to pay from 2*s.* 6*d.* to 4*s.* a day, in addition to food, though occasionally an inferior workman could be hired at 2*l.* a month. After paying wages at this rate, and deducting the Company's dues, he could not sell wheat at 9*s.* 4*d.* the muid. The landdrost and heemraden were of the same opinion, and they requested the governor and council of policy to petition the Indian authorities to raise the price again to 10*s.* 8*d.* In June 1745 the governor-general and council of India agreed to what was asked of them.

The farmers were now in this position. The Company purchased from them as much ordinary wine as it needed at 5*l.* 5*s.* 10*d.* a legger clear, and as much wheat as it needed at 10*s.* 8*d.* a muid, from which was deducted the tithe, leaving 9*s.* 7⅛*d.* clear for the grower. They could sell surplus produce of any kind to any one who chose to buy, upon paying first the Company's dues of 10*s.* 8*d.* upon every ten muids of wheat and 12*s.* 6*d.* upon every legger of wine, secondly 1*l.* 0*s.* 10*d.* a legger to the licensed dealers in wine if this article were sold to the master or purser of a ship, and thirdly a fee to the fiscal when ships' people were purchasers of produce.

Complaints of the quality of the wine were frequently made by the Indian authorities. The directors sent out skilled persons from Europe to instruct the farmers in its proper manufacture, and the authorities at the Cape tested every legger that was purchased, but the complaints continued as before.

In 1744 M. La Bourdonnais, governor of the French island of Mauritius, proposed to the council of policy at the Cape a free exchange of the productions of the two countries, and stated that fifty or sixty leggers of wine would be needed yearly by the colony under his rule, exclusive of the shipping. The council replied that they could not establish a regular trade, nor receive the produce of Mauritius in barter; but that Frenchmen could purchase at the Cape as much wine as they chose, upon paying cash for it, and could then remove it at their pleasure.

The farmers were generally in such a condition that the accumulation of wealth was impossible. In 1750 the directors mooted the subject of increasing the number of colonists, and the council of policy called for reports. The reply of the board of heemraden of Stellenbosch and Drakenstein is dated 11th of January 1751. In it the heemraden express their opinion that there were too many European families then in the country to get a good living, and that people were anxious about the future for their children's sake. The burgher councillors went to the very root of the matter. In their reply they state they knew of no means by which a greater number of people could obtain a living unless free exportation of produce to all countries was permitted.

In their report the heemraden incidentally refer to the change then rapidly taking place in the old settled districts, in the disappearance of grass and the springing up of small bushy plants in its stead.

The village of Stellenbosch was by this time quite embowered among its oaks. It had been quickly rebuilt after the fire of 1710, and all travellers who now visited it described its beauty in glowing terms. The board of landdrost and heemraden acted as a court of justice, and performed also the duties which are now undertaken by municipal and divisional councils. A few of its enactments will illustrate its powers and the way in which it used them.

A contract was made with a farmer to place a pontoon upon the Berg river and to keep in repair the road over the Roodezand pass, for which he was to receive yearly from every family residing beyond the Berg river either a muid of wheat or eleven shillings in money.

In December 1742 permission was given to the burgher

Pieter Wion to open a butcher's shop in the village, on the following conditions. Every Wednesday and Saturday he was to offer for sale good wholesome fresh mutton at the rate of two pence for a single pound, or six pence for four pounds, and to refuse no one at that price. Four times a year he was to offer beef for sale at the same rates. Failing these conditions he was to pay a fine of 5*l.* to the deacons for the benefit of the poor.

Some of the burghers were in the habit of grinding their corn with hand mills or little water mills of their own construction. From this custom the board anticipated a serious decrease in the price paid for the leases of the public mills at Stellenbosch and Drakenstein, which carried with them the exclusive privilege of grinding all the corn consumed within fixed limits at certain stated charges. The district was then receiving 126*l.* 13*s.* 4*d.* a year for the lease of each of these mills. Yet the members of the board were very willing to assist their fellow burghers, if it could be done without affecting the revenue, and generally an arrangement was made that the owner of the hand mill should satisfy the lessee, and be allowed to grind his own corn. As an instance, it is recorded that the burgher Michiel Otto, of Hottentots Holland, petitioned to be allowed to grind sufficient corn for the use of his household with a small water mill which he had erected on his farm. His request was acceded to, upon condition that he should pay to the miller of Stellenbosch the same fees as if he had his corn ground at the district mill, and that this permission should not form a precedent.

The convulsions in Europe which followed the death of the emperor Charles VI (20th of October 1740), and which began by the king of Prussia invading Silesia, largely affected the Dutch East India Company. In September 1744 despatches were received here announcing that France and England were at war, and that there was a likelihood of the Netherlands being involved at no distant date. The council was informed that the Company had resolved to construct a line of fortifications along the shore of Table Bay, and to strengthen the garrison of the Cape.

The fortifications then existing consisted of the castle and a battery on the shore where the breakwater now runs into the bay. The latter was commenced in February 1715 and completed in April 1726. It was at first termed Mauritius, but afterwards came to be popularly called the Chavonnes battery, a name which was officially conferred upon it in November 1744. On the opposite side of the castle a fort was being built, the foundation stone of which was laid on the 24th of October 1743. It was completed in October 1744, and received the name Fort Knokke, which it still bears.

A line of batteries was now thrown up along the shore, only one of which—the Imhof—still remains. This was intended to cover the face of the castle, and rose from the margin of the sea, where the waves in winter storms dashed against its walls. Its foundation stone was laid on the 23rd of November 1744, and cannon were mounted on it in July of the following year. The others were less solidly built. There were four between the castle and the mouth of Salt River, named Swellengrebel, Elizabeth, Helena, and Tulbagh. Between the castle and the Chavonnes battery there was one, called Heeren Hendriks Kinderen, on which ten guns were mounted.

During the time that it was feared the colony might be attacked by an enemy, the burghers of the country districts were required to furnish a contingent of fifty mounted men to assist in keeping guard at the Cape. Every month they were relieved by fifty others, so as to make the task less heavy for individuals. It was felt as a great relief by the burghers, however, when on the 26th of September 1748 the British man-of-war *Tartar* brought intelligence that a truce had been arranged between the belligerents, and a little later the conclusion of peace at Aix-la-Chapelle permitted them to be relieved of military duty. A temporary outpost at St. Helena Bay, which had been established to give notice of any ships that might touch there, was broken up at the same time. The Waveren outpost, which had been maintained since 1700, was withdrawn in October 1743, when the building with sixty morgen of ground about it was sold by auction to Pieter de Vos for 266*l.* 13*s.* 4*d.* The other military outposts—Saldanha Bay, Klapmuts, Groen Kloof, Ziekenhuis, and Riet Vlei—remained as before.

In November 1740 a good deal of excitement was created at the Cape by a report from a man named Frans Diederik Muller, who professed to be an experienced mineralogist, that he had discovered a rich silver mine at Groot Drakenstein, close to Simonsberg. The governor immediately left to inspect the locality, and was persuaded by Muller that ore was to be had in enormous quantities, only requiring capital to extract it. As the Cape government could not incur the estimated expense without authority from the directors, an association was formed by some burghers to work the mine. This met with the approval of the Assembly of Seventeen, and early in 1743 a charter was granted to Mr. Olof de Wet, for himself and his associates, in which they were granted the exclusive right of searching for and extracting metals within the area bounded by the Paarl, French Hoek, and Hottentots Holland mountains, upon condition of paying to the Company fifteen per cent of everything valuable obtained and delivering the surplus at prices which were specified for almost all known metals.

Mr. De Wet, who was the chief director of the mining association, then engaged a large number of men to whom the government had granted passes for the purpose, and the work of prospecting in the mountains and excavating at the so-called silver mine was commenced. Muller was engaged as master miner. For more than five years the clever rogue managed to keep up the hopes of his employers without producing anything valuable. The ore which was found he first pronounced to be silver, then he termed it copper, and finally he asserted it to be gold. At this stage some of it was sent to Holland to be tested by competent persons, when it was found to contain only 'a very inexpensive metal which was mixed in small quantities with other materials in casting bells to improve their sound.' The work then ceased. Muller was brought before the council, who declared him an impostor, confiscated his property, and banished him to Batavia. The pits and underground passages, which had cost the association a great deal of money, are still objects of curiosity to strangers.

In the staff of clergymen several changes were caused by death or removal. The Rev. Mr. Le Sueur, having purchased a farm at Rondebosch on the estate of his wife's father, Johannes Swellengrebel, was obliged to resign his position in the Company's service, and in August 1746 was succeeded by the Rev. Ruwardus Cloppenburg, who was sent out by the directors. Three weeks later the Rev. Petrus van der Spuy arrived from Holland to fill the post of second clergyman at the Cape, which had long been vacant. Mr. Cloppenburg's domestic life was such that in January 1748 he was suspended by the consistory, and in March of the same year was dismissed by the council and sent back to Europe without rank or salary. Mr. Van der Spuy then remained for some time sole clergyman of the Cape congregation, but was greatly assisted by Mr. Le Sueur, who was very highly esteemed, though in accordance with the law he could not draw a salary from the Company while he was owner of more than two morgen of land.

In October 1744 the Rev. Willem van Gendt died, from which date the church at Stellenbosch was without a resident clergyman until September 1747, when the post was filled by the Rev. Edward Arendsen, who was sent out by the directors. Mr. Arendsen died in July 1749. The Rev. Mr. Van Echten, of Drakenstein, was then required to act as consulent of Stellenbosch until the directors could make another appointment.

The Rev. Mr. Meyring remained at Roodezands kerk.

In December 1748 the Rev. Mr. Weerman, of Zwartlands kerk, at his own desire was transferred to Batavia. The congregation remained without a clergyman until August 1750, when the Rev. Christiaan Benjamin Voltelen arrived from the Netherlands, and took over the duty.

In the thirteen years 1738–1750 there put into Table Bay 640 ships belonging to the Dutch East India Company, 193

English, 23 French, and 20 Danish. Simon's Bay began to be used in 1742, and before the close of 1750 seventy-seven ships, all belonging to the Company, put into that harbour. The average number touching at South African ports was thus 73 yearly.

Among the English ships that called was the *Centurion*, Commodore George Anson, bound homeward after her famous cruise in the Pacific. She was here in March and April 1744. Admiral Boscawen also, in April 1748, put into Table Bay with 26 men-of-war and transports, when on his way to India with a force intended to restore English power after the capture of Madras by the French. Great Britain and the Netherlands were then in alliance, and all possible assistance was therefore given to the English fleet. The troops were landed, and formed a camp just above the Company's garden, where they were drilled for some weeks, as many of them were recruits.

In the following year some ships of this fleet put into Table Bay when returning home. A large number of Englishmen being on shore, the commodore requested one Sunday that his chaplain might be permitted to preach in the church. Leave was granted without demur, and on the 20th of April 1749 divine service according to the rites of the church of England was held in the Dutch church in Table Valley.

On the 9th of February 1751 another English service was held in the same building. Mr. William Wake, recently governor of Bombay, died here while on his passage home, when his widow and the captain of the ship in which he was returning requested the government that his body might be buried in the church with the state due to his rank. The request was complied with. The Dutch officers took part in the funeral procession, the flag on the castle was lowered, the bell was tolled, and minute guns were fired from the batteries. The surgeon of the *Boscawen* read the English burial service, and the body was deposited in a vault below the floor of the church. There was another instance of the kind on the 5th of February 1752, when an English officer

K 2

of rank—Commander Lisle—was buried under the pavement of the church, the surgeon of the *Vigilant* reading the funeral service.

Several wrecks took place on the South African coast during this period.

In the night between the 5th and 6th of May 1740 the Company's outward bound ship *Visch*, when attempting to come to anchor in Table Bay in a stiff gale, ran ashore above the castle, and became a complete wreck. Her sick men, who were between decks, were drowned; the others, with one exception, reached the shore safely by means of a hawser.

On the 25th of October 1747 the Company's outward bound ship *Reygersdaal* ran ashore on the coast between Dassen and Robben islands, and went to pieces at once, only twenty men getting to land. She was four months and a half from Holland, and had lost one hundred and twenty-five men from scurvy. Eighty-three of the remaining crew were too ill with the same disease to keep their feet, and the few who were able to work could not manage the ship. They were trying to get into Saldanha Bay when the final disaster took place.

At dawn of the 19th of January 1750 the French ship *Centaur*, homeward bound from Mauritius, ran ashore near Cape Agulhas in perfectly fine weather. Her crew of 300 souls and about 100 passengers, including 9 ladies and several children, got safely to land; but suffered great hardships before they reached the Cape, though as soon as intelligence of the disaster was received, waggons and provisions were sent to meet them.

On the 8th of August 1750 a Danish ship named the *Elephant*, homeward bound from Tranquebar, was purposely run ashore close to the mouth of the Gauritz river, where some days later she went to pieces. She had made a long and disastrous passage, during which her provisions ran short, and when land was sighted there was not a drop of fresh water on board. The crew therefore ran her ashore as the only means of saving their lives. They, to the number of 65 men, got safely to land, and after a time reached the Cape.

During the thirteen years 1738–1750 there were several bad seasons and one exceptionally good one. The exports therefore fluctuated greatly. The year 1738 was one of drought, and consequently the harvest was so poor that in 1739 only 340 muids of wheat and 85 muids of rye could be sent abroad. The next crops were almost destroyed by rust, so that in 1740 not only could no grain be exported, but famine at home was feared. The government was obliged to regulate the issue of bread very carefully. As those who had a supply of grain in store naturally demanded a high price for it, a placaat was issued declaring such demands extortionate, and prohibiting the sale of wheat at a higher rate than 11*s.* 1*d.* a muid. Following the famine, the wheat crop of 1740 was the best ever known in the country, and after the magazines had been filled, 17,000 muids were exported, a larger quantity than in any previous year.

In 1746 abundance of rain fell, and the wheat crop harvested was an exceedingly good one, but before the beans and peas were off the ground enormous swarms of locusts made their appearance, a plague from which the colony had been free since 1695. On the 28th of December they found their way in such vast numbers into Table Valley that the air seemed filled with them, and in a few days there was nothing edible left, not even leaves on the trees. The council appointed the 22nd of February 1747 to be observed as a day of fasting and prayer that God would be pleased to remove the plague. In the country districts the gardens were completely destroyed, and as there was nothing left for the cattle to eat, so many oxen and sheep died that meat, which, owing to there having been no disease among cattle for many years, had been previously sold at less than ¾*d.* a pound, at once doubled in price. By the end of April 1747, however, the locusts had almost disappeared.

The remaining years were free from excessive drought and insect plagues. The average exports to India during the period were 7,539 muids of wheat, 115 muids of rye,

289 muids of peas, and 271 muids of beans. Of ordinary wine, every year on an average 384 leggers were sent to Batavia, exclusive of that supplied to the ships. All the Constantia wine that could be obtained was exported, and ten times the quantity would have found a ready sale. Ivory, skins of wild animals, ostrich plumes, and dried fruit were also among the exports of the colony.

The Europeans and the Hottentots were living together on friendly terms, but occasionally the peace was disturbed by Bushman marauders. In 1747, and again in 1750, rumours reached the Cape that certain farmers on the distant border of Swellendam had not scrupled to shoot down women and children as well as men, when they were endeavouring to recover cattle and punish the murderers of their servants. The government caused strict inquiry to be made, with the object of bringing the offenders to justice; but it was impossible to obtain evidence sufficient to secure conviction.

The country along the coast was now occupied by Europeans a few miles farther eastward than Mossel Bay. Some graziers had taken possession of land on the banks of the Gamtoos, but in January 1745 the landdrost of Stellenbosch, acting under orders from the governor, had required them to return to the westward of the Great Brak river. The circumstances under which the graziers lived were, however, so favourable to expansion of the colony, that they could not long be kept within the assigned limits.

That the Cape is subject to occasional shocks of earthquake was experienced in the early morning of the 5th of September 1739, and again at daybreak on the 27th of August 1749. In the first instance there was a single shock, in the second there were two in quick succession. On both occasions there was a rolling noise, as of passing thunder. Beyond causing alarm, no damage was done.

The East India Company had recently undergone a change in its constitution. During the late war the office of stadtholder had been again created in the Netherlands, after its abrogation for a number of years; and Willem Carel

Hendrik Friso, prince of Orange, had been raised to the dignity, which was declared to be hereditary, with the additional title of captain and admiral general of the republic. On the 25th of March 1749 he was created chief director and governor-general of the East India Company, and thenceforth all appointments to office were made by him upon recommendations from the Assembly of Seventeen.

At the Cape the officers of government were enthusiastic partisans of the Orange, as against the pure republican faction, and intelligence of the resumption of the stadtholderate was received with great rejoicing. The 29th of November 1747 was kept on this account as a public holiday. There were processions through the streets, ringing of bells, and firing of salutes, every person being decorated with orange cockades, while above the towers of the church and the castle orange banners were streaming. In the evening the houses were illuminated. For two nights in succession there were balls at the governor's residence; but in those days guests retired before midnight.

Governor Swellengrebel gave contentment to the colonists by his administration, though his talents were not of a brilliant order. The directors were also satisfied with him, and, as a mark of their approbation, in March 1744 he received the rank and title of councillor extraordinary of Netherlands India. After holding the office of governor ten years, and having been in continuous service since 1713, in April 1749 he wrote to the directors for permission to retire. He assigned as his reason that he wished to spend the remainder of his life in the Netherlands. This was then the prevailing custom with most of the Company's servants who attained high rank and who had accumulated wealth, and with him such a desire could only be compliance with fashion. Except two of his sons who were studying at Utrecht, all his near relatives were living at the Cape. He was a widower, his wife having died in December 1746, and as an old man he was going to a country which was not his fatherland in any other sense than that his mother was a Dutch woman. His father was by birth a Russian.

The same despatch that announced Governor Swellengrebel's wish to retire contained a request from the remaining members of the council that if the directors consented to relieve him, the secunde Ryk Tulbagh might be appointed in his stead. The directors and the stadtholder consented to what was asked, and on the 1st of April 1750 a despatch was received announcing the appointment of Mr. Tulbagh as governor and of Mr. Sergius Swellengrebel as secunde. The retiring governor was permitted to transfer the administration whenever he chose, and to proceed to Europe as admiral of a homeward bound fleet. It was nearly a year before the final arrangements were made, for it was only on the 27th of February 1751 that the administration was handed over to Mr. Tulbagh. On the following day the late governor embarked, and on the 2nd of March he sailed for Europe with a fleet of five ships. He took up his residence at Utrecht, to be near his sons, and died in that city in 1763.

CHAPTER XXII.

RYK TULBAGH, GOVERNOR, ASSUMED OFFICE 27 FEBRUARY 1751, DIED 11 AUGUST 1771.

Early life of Ryk Tulbagh—His arrival in South Africa—Various offices filled by him—His character and conduct—Corruption in the Company's service —Suppression by the governor of fraudulent practices—Tax in aid of the Netherlands—Work of the astronomer De la Caille in South Africa—Commemoration of the first century of the colony's existence—Exploration of the country beyond the eastern border of the settlement—Character of legislation in the middle of the eighteenth century—The slave code—Horrors of the slave trade—Sumptuary laws—Etiquette of salutes—Compulsory education—Proposed new taxes—Experiments in agriculture—Second outbreak of small pox in the colony—Wreck of the English ship *Doddington* — Leprosy in South Africa — The wine trade—Trade with foreigners—Establishment of a public library by bequest of Mr. Van Dessin—English astronomers at the Cape—Treatment of English visitors —Exploration of Great Namaqualand—Shock of earthquake—Third outbreak of small pox—Improvements in Cape Town, Simon's Town, Stellenbosch, and Swellendam—Dealings with the natives—Boundaries of districts and of the colony—The seasons—Exports—Succession of clergymen in the various churches—Statistics of shipping—Notable visitors—Wrecks on the coast—Death of Governor Tulbagh—Changes in the official staff—Arrangements made by the council for carrying on the government—Names of new colonists.

THE memory of Governor Ryk Tulbagh is still preserved by tradition in South Africa as that of a wise, just, and benevolent ruler. The eldest son of Dirk Tulbagh and Catharina Cattepoel, he was born in the city of Utrecht on the 21st of May 1699. He was of a plain, but honest and respectable family, many of the members of which had done good service for their country in time of war. Several of his near relatives, and among them in later years his father, laid down their lives on the battle field, fighting in the cause of the Netherlands. His parents removed from Utrecht to Bergen-op-Zoom while he was still an infant, and at this place his early life was spent. Here he remained at school until he was sixteen years of age, when his friends considered him sufficiently well educated to make his way in the world. Other capital than his own good qualities and the knowledge gained at school he had none.

In those days, although its purest period was past, the East India Company's service offered special inducements to lads like young Tulbagh. Whatever were the faults in colonising and ruling immense territories by means of such an Association, there were merits also which ordinary governments do not possess. One of these merits was that the Company regarded ability in its officers as so much capital to be turned to account. Its agents abroad were far more competent, taken man for man, than the civil servants of the mother country. Men of genius and intellect, of energy and industry, were sure of rapid promotion, while the dullard and the idler were equally certain of remaining in the lowest ranks.

Tulbagh entered the Company's service under an agreement for five years to act in whatever capacity he should be found most competent. The directors resolved to send him to South Africa, and in the year 1716 he bade his friends at Bergen-op-Zoom farewell and embarked in the ship *Terhorst*. He was not quite seventeen years of age when he landed in this country.

The lad had not been long here when he attracted the attention of his superiors by his excellent conduct. There was an earnestness in his demeanour that recommended him, and it was observed that whatever was given him to do, no matter how trivial it might be, was thoroughly well done. His obliging disposition, his utter forgetfulness of self when he could serve others, made him a general favourite.

Colonel De Chavonnes, who was then governor, observed that young Tulbagh spent his leisure hours principally in reading useful books. He found, on inquiry, that the youth was a fair accountant, and that his style of composition was much better than that of many old clerks. The neatness of his papers and the clearness of his handwriting pointed in the same direction. The governor, therefore, in 1718, placed him as an assistant clerk in the office of the secretary of the council of policy.

This appointment gave him a slight increase of pay, which he much needed, and it afforded him greater opportunities for study. His memory to the day of his death was exceedingly retentive, and it was at this period of his life that he laid by much of that great store of knowledge which those who came in contact with him half a century later considered marvellous in one whose schooldays had been so short. In his new employment his first care was to make himself master of his work, and thereafter to do it in a masterly manner.

It was a peculiarity in the religious teaching of those days, and especially in the pulpit utterances, that models for imitation were almost invariably selected from the old testament, not from the new. Of the numerous sermons and texts of sermons that have been handed down to us, nearly all are taken from that source. The power and majesty and wrath of God are continually dwelt upon, and the terrible judgments that overtake the wicked may almost be termed a favourite theme. Under this tuition men grew up to fear God, as undoubtedly they ought to do, but generosity and sympathy with distress were in most instances undeveloped.

With Ryk Tulbagh this was not the case. In all his dealings with others he did as he would have wished to be done by. His word was ever known to be strictly the truth. He often left himself without comforts, such as most men in his position would have regarded as necessaries of life, and no one would know the reason why until some poor widow or orphan or other distressed person would give the explanation. The Company's books in our archives show that a large proportion of his salary was transmitted every year to his widowed mother, Catharina Cattepoel, until her death in 1757. He disliked to have his charity spoken of, and it was remarked of him that his judgment was never at fault except in the estimation of his own good deeds. Of these he was sure to make light.

Tulbagh remained as junior until 1722, when he was

raised to the post of chief clerk to the secretary of the council of policy. In the following year, upon the promotion of Mr. Hendrik Swellengrebel to be master of the warehouses, Tulbagh was chosen to succeed him as clerk in that department. In 1725 the secretary, Adriaan van Kervel, became fiscal, when Tulbagh was appointed to the vacant office. He remained in it without a vote until the 16th of September 1728, when he became a member of the council of policy, and at the same time had a seat given to him in the high court of justice. In 1726 he had been named by the local authorities a junior merchant on approbation, and this dignity was now confirmed by the directors. In 1732 he was further elevated in rank by having the title of merchant conferred upon him.

Thus gradually he was making his way upward in society, in every post giving entire satisfaction, and always esteemed and beloved by his colleagues. He had taken to wife a young lady who was by birth a colonist. Several of her relatives were then in the service of the East India Company, and among them her brother, Mr. Hendrik Swellengrebel, who was on several occasions Tulbagh's immediate superior in office.

He remained secretary of the council of policy until the 14th of April 1739, when by order of the Assembly of Seventeen he became secunde. At the same time he was raised to the dignity of senior merchant. He had long been a member of the high court of justice, and now he became its president, an office at this period always held by the secunde.

He was not quite fifty-two years of age when, on the 27th of February 1751, he became governor of the colony. The ceremony of public presentation to the burghers and of receiving the promise of fidelity from the various official boards did not take place until the 15th of April.

As governor, the high qualities which he possessed were prominently shown. He was accessible without the least difficulty to all who wished to see him. The humblest individual could pour his grievances, if he had any, into the ears of the father of the country, and be sure of a patient hearing. If his complaints were well grounded, he obtained speedy redress, and in any case he was sure of good counsel. It was this quality that more than any other endeared him to the people. They knew that he studied their interests, that although he was their governor he was still their adviser and friend. No man, however good and wise he might be, could ever gain the affections of a people like the South African colonists if he held himself aloof from them.

His probity was beyond suspicion, and that in an age when probity was hardly looked for in men holding positions such as his. The salaries of officers in the Company's service were small, and it was taken almost as a matter of course that all who could do so would supplement their incomes in any way not punishable by law. Some of the practices resorted to were perhaps harmless, but others had a tendency to lead on to real pilfering. They had further the effect of causing men to look upon commercial immorality as after all not a very serious crime. He who became wealthy through dishonest, even fraudulent, transactions was too often admired as a sharp, clever, business man, and not regarded as a swindler should be. Governor Tulbagh set his face firmly against everything of this nature. He neither traded on his own account, nor would he allow any other officer of the government to do so. The fees which they were permitted to receive in certain transactions were fixed, and they were restricted from taking more. As for himself, he regulated his expenses so that he lived well within his income and allowances, and used what he had to spare in relieving the wants of others.

Under his administration every man was certain of getting his dues. The petty, shameless, pilfering system, often previously in vogue, under which farmers were compelled to bribe the Company's officers before they would receive produce, and then bribe them again before proper accounts could be had, was not tolerated. The governor took care that no man was put to unnecessary delay, and that no bribes were received or false accounts rendered, so that the farmers were not exposed to injustice or vexatious treatment.

During the war in Europe which was brought to a close by the treaty of Aix-la-Chapelle, the United Netherlands had been put to enormous expense. The public finances were in such a condition that it became necessary to resort to special taxation for the purpose of raising a large sum of money. On the 29th of December 1750, the States General imposed a tax called the fiftieth penny upon the inhabitants of the United Provinces, that is, every one was obliged to pay a rate nearly equal to five pence in the pound upon the value of his property. The governor-general, Jacob Mossel, and the council of India, on the 20th of December 1751, decreed that the tax should be paid by all Europeans in the Company's possessions.

The first names upon the list of those who paid in South Africa are those of Ryk Tulbagh and his wife Elizabeth Swellengrebel. Then come those of the members of the council of policy as follows: the independent fiscal Pieter van Reede van Oudtshoorn, his wife Sophia Boesses, and eight children; Lieutenant-Colonel Izaak Meinertzhagen; Captain Rudolph Sigfried Allemann, his wife Alberta Meyboom, and eight children; the issuer of stores Nicholas Heyning, his wife Gertruyd Vermey, and six children; the master of the warehouses Christoffel Brand, and his wife Sarah van Brakel, also for the children of Burgert Brand, and his wife Anna van der Byl; the chief salesman Cornelis Eelders, his wife Johanna Catharina van der Poel, and three children; the secretary Joseph de Grandpreez, and his wife Adriana Slotsboo.

On the 19th of April 1751 the Abbé Nicolas Louis de la Caille, member of the Royal Academy of Sciences at Paris, arrived in South Africa. He had already attained celebrity in France by his astronomical researches and his writings, when he resolved to visit the Cape of Good Hope with the object of making a sidereal chart of the southern skies and of measuring an arc of the meridian. He brought a letter of recommendation from the Prince of Orange to the authorities at the Cape. From Governor Tulbagh, who took a warm interest in his work, he received all the assistance that it was possible to give. He remained in the colony until the 8th of March 1753. During his stay he performed an almost incredible amount of astronomical work, and all that he did was surprisingly well done. When measuring his base line on a plain east of Saldanha Bay he had the aid of an engineer officer named Muller, belonging to the Cape garrison, but for the remainder of his work in the field his only assistants were untrained and uneducated men. The arc which he measured by triangulation extended from a point within a few yards of the corner of Strand and Adderley streets in Cape Town to Klipfontein in Piketberg, 1° 13′ 17·5″ according to his computation. He found the degree of latitude to be 364,728·4 English feet.

Sir Thomas Maclear, astronomer royal at the Cape of Good Hope, was employed from 1840 to 1848, with an able staff of assistants, in verifying and extending De la Caille's arc of the meridian. With the greatly improved instruments of his time, he ascertained that the French astronomer's latitude of his observatory was incorrect by only 2·01″, and that the true length of a degree of latitude northward from it is 364,439 English feet. The difference between the two calculations amounts to less than twenty miles for the whole circumference of the earth. The position of the stars in De la Caille's chart was found to be equally accurate.

Saturday, the 8th of April 1752, was observed by the Europeans in South Africa as a day of thanksgiving to Almighty God for the undisturbed possession of the colony by the Company for a hundred years. Special services were held in the churches at Cape Town, Stellenbosch, Drakenstein, Roodezand, and Zwartland.

On the 29th of February 1752 an expedition left the Cape to explore the country to the eastward of the settlement and report upon any changes that had taken place since 1688. It was under command of Ensign August Frederik Beutler, and was of sufficient strength to defend itself in case of sudden attack by Kaffirs. There were thirty-seven petty officers and soldiers, twenty-five waggon drivers and leaders, a superintendent of the train, a botanist, a blacksmith, and a waggonmaker. The clerk Carel Albrecht Haupt went as journalist, the marine officer Pieter Clement to determine latitudes and distances, the surveyor Carel David Wentzel to make a map, and the surgeon Jan van Elleve to attend to the sick. They had eleven waggons to transport baggage, stores, presents for native chiefs, and a boat to convey them across flooded rivers. No expedition fitted out on such a scale had ever left the Cape before, except when Commander Simon van der Stel visited the copper mountain in Namaqualand.

By the 31st of March the Gaurits river was reached, and while resting there the party was joined by a French sailor in a half-famished condition. He had come from Mauritius in a brig named the *Nécessaire*, which was one of three vessels sent to explore the south-eastern coast of Africa and look for a suitable place for a French settlement. At Algoa Bay a boat with an officer and eight men had been sent ashore, when the boat was swamped, and the *Nécessaire* sailed away without an attempt to rescue the crew.

For thirty-four days the man who gave this account of himself had been travelling westward, and he did not know what had become of his companions. Ensign Beutler sent him to Swellendam, with a letter to Mr. Jan Andries Horak, who in April 1749 had succeeded Mr. Rhenius as landdrost, requesting that he should be forwarded to the Cape.

On the 2nd of April the farm of Esaias Meyer at Mossel Bay was reached. Here the officer of the French boat met them, and corroborated the account of the sailor in every particular. He could give no information as to the fate of the remainder of the crew, except that he knew one man had died from eating part of a poisonous fish. The ensign directed him to the farm of Ignatius Ferreira, who sent him on to the Cape.

On the 4th of April the Little Brak river was passed, and on the following day the farm of the widow Hasewinkel, the last occupied by Europeans, was reached. On the 7th the expedition came to the foot of a formidable mountain, at the place now called Montagu Pass. It took three days of excessive toil to get the waggons across the mountain, in some places a tackle being used to assist the oxen, in other places the waggons needing to be steadied by ropes held by the soldiers.

Having got safely over this barrier, the expedition found itself in the long kloof, a narrow valley of great length between two ranges of mountains running nearly parallel to the coast. That section of it had already been named Cannaland by the elephant hunters, on account of the canna plant, which was used by the Hottentots as a purgative, being found there in great abundance. Very little grass was to be seen, but rhenoster bush was plentiful.

On the 17th of April they passed the head waters of the Keurbooms river, their chief trouble now being the numerous lions that infested the valley. On the 20th they encamped at the Moordenaar's river, which had received its name from a deserter who had been living with a Hottentot clan being murdered on its bank some years before.

On the 4th of May they came to the end of the long kloof, and found that the mountain range on their right terminated on the shore of the sea. For some days they had been travelling along a stream which was a branch of the Gamtoos, but they left it before reaching the junction, and proceeded to the beach to examine the curve that now bears the name of St. Francis Bay. They found it an open roadstead, protected only on the north and west. At the mouth of the Kabeljaauw river they set up a beacon with the Company's mark upon it, as a token of possession, and then proceeded onward.

The Gamtoos river was crossed on the 6th of May, and three days later the expedition reached the Galgenbosch. The manner in which names were given to places from the most trivial events was here exemplified. Some elephant hunters had carved their names in the bark of a tree, and a later traveller had cut the figure of a gallows above the signatures, from which circumstance the forest was called the Galgenbosch.

On the 13th of May the expedition encamped at the

mouth of the Zwartkops river. The broken boat of the *Nécessaire* was lying on the beach, but there was no other trace of European handiwork. The salt pans in the neighbourhood were visited, and the bearings of the shore around Algoa Bay were taken. The ensign regarded the roadstead as too exposed to be of any use for shipping. A beacon, however, was set up at the mouth of the Zwartkops, with the letters V O C (Vereenigde Oost-Indische Compagnie) upon it, to denote that possession had been taken on behalf of the Company.

On the 16th of May they passed the Sunday river, on the 17th a place called by the Hottentots Koernoe—meaning small forest—but which they named Hoender Kraal on account of the great number of Guinea fowls seen there, and on the 20th they crossed the Bushman's river. Keeping near the sea, on the 2nd of June they passed the Fish river, and on the 5th reached the Keiskama.

So far they had met only Hottentots. The names of the tribes are given in the report of the expedition, but they need not be repeated, as they have long since passed into oblivion. From Cannaland to the Keiskama the Hottentots were found in a condition of great poverty, arising partly from depredations by Bushmen, partly from wars with the Kaffirs, and partly from feuds among themselves. They were very thinly scattered over the country. The Europeans noticed some of the heaps of stones which are still to be seen near the Fish river, and observed that the Hottentots who had joined their train threw green branches of trees upon the cairns as they passed, at the same time muttering some words or phrases. When questioned why they did so, the most intelligent among them replied that the devil had made the cairns, and that in this way they prayed for good luck and a long life. The Gonaquas, living between the Fish river and the Keiskama, were on good terms with the Kaffirs.

As the Keiskama was considered the boundary between the Bantu and Hottentot tribes, the party was now divided into three watches, one of which was constantly armed and on guard. Two burghers—Andries Arendsdorp and Gerrit van Nimwegen—had joined them, and there was a large number of Hottentots in the train. After crossing the river, several Kaffirs came to meet them, and with these and some Gonaquas presents were sent on in advance to the great chief Palo and to another of lower rank whom they called Banke.

As the expedition advanced, the country was found to be more thickly peopled. It was the winter season, and the district had been subject to a long and severe drought, still there was ample proof that the inhabitants were agriculturists. Gardens were seen, in which millet stalks were still standing, and leaf tobacco was also noticed. Before they reached the Buffalo river, which they crossed on the 17th of June, all the Hottentots with the train, except a few Gonaquas, deserted through fear of the Kaffirs.

On the 24th of June the Gonubie river was reached. On the 28th the expedition halted at the kraal of Galeka (correct Kaffir spelling Gcaleka), great son of Palo, somewhere near the present village of Komgha. The place where Hubner's party had been massacred was not far off. Upon being questioned as to the massacre, the Kaffirs tried to throw the blame upon Hubner's interpreters, who, they said, had caused a misunderstanding. It may have been so; but the declarations of the survivors record an event similar to some of our own day, in which misunderstanding certainly had no part.

After resting a little, the party crossed the Kei on the 3rd of July, and on the following day encamped at the Toleni river. Here messengers whom they had sent in advance to the Tembu chief Tzeba met them and delivered a friendly greeting. To the east of the Kei only Tembus were found, and in Ensign Beutler's report that river is stated to be the boundary between them and the Kosas. As these tribes were frequently at war, it is evident that the Kosas had been defeated and driven for a time from the district between the Kei and the Bashee. Five days longer the party marched north-eastward, without making any discovery of note. The oxen were now beginning to die from fatigue and scarcity of food, and the members of the expedition were almost wearied out. Travelling over a broken country, where at every brook a road had to be made, was no easy task. The ensign took counsel with the leading men of the party, and all decided that it was advisable to go no further. On the 10th of July therefore they turned towards home.

Palo, the head of the Kosa tribe, was then living at the foot of the Amatola mountains. They were desirous of seeing him, but he probably feared meeting a strong party of Europeans, for no one would guide them to him. They noticed that from the eastern side the peak which the elephant hunters called Kaffirland's Berg, because they considered the Kaffir country commenced there, could be seen at as great a distance as when approaching in the opposite direction. This is the Intaba-ka-Ndoda—the Mountain of the Man—of the present day.

Keeping close to the foot of the mountain chain, the expedition, after leaving the Kaffir country, passed the Tyumie, Kat, Koonap, Baviaan's, Tarka, and Fish rivers. The only inhabitants of this tract of country were Bushmen, with whom it was impossible to have much intercourse. In the report it is stated that one division of these savages practised polyandry as well as polygamy, but this may be doubted, as there is not sufficient evidence in support of the assertion. The Bushmen along the Fish river—called Little Chinese by the Europeans—were reported to be monogamists. Many rock paintings made by these people were noticed. The country was so parched by a long drought that the cattle were half famished, and large thorn trees were perishing through want of moisture. The ensign had not been able to purchase from the Kaffirs as many oxen as he needed, so after keeping upward along the bank of the Fish river until the 18th of August without discovering anything of importance, he turned again towards the sea. For many days nothing more noteworthy occurred than the recovery of a runaway slave of the burgher Willem Landman.

When resting at the farm of Hendrik Blankenberg at

Zoetmelks river, the ensign received a letter from the landdrost of Swellendam, written under instructions from the governor, directing him to search for a bay that was reported to have been found by some hunters on the coast of Outeniqualand. He accordingly sent part of the train on to the Cape, and with a few men on horseback he endeavoured to find a way to the shore. He reached the two lakelets nearest the present village of George, and supposing them to have been mistaken for a bay, he turned back without seeing the Knysna lagoon. On the 6th of November he reached the Cape, after an absence of a little over eight months.

The laws of the colony at this time were much harsher than they are in our days. They were, however, seldom enforced in all their severity, the object of legislation being to lay down the heaviest punishment which could be inflicted for offences, rather than the ordinary penalties. Far greater power was thus placed in the hands of administrators and judges than is now the case.

It was held to be one of the duties of government to regulate many matters which are now left to settle themselves under the action of demand upon supply. Thus in 1744 a proclamation of Governor Swellengrebel and the council was issued, in which the price to be charged by waggonmakers and blacksmiths for every part of their work was minutely fixed.

In 1753 a regulation was made concerning the sale of ivory. It fixed the price of prime tusks at one shilling and four pence per pound, and of inferior tusks in proportion. Any one detected disposing of ivory, except to the Company, was made liable to a heavy fine and to be banished from South Africa. The purchaser was to be punished in the same manner. Any petty officer or soldier of the patrol who should through want of proper diligence allow a tusk to pass the barrier by day or by night, except to the Company's stores, was made liable to be severely flogged, to be branded, and to serve ten years in chains.

In the slave code the wide difference between the spirit of those times and these in which we live is very observable.

There were then more slaves than Europeans in South Africa, notwithstanding the manumission of such as were considered deserving of freedom and of those who could lay claim to it under the law. Some were sent here from Batavia, sentenced to periods of servitude varying in length. Officers of ships and private individuals regarded them as the most profitable article in which they could carry on a small trade, and brought so many from India that the government became apprehensive that this class of the population might too greatly preponderate, for when excited they were prone to commit appalling crimes. The council of India was therefore earnestly requested to prohibit the exportation of Asiatic slaves to this colony, but they continued to arrive in considerable numbers until 1767, when the request of the Cape government was complied with, and further importations ceased. A few were brought from the east coast of Africa. With Madagascar there was a regular trade in slaves, small vessels being sent frequently from the Cape to procure them. They cost there less than three pounds sterling each, though the rivalry of the English, French, and Portuguese was complained of as increasing the price and making it difficult to obtain cargoes.

It was nothing unusual when one fourth to one third of the number taken on board died during the passage. And frequently from one third to half of those landed died within three months, from despondency and change of climate and food. After the arrival of a slave-ship, it is not uncommon to find in the journal whole pages of names of those who died during the preceding month, with an occasional comment as to the loss to the Company, but never a word of compassion for the wretched negroes. And this during the government of such a thoroughly good man, according to the views of his time, as Ryk Tulbagh. More pity would be expressed to-day for a shipment of horses.

Occasionally captives on board ship made attempts to regain their liberty, but in general such precautions were taken that they were utterly helpless.

There is in the Cape archives of the early years of the

eighteenth century a statement that exhibits in a very clear light the views of those times regarding negro slaves. It was made by the master of an English slave-ship bound to the West Indies, who put into Table Bay for provisions, and who asked to be treated with exceptional favour, on the ground of his voyage having been disastrous. On the passage from Madagascar he had observed symptoms of discontent among the negroes, he said, and to prevent them from rising and murdering his crew, he had considered it necessary to throw the sturdiest of them overboard. The event is recorded with no more feeling for the blacks than if they had been bales of calico.

In 1765 the Cape packet *Meermin* was sent to Madagascar to procure slaves for the Company. Her supercargo called at several ports in the island, and succeeded in purchasing one hundred and forty of both sexes. On the passage back, the skipper—Gerrit Mulder—caused the irons to be taken off the slaves, and a few days afterwards—18th of February 1766—the supercargo very imprudently gave some of them a number of assagais to polish. They seized the opportunity, rose suddenly, and killed the supercargo and the whole of the watch on deck, twenty-four men all told. There were twenty-nine men below. None of these were allowed to come on deck for the next forty-eight hours, but at the end of that time, through the medium of a woman, an agreement was made that no harm should be done to the white men, they on their part promising to convey the negroes back to Madagascar.

The way the crew of the *Meermin* kept their promise was by steering for Cape Agulhas. After four days sail, land was seen, and the negroes were assured that it was their own country. At a distance of some miles from the coast they required the sailors to drop the anchor and get out the long-boat and pinnace, in which over fifty of them, male and female, went ashore, after promising to make signal fires if all was right, and send the boats back for their companions as soon as they could. Near the place where they landed was a farm belonging to Matthys Rostock. Upon seeing the house, the negroes first became aware that they had been deceived. Intelligence of their landing soon spread, and the neighbouring farmers assembled. As the blacks would not surrender they were attacked, when fourteen were shot and the others were taken prisoners.

The negroes on board the *Meermin* became very impatient when the boats did not return for them. There was a current setting towards the land, so the crew wrote an account of their condition, and put the papers in bottles which they dropped overboard. They begged that three fires might be kindled on the shore. Two of the bottles were picked up on the beach, and the fires were kindled, as requested. The negroes then cut the cable, and when the *Meermin* drifted close to the shore, a canoe was got out in which six of them landed. They had hardly touched the beach when they were surrounded. One was shot, the other five were made prisoners. Those still on board, on seeing this, attacked the crew; but the sailors were able to defend themselves until the vessel ran ashore, when the blacks surrendered. One hundred and twelve of the slaves finally reached the Cape. The *Meermin* could not be got off again, and went to pieces where she struck.

The nature of the industries carried on in the colony prevented slávery from becoming here what it was on an American cotton or sugar plantation, and few instances of extreme cruelty are on record; but under the law bondsmen were in a very abject position.

In the preamble of a slave code drawn up by Governor Tulbagh and the council it is stated that notwithstanding the stringent proclamations that had from time to time been issued, the misconduct of the slaves was such that for the preservation of peace and good order it was necessary to collect all the laws into one ordinance, and to amplify them to meet existing circumstances. After mature deliberation, the code was drawn up in the castle of Good Hope on the 3rd of September 1754, and two days later was published by being affixed to the notice board, with the great seal of the Company attached to it.

The second paragraph condemns to death without mercy any male or female slave who shall raise his or her hand, though without weapons, against master or mistress. The twenty-third condemns every slave found loitering about the entrance of a church, when the congregation was leaving, to be severely flogged by the ministers of justice. The twenty-fourth subjects to the same punishment any slave, adult or child, found within a churchyard at the time of a funeral. The twenty-eighth prohibits more than twenty slaves from following the corpse of a companion to its burial. The number was to be regulated according to the rank of the owner of the deceased, by whom a fine of *5l.* was to be paid if the rule was transgressed.

For many offences slaves could be flogged at once by the officers of justice, without any trial. When convicted of ordinary crimes, they were punished much more severely than freemen. Some of the death sentences recorded against them horrify the reader by their barbarity. It is sufficient to say that impalement, breaking the limbs on a wheel, and slow strangulation were among the methods of execution.

In the Indies there had been of late years a growing tendency with Europeans towards luxurious habits, and the authorities feared that the descendants of the sturdy pioneers would sink into effeminacy. It was observed that the children or grandchildren of men who had toiled with their hands to earn their food were not content unless they could ride in carriages and be waited upon by menials. The directors did not reflect that this was inevitable in countries where there were inferior races and where the road to wealth was open to colonists; they regarded it simply as an evil that would lead to ruin, unless checked in time. They attempted, therefore, to prevent it by issuing stringent sumptuary laws, by which all undue display was prohibited. These laws failed in their object, but while they were still on trial the council of India sent a copy of them to the Cape with orders to enforce them here also.

There was no dependency of the Company in which such regulations could have less effect than in this colony, because there was very little accumulated wealth here except in the form of farming stock. The people generally were above fear of want, but there were few who could pretend to live in luxury. Yet Governor Tulbagh favoured the sumptuary laws, not only because he was instructed to put them in force, but because he believed them to be well adapted to form a simple, honest, manly race of colonists, to preserve the hardy virtues which had made the people of the Netherlands a powerful nation.

On the 25th of March 1755 the sumptuary laws of India were referred to a committee to make such alterations as were necessary to adapt them to the condition of this country, and they were thereafter promulgated. They comprised such regulations as the following: no one except the governor may use a gilded coach or one with a coat of arms emblazoned on it; no one except a member of the council of policy may dress his coachman in livery; no one may use large umbrellas except senior merchants and ladies whose husbands or fathers have seats at any of the public boards.

There were other regulations hardly less than the foregoing in accordance with modern ideas.

Every foreign vessel that put into Table Bay was required to fire a salute of nine guns, upon which the castle replied with seven. A French ship came to anchor in March 1754, and her captain declined to salute unless the fortress would return an equal number of shots. The governor was at his country seat at Newlands, but the secunde Swellengrebel informed the French captain, who had come on shore, that no provisions would be supplied until he conformed to the usual custom. He could get water and firewood, but nothing more. The Frenchman returned to his vessel, but disdained to fire a shot. Early in April another French ship came in, and met with the same reception. Governor Tulbagh would not allow even a boat to go off to either of them. At length one of the French captains offered to fire the required number of guns for both vessels. The governor replied that each must fire. They held out a little longer, but at length submitted, fired their guns, and were afterwards treated in the most friendly manner and supplied with whatever provisions they needed.

In the same year there was a widow living in the town who refused to allow her two children to attend school. The elders of the church reminded her of her duty, and the clergyman reprimanded her, but to no purpose. The consistory next reported the circumstance to the council of policy, and by that body she was admonished not to bring up her children as heathens. Still she remained obdurate, maintaining her right to have the children educated or not, as she pleased. The matter came again before the council, but now the governor settled it. The widow was ordered at once to consign her children to the church authorities that they might be instructed in the duties of Christians. If she did not comply, it was added, she should be flogged. Upon this she wisely submitted.

In 1754 the council of India, in order to derive greater benefit than previously from this colony, proposed to reduce by one-third the prices paid by the Company for produce, to charge a duty of a penny a pound upon meat, two shillings and eight pence a muid upon meal, and thirty-two shillings a legger upon wine supplied to foreign ships, also to permit the importation of clothing materials in foreign ships upon payment of a duty of twenty per cent upon the value. The council of policy, guided by Governor Tulbagh, objected to these proposals, for the following reasons. The prices of colonial produce were already so low that a reduction of one-third would ruin the farmers. A duty of a penny a pound upon meat supplied to foreign ships would not benefit the Company in the least. Already foreigners were complaining because they had to pay twice as much as the inhabitants for meat, and it was this privilege of charging double prices to them which enabled the contractors to supply the Company at very cheap rates. The proposed duties on meat, meal, and wine would drive foreigners from the port, and from them the burghers made their largest profits. As for the importation of clothing materials in foreign bottoms, it would hardly be worth while to make one class of merchandise an exception to the general rules. The question was submitted to the directors, by whom these views were endorsed, and matters were left as they always had been.

Instructions were at this time given by the directors to renew experiments in the cultivation of indigo, and also to try if cotton could not be successfully grown in South Africa. These orders were carried out in the Company's gardens at the Cape, Rondebosch, and Newlands, with the result of showing that neither indigo nor cotton could be produced with profit.

For forty-two years the colony had been free of small pox when in 1755 that scourge made its appearance again. It was introduced at the beginning of winter by a homeward-bound fleet from Ceylon. At first the disease was supposed to be a kind of fever, but after a few days there were cases that admitted of no doubt. It assumed, however, various forms, and among some of the distant Hottentot tribes differed in appearance so much from what was held to be true small pox that the Europeans termed it gall sickness.

In Table Valley it was of such a malignant type that hardly a single adult who was attacked recovered. In July the weather was colder than usual, and during that month four hundred and eighty-nine Europeans, thirty-three free blacks, and five hundred and eighty slaves perished. If that death rate had continued, before the close of the year there would have been no one remaining, but as soon as the warm weather set in the virulence of the disease abated. Two great hospitals were established: one for poor Europeans, supported by the board of deacons, the other for blacks. To the latter all slaves who were attacked were sent, the expense being borne by their owners, who were required to pay one shilling and four pence a day for each. Those who recovered were employed as nurses. In Table Valley from the 1st of May to the 31st of October nine hundred and sixty-three Europeans and eleven hundred and nine blacks died.

In the country the European inhabitants did not suffer very severely, as they remained so secluded on their farms that for several months hardly a waggon load of produce was taken to the Cape for sale. The dead were not removed from the farms for burial. The government excused the muster of the militia for drill, and even the services in the churches were not attended by people from a distance.

In the census returns of 1754 the number of colonists of both sexes and all ages is given as 5,510, and the number of slaves owned by them as 6,279; in those of 1756 the number of colonists is given as 5,123, and of their slaves as 5,787. In ordinary years the number of deaths was in proportion to the number of baptisms as 100 to 261,[1] and there was a constant accession to the colonial population by servants of the Company taking their discharge, so that these figures, though they cannot be depended upon as absolutely accurate, give an idea of the heavy loss of life by the small pox.

With the Hottentots also it created great havoc, for it spread further inland than in 1713. It is not possible to say exactly how far it extended, but its ravages were felt in Great Namaqualand at least to the twenty-sixth parallel of latitude, and in the east to the Great Fish river.

Before midsummer it entirely died out.

A shipwreck which took place at this time was made famous by the display on the part of a few survivors of such industry and ability to overcome difficulties as have seldom or never been surpassed.

The English East India Company's ship *Doddington* sailed from the Downs on the 23rd of April 1755. At a quarter to one in the morning of Thursday the 17th of July, while no one on board suspected danger, she struck a rock on the eastern side of Algoa Bay, and at once went to pieces. Of two hundred and seventy persons on board, all perished but twenty-three. Those saved found themselves upon a barren islet frequented only by sea-birds. Fortunately for them, a quantity of provisions, a small boat, a

[1] A mean of the entries for eight years of deaths and baptisms, excluding deaths of seamen in the hospital and of the troops. The returns of deaths in the country districts are, however, not to be too firmly relied on, and these figures can therefore only be regarded as approximately correct.

smith's bellows, much timber, and numerous other useful articles washed up from the wreck. They at once set to work to build a sloop of twelve feet beam and thirty feet keel, with which to make their escape. They had no nails; but a Swedish sailor, who had once been a blacksmith, put up a forge, and with iron obtained from pieces of the wreck managed to make as many as were needed.

As smoke was often seen on the mainland, on the 3rd of September three men left in the little boat to find out something of the country and its people. They steered for a point about nine or ten miles east of the islet, but when attempting to land the boat was overturned in the surf, and one man was drowned. The other two passed the night on the shore. Next day they found the boat, and managed to pull it up on the beach. That night, weary and almost exhausted from want of food, they turned the boat over and lay down under it to sleep, but were disturbed by wild animals prowling about. Next morning a party of Hottentots appeared, who took from them a pistol and the greater part of their clothing, though otherwise the wild people were friendly and, seeing their distress from hunger, gave them some roots to eat. The wind was adverse that day, and they were obliged to pass another night under the boat, but on the following morning they returned to the islet.

During the last months of the year the wrecked people had as many sea-birds' eggs as they chose to gather, and at all times fish could be obtained, so that they did not suffer from hunger. On the 16th of February 1756 they launched their sloop and named her the *Happy Deliverance*. Two days later they sailed from the rock, to which they gave the name Bird Island, which it still bears. They reached Delagoa Bay safely, and there found a ship in which some of them obtained a passage home. The others proceeded to Bombay in their sloop.

Two burghers—Andries du Pré and Pieter Ferreira—who were hunting elephants along the Bushman's and Sunday rivers, heard from some Hottentots rumours of the landing of the boat, and sent a report to the landdrost of Swellendam. Mr. Horak thereupon directed the farmers Nicholas Haarhof and Pieter van Vuuren to make inquiries among the natives, and they obtained the pistol which had been taken from the English sailors, but could learn nothing of a wreck. For anything they could gather, the boat might have belonged to a passing ship. In December 1755, by order of the government, the landdrost sent Dirk Marx, a hunter who was well acquainted with the country, to look for any white people who might be in distress; but he could hear of none, nor could he find any trace of a wreck. He reported having met Kaffirs as far west as the Great Fish river.

The coloured races of South Africa, though singularly free of disease, were subject to one of the most dreadful maladies with which mankind is afflicted. There are no means of ascertaining the ravages made by leprosy among the Hottentots, but it is tolerably certain that though they were acquainted with the disease, the number of individuals affected was very small. It is not once named in the early records, and it is only from tradition that it is known to have existed among these people before their intercourse with strangers. Whether the Bushmen were liable to be attacked by it is uncertain. Among the Bantu tribes it was by no means rare, and the slaves of all nationalities who were brought into the colony were subject to it. It was now proved that Europeans also were liable to its attacks. Some cases having been suspected, in May 1756 a commission of medical men was appointed, who examined the sufferers, and reported that one man, who had been eighteen years ill, was afflicted with leprosy, that his eldest daughter was showing symptoms, and that another man, who had been nine years ill, was suffering from the same disease. The government recommended isolation of the sufferers, but did nothing more.

The quality of the wine sent to India was frequently complained of, but no improvement was made in it. The master of the Company's wine stores at the Cape professed that the greatest care was taken to reject the worst that was brought for sale, and that he could not obtain a better article than was forwarded. The result was that the council of India declined to take as large a quantity as previously, and the exportation to Batavia, which for the five years 1751–5 had averaged 558 leggers, fell off to 262 leggers on an average during the next ten years. There was some correspondence with the directors concerning the conversion of the wine into brandy, and it was ascertained that if more stills were introduced there would be no difficulty in procuring annually 400 leggers at a price not exceeding 14*l*. 11*s*. 8*d*. a legger. But the quality of the brandy sent as samples was so objectionable that the project fell through.

The directors just at this time also saw fit to make wine a special object of taxation. The colonial revenue and the profit on goods sold here now amounted to between 11,000*l*. and 12,000*l*. a year, but the sum paid out of the Company's treasury at the Cape was in round numbers 20,000*l*. more, taking one year with another. To increase the revenue, in 1756 an export duty of 1*l*. per legger was laid by the directors upon all wine and brandy sold to strangers in bulk. This was in addition to the dues previously levied. The duty was farmed out by auction, and in the first year was sold for no more than 33*l*. 6*s*. 8*d*. Four years later it rose to 400*l*.

In 1756 and 1757 only twelve foreign ships called, and though three of these were sent from Mauritius to procure provisions for the French troops there, the supply of wine far exceeded the demand. Insolvencies of wine-farmers became alarmingly frequent. The governor-general Van Imhof in 1743 had allowed the fiscal a fee of four shillings and twopence upon every legger of wine sold to a foreigner. Governor Tulbagh, as the only measure of relief which he could think of, arranged with the independent fiscal Van Oudtshoorn that he should abandon his claim to this fee, and in its stead receive one shilling and fourpence on every hundred pounds of grain or meal sold to a foreigner.

Matters were at their worst when in December 1758 and January 1759 a fleet of seventeen French men-of-war and transports with troops arrived from Mauritius. They were sent here purposely to refresh and lay in a supply of provisions. At once the price of farm produce doubled or trebled, all the surplus stock was disposed of, and everything was paid for in money.

From this date until the termination of the war in India between the English and the French, the farmers were in a prosperous condition. French men-of-war until 1761, and after that date ships of both nations, came here to refresh and take in supplies. The officers of French packets from Mauritius and of English packets from St. Helena bid against each other for cattle and meal and wine. On more than one occasion the government was unable to procure as much provision as was needed for the Company's ships, as the burghers were desirous of selling at high prices to strangers. There was a remedy for this, however. In August 1762 a placaat was issued prohibiting the sale of wine to foreigners under penalty of confiscation of all that was offered and a fine of 66*l.* 13*s.* 4*d.* This had the desired effect, the Company obtained as much as was needed, and four weeks from the date of its issue the placaat was withdrawn. In January 1763 it was necessary to resort to the same means to procure a supply of butter.

The government, as well as individuals, profited by the strangers. The revenue was increased, a quantity of surplus wheat in the magazines was disposed of, and some shipments of Bourbon coffee were purchased at the low price of twenty-five shillings per hundred pounds for transmission to Europe. This season of prosperity lasted until March 1763, when intelligence was received of the conclusion of peace between France and England.

On the 8th of December 1760 the secunde Sergius Swellengrebel died. On the 12th the council of policy decided that the independent fiscal Pieter van Reede van Oudtshoorn should fill the vacant office until the pleasure of the supreme authorities could be known. Mr. Van Oudtshoorn was confirmed in the appointment by the directors, and Mr. Jan Willem Cloppenburg was sent out as fiscal. The latter officer arrived in September 1762.

In 1761 Mr. Joachim Nicholas van Dessin, who had been for nearly a quarter of a century secretary of the orphan chamber, bequeathed to the colony his library consisting of three thousand eight hundred printed books, many manuscripts, some mathematical and astronomical instruments, several oil paintings, &c. He appointed the consistory of the Cape guardians of this bequest. He also left the sum of one thousand rixdollars—then equal to 208*l.* 6*s.* 8*d.*—to form a capital fund, the interest of which was to be applied to the preservation and enlargement of the library. The books were placed in a building near the church, and the sexton was required to perform the duty of librarian. The institution, however, was not much used, and in course of time several of the most interesting volumes disappeared, without any record being left of the manner in which they were lost. Those which remain are known as the Dessinian collection, now kept in the gallery of the South African Public Library. Among them are still many works of permanent value.

On the 27th of April 1761 Messrs. Charles Mason and Jeremiah Dixon, two astronomers who had left England with the intention of observing at Bencoolen the transit of Venus on the 6th of June following, arrived at the Cape. They had been delayed on the passage, and therefore resolved to observe the transit here. From Governor Tulbagh they received all the assistance that he could possibly give. The 6th of June was showery, but at the time of the transit there were no clouds over the sun's disc, so that they were able to observe it. Their instruments were two reflecting telescopes of two feet focal length and magnifying one hundred and twenty times, a quadrant of a foot radius, and an astronomical clock. They remained at the Cape until the 3rd of October.

In 1759 an armament was sent by the government at Batavia to reinforce the garrison of the Dutch factory of Chinsurah on the Ganges. Colonel Clive was then the representative of the English East India Company at Fort William. He apprehended that if the Dutch forces were increased, the nabob Meer Jaffier, who had been raised to power by his assistance, would form an alliance with them to the detriment of English interests in Bengal. England and the Netherlands were at peace, but Clive resisted the passage of the Dutch fleet up the Hoogly, captured the ships, and destroyed the army. Conditions were imposed upon the authorities at the Dutch factory, under which they were prohibited from building fortifications or raising troops.

When intelligence of this event reached Europe, the friendly feeling that had existed between Great Britain and the United Provinces was disturbed, and for a time it was doubtful whether peace would be maintained. Orders were issued by the directors that nothing which could be refused under existing treaties should be supplied to English ships touching at the Cape. The matter, however, was adjusted without a rupture, and in 1761 instructions were received that English visitors were to be treated in a liberal manner.

In January 1762 his Britannic Majesty's ships of war *Chatham* and *York* put into Table Bay, where they were supplied with whatever they needed. The commodore, Thomas Lynn, taking Governor Tulbagh to be an obliging, good-natured individual, who would do almost anything he was requested to, asked that all the English seamen in Dutch ships in the bay should be sent on board his vessel. But he met with a decided refusal, for in this the governor and council held that the honour of their flag was at stake.

In 1760 a burgher named Jacobus Coetsee with twelve Hottentots proceeded northward from his farm at Piketberg, and hunted elephants beyond the river known to us as the Orange, which it was believed had never been crossed by a white man before. Some time after his return he informed Hendrik Hop, one of the captains of the burgher militia, who occupied the farm Slot van de Paarl, that he had heard of a tribe of black people called Damrocquas living ten days journey beyond the farthest point which he had reached, and that they had long hair and wore clothes made of linen cloth. In June 1761 Captain Hop reported this to the government, and offered to lead an exploring party in that direction. The offer was accepted, and the captain then called for burghers to volunteer for the expedition. Such an undertaking was no longer so formidable as in the days of Simon van der Stel, for white men were now in permanent occupation of cattle runs as far north as the mouth of the Elephant river. Since 1685 the base of supplies had been moved inland nearly two hundred miles. The services were secured of the botanist Jan Andries Auge, who was to collect information on plants, the surgeon Carel Christoffel Rykvoet, who went in the capacity of mineralogist, and the surveyor Carel Frederik Brink, whose duty it was to determine positions, to make a map, and to keep a journal.

It was arranged that the members of the expedition should assemble at a place called the Bakoven, near the mouth of the Elephant river, and from that point commence the journey. On the 16th of August 1761 all was ready, and the caravan left the Bakoven for the north. Beside the four Europeans named, there were thirteen colonists: Jacobus and Joris Coetsee, Abraham Russouw, Hendrik Kruger, Andries Greef, Jan van Niekerk, Tieleman Roos, Pieter Marais, Casper and Jan Badenhorst, Josua Joubert, Coenraad Scheepers, and Ocker Heyns. They had fifteen waggons and sixty-eight half-breed Hottentot servants.

They passed by the copper mountains of Little Namaqualand that had been first visited by Europeans in 1685, and keeping in a direction almost due north, crossed the great river on the 29th of September, at a ford where the stream was nearly eleven hundred feet in width. The Little Namaquas were found in an impoverished condition. They had been robbed by Bushmen of the greater part of their cattle, and it seemed as if they must eventually be utterly destroyed. The Great Namaquas had migrated to the north about twenty years before.

The names given by Captain Hop to places north of the great river have long since been replaced by others, but there is no difficulty in following the route of the expedition. They passed the hot spring now known as Nisbett's Bath, and kept along the western base of the Karas mountains, between the eighteenth and nineteenth meridians from Greenwich, the same route as that of Sir James Alexander in 1838. They found giraffes soon after crossing the great river, and killed several. Governor Tulbagh, who had already enriched the chief museums of the Netherlands with many specimens illustrating the botany and zoology of the colony, sent the skin of one of these giraffes to the museum of the University of Leiden. It was the first taken to Europe from South Africa.

The expedition reached latitude 26° 18′ S., and two of the burghers penetrated the country some miles further. But the heat had now become almost insupportable; there was such a scarcity of food for the cattle that they were dying off rapidly, and though numerous beds of rivers were found, there was no water in any of them except at distant points where the natives had made deep pits in the sand. Captain Hop called a council, and there was but one opinion expressed, that it was impossible to go further.

On the 7th of December the caravan turned to the south. At the great river some time was spent in refreshing the worn-out cattle, which afforded an opportunity to examine the country around. In the mountains bordering on the river copper was discovered, but the conclusion which Captain Hop and his assistants came to was that it would not pay to extract it. They observed first that there was no wood in the neighbourhood which could be used as fuel, consequently the ore must needs be taken away in its crude state. Next, there were obstructions in the river which would prevent the use of boats to transport the ore to the sea, so that it would be necessary to remove it in waggons. And lastly, the country was not only very difficult to traverse, but it was so parched by the summer heat as not to afford a supply of food for draught cattle. The mouth of the river was too distant to be examined.

During the night of the 11th of January 1762 the water in the Great river rose suddenly. The expedition was encamped on the bank, unsuspicious of danger, and it was with difficulty that the waggons were removed to a place of safety. One night a little later thirty of the oxen were stolen by Bushmen. The colonists had volunteered to accompany the expedition, chiefly with a view of obtaining a large number of cattle in barter, but they had not succeeded according to their anticipations.

No information of a positive kind was obtained concerning the black people to the north, then called Damrocquas, now Damaras. But the wild stories that had previously been current of their having long hair and wearing linen clothing were found to be incorrect, for the Great Namaquas knew of no people answering that description except Europeans. Information was obtained concerning the Betshuana, then called Briquas or Birinas, living east of the Kalahari. And it was ascertained that the small pox in 1755 had spread into Great Namaqualand and caused the loss of many lives.

Pieter Marais, one of the burghers who accompanied the expedition, understood the Hottentot language, and was a man given to inquiry. He and Tieleman Roos drew up a report upon the natives, showing that the different clans which were met were members of one tribe. They had witnessed the method of worshipping the new moon by singing, dancing, and invocations; and they had learned that the Great Namaquas had some faint conception of a supreme being, whom they called Chuyn, but what the nature of this being was supposed to be they had not ascertained. They had seen the natives smelting copper and working it into ornaments by means of a stone hammer and anvil. The Great river was called by the Namaquas Chari or Eyn. The last word was the same as that given to Commander Van der Stel by the Little Namaquas in 1685. The first word Chari is the same as Gariep of our days.

On the 27th of April 1762 the expedition reached the castle, none of its members having died or suffered serious illness during the journey.

A little before two o'clock in the morning of the 14th of

July 1766 a slight shock of earthquake was felt throughout the Cape peninsula. It was accompanied by a noise like rolling thunder. No damage was caused by it, though at Simon's Town it was sufficiently violent to throw the bedsteads in the hospital against the walls of the wards.

In 1767 the small pox was again brought into the colony. On this occasion it was introduced by a Danish ship returning to Europe. From May until November it was prevalent in Cape Town, but owing to precautions which were taken, only a few families in the country districts were attacked by it. In 1713 and 1755 it died out entirely when the hot weather set in; but there were occasional cases throughout the summer of 1767–8, and it was not until April 1769 that it quite disappeared. Altogether between eighteen and nineteen hundred persons were attacked, of whom one hundred and seventy-nine Europeans, one hundred and forty-five free blacks, and two hundred and fifty-one slaves died. The ravages of the disease were thus slight when compared with earlier years.

During the period that Governor Tulbagh was at the head of the colony, the town in Table Valley was considerably enlarged, and strangers began to know it by its present name of Cape Town, though by the colonists it was still termed the Cape. Several new streets were laid out. The parade ground was again levelled, and an oak hedge was planted round it. The artificial fountains from which the inhabitants got water were renewed. The town house—the same that is still in use—was built by the burgher council. The tower of the church was raised a few feet higher by the consistory, and a clock was placed in it, which did not, however, indicate the time until the 25th of November 1771. The graveyard round the church was closed, and early in 1770 the cemetery between the Lion's Rump and the shore of the bay was opened for use. The hospital was falling to ruins, and it had been resolved by the directors to build a new one, but the work was not yet commenced, though the materials were being collected. The fortifications were repaired, and a new battery was constructed near the mouth of Salt River.

At Simon's Town expensive works were carried out. The hospital—a square building of 130 feet frontage—was commenced in 1760 and completed in 1765. Substantial storehouses were then put up, and when these were finished, in 1768 a stone pier was constructed. A slaughter house, a bakery, workshops for smiths and carpenters, and a dwelling house for the officer in charge of the station, followed. The building erected in the time of Governor Swellengrebel—which was 450 feet in length and had previously served for all purposes—was now used solely as quarters for the garrison and workmen. In March 1751 Adriaan de Nys was appointed postholder in succession to Justinus Blas. Mr. De Nys died in May 1761, when Jan Frederik Kirsten was appointed officer in charge at Simon's Town, with the title of resident.

The village of Stellenbosch was also considerably enlarged and improved in appearance during this period. On the 31st of October 1762 the drostdy buildings were destroyed by fire, but they were shortly rebuilt in a handsomer style. On the 30th of May 1768 much damage was done to the village by a flood, which for some hours threatened the total destruction of the place. The same thing had occurred once before—on the 13th of October 1716. To prevent similar disasters in future, the course of the river was altered, according to plans furnished by the heemraad Martin Melk, under whose supervision the work was carried out. In September 1748, upon the death of Pieter Lourens, Adriaan van Schoor had been appointed landdrost of Stellenbosch and Drakenstein. In August 1763 this gentleman was promoted to an office in Cape Town, and Jacobus Johannes le Sueur succeeded him as landdrost. Mr. Le Sueur held the appointment until June 1769, when he was promoted and was succeeded by Lucas Sigismundus Faber.

Swellendam remained a mere hamlet. To facilitate access to it from the Cape, in 1757 a pontoon was placed on the Breede river, close to the junction of the Zonder End.

In 1766 Mr. Horak retired from the Company's service and became a burgher, when Joachim Frederik Mentz, who had previously been secretary of the district, was appointed landdrost.

During the administration of Mr. Tulbagh the natives gave very little trouble to the colonists. The Hottentot clans that still held together in compact bodies within the limits of the European settlement retained their own government, though their chiefs were practically appointed by the Dutch authorities. Only when Europeans or slaves were also concerned were they made amenable to colonial law. But the greater number of these people had lost their old tribal distinctions, and recognised no chief of their own race. Many of them were living as dependents of farmers, or wandered about the country, taking service occasionally as they felt so disposed. These were of necessity amenable to colonial law, even in matters affecting their relationship to each other.

There were instances of harsh and unjust treatment of Hottentots by colonists, especially on the remote border; but the courts of law were open for their protection, and the heavy sentences that are found recorded against European criminals in such cases prove that the law was not a dead letter. The government of Mr. Tulbagh, being popular, was strong; and oppression of the Hottentots on any large scale could only take place in times of anarchy. Land was allotted to colonists without consulting them, which will be considered just or unjust according as one regards the right of property in the soil by a race of nomads unacquainted with agriculture. As yet there was plenty of land left for them and their cattle, so that this question was not a pressing one. It had already been noticed, and was as well recognised then as it is now, that nearly every case of cruelty by colonists was committed by men who either had coloured blood in their veins or who had mixed with the uncivilised coloured people on terms of equality.

The government was anxious to prevent the Hottentots from becoming possessed of guns and horses, as many of those who accompanied the elephant hunters in their expeditions had learned to be expert marksmen, and might prove dangerous to the peace of the colony if mounted and armed. In 1755 some Hottentots in the district of Swellendam acquired several horses and a couple of muskets as wages from burghers, when the landdrost was instructed to endeavour to procure the forbidden property in a friendly way in exchange for something else, and strictly to prohibit such actions in future.

With Bushmen there were occasional contests.

In the spring of 1754 a large party of these savages made their appearance in the Roggevelden, and drove off great herds of cattle. Only one individual—a Hottentot—was murdered by them; but the farmers on the north-western frontier abandoned their homes in alarm. The military board (krygsraad) of Stellenbosch and Drakenstein instructed the field corporals Willem van Wyk, Godlieb Opperman, Nicholas Ryk, Pieter van Zyl, Barend Lubbe, and Barend Forster to proceed with their forces against the robbers. For six weeks the commando was in the field, as the Bushmen retired to mountains, where they made an obstinate resistance. One stronghold was besieged in vain, the robbers from secure positions shouting defiance and declaring they would have the whole of the cattle in the country. In other places, however, sixty-four Bushmen were killed, at a cost on the farmers' side of one white man and two Hottentots wounded. The commando then returned home, with only seven head of cattle out of all that had been lost.

A little later in the same year the cattle of Jacobus Gildenhuis were driven away from his farm in the Bokkeveld. Gildenhuis's neighbours—Dirk Koekemoer, Jan van Aswegen, and Andries van der Heiden, with twenty Hottentots, pursued, shot down twenty-six of the robbers, wounded eight others, and recovered nearly all the cattle.

The Bushmen in that part of the country then promised to abstain from robbery, and peace was made with them.

In May 1758 a party of about two hundred Bushmen

from beyond the interior range of mountains made a raid into the Roggeveld, and drove off some four hundred head of cattle. A commando, under David van der Merwe, assembled and pursued the robbers for fourteen days. The Bushmen were overtaken in a mountain, when fifty-six were shot, and all the cattle but forty-eight were recovered. Commandant Van der Merwe was slightly wounded, but there was no other casualty on the European side.

In the winter of 1763 a party of Bushmen drove off the cattle of Pieter Loubser from his farm in the Bokkeveld. A European named Hermanus Vos and a few Hottentots pursued the robbers, but upon being overtaken the Bushmen turned and killed Vos with poisoned arrows, when the Hottentots retreated. Landdrost Van Schoor called out a commando, which was placed under order of Dirk Koekemoer. The commando searched for the Bushmen for three weeks without success, and then broke up. In January following the farms of Nicholas Loubser and Willem Engelbrecht were in the same way cleared of cattle. On this occasion a commando assembled more hastily, when the Bushmen were surrounded, and the whole of them were shot.

In June 1764 some Bushmen visited a cattle station on the Zak river, where the burgher Jacob van Reenen had some sheep running. They murdered Van Reenen's European servant, who was in charge of the station, and drove off three hundred sheep. Upon hearing what had occurred, Gerrit van Wyk, who was the nearest field corporal, raised a commando and hunted up the robbers. Their retreat was discovered, and they were attacked, when twenty-five of them were shot, and ten children were taken away. Only sixty-three sheep were recovered. The children were distributed as servants among some of the members of the commando, on the ground that it would be unjust to shoot them for the sins of their parents, that to leave behind those whose parents were killed would be to leave them to perish, and that those who had relatives to provide for them would assuredly become robbers if not removed from evil influences.

In May 1770 some Bushmen drove off thirty-four head of cattle from the farm of Casper Scholtz on the Salt river, between the present villages of Beaufort West and Murraysburg. Adriaan van Jaarsveld, a man whose name was afterwards to be well known throughout South Africa, was then field corporal of that part of the country. He mustered a commando, followed the Bushmen, and shot six of them, the others managing to escape. The cattle were found dead. The commando, before dispersing, came across a party of Bushmen in the act of lifting the cattle of David van Heerden. They shot two, and made prisoners of the others, who were afterwards distributed as servants.

Later in the same year many of the farms along both sides of the Roggeveld and Nieuwveld mountains were plundered by Bushmen, and three servants of Barend Lubbe, Cornelis van Wyk, and Willem van Zyl were murdered. The field corporals assembled their forces, hunted up the plunderers, and shot a good many, the exact number not being given. Some of the cattle were recovered, and for a time it was hoped that there would be no more depredations. But early in 1771 the Bushmen mustered in force, laid siege to several houses, murdered three of Jacob Joubert's servants, and drove off large herds of cattle. Adriaan van Jaarsveld determined upon giving the marauders a severe lesson. With thirty picked men, well mounted, he took the field, and did not return until he had counted ninety-two dead Bushmen. After that there was quietness for a short time.

In December 1769 a commission consisting of Lucas Sigismundus Faber, landdrost of Stellenbosch, Joachim Frederik Mentz, landdrost of Swellendam, two heemraden from each court, and the two secretaries, was directed to lay down a permanent boundary between the two districts. The Zwartberg range was settled upon as a good dividing line, the country to the north being allotted to Stellenbosch, and that to the south to Swellendam.

The commission was also required to inspect the most distant farms and ascertain the state of affairs on the frontier. They reported that they found between the Gamtoos and Fish rivers many persons with large herds of cattle, who were not paying rent to the Company, and others who were paying for a farm within the colonial limits, but who were moving about with their cattle wherever they pleased. They had reason also to believe that notwithstanding the placaat of the 8th of December 1739, which prohibited the purchase of cattle from natives, a large trade with the Kosas was being carried on, for they found a well-beaten waggon-road from Swellendam into Kaffirland.

The council of policy therefore resolved—13th of February 1770—that on the northern or Stellenbosch side of the Zwartberg and the corresponding range further eastward the colonial boundary should be the hills known as Bruintjes Hoogte, that on the southern or Swellendam side it should be the Gamtoos river, that all persons then beyond these limits should be called upon to return to the colonial side, that all cattle found away from farms held on lease as well as all found in possession of nomads should be forfeited to the Company, and that landdrosts who neglected to prevent such irregularities should be dismissed and declared incapable of serving the Company.

During the period 1st of January 1751 to 31st of December 1771 there were five years of drought, more or less severe, in the corn-growing districts. These years were 1755, 1756, 1763, 1764, and 1771. In 1755 the drought was severe during the early months, and many cattle died of starvation, but after June abundance of rain fell, and the corn crop was a very good one. In 1756 the rain that fell was insufficient for wheat, and only a poor crop was gathered. There was such a quantity in reserve, however, that as much as usual was exported. In 1763 not only was the drought severe, but south-east gales set in early and with such force as partly to destroy what wheat was growing, and a plague of caterpillars followed, so that little or nothing was reaped. There was plenty of grain in reserve, but it was considered prudent only to send one-fourth of the usual quantity to

India. In 1765 the drought continued, and there was hardly any harvest. Of the grain which remained in stock, a small quantity was sent to India, but rice was imported to compensate for it. In 1771 the drought was not very severe, though the crop gathered was poor.

During these twenty-one years the average quantity of farm produce exported to India was 11,791 muids of wheat, 202 muids of rye, 68 muids of barley, 202 muids of peas, 174 muids of beans, and 346 leggers of common wine. In 1754 butter was first exported to India. During the next eighteen years the quantity sent abroad annually averaged 22,322 pounds. It was usually purchased at the Company's stores at six pence to eight pence a pound, but occasionally in times of scarcity as much as a shilling a pound was paid for it. A small quantity of dried fruit and a little ivory were also exported to India.

To Europe were sent yearly rather over 100 leggers of common wine and as much Constantia wine as could be obtained, which was usually not more than 14 or 15 leggers. From 1736 to 1761 the price paid by the Company for red Constantia wine was 20*l.* 16*s.* 8*d.* and for white Constantia wine 10*l.* 8*s.* 4*d.* the legger, the proprietors of the farms into which the original estate was divided being obliged under an old contract to sell at that price. But as they could easily get double those sums from foreigners, they were loud in complaining, and in 1761 an agreement was made with Jacobus van der Spuy, then owner of High Constantia, that he should deliver to the Company two-thirds of all the red wine made by him at 31*l.* 5*s.*, and two-thirds of all the white wine at 15*l.* 12*s.* 6*d.*[1] the legger, he to be at liberty to sell the remaining third to whom he chose at the best price which he could obtain. A similar agreement was subse-

[1] The agreement was made in rixdollars, at that time current at two and a half gulden of Holland, or four shillings and two pence English money each. In 1770 the supreme authorities issued instructions that the rixdollar was to be valued at $2\frac{4}{10}$ gulden of Holland, equal to four shillings English money. The prices named must be reduced by four per cent after that date, for the sellers had to bear the loss in the difference of exchange.

quently made with Lambert Myburgh, owner of Great Constantia.

In 1761 the first aloes were exported from South Africa. A quantity of two hundred and eighteen pounds in weight was produced by the old burgher councillor Petrus Johannes de Wit, who lived at the Cape, but who had a farm in the country, and had caused the drug to be prepared there. The council of policy decided to send it to Europe, where it was pronounced to be of good quality. The directors issued instructions to purchase it at the stores at a price not exceeding two shillings and three pence half-penny a pound. From that date it has been an article of export to Europe, but the quantity in demand being inconsiderable, it has not been of much advantage to the colony.

The first horses were exported from South Africa in 1769. Six years earlier the horse sickness had been unusually severe, the burghers losing over 2,500 within a few months; but the loss had been made good by breeding, and when some English officers visited the Cape to procure remounts for India, there were plenty to be had, though they were small and not very handsome. On the 25th of December 1769 the *Duke of Kingston* sailed from Table Bay with a shipment for Madras.

The various churches in the colony were well supplied with clergymen during the administration of Mr. Tulbagh. When he became governor, Mr. Van der Spuy was alone at the Cape, Stellenbosch was vacant, Mr. Van Echten was at Drakenstein, Mr. Meyring was at Waveren, and Mr. Voltelen was at Zwartland.

In October 1752 the Rev. Hendrik Kroonenburg arrived from Europe and was stationed at the Cape. In January 1753 Mr. Van der Spuy was transferred to Drakenstein, at his own request, when Mr. Van Echten returned to Holland. The Cape church was then again under the care of a single clergyman until September 1754, when the Rev. Gerhardus Croeser arrived from Europe, and was inducted as assistant pastor. In November 1755, under an arrangement between themselves of which the government approved, Mr. Croeser went to Zwartland and Mr. Voltelen came to the Cape. In April 1758 Mr. Voltelen died, but his place was filled in November of the same year by the Rev. Johannes Frederik Bode, who was sent out by the directors.

In March 1760 the Rev. Johannes Petrus Serrurier arrived from Europe. The council of policy decided to keep him at the Cape, and to send Mr. Bode to Waveren. But Mr. Bode declined to remove, on the ground that having been inducted as clergyman of the Cape he could not be required to fill a position of less dignity, without being found guilty of misconduct. Some members of the council were also of this view, but the majority suspended him from duty and stopped his pay until the opinion of the directors could be made known. The directors decided that his contention was just, and they issued instructions—which were received here in April 1761—that Mr. Serrurier should be inducted as third clergyman of the Cape, that Mr. Bode should resume duty as second clergyman and be paid his arrear salary, and that upon the first death or removal of either Mr. Kroonenburg, Mr. Bode, or Mr. Serrurier, no successor should be appointed. They were all in active service at the close of the period embraced in this chapter.

In September 1753 the Rev. Johannes Appeldoorn arrived from Europe, and in the following month was stationed at Stellenbosch. He was still there in 1771, as was Mr. Van der Spuy at Drakenstein.

In May 1757 the Rev. Mr. Meyring died. In January 1758 the commissioner Johan Gideon Looten, who was then at the Cape, removed the Rev. Remmerus Harders from a ship of which he was chaplain, and sent him to minister to the congregation at Waveren until the place should be filled by an appointment from the Netherlands. In 1761 the directors issued instructions that Mr. Harders was to remain there permanently, and he was still doing duty in 1771.

In May 1770 the Rev. Gerhardus Croeser died. No successor had been appointed in 1771, but the three clergymen of the Cape were required by the council of policy to hold service at Zwartland monthly in succession.

In 1759, by order of the council of policy, the yearly meetings of the combined consistories ceased to be held. The council considered that the meetings were serving no useful purpose, and that the travelling charges of the clergymen and elders were burthens too heavy to be borne by the congregations.

During the 21 years 1751–1771 there put into Table Bay 938 ships belonging to the Dutch East India Company, 168 English, 147 French, 31 Danish, 13 Swedish, 4 Prussian, 1 Portuguese, and 1 Spanish. During the same period 129 ships belonging to the Dutch East India Company, 14 English, 11 French, 13 Danish, and 2 Swedish put into Simon's Bay. The whole number that touched at the two ports was 1,472, and the average yearly number 70.

The Prussian flag was first seen on a ship in Table Bay in 1755, and the Swedish in 1759. The Spanish ship touched here in 1770. According to the treaties of Münster and Utrecht, the Spaniards were prohibited from sending vessels to India by the way of the Cape of Good Hope. The government therefore refused to allow the captain of this ship, which was a man-of-war, to procure any supplies except water and fuel. The other foreigners obtained whatever they chose to pay for, excepting when the council thought it necessary to prohibit the sale of such articles as the Company needed and of which the supply was insufficient for all.

Among persons of note that called at the Cape during the government of Mr. Tulbagh was Lord Clive, who touched here when on his way to India for the last time, on the 17th of December 1764. Shortly after the anchor of his ship—the *Kent*—was dropped, a stiff south-easter set in, but Clive determined to try and get ashore. He left the ship in a large boat well manned, but could not reach the jetty, and after a long struggle against the gale, was obliged to run to Robben Island and pass the night there.

On landing at the Cape next morning, Lord Clive was received with all possible honour, and during his stay he resided in government house in the garden as the guest of the Company. He was provided with a military guard, not only for himself, but for the colonels who accompanied him. Captain Collins, who commanded an English man-of-war lying in the bay, took offence at this. He was lodging on shore, and ascertaining late one evening that Clive's colonels had a guard of soldiers, he sent to request the immediate attendance of the government secretary. When that gentleman arrived, Captain Collins demanded that he should be informed on the authority of the governor why he, who held the king's commission, was treated with less courtesy than officers who held their rank from Lord Clive. It was with difficulty that the offended captain could be induced to let the matter rest for that night, as the governor had retired, and the secretary did not wish to disturb him. In the morning the matter was laid before Governor Tulbagh, who assured the captain that no slight whatever had been intended; and a guard was placed at his service, as he desired it.

Lord Clive remained ashore until the 12th of January 1765, when he embarked, and sailed on the 16th. On the 22nd of April 1767 he arrived at the Cape again, on his return passage to England. On this occasion also the government house in the garden was placed at his disposal, but he declined it with thanks, and took lodgings with the burgher Petrus Johannes de Wit. He left on the 4th of May.

A visitor scarcely less eminent was Captain James Cook, who called at Table Bay in the *Endeavour* on his homeward passage, on the 15th of March 1771. After refreshing his crew and taking in a stock of provisions, he sailed again on the 14th of April.

Bernardin de St. Pierre, author of *Paul et Virginie*, also spent about six weeks at the Cape in 1771.

There were but few disasters on our coast at this period. The loss of the *Doddington* and the drifting ashore of the *Meermin* have already been mentioned. The only other casualties were the following:

On the 9th of June 1752 the Danish ship *Crown Princess of Denmark*, homeward bound from Tranquebar, put into Mossel Bay disabled, having sustained great damage in a gale. The cargo was landed and stored in sheds until it could be forwarded to Copenhagen, and the wreck was then abandoned. All possible assistance was given to the crew by the Cape authorities.

On the 19th of March 1756 the French ship *Cybelle*, bound to Mauritius from the coast of Guinea with slaves, in trying to beat into Table Bay ran ashore a little above Blueberg, and shortly went to pieces. Her crew, with the slaves, got safely aboard another French ship lying at anchor in the bay.

On the 3rd of June 1756 the Cape packet *Schuylenburg* left Table Bay to take some stores to Simon's Bay. That night there was a violent storm, and the *Schuylenburg* was never afterwards heard of.

On the 8th of June 1757 the Company's provision ship *Voorsigtigheid*, which had recently arrived from Batavia with goods for the Cape, in a gale from the north-west went ashore near Salt River mouth, and became a wreck. Her crew of fifty-nine men got safely to land.

In January 1757 the Company's ship *Naarstigheid* sailed from Bengal with a valuable cargo, and on the 9th of the following April was dismasted in a hurricane. During six weeks her crew did their best to reach False Bay under jury masts, but finding this impossible, and being in great distress, they put the ship about and steered for Mozambique. The Agulhas current being now against them, they found they could not get so far north, so on the 1st of July they put into Delagoa Bay, and cast anchor before the ruins of the abandoned Dutch fort. They then sent out parties to endeavour to reach the Cape and Mozambique overland, but these were soon obliged to return unsuccessful. In May 1758 a boat with an officer and five men left to try and reach Mozambique, but she was never afterwards heard of. After being dismasted, the *Naarstigheid* was spoken by the English ship *Delaware*, homeward bound, whose master reported the circumstance to the Chamber of Delft. The directors thereupon issued instructions to the Cape government to cause a search to be made, and towards the close of 1758 the packet

Hector left Table Bay for this purpose. She found the wreck, with fifty-nine individuals—including some passengers—still living. The greater portion of the cargo was undamaged. The *Hector* returned to the Cape with the intelligence, when some vessels were sent for the crew and cargo. As she also brought word that elephants in large numbers had been seen in the neighbourhood of the wreck, four experienced hunters from the district of Swellendam, who volunteered for the purpose, were sent to Delagoa Bay by this opportunity. Two of them died of fever immediately after landing, and the other two—Hans Ditlof and Jacob Kock—only shot twenty elephants, most of the animals having gone inland before their arrival.

On the 11th of September 1763 the French man-of-war *Fortuné*, homeward bound from Mauritius, after encountering a heavy gale off the coast put into Fish Bay in a sinking condition. She was kept afloat until everything of value was landed, but was abandoned on the 27th, when she went down at her anchorage. Two days later she broke up in a storm. Her crew and some troops on board, 441 in all, proceeded overland to the Cape, where they embarked in French ships returning to Europe.

Governor Tulbagh was regarded as a model officer by his superiors in Europe and India. In March 1755 he was raised to the dignity of councillor extraordinary of Netherlands India, a position which gave him higher rank than that of governor, though it did not add to his duties. In March 1767 he was further elevated to be an ordinary councillor. He had now only two superiors out of Europe, the governor-general and the director-general.

In his declining years he was often laid upon a bed of sickness. In 1766 his life was despaired of, but he rallied, though he did not recover his former strength. At length, in the winter of 1771, he was prostrated by illness which he felt was to be his last, for to other ailments was now added a painful attack of gout in the feet. His deathbed, on which he lay for eleven weeks, was one of patient suffering and contemplation of the hereafter. In the afternoon of the 11th of August he appeared to be better than usual, but between five and six o'clock in the evening, without a struggle, his spirit passed away. He died at the age of seventy-two years and nearly three months.

A quarter of a century earlier he had been surrounded by his wife's relatives, who then formed a very numerous family. At the time of his death he had no nearer connection in South Africa than the three brothers Le Sueur, who were his wife's nephews. The whole of the Swellengrebel family had moved to other countries or had died out. The governor had no children, and he had been a widower since October 1753. By will he left his property to his younger brother, Johannes Tulbagh, a retired captain of the national army, who was living at Bergen-op-Zoom, and to whom for a long time he had made an allowance of 200*l.* a year.

On the morning after Mr. Tulbagh's death, the council of policy met to make provision for carrying on the government. The principal offices at the time were filled by men with only acting appointments. In April 1766 the secunde Van Oudtshoorn had gone to Europe on leave of absence to attend to his private affairs, when the fiscal Cloppenburg was chosen to act for him, and Mr. Otto Luder Hemmy was directed to act as fiscal. In March 1767 a despatch from the directors was received, announcing that Mr. Van Oudtshoorn had resigned, that Mr. Cloppenburg was to succeed as secunde, and Mr. Joachim van Plettenberg—then a member of the high court of justice at Batavia—was appointed fiscal. On the 21st of December of the same year Mr. Van Plettenberg arrived in South Africa. On the 30th of May 1770 Mr. Cloppenburg died, and the council then directed Mr. Van Plettenberg to act as secunde until the directors could make their wishes known. He was also to perform the most important duties of fiscal, but his assistant, Mr. Olof Godlieb de Wet, was to relieve him of the routine work of the office. This was the condition of matters at the time of Mr. Tulbagh's death, for the directors had not yet expressed their pleasure.

The council decided that Mr. Van Plettenberg should act

both as governor and secunde, and that the secretary, Mr. Olof Martini Bergh, should act also as fiscal until the supreme authorities could make new appointments. They then resolved to go into full mourning with their families for six weeks. The principal townspeople did the same. The funeral of the late governor was kept back till the 17th, to allow the country people to attend. On that day the town was filled as it never had been before, and with all the solemnity and state that was possible the remains of the landsfather were laid beneath the pavement of the church.

The records during these years contain many names of individuals then recently arrived, whose descendants are still in South Africa. They were chiefly officers in the Company's service, who subsequently settled here as burghers. Among them are:

Hendrik Albertyn
Eric Gustaf Aspeling
Anthonie Berrange
Christiaan Bester
Johannes Bresler
Willem Buissinne
Jan Hendrik Coenradi
Willem Dempers
Andries Dreyer
Jan Augustus Dreyer
Hendrik Jacobus Eckard
Jan Zacharias Eelhof
Jan Fischer
Carel Augustus Freislich
Jan Coenraad Gie
Adriaan de Graaff
Jan Greyling
Jan Adam Hartman
Godfried Gabriel Hauptfleisch
Pieter van den Heever
Albert Herhold
Jan Frederik Heydenryk
Jan Hendrik Hofmeyr
Rutger van Huysteen
Job Ludolf Immelman
Joachim Kannemeyer
Rynard Keet
Johan Bernard Koch
Johan Frederik Koch
Willem Adolf Kriege
George Frederik Langejan
Jan Liebenberg
Andries Christoffel Lind
Jan Adam Luckhof
Hartwich Jan Luttig
Honoratius Maynier
Nicholas Meeser
Godfried Mocke
Christiaan Ludolf Neethling
Coenraad Nelson
Jan Hermanus Redelinghuis
Johan Frans Reyneke
Jan van der Riet
Daniel van Ryneveld
Hercules Sandenberg
Simon Jacobus Sandenberg
Johan Frederik Schikkerling
Christiaan Sederblad

Hendrik Stander
Johan Godlieb Stegmann
Matthias Taute
Martin Theunissen
Jacobus Gustaf Triegard
Jacobus Verster
Kenne Nicholas Volsteedt
Abraham Wannenburg
Jan Carel Winterbach
Maurits Herman Otto Woeke
Matthys Zondag

CHAPTER XXIII.

DESCRIPTION OF THE NATIVE RACES OF SOUTH AFRICA.

Dividing line between the Hottentot and Bantu tribes—Territory occupied by the Bushmen—Characteristics of the Bantu, of the Hottentots, and of the Bushmen—The Hottentots—Division into tribes—Property—Food—Clothing—Dwellings—Weapons—Arts—Government—Superstition — Character —Language—The Bushmen — Language — Dwellings—Food—Weapons—Stone implements—Character—Independence—Superstition—Art of painting on rocks—The Bantu—Personal appearance—Tribal divisions—Clicks in the Kosa dialect—Formation of the tribes—Government—System of law—Tribunals of justice—Religion—Belief in witchcraft—Witchfinders—Rainmakers—Herbalists—Charms—Method of computing time—Folklore —Practice of circumcision—Weapons—Domestic life—Agriculture—Food —Land tenure—Villages—Dwellings—Wealth in cattle—Law of inheritance—Clothing—Manufactures—Habits—Line of descent of Kosa chiefs—Traditional history of the Kosa tribe.

As the colonists were rapidly approaching territory occupied by Bantu tribes, it is necessary to devote a chapter to explain in what respects these people differed from the natives with whom Europeans had long been in contact. A short review of the condition of the Hottentots and Bushmen when white people began to colonise the country must first be given.

In 1652 the south-western portion of the African continent was inhabited by the people whom we call Hottentots. A totally distinct race, now termed the Bantu, occupied the eastern seaboard and the country to the north. A straight line drawn on a map from Walfish Bay to the mouth of the Kei would form a fairly correct boundary of the Hottentot territory at that time. On the north-eastern side the Bantu tribes did not touch that line along its whole length, as there were large tracts of land without other inhabitants than Bushmen. Between the Bantu and the Hottentots there was nearly always deadly enmity. At only two points along the border was there anything like a mingling of blood. At its south-eastern extremity this was being effected to a slight extent by the extermination of Hottentot tribes with the exception of young females, and nearly midway between the oceans a few of the feeblest of the Bantu were in the habit of marrying Hottentot women in the intervals of peace.

Another class of people, known to us as Bushmen, roamed over the entire country. They were to be found in the interior at least as far as the Zambezi, and probably very much farther; but owing to the Bantu possessing greater means for their extermination than the Hottentots had at their disposal, they were most numerous in the territory of the latter. They were of the same branch of the human family as the Hottentots, but as distantly related as Celts to Teutons. The enmity between them was constant and strong.

The greatest differences between these divisions of people are now known to be in the constitution of their minds, but early observers did not detect these. The variations which they noticed were chiefly the following:

Bantu: frame of those on the coast generally robust and as well formed as that of Europeans, head covered closely with crispy hair, cheeks full, nose usually flat but occasionally prominent, hands and feet large, colour brown to deep black; weapons assagai, knobkerie, shield; pursuits agricultural, pastoral, and metallurgic; government firmly constituted, with perfect system of laws; habitations strong framework of wood covered with thatch; domestic animals ox, goat, dog, barnyard poultry; demeanour ceremonious, grave, respectful to superiors in rank; language musical, words abounding in vowels and inflected to produce harmony in sound.

Hottentots: frame slight but sometimes tall, back hollow, head scantily covered with little tufts of short crisped hair, cheeks hollow, nose always flat, eyes far apart and often set obliquely, hands and feet small, colour yellow to olive; weapons assagai, knobkerie, bow and poisoned arrow, shield;

pursuits pastoral and to a very limited extent metallurgic; government feeble; habitations slender wickerwork covered with skins or reed mats; domestic animals ox, sheep, and dog; demeanour inconstant, marked by levity; language abounding in clicks.

Bushmen: frame dwarfish, colour and general appearance those of the ugliest specimens of Hottentots; weapons bow and poisoned arrow; pursuits those of a hunter; government none but parental; habitations caverns or mats spread over branches of trees; domestic animal the dog; demeanour that of perfect independence; language abounding in clicks even more than that of the Hottentots, and in deep guttural sounds from which that of the Hottentots is free.

The investigations of the late Dr. Bleek have shown that the language of the Bushmen differs in construction from that of the Hottentots, that the Bushmen are monogamists while the Hottentots are polygamous, and that in many other respects they vary so greatly that the relationship between them must be very remote.

To a European ear the Hottentot language sounds like a continuous clapping of the tongue and clattering of the teeth. Most of the words are monosyllables or composites, and much the greater number contain clicks. The liquid consonant *l* is wanting. Missionaries have reduced the Nama dialect to writing, and a considerable amount of literature exists in it. But at the present day, excepting a few Namaquas and Koranas, there are no Hottentots who use the language of their ancestors. Nearly all now speak a patois of the Dutch.

The Hottentots were divided into a great number of tribes, each tribe being usually composed of several clans loosely joined together. They were frequently at war with each other. The chiefs were hereditary, but their authority was very slight.

Their principal property consisted of horned cattle and sheep. They had great skill in training oxen to obey certain calls, as well as to carry burdens. The milk of their cows was the chief article of their diet. They did not kill horned cattle for food, except on occasions of feasting, but they ate all that died a natural death. The ox of the Hottentot was an inferior animal to that of Europe. He was a gaunt, bony creature, with immense horns and long legs, but he was hardy and well adapted to supply the wants of his owner. The sheep were covered with hair instead of wool, were of various colours, and had long lapping ears and tails six or seven pounds in weight. The milk as well as the flesh was used for food. Children were taught to suck the ewes, and often derived their whole sustenance from this source. The only other domestic animal was the dog. He was an ugly creature, his body being shaped like that of a jackal and the hair on his spine being turned in the wrong direction; but he was a faithful, serviceable animal of his kind.

The food of the Hottentots consisted of milk, the flesh of game obtained in the chase, the meat of tame animals, locusts, and wild roots and fruits. Some impoverished clans on the coast lived chiefly on shellfish and the produce of the sea. They rejected no part of an animal except the gall. Agriculture, even in its simplest forms, was not practised by them, but they collected for food many kinds of wild plants with whose properties they were acquainted. They knew how to make an intoxicating drink of honey, large quantities of which were to be had in the season of flowers. With a pipe made of the horn of an antelope, they smoked dacha, a species of wild hemp, when it was procurable. This is one of the most powerful intoxicants known.

Their clothing was made of skins, usually prepared with the hair on. When removed from the animal, the skin was cleansed of any fleshy matter adhering to it, and then rubbed with fat till it became soft and pliable. The ordinary costume of a man was merely a piece of jackal skin suspended in front, and a triangular piece of leather behind. In cold weather he wrapped himself in a kaross or mantle of skins sewed together with sinews. The women wore at all times a headdress of fur, an apron, and a wrapper or a girdle of leather strings suspended from the waist. In cold weather they added a scanty kaross. Children wore no clothing whatever. Round their legs the females sewed strips of raw hide, like rings, which, when dry, rattled against each other and made a noise when they moved. Both sexes ornamented their heads with copper trinkets, and hung round their necks and waists strings of shells, leopards' teeth, or any other glittering objects they could obtain. Ivory armlets were worn by the men. From earliest infancy their bodies were smeared with fat and rubbed over with clay or soot, and to this may partly be attributed the stench of their persons. The coat of fat and clay was not intended for ornament alone. It protected them from the weather and from the vermin that infested their huts and clothing.

Their dwellings were oval or circular frames of light undressed wood, sometimes covered with skins, but usually with mats made of rushes. They were not more than five feet in height, and had but one small opening through which the inmates crawled. In cold weather a fire was made in a cavity in the centre. The huts of a village were arranged in the form of a circle, the space enclosed being used as a fold for cattle. They could be taken to pieces, placed on pack oxen, removed to a distance, and set up again, with very little labour and no waste.

The weapons used by the Hottentots in war and the chase were bows and arrows, sticks with clubbed heads, and assagais. They usually covered the head of the arrow with poison, so that a wound from one, however slight, was mortal.

The assagai could be hurled with precision to a distance of thirty yards. The knobkerie or clubbed stick was almost as formidable a weapon. It was rather stouter than an ordinary walking cane, and had a round head two or three inches in diameter. Boys were trained to throw this with so accurate an aim as to hit a bird on the wing at twenty or thirty yards distance. It was projected in such a manner as to bring the heavy knob into contact with the object aimed at, and antelopes as large as goats were killed with it. The bow was a weapon of little force, and the arrows would have been harmless to large game if they had not been poisoned.

The Hottentots were acquainted with the art of smelting iron, but were too indolent to make much use of it. Only a few assagai and arrow heads were made of that metal. Horn was ready at hand, was easily worked, and was commonly used to point weapons. Masses of almost solid copper were obtained in Namaqualand, and this metal was spread over the neighbouring country by means of barter, but was never used for any other purpose than that of making ornaments for the person.

They could also manufacture earthenware pots for cooking utensils. Milk was kept in skin bags or in large bowls made by hollowing out a block of wood. Ostrich egg shells and ox horns were used for carrying water and other domestic purposes.

Each kraal or village was under the government of a chief, whose authority, however, was very limited, as his subjects were impatient of control. The succession was usually from father to son, but sometimes to brother or nephew.

The Hottentots were a superstitious people, who placed great faith in the efficacy of charms to ward off evil. They believed that certain occurrences foreboded good or ill luck, that a mantis alighting on a hut brought prosperity with it, and many other absurdities of a like nature. They were in dread of ghosts and evil spirits. They invoked blessings from the moon, to whose praise they sang and danced when it appeared as new. They also invoked blessings from dead ancestors, to whose shades sacrifices were offered by priests on important occasions, and they implored protection and favour from a mythical hero named Heitsi-eibib, whose worship consisted in throwing a bit of wood or an additional stone upon a cairn. Cairns of great size raised in this manner are to be found at the present day far within the territory occupied by Bantu tribes, showing, like many other indications, that the Hottentots in times long gone by occupied a much larger area than when Europeans became acquainted with them. They made offerings also to a powerful evil spirit, with a view of averting his wrath. Their system of religion could not be explained by themselves, what they understood being little more than that the customs connected with it had come down to them from their ancestors. They had not the faintest expectation of their own resurrection, or conception of a heaven and a hell.

A more improvident, unstable, thoughtless people never existed. So long as they had food they were without care or grief. They delighted in dancing, and many early travellers speak with astonishment and admiration of the music which they were able to produce from reeds. Active in this amusement and in hunting, in all other respects they were extremely indolent. Their filthiness was disgusting to Europeans. They were in the habit of abandoning aged and helpless persons as well as sickly and deformed children, and allowing them to perish of hunger. But they regarded this as mercy, not as cruelty. Better that a helpless wretch or a cripple should give up life at once than linger on in misery. For the same reason, when a woman giving suck died, the child was buried with its parent.

It was customary with some, perhaps with all, to take wives not from their own but from some other clan. Cattle were given by the bridegroom to the nearest relatives of the bride. A system almost as bad as that of free love prevailed, for the marriage tie on both sides was very lightly regarded.

The women were more nearly the equals of the men than among most barbarians. They were mistresses within the huts. The stores of milk were under their control, not under that of their husbands, as is the case with the Bantu tribes. The men tended the cattle, but their daughters milked the cows. The females exercised much greater freedom of speech in domestic disputes than is usually tolerated by savages.

The Hottentots termed themselves Khoikhoi, men of men, as they flattered themselves that they were models for the rest of mankind. Their language was divided into many dialects, but these did not vary greatly,—not more than some dialects of English. When this language was thoroughly examined by competent persons, it was found to be of a high order, notwithstanding its numerous clicks. Its roots are monosyllabic, and end in vowels. It is inflected by means of affixes only, which places it in contrast with the Bantu languages, as these are inflected chiefly by prefixes. It has three numbers, singular, dual, and plural. Its system of counting is decimal, and is perfect at least up to a hundred. From common nouns, abstract nouns and adjectives are formed by regular rules, and in other respects the language is so flexible that there is no lack of means of expressing ideas in it.

The people who termed themselves Khoikhoi, and who were termed Hottentots by Europeans, called the pigmy hunters who lived on the same soil and looked so much like themselves Sana. The early Dutch residents in South Africa gave them the title of Bushmen. Their language has not been examined as carefully as that of the Hottentots, except by the late Dr. Bleek and by Miss L. Lloyd, whose researches have not yet been published. It is known, however, to be divided into a great number of dialects, some of which vary as widely as English from German. Many of its apparent roots are polysyllabic, but there is a doubt whether some of the supposed roots are not really composites. It is irregular in its formation. Only one instance of a dual form has been discovered, that of the first personal pronoun. The plural of nouns is often formed by reduplication. Sometimes a plural idea is expressed by a word which has nothing in common with the one which expresses the singular. In none of the dialects has any word for a numeral higher than three been discovered.

When the white man came to South Africa he found the Bushmen inhabiting the mountains and deserts, and carrying on incessant war with the Hottentot and Bantu tribes. A cave with its opening protected by a few branches of trees, or the centre of a small circle of bushes round which skins of wild animals were stretched, was the best dwelling that they aspired to possess. Failing either of these, they scooped a hole in the ground, placed a few sticks or stones round it, and spread a skin above to serve as a roof. A little grass at the bottom of the hole formed a bed, and though it was not much larger than the nest of an ostrich, a whole family could manage to lie down in it.

Their ordinary food consisted of roots, berries, wild plants, locusts, white ants, reptiles, birds, and mammalia of all kinds. No chance of plundering the pastoral tribes of domestic cattle was allowed to escape them. They were capable of remaining a long time without food, and could then gorge immense quantities of meat without any ill effects. They were careless of the future, and were happy if the wants of the moment were supplied. Thus, when a large animal was killed, no trouble was taken to preserve a portion of its flesh, but the time was spent in alternate gorging and sleeping until not a particle of carrion was left. When a drove of domestic cattle was stolen, several were slaughtered at once and their carcases shared with birds of prey, while if their recapture was considered possible, every animal was killed. Such wanton destruction caused them to be detested by all other dwellers in the land.

Their weapons were bows and arrows. The bows were nothing more than pieces of saplings or branches of trees about four feet in length, dressed down a little, and strung with a cord formed by twisting together the sinews of animals. The arrows were from twenty to thirty inches in length, made of reed pointed generally with bone. The arrowhead and the lashing by which it was secured to the reed were coated with a deadly poison, so that the slightest wound caused death. The arrows were carried in a quiver made of the bark of a species of euphorbia, which is still called by Europeans in South Africa the kokerboom or quiver tree. They were formidable solely on account of the poison, as they could not be projected with accuracy to any great distance, and had but little force. In after years the colonists considered their clothing ample protection at fifty yards distance. The Bushmen made pits for entrapping game, and also poisoned pools of water, so that any animal that drank perished.

They used stone flakes for various purposes, but took no trouble to polish them or give them a neat appearance. Their knives, scrapers, awls for piercing skins, and arrow-heads were commonly made of horn or bone. There was a stone implement, however, which was in general use. It was a little spherical boulder, from three to six inches in diameter, such as may be picked up in abundance all over the country, through the centre of which the Bushman drilled a hole large enough to receive a digging stick, to which it gave weight. With the tools at his disposal, this must have required much time and patience, so that in his eyes a stone when drilled undoubtedly had a very high value. On it he depended for food in seasons of intense drought, when all the game had fled from his part of the country. Drilled stones from an inch to three inches in diameter have been found in considerable numbers in tracts of country once inhabited by Bushmen, but from which those savages have long since disappeared. None so small as these have been noticed in use in recent times. It is conjectured that they were probably intended as toys for children.

The Bushmen wore few ornaments. Their clothing was similar to that of the Hottentots. They rubbed their bodies with fat and clay or ashes, which made them even more hideous in appearance than they were by nature. When they expected to meet an enemy, they fastened their arrows in an erect position round their heads, so as to appear as formidable as possible. In times of scarcity they wore a belt, which they tightened to assuage the pangs of hunger.

They lived in small societies, often consisting of only a couple of families. They were vindictive, passionate, and cruel in the extreme. Human life, even that of their nearest kindred, was sacrificed on the slightest provocation. They did not understand what quarter in battle meant, and when surrounded so that all hope of escape was gone, they fought till their last man fell. They never spared an enemy who was in their power. Their manner of living was such as to develop only qualities essential to hunters. In keenness of vision and fleetness of foot they far surpassed

Europeans; they could travel immense distances without taking rest, and yet their frames were so feeble as to be incapable of labour.

They possessed an intense love of liberty and of their wild wandering way of life. To this day, though strenuous and long-continued efforts have been made by various missionary societies for their reclamation, there is not a single instance of a Bushman of pure blood having permanently adopted the habits of European civilisation. Hereditary chieftainship was not recognised by them. It sometimes happened that the bravest or most expert of a party became a leader in predatory excursions, but his authority did not extend to the exercise of judicial control. Each man was independent of every other. Even parental authority was commonly disregarded by a youth as soon as he could provide for his own wants.

They were firm believers in charms and witchcraft. In some localities they have been found performing ceremonies and making offerings to propitiate an evil spirit, but it is doubtful whether this belief was general. Dr. Bleek and Miss Lloyd obtained from several individuals prayers to the moon and to stars. But all their religious ideas were vague and childish. They could not explain them any more than they could explain the structure of their language. And Europeans have not yet placed on record a sufficient number of reliable observations upon either the one or the other to make any deductions from them authoritative and final.

It is difficult to conceive of human beings in a more degraded condition than that of the Bushmen. The rearing of cattle placed the Hottentot on a much higher level, low as that level seems to Europeans. Yet in one respect the Bushman was in advance of the other. He was an artist. On the walls of caves and the sheltered sides of great rocks he drew rude pictures in profile of the animals with which he was acquainted. The tints were made with different kinds of ochre having considerable capability of withstanding the decay of time. There are caves on the margins of rivers in Kaffraria containing paintings which have been exposed to the action of water during occasional floods for at least a hundred years, and the colours are yet unfaded where the rock has not crumbled away.

In point of artistic merit, however, the paintings are not superior to the drawings on slates of European children eight or nine years of age. No knowledge of perspective or of shading is displayed. Two colours are sometimes used, as, for instance, the head or legs of an animal may be white, and the remainder of the body brown. But each colour is evenly laid on as far as it goes. In short, the paintings might be mistaken by strangers for the work of children, but for the impressions of the hands often accompanying them, and the scenes being chiefly those of the chase.

The Bantu have no word to signify the whole of their race, *ntu* in their language meaning a human being or person of any colour or country; but ethnologists felt the want of a name to distinguish the group to which they belong from the rest of mankind, and chose this as a convenient one. The Bantu occupy the larger portion of the African continent, and though some of the tribes are more degraded than others, everywhere their principal characteristics are the same.

The black man who occupies the land along the coast north of the Great Fish river is in general large without being corpulent, strong, muscular, erect in bearing, and with all his limbs in perfect symmetry. His skull is shaped like that of a European, but the bone is thicker. His intellectual abilities are considerable, his reasoning powers when defending himself in a controversy being equal to those of an ordinary white man. He is haughty in demeanour, and possesses a large amount of vanity. The men are handsomer than the women, owing to the girls being stunted in growth and hardened in limb by carrying burdens on their heads and toiling in the gardens at an early age.

In 1771 the tribes that inhabited the lower plateaux of the belt of country between the Kathlamba mountains and the sea were, first or adjoining the colony the Kosas, next the Tembus, following them the Pondos, the Pondomisis, and the Kesibes. Further northward it is unnecessary to proceed in this chapter. Each of these was independent of all the others, and wars between them were not uncommon.

The Kosas,—Amaxosa they style themselves,—having a click in their tribal name which is unpronounceable by European tongue, have been usually called Kaffirs by the colonists. But they find as much difficulty in repeating this word as white people find in their correct title, for the English sound of the letter r is wanting in their language. In the Kosa literature of the present day r is used to signify the sound which g has in Dutch or ch in the Scotch word loch. C, q, and x are used to denote the clicks. The other letters of the English alphabet represent the same sounds as with us, but there are combinations of consonants which it is very difficult for strangers of mature years to master.

The clicks are only found in a few dialects of the language spoken by the Bantu family. They seem to have been derived in the south from Hottentot, and in the north from Bushman sources, though further investigation is needed as to those beyond the equator. The group presents this peculiarity, that some of the dialects on the opposite borders bear a closer resemblance to each other than to those between them. The tribes seem to have been scattered and mixed together again by violent convulsions in some long-forgotten time.

However that may be, it is certain that at least a large proportion of the clicks in the dialect of the Kosa and adjoining tribes came from Hottentot sources. They were introduced by females who were spared when the hordes to which they belonged were conquered, as is evident not only from tradition, but from the words in which they occur being chiefly those pertaining to occupations of women. A few names of places east of the Kei are Hottentot words slightly changed. The Kosa names of rivers and mountains west of the Kei are all Hottentot words, and contain clicks, but this circumstance arises from recent events. Many of the people of this tribe show traces of Hottentot blood in their features and in the lightness of their colour. They are also more volatile in disposition than their neighbours higher up the coast.

The Kosa and Tembu, like most other Bantu tribes, are composed of a number of clans, each under its own chief, but all acknowledging the supreme authority of one particular individual. In the case of the Kosas, the chiefs of all the clans, with a solitary exception, are members of the same family, of which the paramount ruler is the head. Some of them are cousins seven or eight degrees removed from others, but all, with the exception referred to, trace their descent from a great-grandson of Kosa. It is different with the Tembus, many of whose clans are remnants of tribes which were broken up by wars in bygone times, and which kept their own hereditary chiefs when they were incorporated as vassals. The cohesion of the members is much weaker than with the Kosas.

In times of peace the government of the supreme chief is in ordinary matters hardly felt beyond his own village. Each clan possesses all the machinery of administration, and in general it is only in cases of appeal or serious quarrels that the tribal head uses his authority. In war he issues commands to all, and on important occasions he summons the minor chiefs to aid him with advice. The members of the ruling family, even to the most distant branches, are of aristocratic rank, and enjoy many privileges. Their persons are inviolable, and an indignity offered to one of them is considered a crime of the gravest nature.

With regard to the common people, the theory of the law is that they are the property of the rulers, consequently an offence against any of their persons is atoned for by a fine to the chief. Murder and assaults are punished in this manner. Thus in theory the government is despotic, but in practice it has many checks. The first is the existence of a body of councillors about the person of each chief, whose advice he is compelled to listen to. A second is a custom that fugitives must be protected by strangers with whom they take refuge, so that an arbitrary or unpopular ruler is in constant danger of losing his followers.

The law of succession to the chieftainship favours the formation of new tribes. The first wives of a chief are usually the daughters of some of his father's principal retainers; but as he grows older and increases in power his alliance is courted by great families, and thus it generally happens that his consort of highest rank is taken when he is of advanced age. Usually she is the daughter of a neighbouring ruler and is selected for him by the great council of the tribe, who provide the cattle required by her relatives. She is termed the great wife, and her eldest son is the principal heir. Another of his wives is invested at an earlier period of his life, by the advice of his councillors and friends, with the title of wife of the right hand, and to her eldest son some of his father's retainers are given, with whom he forms a new clan. The government of this is intrusted to him as soon as he is full grown, so that while his brother is still a child he has opportunities of increasing his power. If he is the abler ruler of the two, a quarrel between them arises almost to a certainty as soon as the great heir reaches manhood and is also invested with a separate command. Should peace be maintained, upon the death of his father the son of the right hand acknowledges his brother as superior in rank, but neither pays him tribute nor admits his right to interfere in the internal government of the new clan.

Since Europeans became acquainted with the coast tribes, the Kosas in this way separated into two branches, which, but for outside pressure, would certainly before this date have become quite independent of each other; the Pondomisis broke into two sections, thereafter almost constantly at war until both came under the colonial government; and in our own days the Pondos have become two practically independent tribes. The Tembu tribe was divided for a time in another way. A hostile invading force, acting like a wedge, broke off a large section, which but for the action of the colonial government would have become independent.

There is always a tendency towards division and subdivision of the tribes into little clans. In some of them two, in others three, sons of every chief divide their father's adherents among them. In the latter case the third heir is termed the representative of the ancients, or the son of the left hand. In olden times this disintegrating process was to some extent checked by constant feuds and wars, but since the tribes have been compelled to live in comparative peace it has been in active operation. Every little Kosa kraal at the present day is practically a separate clan.

The Bantu have a system of common law and perfectly organised tribunals of justice. Their laws have come down to them from a time to which even tradition does not reach, and those which relate to ordinary matters are so well known to every member of the community that trials are mere investigations into statements and proofs of occurrences. When complicated cases arise, precedents are sought for, antiquaries are referred to, and celebrated jurists even in other tribes are consulted. Should all these means of ascertaining the law fail, and the chief before whom the case is being tried not be a man of generally recognised ability, it often happens that no judgment is given, for fear of establishing a faulty precedent. From the decisions of the minor chiefs there is a right of appeal to the head of the tribe.

A lawsuit among these people is commonly attended by all the men of the kraal where it takes place. Nothing is more congenial than to sit and listen to the efforts of the querists to elicit the truth, or for the ablest among them to assist in the investigation. The trial takes place in the open air. The person charged with crime or the defendant in a civil case undergoes a rigorous examination, and must give a satisfactory account of himself or be condemned. The sentiment of considering a man innocent until he is proved guilty has little sympathy from them, and the English practice of warning an individual on trial against criminating himself is held to be perversion of justice.

The accuser or plaintiff or a friend prosecutes, and a friend of the individual on trial conducts the defence; the councillors, who act as assessors, put any questions they choose; and the mass of spectators observe the utmost silence and decorum. At the conclusion of the trial, the councillors express their opinions, and the chief then pronounces judgment.

There are only two modes of punishment, fines and death, except in cases where an individual is charged with having dealt in witchcraft, when torture, often of a horrible kind, is practised. In this class of trials every one is actuated by fear, and is in a state of strong excitement, so that the formalities required on other occasions are dispensed with. The whole clan is assembled and seated in a circle; the witch-finder, who is fantastically painted and attired, goes through certain incantations; and when all are worked into a state of frenzy he points to some individual as the one who has by bewitchment caused death or sickness among the people, murrain among cattle, blight in crops, or some other disaster. The result to the person so pointed out is confiscation of property and torture, often causing death.

The Bantu are seen in the most favourable light at the ordinary lawsuits before the chief and councillors, and in the most unfavourable light at the trials for the discovery of wizards and witches. In the one case men are found conducting themselves with the strictest gravity and propriety, astonishing even highly educated Europeans by the acuteness of their reasoning and the skilful method of their inquiries. In the other case the same people are seen as a panic-stricken horde, deaf to all reason, and ready to perform the most atrocious acts of cruelty, even upon persons who just previously were their companions.

The sentences pronounced in ordinary cases often seem to Europeans unjust, but that is because our standard of comparative crime is not the same as theirs, and because with us there is no difference of punishment according to the rank of the criminal. With them the ruling family in all its branches has the privilege of doing many things with impunity that a commoner would be severely punished for. Bribery is not unknown, but in courts as open as those of the Southern Bantu, and where there is the utmost freedom of inquiry, it cannot be practised to any great extent.

When a case is talked out, everyone present is usually acquainted with its minutest details.

The religion of the Bantu is based upon the supposition of the existence of spirits that can interfere with the affairs of this world. These spirits are those of their ancestors and their deceased chiefs, the greatest of whom has control over lightning. When the spirits become hungry they send a plague or disaster until sacrifices are offered and their hunger is appeased. When a person is killed by lightning no lamentation is made, as it would be considered rebellion to mourn for one whom the great chief has sent for. They have no idea of reward or punishment in a world to come for acts committed in this life, and each one denies his own immortality.

In olden times, when common people died, their corpses were dragged a short distance from the kraal, and there left to be devoured by beasts of prey; but chiefs and great men were interred with much ceremony. A grave was dug, in which the body was placed in a sitting posture, and by it were deposited the weapons of war and ornaments used in life. When the grave was closed, such expressions as these were used: 'Remember us from the place where you are; you have gone to high places; cause us to prosper.'

The Kosas have a dim belief in the existence of a powerful Being, whom they term Qamata, and to whom they sometimes pray, though they never offer sacrifices to him. In a time of great danger, one of them will exclaim, 'O Qamata, help me,' and when the danger is over, he will attribute his deliverance to the same Being. But of Qamata nothing more is known than that he is high and mighty, and that though at times he helps individuals, in general he does not interfere with the destinies of men. They are not given to inquiry or speculations upon matters of this kind. Recent investigations have shown that the belief in Qamata does not extend far among the Bantu tribes, and it is now supposed to have been acquired from the Hottentots. Not that the Hottentots venerated a deity under that name, but that a knowledge of some other object of worship than their own ancestral shades having been obtained through the Hottentot females whom they took to themselves, this name was given to the unknown divinity.

Nearer than the spirits of deceased chiefs or of their own ancestors is a whole host of hobgoblins, water sprites, and malevolent demons, who meet the Bantu turn which way they will. There is no beautiful fairyland for them, for all these beings who haunt the mountains, the plains, and the rivers are ministers of evil.

No days or seasons are considered more sacred than others. The rites of religion consist merely in sacrifices to appease the spirits. When an individual is ill or some domestic calamity occurs, the head of the family sacrifices an animal. The flesh is eaten, it being supposed that the spirit who is hungry will be satisfied with the smoke. In cases of tribal disaster, or when a member of the great chief's family is ill, animals are sacrificed with much ceremony by the tribal priest. This man possesses enormous influence throughout all the branches of the tribe that are not of alien origin. In addition to his duties as a priest, he prepares the army for the field, by administering medicines and supplying charms to make the warriors brave and all who do their duty invulnerable. Each ruling family has its own priest. When a community is broken in war and compelled to become a vassal clan of some other tribe, it retains its priest until by time or circumstances a thorough incorporation takes place. This is a process, however, that is not usually completed until several generations have passed away.

This religion is the principal counteracting force against the tendency of the Bantu tribes to break into fragments. The fear of offending the spirits of the deceased chiefs, and so bringing evil upon themselves, keeps the clans loyal to their head. He is the representative, the descendant in the great line, of those whose wrath they appease by sacrifices. A tribe all of whose clans are governed by offshoots of the family of the paramount chief is thus immensely stronger in war than one of equal size made up of clans thrown together by chance. In the one case the religious head is the same as the political, in the other they are separated. The Kosas are more powerful than the Tembus for this reason. With one exception, the chiefs of every clan in the Kosa tribe trace their descent from Tshawe, Kosa's great-grandson. In the Tembu tribe, a large proportion of the clans are aliens, under chiefs not related to the paramount family.

The belief in witchcraft is deep-seated and universal. The theory is that certain evil-disposed persons obtain power from the demons to bewitch others, and cause sickness, death, or disaster of some kind. They can only be discovered by individuals who go through a very severe novitiate, and to whom the necessary knowledge is imparted by people who live under water. The witchfinders are commonly regarded by Europeans as impostors; but they are really monomaniacs, and have the firmest conviction in their own ability to do what they profess.

Occasionally a person believes that he has received revelations from the spirit world. If his statements are credited, his power at once becomes equal to that of the highest chief, and his commands are implicitly obeyed. Crafty chiefs have sometimes made use of such deranged beings for the purpose of exciting the people to war, or of inducing them to approve of measures which would otherwise have been unpopular.

There are individuals who profess to be able to make rain. There are also persons who are skilful in the use of herbs as remedies for diseases, and who are well acquainted with different kinds of poison. It often happens that the three offices of witchfinder, rainmaker, and herbalist are combined in the same person, but this is not always the case, and the occupations are distinct. When practising, these individuals attire themselves fantastically, being painted with various colours, and having the tails of wild animals suspended around them.

Charms are largely depended upon to preserve the wearers against accident or to produce good luck. They are merely bits of wood or bone, which are hung about the neck, and are regarded just as lucky pennies and fortunate days are by some silly Europeans. But the belief is firm in charms and medicines which give to a gun the property of shooting straight, to an individual the property of winning favour, and such like. Some events, which to us appear natural, are regarded by them very differently. A party of Kosas, for instance, when travelling come to the banks of a river. Each one picks up a stone and throws it upon a heap to propitiate the spirit of the stream. In crossing, one of them gets into deep water and is in danger of being drowned. The others make no effort whatever to save him, but rush away frantically in search of cattle, which they drive hastily into the river, hoping that the spirit will be satisfied with an ox and release their comrade. Cases precisely similar to this still occur frequently, even among those who have been in contact with civilisation for many years.

The Bantu know of no other periods in reckoning time than the day and the lunar month, and can describe events only as happening before or after some remarkable occurrence, such as the death of a chief, a season of famine, or an unusually heavy flood. The rising of particular constellations just after sunset is regarded as indicating the approach of the planting season. To these constellations, as well as to several of the prominent stars and planets, they have given expressive names. They have formed no theories concerning the nature of the heavenly bodies and their motions, and are not given to thinking of such things. If questioned by a European, they may venture to remark that the sky is smoke which has risen from fires, but in such cases it is evident that the effort to find a solution to a query of this kind is new to them.

Their folklore, of which sufficient to fill many volumes can be collected in every kraal, is neither of a moral character, nor does it convey any useful lessons. The actors in it are animals which speak as human beings, persons who are bewitched and compelled to appear as beasts, individuals with magical powers, fantastic creatures, imps, cannibals, young chiefs, girls, &c., &c. The characters in the tales told round an evening fire by Kosa women to their children are identical with those told under similar circumstances on the shores of Lake Nyassa or on the banks of the Limpopo. There is nothing that partakes of the nature of true poetry or that leads to elevation of thought in any of these stories. To European minds there is very little that is even amusing in them, but they give a large amount of pleasure to those among whom they pass current. Many of the proverbs in common use, on the contrary, convey excellent lessons of prudence and wisdom.

When about fifteen or sixteen years of age, Kosa boys are circumcised. The rite is purely civil. By it a youth is enabled to emerge from the society of women and boys, and is admitted to the privileges of manhood. Its performance is attended with many ceremonies, some of a harmless, others to European ideas of a criminal nature. At a certain period in every year, unless it is a time of calamity or the chief has a son not yet ready, all the youths of a village who are old enough are circumcised. Thereafter for a couple of months or longer they live by themselves, and are distinguished by wearing a peculiar head-dress and a girdle of long grass about the loins, besides having their bodies covered with white clay. During this period they have license to steal freely from their relatives, provided they can do so without being caught in the act. After returning to their homes they are brought before the old men of the tribe, who lecture them upon the duties and responsibilities which they have taken upon themselves. Presents of cattle and weapons are afterwards made by their friends to give them a start in life. A free rein is then given to all kinds of immorality, without let or hindrance from their elders.

In case a scion of the ruling house is growing up, the performance of the rite of circumcision is generally allowed to stand over for a year or two, so that he may have a large number of companions. These are all supposed to be bound to him by a very strong tie. In after years they are to be his councillors and attendants, and in case of danger are to form his body guard. There is no instance on record of any one who was circumcised at the same time as a chief afterwards proving unfaithful to him, but numerous instances have come under the notice of Europeans where such persons have sacrificed their lives for him.

Females who arrive at the age of puberty are introduced into the state of womanhood by peculiar ceremonies, which extinguish all virtuous feelings within them. Originally, however, the very worst of the observances on these occasions was a test of self-discipline. The object of the education which a people like the Kosas go through is to make a man entirely master of himself. He must be able to control himself so that no trace of his emotions shall appear on his countenance, he must not wince when undergoing the most severe punishment. In olden times a further test was applied, which has degenerated into the most abominable licentiousness. It will be sufficient to say that the young women who attend the revels on these occasions are allowed to select temporary companions of the other sex, and if they decline to do so, the chief distributes them at his pleasure. As these pages are being prepared, a Kosa chief who is considered one of the most advanced of his tribe in civilisation has come into legal collision with the colonial authorities for distributing, in a district annexed to the colony, a large number of girls in this manner.

The Bantu of the coast belt are warlike in disposition and brave in the field, though they have not often ventured upon a pitched battle with Europeans. In olden times, their weapons of offence were wooden clubs with heavy heads and assagais or javelins. The assagai consists of a long, thin, iron head, with both edges sharp, and is attached by thongs to a slender shaft or rod. Poising this first in his uplifted hand and imparting to it a quivering motion, the warrior hurls it forth with great force and accuracy of aim; but, formidable as this weapon is in native encounters, it is of little effect when opposed to firearms. The club is used at close quarters, and can also be thrown to a considerable distance. Boys are trained from an early age to the use of both these weapons. Of late years firearms have come into general use, but the assagai and clubbed stick have not yet been discarded. Before they became acquainted with European weapons, the warriors carried shields made of oxhide, which varied in size and pattern among the tribes. These are now seldom seen.

The Bantu are polygamists, and women occupy a much lower position than men in their society. A woman is a drudge, upon whom the cultivation of the ground and other severe labour falls; her affections are not consulted in the choice of a husband, but a match is made for her by her nearest male relatives; she can inherit nothing; and she is liable to severe castigation from her husband, without protection from the law. She can only obtain redress when she is permanently maimed. Wealth is estimated by the number of wives and cattle a man possesses, and the one is always made use of to increase the other. The husband is head or lord of the establishment, and the wives are required to provide the food. Each has a hut of her own, which she and her children occupy, and the husband uses his caprice as to which he shall honour with his society at any time.

In conversation a Kosa woman uses for many purposes different words from those used by everyone around her. This arises from a custom which prohibits females from pronouncing the names of any of their husband's male relatives in the ascending line, or any words whatever in which the principal syllables of such names occur. The violation of this custom is considered as showing a want of proper respect for connections by marriage. Women avoid meeting their husband's male relatives in the ascending line, whenever it is possible to do so, and never sit in their presence.

All the Bantu practise agriculture. A species of millet, called by the colonists kaffir-corn, was the grain exclusively cultivated by the Kosas before their intercourse with Europeans. They raised large quantities of this, which they used either boiled or bruised into a paste from which bread was made. They were acquainted with the art of brewing, and in good seasons turned much of their millet into beer. A supply of grain sufficient to last until the next season was preserved from the attacks of weevil by burying it in air-tight holes excavated beneath the cattle folds. When kept for a long time in these granaries, the grain loses the power of germinating, and acquires a rank taste and smell. It is, however, none the less agreeable to the Kosa palate, though it is offensive to Europeans. The Kosas had also pumpkins, a species of gourd, a cane containing saccharine matter in large quantities, and a sort of ground nut. The other productions of their gardens, as we see them at present, have been introduced since they became acquainted with white men.

Of those mentioned their food consisted, with the addition of milk and occasionally flesh. Milk is kept in skin bags, where it ferments and acquires a sharp acid taste. As it is drawn off, new milk is added, for it is only in this state that it is used. Europeans soon come to be as fond of it as are the natives themselves, and in warm weather it is perhaps the most agreeable and healthy beverage that can be used. The art of making butter and cheese is unknown to the Kosas. They have two meals every day: a slight breakfast in the morning, and a substantial repast at sunset. Boys before being circumcised are permitted to eat any kind of meat, even that of wild cats and other carnivora, but after that ceremony is performed the flesh of all unclean animals is rejected by them. They do not use fish as food.

They have an admirable system of land tenure. The chief apportions to each head of a family sufficient ground for a garden according to his needs, and it remains in that individual's possession as long as it is cultivated. He can even remove for years, with the consent of the chief, and resume occupation upon his return. He cannot lend, much less alienate it. But if he ceases to make use of it, or goes away for a long time without the chief's permission, he loses his right. Under the same conditions he has possession of the ground upon which his hut stands, and of a yard about it. All other ground is common pasturage, but the chief has power to set aside portions of it for use in particular seasons only. No taxes of any kind are paid to a chief for land, air, or water.

Villages are usually built in situations commanding an extensive view of the surrounding country, and always on ground with good natural drainage. The brow of a hill, with a clear flowing stream at its base and fertile garden ground beyond, is the site most favoured.

The huts are shaped like beehives, and are formed of strong frames, thatched with reeds or grass. They are proof against rain or wind. The largest are about twenty-five feet in diameter, and seven or eight feet in height at the centre. They are entered by a low, narrow aperture, which is the only opening in the structure. A hard and smooth floor is made of antheaps, moistened with water and then kneaded with a round stone. When this has set, it is painted with a mixture of cowdung and water, which is the material used ever afterwards for keeping it in good order. In the centre of the floor a fireplace is made, by raising a band an inch or two in height and three or four feet in diameter, and slightly hollowing the enclosed space. Many women bestow a great deal of attention upon their fire-circles, often enclosing them with three bands, a large one in the centre and a smaller one on each side of it, differently coloured, and resembling a coil of large rope lying between concentric coils of less thickness. Against the wall of the hut are ranged various utensils in common use, the space around the fire-circle being reserved for sleeping on. Here in the evening mats are spread, upon which the inmates lie down to rest, each one's feet being towards the centre. Above their heads the roof is glossy with soot, and vermin swarm on every side. It is only in cold or stormy weather that huts are occupied during the day, for the people spend the greater portion of their waking hours in the open air.

Horned cattle constitute their principal wealth, and in days of old formed a convenient medium of exchange throughout the country. Great care is taken of them, and much skill is exhibited in their training. They are taught to obey signals, as, for instance, to run home upon a certain call or whistle being given. In former times every man of note had his racing oxen, and prided himself upon their good qualities as much as an English squire does upon his blood horses. Until quite recently ox racing was connected with all kinds of festivities. The care of cattle is considered the most honourable employment, and falls entirely to the men. They milk the cows, take charge of the dairy, and will not permit a woman so much as to touch a milksack.

The descent of property is regulated in the same manner as the succession to the chieftainship, so that there are always a great number of poor among them.

Their dress was formerly composed of skins of animals formed into a square mantle the size of a large blanket, which they wrapped about their persons. The skin of the leopard was reserved for chiefs and their principal councillors, but any other could be used by common people. Within the last half century woollen and cotton blankets have come into such general use that a fur robe is now rarely seen. Married women wear a leather petticoat at all times. In warm weather men and small children usually go quite naked. They are fond of decorating their persons with ornaments, such as necklaces of shells and teeth of animals, arm rings of copper and ivory, head plumes, &c. They rub themselves from head to foot with fat and red clay, which makes them look like polished bronze. Their clothing is greased and coloured in the same manner.

Their manufactures are not of a very high order. Foremost among them must be reckoned metallic wares, which include implements of war and husbandry and ornaments for the person. In many parts of the country iron ore is abundant, and this they smelt in a simple manner. Forming a furnace of clay or a boulder with a hollow surface, out of which a groove is made to allow the liquid metal to escape, and into which a hole is pierced for the purpose of introducing a current of air, they pile up a heap of charcoal and virgin ore, which they afterwards cover in such a way as to prevent the escape of heat. The bellows by which air is introduced are made of skins, the mouthpiece being the horn of a large antelope. The molten iron, escaping from the crude yet effective furnace, runs into clay moulds prepared to receive it, which are as nearly as possible of the same magnitude as the implements they wish to make. These are never of great size, the largest being the picks or heavy hoes used in gardening.

The smith, using a boulder for an anvil and a hammer of iron or stone, next proceeds to shape the lump of metal into an assagai head, an axe, a pick, or whatever is required. In this laborious operation a vast amount of patience and perseverance is exercised. The neatly grooved assagai heads of our own day are made of iron obtained in trade from the colonists, but their manufacture is still the same as it was a century ago. Now that all kinds of goods of European manufacture are to be had in every part of the country, native smelting furnaces are seldom seen, but there are a few rigid conservatives who scorn to depart from the customs of their ancestors, and who therefore still obtain their iron in the ancient manner. Before the arrival of Europeans the Bantu of the coast were also acquainted with copper, which they wrought into a variety of ornaments for their persons.

In the manufacture of wooden articles, such as spoons, bowls, fighting sticks, pipes, &c., they are tolerably expert. Each article is made of a single block of wood, requiring much time and patience to complete it, and upon it is frequently carved some simple pattern.

Skins for clothing are prepared by rubbing them for a length of time with grease, by which means they are made nearly as soft and pliable as cloth.

In their department the women are equally skilful. Earthenware vessels containing from half a pint to fifty gallons are constructed by them, some of which are almost as perfect in form as if they had been turned on a wheel. Though they are frequently not more than an eighth of an inch in thickness, they are so finely tempered that the most intense heat does not damage them. These vessels are used for beer pots, grain jars, and cooking utensils. The manufacture of earthenware vessels, however, bids fair to be lost

P 2

at no distant date. Already wooden casks have taken the place of the larger ones, as it has been found by experience that less labour is required to furnish the means of purchasing a cask than is needed to make a jar, and the one answers all the purposes of the other. Iron pots, too, are everywhere superseding the native cooking utensils.

Baskets for holding grain, rush mats, and grass bags are made by the women. The last are so carefully and strongly woven that they are used to hold water or any other liquid.

When not engaged in the trifling industries that have been mentioned, the men are habitual idlers. A great portion of their time is spent in visiting and gossip, of which they are exceedingly fond. They spend days together engaged in small talk, and are perfect masters of that kind of argument which consists in parrying a question by means of putting another. They pay very little regard to truth, and, though not pilferers, are inveterate cattle thieves. According to their ideas, cattle stealing is not a crime: it is a civil offence, and a thief when detected is compelled to make ample restitution; but no disgrace is attached to it, and they have no religious scruples concerning it.

Before the arrival of Europeans, the Southern Bantu had no knowledge of letters or of any signs by which ideas could be expressed. Their history is thus traditional, and can only be considered trustworthy for five or six generations. There are old men in every tribe who profess to be acquainted with the deeds of the past, but their accounts of events more than a century distant from their own birth seldom correspond in details. The genealogy of the great chiefs is preserved in all the tribes for twelve or fourteen generations.

The Kosa antiquaries give the line of descent of their great chiefs as follows: (1) Kosa (correct Kaffir spelling Xosa), (2) Malangana, (3) Nkoziyamtu, (4) Tshawe, (5) Ncwangu, (6) Sikomo, (7) Togu, (8) Gonde (correct Kaffir spelling Gconde), (9) Tshiwo, (10) Palo, (11) Galeka (correct Kaffir spelling Gcaleka), (12) Kawuta, (13) Hintsa, (14) Sarili, called by Europeans Kreli, the present chief.

Before the time of Nkoziyamtu there was a law that a chief might have as many wives as he chose, but only one son must be allowed to live. All the others were destroyed in infancy. Nkoziyamtu introduced the custom of the right hand wife, and thus preserved two sons alive. These were Cira, great son, and Jwara, right hand son.

A third, who was destined to surpass both his brothers in barbarian fame, was preserved by the flight of his mother to her father's people, the Abambo. Among them the boy, Tshawe by name, grew up, and proved himself so valiant that a large number of young men were given to him as followers by the chief, for he was known to be the son of Nkoziyamtu. At length he became desirous of visiting his father and showing him his greatness, so at the head of his followers and with immense herds of cattle he journeyed southward from Embo. On the way he was joined by many people whose only weapons were clubs and stones, and who were glad of the opportunity of ranging themselves under such a famous leader.

Upon arriving in the country of his father, he found that Nkoziyamtu was dead. His two brothers assembled their followers to oppose him, and a great battle took place, in which they were completely defeated, owing to Tshawe's original retainers being armed with assagais, weapons unknown before to the Amakosa. This battle established Tshawe's supremacy in the land, and he was joined thereafter by nearly all his father's people, though he still acknowledged the superiority in rank of Cira. As for Jwara, after the battle he wandered away with a few followers to the north, and died there.

This legend shows that very remote events may easily become grouped round a comparatively modern hero. The assagai was to a certainty in use by all the Bantu long before the time of Tshawe. In the Kosa folklore there are tales of people using stone weapons, which must have had their origin ages ago, for there cannot be a shadow of doubt that iron was known to the Southern Bantu before they broke up into the existing sections. But being aware that there was a time when their ancestors were unacquainted with that metal, and Tshawe being their great hero, they attributed its introduction to him. The Kosas are not alone in this respect, for there are other tribes in South Africa who have traditions in which the use of iron was made known to them by their most famous chief.

There is some corroborative evidence of the battle in which Tshawe was victorious, in traditions among the tribes north of the mountains of the defeat of Jwara and his subsequent wanderings. The traditions are dim and devoid of particulars, but the name of the chief has been preserved, together with the fact of his having been driven by war from his own country to die in exile.

Tshawe is the hero of many legends, and stands prominently out among the great ones of the misty past. The two chiefs before him are often omitted in the line of descent, and he is then termed the great one of Kosa's sons. He deserves, indeed, to be considered the real founder of the tribe, for in him the direct line of the great chiefs was lost. To this day all his descendants are of aristocratic rank in the Kosa tribe.

To Tshawe succeeded his son Ncwangu, and to him again Sikomo, of neither of whom is much known. The great son of Sikomo was Togu, during whose government according to tradition the tribe moved westward as far as the Kei. Here there is an opportunity of comparing tradition with contemporaneous records. Togu was the great chief of the Kosa tribe when the wrecked sailors of the *Stavenisse* were in his country, and they found an offshoot as far west as the mouth of the Buffalo. But that offshoot cannot have been a clan of any importance, for the closest inquiry made by and for the writer of this history from the recognised antiquaries of the tribe has failed to recover any trace of it or of a chief of the name given by the wrecked sailors. It may have been merely a small section of a clan driven out for a time by some petty feud.

The great son of Togu was Gonde, who died young, and left Tshiwo, great son, Umdange, right hand son, and Tinde, left hand son. The mother of Tinde was of Hottentot blood.

During the government of Tshiwo an event took place by which an individual who did not belong to the family of hereditary chiefs was raised to the rank of head of a clan. Among the Southern Bantu it often happens that an individual of considerable wealth is accused by a witchfinder of having caused some calamity. In the phraseology of the country such a person is 'smelt out.' He is allowed no opportunity to defend himself, but is kept quite unconscious of there being a charge against him. A party of executioners is sent, who fall upon the person accused, usually during the night, and kill him and his family. His cattle are taken to the chief, who reserves the greater number for himself, but allows the witchfinder and the executioners a share. In Tshiwo's time a succession of disasters was followed by an unusually large number of people being smelt out.

The principal attendant of the chief, who was generally entrusted with the duty of carrying out decisions in these cases, was a man named Kwane. Instead of literally obeying orders, Kwane was in the habit of allowing many of those to escape whom he was sent to destroy, and contenting himself with seizing their cattle. The fugitives took refuge with the Gonaqua tribe of Hottentots, by whom they were kindly received as being outcasts from their own people. On one occasion towards the close of his life, when Tshiwo was sore pressed and greatly in need of reinforcements, Kwane boldly presented himself at the head of a strong band of those whom he had saved, and tendered their services. Tshiwo was so delighted at receiving aid thus opportunely that he appointed Kwane to be chief with hereditary rights over the former fugitives. By this time these were so mixed in interests and family connections with the Gonaquas that separation was impracticable. The whole horde thereupon received Kwane as its chief, and was thenceforth regarded as a Kosa clan. In the time of Cungwa, third in descent from Kwane, we shall find it a formidable enemy of the colony. It had then entirely adopted the Kosa language and customs, and termed itself the Gunukwebe (correct Kaffir: Amagqunukwebe).

Tshiwo's great son Palo was not born until after his father's death. Gwali, Tshiwo's right hand son, was then in the prime of life, and being ambitious he attempted to make away with his brother. A portion of the tribe, however, rallied round the guardians of the infant chief, and Gwali was compelled to flee. With his own adherents and the Tinde clan he crossed the Kei and took refuge with a Hottentot chief named Hintsati, who resided near the site of the present village of Somerset East. Tradition points these out as the first compact bodies of Bantu to cross the Kei. The date was the year 1702. They were the people encountered by the European marauding party mentioned in chapter seventeen.

Gwali was received in a friendly manner by Hintsati, to whom he gave one of his sisters in marriage. After a long time an army was organised to follow him up. Hintsati's kraal was surrounded in the night, the chief was killed with many of his people, and his cattle were taken. The army at once commenced its return march, but was followed closely by the Hottentots. At the Koonap river it was overtaken, and an indecisive battle was fought. Further on, at the broad ford of the Keiskama, another engagement took place, and yet another on the Debe flats, where the Hottentots recovered many of their cattle.

About this time the clans terming themselves the Imidange and the Kosini (correct Kaffir: Amangqosini) crossed the Kei, and they have remained west of that river ever since.

The left hand son of Tshiwo was named Tiso. He died without issue, when Palo placed his son Langa at the head of the clan. This petty chief and his people crossed the Kei some time before the year 1740, and never returned. There had thus been for a considerable time a tendency on the part of the Kosa tribe to throw its offshoots over the Kei. These appear to have avoided a conflict with the Hottentots, who still occupied the greater portion of country on the right bank of that river, and even had outposts as far eastward as the Tsomo. There are no traditions of wars between them, but Kosa antiquaries cannot explain why they did not fight. It may have been that the migratory clans were regarded by the Hottentots as refugees, as was the case with the individuals who took shelter with the Gonaquas.

The great son of Palo was named Galeka. The right hand son, Rarabe, was a man of mature years when the great son attained his majority, and was in intellectual power the higher of the two. War between the brothers followed, and was waged with great bitterness. When the strife commenced, the principal sections of the tribe were beyond the Kei, and they alone took part in it. Numbers were on the side of Galeka, but skill on that of Rarabe. It was a natural consequence of a civil war of this kind that the weaker of the two combatants should endeavour to remove from the neighbourhood of the other. To the westward stretched a tract of country of unknown extent, inhabited by hereditary foes. In that direction Rarabe cast his eyes.

With a great body of followers, he reached the Kei, at the place now known as the lower drift, and found there a Hottentot army ready to dispute his passage. If half of what Kosa antiquaries relate of the action that followed be true, the Hottentots fought bravely and well. Each side pressed its foremost men against the enemy and compelled them thus to battle to the death. They met in the stream, which was soon so choked with corpses that its water was red with blood. At last, by sheer force of pressure, the Hottentots were driven back, and Rarabe won a footing on the western bank. But this success was so dearly bought that he preferred to negotiate rather than risk another such encounter, and so for a great number of cattle he purchased a tract of country between the head waters of the Keiskama and Buffalo rivers, including the Amatola mountains, from the wife and followers of the chief who had fallen in the struggle. The name of this Hottentot chieftainess was Hoho, and after her the Perie forest is still called by the Kosas 'the forest of Hoho.'

The Kosas soon acquired sole dominion as far as the Great Fish river, though many Hottentots held honourable positions among them, while matrimonial connections tended to obliterate all distinctions between the two races.

Native traditions agree with European records as to the recent advance westward of the Kosas. The exploring expedition of 1752 found the Keiskama the dividing line between the Bantu and the Hottentots, but in 1756 the hunter Dirk Marx reported that he met Kaffirs as far westward as the Great Fish river.

Rarabe, for a barbarian, was a man of considerable ability. He governed his people wisely, and was so greatly esteemed that his name was adopted and is still retained by all the Ciskeian Kosa clans, who term themselves Amararabe in distinction to the other branch of the tribe, which is known as the Amagaleka. He was the favourite son of his father Palo, who crossed the river and continued to reside near him until the death of the old chief, which occurred about the year 1770.

At this time Rarabe's paramount authority was recognised throughout the whole district between the Great Fish river and the Kei. But each clan had its own head, and these often acted in important matters without consulting him. The Imidange clan, under the chief Mahuta, was then the farthest western outpost of the tribe, occupying, as it did, the country along the right bank of the Koonap. Galeka, who usually resided beyond the Kei—though found by Europeans on one occasion on the right bank—was acknowledged in name as the head of the whole Kosa tribe; but practically the adherents of Rarabe were not in any way subject to his authority. Two generations later, the nominal head recovered considerable influence with the western section, but that was almost entirely owing to pressure by Europeans.

A few years after this date Rarabe died in battle. He had sent one of his daughters to be the wife of a Tembu chief, who returned only a hundred head of cattle. Rarabe was indignant that his daughter should be valued at so low a rate, and with his bravest warriors he marched against his son-in-law and attacked him. His forces were victorious, but he fell pierced with an assagai in the thickest of the fight. His son Ndlambe then became regent, as the heir in the great line was a minor.

The Kosa tribe at this time occupied, or rather was thinly scattered over, the country between the sea and the range of mountains of which the Winterberg and the Amatolas form part. North of that range as far east as the Tsomo river the only inhabitants were Hottentots and Bushmen. Beyond the Kosas, in the district between the Bashee and Umtata rivers, were the Tembus; but as it was not until 1827 that the colonists came in contact with this tribe, it is unnecessary to enter into their history in this chapter.

CHAPTER XXIV.

JOACHIM VAN PLETTENBERG, FISCAL AND SECUNDE, ACTING HEAD OF THE GOVERNMENT, 12 AUGUST 1771 TO 18 MAY 1774; GOVERNOR, INSTALLED 18 MAY 1774, RETIRED 14 FEBRUARY 1785.

Appointment of Mr. Van Oudtshoorn as governor—Death of that gentleman on the passage out—Appointment of Mr. Van Plettenberg as governor, Mr. Hemmy as secunde, and Advocate Boers as fiscal—Extension of the colony eastward—Erection of a new hospital—Exportation of Cape produce to the Netherlands and to India—Statistics of shipping—Trade with foreigners—Regulations regarding half-breed children born on farms—Petition of frontier colonists for a landdrost's court and a church—Visit of the governor to the eastern frontier—Meeting and arrangement with Kosa chiefs—Naming of Plettenberg's Bay—Naming of the Orange river by Captain Gordon—Extension of jurisdiction of the country courts—Declaration of the Fish river as the eastern boundary of the colony—Discovery of the Cango caverns—Character of the administration of Governor Van Plettenberg—Sending of a deputation by the colonists to the Netherlands to complain of the corruption and tyranny of the government—Action of the directors—Defence of the Cape officials—War between England and the Netherlands—Defenceless state of the colony—Constant warfare with Bushmen—War between the colonists and the Kosas—Sending of several return ships to Saldanha Bay to be out of danger—Expedition under Commodore Johnstone sent from England to seize the colony—Expedition under Admiral Suffren sent from France to oppose the English—Naval battle at Porto Praya—Arrival of the French fleet and troops at the Cape—Seizure by Commodore Johnstone of the Dutch ships in Saldanha Bay—Issue of paper money—Composition of the garrison at the Cape—Resignation of the fiscal Boers—Decision of the directors regarding the complaints of the colonists—Appeal of the colonists to the States-General of the Netherlands—Changes in the administration—Great damage sustained by the Company in the war with England—Increase of foreign shipping at the Cape—Distinguished visitors—Wrecks on the South African coast—Succession of clergymen in the various churches—Permission obtained by the Lutherans to establish a church—Succession of officers in the country districts.

JOACHIM VAN PLETTENBERG, who was elected by the council to act as head of the government until the pleasure of the directors could be known, had been educated as a lawyer, and had very little experience in any other employment. Before the death of Mr. Tulbagh was known in the Netherlands, the Prince of Orange, acting upon the nomination of the directors, appointed Mr. Pieter van Reede van Oudtshoorn secunde, as that gentleman had applied for employment again in South Africa, where some of his children were residing. It was then intended that Mr. Van Plettenberg should resume the duties of fiscal.

Despatches announcing the death of Mr. Tulbagh arrived from the Cape, however, before Mr. Van Oudtshoorn could leave Holland, and he then had the office of governor conferred upon him, Mr. Van Plettenberg being at the same time appointed secunde. This information was received at the Cape on the 4th of September 1772.

The newly appointed governor embarked in the ship *Asia*, but was taken ill at sea, and after nineteen days confinement to his bed, died on the 23rd of January 1773. His body was placed in a leaden coffin which he had taken on board with him, and a few days after the arrival of the ship was buried with state under the pavement of the church.

The Prince of Orange then, upon the nomination of the directors, appointed Mr. Van Plettenberg governor, Mr. Otto Luder Hemmy secunde, and Advocate Willem Cornelis Boers fiscal. The ceremony of installation of the new governor took place on the 18th of May 1774. Mr. Hemmy, who had previously filled the post of chief salesman, took over the duty of secunde some three weeks earlier. Advocate Boers, who was practising at the Hague when he received his appointment, did not arrive in the colony until the 10th of the following December. The office of master of the naval establishment had become vacant in April 1773, and the council had filled it provisionally by detaining here an energetic skipper, named Damien Hugo Staring, whose appointment was now confirmed by the supreme authorities.

The eastern boundary of the colony at this time was, according to the resolution of the council of policy, Bruintjes Hoogte and the Gamtoos river; but, in defiance of the prohibition of the 13th of February 1770, Europeans were [illegible] Villem [illegible] 1770 the [illegible] removed [illegible] Swellendam eastward to the [illegible] River [illegible] of Swellendam to the [illegible]'s River.

The boundary between the new portions of the two [illegible] was [illegible] fixed upon the mountain range [illegible] Zuurberg and parallel to the coast. The district of Swellendam was thus nearly defined on all sides [illegible] fixed limit on the north. [illegible] Kamdeboo, [illegible] mountain [illegible] about the sources of [illegible] mountains, and the Sneeuw- [illegible] for several years.

The ground upon which the new hospital was to stand [illegible] of Governor Tulbagh, [illegible] commenced. It was designed for the accommodation of [illegible] four hundred and fifty [illegible] for the medical officers and attendants, with [illegible]. The foundation stone was laid by Mr. Van Plettenberg on the 2nd of November 1772.

As most of the materials used in the construction of this building—now the military barracks—were sent from the Netherlands, the Directors, in a despatch dated 18th of October 1771, required the council to provide return cargoes of Cape produce for the ships bringing them out, provided produce of good quality could be had at reasonable rates. They complained of the high prices and inferior quality of various samples previously sent home, excepting wheat, and they therefore issued orders that the bulk of the cargoes should consist of that grain.

When these instructions arrived in South Africa, the French were laying in large supplies of meal, wine, and meat for their men-of-war and magazines at Mauritius, and the preceding harvest had not been quite as good as usual, so that prices were ruling high. In 1772 only one ship laden with materials for the Cape arrived, but she was a large one, and brought out reinforcements of troops also. The council found it would not be possible to get a full cargo for her, so they sent her to Batavia for orders, and prepared the Cape packet *Zon*, a vessel of about three hundred tons burden, to take produce to Europe. To obtain even this quantity, it was necessary to prohibit for a time the sale of grain to foreigners for exportation.

This first cargo of Cape produce sent to Holland consisted of 2,997 muids of wheat, purchased at 9*s.* 7⅛*d.* a muid free of the tithe; 37 muids of rye, purchased at 8*s.* 4⅛*d.* a muid; 222 muids of barley, purchased at 4*s.* 9⅜*d.* a muid; 32 leggers of assorted wines, for which the farmers were paid from 5*l.* 8*s.* to 13*l.* 8*s.* a legger according to quality; and 5,300 pounds of tallow, purchased at 20*s.* the hundred pounds. On arrival at Amsterdam, the wheat was sold at 16*s.* 2*d.* to 16*s.* 6*d.* a muid, and the wine at 11*l.* 16*s.* to 48*l.* 19*s.* a legger. These profits were so satisfactory to the directors that they resolved to continue the importation of South African produce, especially as the Cape government wrote that purchases would in future be made at much lower rates.

From this date until the commencement of the war with England, a period of nine years, a quantity of Cape produce was yearly sent to the Netherlands. In 1777 the grain crop was very poor, owing to a severe drought, and after the requirements of the Company in India had been met, on wheat could be spared, but the usual quantity of wine was forwarded. The average exportation to Europe during these nine years, 1772–1780, was 15 leggers Constantia wine, 93 leggers ordinary wines, 10,714 muids of wheat, 23,800 pounds of tallow, and 3,614 pounds of aloes. Small quantities of brandy, rye, barley, vegetable wax, oxhides, sheepskins, coarse wool, skins of wild animals, and leather were also sent to Europe, but neither regularly nor of sufficient value to need further notice.

During these nine years the average export to India was 14,419 muids of wheat, 180 muids of rye, 66 muids of barley, 37 muids of beans, 100 muids of peas, 296 leggers of wine, 13,613 pounds of butter, 11,555 pounds of tallow, and 1,183 pounds of ivory. Some dried and preserved fruits, mustard seed, peltries, and leather, though not to any great value, were also exported to India.

The increase of exports above those of previous years did not, however, cause increased prosperity to the colonists. The prices paid by the Company were ruinously low. For the wheat sent to India the farmers received only 8*s*.9⅝*d* and for that sent to Europe only 5*s*. 11¼*d*. a muid, after the government dues were deducted. The butter was bought at 6*d*. to 8*d*., and the tallow at about 2*d*. a pound.

At the same time there was a constant demand for all kinds of farm produce at more than double the prices which the Company was giving. In the year 1772 there was a sudden and great increase in the foreign shipping that put into South African ports, and the number of vessels did not fall off again until the commencement of the war with England. During these nine years, 1772–1780, there put into Table Bay 418 Dutch ships, 159 English, 192 French, 41 Danish, 7 Swedish, 16 Spanish, 9 Portuguese, and 3 Austrian; and into Simon's Bay 47 Dutch, 85 English, 46 French, 17 Danish, 1 Austrian, and 6 Swedish ships; or, on an average, 52 Dutch ships and 65 under various other flags touched yearly at the two ports.

All of them needed fresh provisions. Some of the French vessels, indeed, were sent there from Mauritius expressly to obtain cargoes of grain, meat, and wine; and occasionally an English vessel arrived from St. Helena for the same purpose. The directors admitted that they should be encouraged to call, as they brought ready money into the country and increased the revenue. Owing to them, the contract for the supply of meat to the Company could now be taken at less than ½*d.* a pound, for the contractor had the privilege of charging foreigners 2*d.* The farmer of the duty of 1*l.* a legger on wine and spirits sold to foreigners for exportation could now afford to pay nearly 1,000*l.* a year for it. The licensed retail dealer in wines and spirits could afford to bid 1,000*l.* a year more for his monopoly. The average production of wine was 3,244 leggers, and the Company needed only 945 leggers for its own use and for sale in Europe and India. The directors were therefore only too glad to know that the surplus could be sold at high rates at the Cape. They protected their own trade, however, for in 1776 when some burghers requested to be allowed to export wine to Holland, they declined to give permission.

With grain it was different. As much of this as could be produced could be sold at a profit, and it therefore became a matter for calculation to get as large a quantity as possible without driving foreigners away. The fiscal took control of the trade, and permitted nothing to be sold to strangers without his leave. The burghers protested against this infringement of their rights, but to no purpose.

The number of male slaves imported was always much larger than that of females, and as a consequence many of those men who were unable to obtain wives of their own colour had formed connections with Hottentot women. A large class of halfbreeds had sprung from such unions, and these were generally indisposed to gain a living by honest industry. From early times it had been observed that Hottentot women who formed connections with either Europeans or slaves had many more children than those who took husbands of their own race. The farmers could not prevent their union with slaves, for if they tried to do so the slaves were certain to run away. And if they permitted the women to remain on the farms, directly or indirectly they were obliged to maintain them and their offspring, without any return in labour.

These circumstances gave rise to a regulation which was first put in force in 1775, and which provided that children born of Hottentot mothers by slave fathers upon attaining the age of eighteen months should be apprenticed to the owner of the farm on which they were living until they were twenty-five years old. In every case a formal application to the board of landdrost and heemraden of the district was to be made by the owner of the farm, and a register of all apprenticeships was to be kept by the secretary of the board. Hottentot mothers were to be at liberty to remove their children under eighteen months of age. The apprentices were to be properly fed and clothed, and were to be otherwise well treated.

In February 1776 a despatch was received, announcing that the governor had been raised to the dignity of councillor extraordinary of Netherlands India. In January 1777 the secunde Hemmy died. The council met on the 1st of February to elect an acting successor, when the fiscal Boers, to whom the post was offered, declined to accept it. Pieter Hacker, who had long been in service at the Cape and then filled the situation of master of the winestores, was thereupon chosen, and his appointment as secunde was shortly afterwards confirmed by the directors. He was succeeded as master of the winestores by Jacobus Johannes le Sueur.

In October 1777 the surveyor Hieronymus Leiste was sent to inspect the country as far as it was occupied by Europeans, and to frame a map. He returned in January following, having made but slight acquaintance with the interior.

In March 1778 a petition was sent to the council by Jan Kruger, Jan Adriaan Venter, Adriaan van Jaarsveld, Jan Oosthuizen, and thirty other heads of families living near the eastern frontier, praying for the establishment of a landdrost's court and a church in that part of the country.

This petition, together with Leiste's report and the

numerous accounts of depredations by the Bushmen, caused the governor to resolve upon visiting the eastern border and ascertaining for himself the condition of affairs there. Four months before he intended to set out, orders were issued to the landdrosts of Stellenbosch and Swellendam to have burgher escorts and cattle ready to forward him on his journey.

On the 3rd of September 1778 he left Cape Town with two travelling and four baggage waggons, taking with him the junior merchant Olof Godlieb de Wet as secretary, the surgeon Johan Michiel Seyd as medical attendant, and the captain Christiaan Philip van Heyden as purveyor and conductor of the train. He travelled by way of the Berg river valley, through the Roodezand kloof, down the valley of the Breede river, past Swellendam, and onward to the Little Fish river, somewhere near the present village of Somerset East. The journal of this important expedition is unfortunately missing from the Cape archives, and it is only from statements in other documents of the time that the chief events can be gathered.

The governor met the frontier farmers who had petitioned for a landdrost and a clergyman, and made himself acquainted with their condition. They represented that owing to the unbridged rivers it was often a journey of a month to the village of Stellenbosch, so that practically they were cut off from a court of justice. It was also a matter of great hardship to them to attend the militia exercises in that village, as during their absence from home their stock was subject to depredations by Bushmen. For the same reason they were unable to attend the church services, and their children were growing up without proper instruction. They were willing to contribute liberally towards the expense of erecting the necessary buildings. The governor admitted that their request was reasonable, and promised to recommend it favourably to the directors, a promise which was fulfilled upon his return to Cape Town, though it was not immediately attended to in Holland.

He also had a conference with several Kosa chiefs, and

arranged with them that the Fish river should be a boundary between the Europeans and the Bantu. Whether these chiefs were men of high position in their tribe it is impossible to say, as their names cannot be recovered.

He proceeded northward to the Zeekoe river, and on the bank of this stream he caused a beacon to be erected to mark the termination of his tour and the north-eastern limit of the colony.

On the 3rd of November the governor was at the bay into which the Keurboom river falls. To this bay he gave his own name, and caused a landmark with the Company's arms upon it to be erected as a sign of possession. The stone is still standing where it was set up. On the 26th of November the party arrived in Cape Town again, having been absent nearly three months.

An officer whose name was to be closely connected with South Africa during the next eighteen years was on the frontier at the same time as the governor. This was Captain Robert Jacob Gordon, previously an officer in the Scotch regiment under Colonel Dundas in the service of the United Provinces, but who had recently been engaged by the East India Company, and had arrived at the Cape on the 1st of June 1777. At this time he was second in command of the garrison, the chief military officer being Lieutenant-Colonel Van Prehn.

In October 1777 Captain Gordon left Cape Town in company with Lieutenant William Paterson, an English traveller, on a journey of exploration. He proceeded by way of the Sneeuwberg to the Great river, which he came upon quite unexpectedly somewhere near the twenty-sixth meridian from Greenwich. He travelled for a day along its southern bank in search of a ford, but did not find one, so was unable to cross. From the summit of a hill he observed that the river was formed by the junction of two streams, at no great distance to the eastward. Lieutenant Paterson had returned to the Cape, in ill health, some time before.

Two years later the same gentlemen made another journey

together, this time travelling northward through Little Namaqualand to the mouth of the great river. Captain Gordon had taken a boat with him, which he placed on the stream, so that he had now a much better opportunity for examining the immense flow of water than in 1777, when he had seen it at a point inland nearly six hundred miles distant. On the 17th of August 1779 he hoisted the Dutch colours to a staff in his boat, and while floating in the centre of the stream he named it the Orange, in honour of the stadtholder. He and Lieutenant Paterson examined it from the mouth upwards some thirty or forty miles. Since that date geographers have usually called the river by the name which Captain Gordon gave it, but the colonists term it indiscriminately the Orange, Great, and Gariep.

In 1779 the jurisdiction of the courts of landdrost and heemraden was enlarged, owing to the difficulty of bringing cases from distant parts for trial before the court of justice in Cape Town. Henceforth civil cases in which the amount in dispute was less than 10*l.* were summarily decided in these courts.

Governor Van Plettenberg had arranged with some Kosa chiefs that the Fish river should not be crossed by either Europeans or Bantu, but this agreement had not been officially recorded. On the 14th of November 1780, however, the council of policy resolved that the Fish river along the whole of its lower course should be the colonial boundary, thus adding to the Company's possessions the tract of country then usually known as the Zuurveld, now the districts of Albany and Bathurst.

In 1780 the Cango caverns, in the present district of Oudtshoorn, were accidentally discovered by a farmer named Van Zyl, who was out hunting. They are of great size, passages having been explored for at least a mile into the mountain, without the end being reached, while on each side openings of unknown depth occur at short intervals. The stalactites in some of the chambers present a very grand appearance when seen by the light of numerous torches. Being saturated with water, they are semi-transparent and of dazzling brightness, while they present innumerable varieties of fanciful and grotesque forms. One of the chambers is eight hundred feet in length, another six hundred feet in length, one hundred in breadth, and sixty to seventy in height.

Ever since the accession of Mr. Van Plettenberg to power there had been a feeling of discontent throughout the colony. There was no sympathy between the governor and the people. If his proclamations be compared with those of his predecessor, and judgment be formed by them alone, the administration of Mr. Tulbagh will be pronounced the harsher of the two. Yet in reality not only was the reverse the case, but a period of misrule had succeeded a period of tranquillity. Governor Tulbagh had kept a watchful eye upon every official, and allowed no one to overstep the directions concerning farming and trading, or to take a fee that he was not entitled to. Governor Van Plettenberg permitted his subordinates to do almost as they chose. The result was a condition of affairs in which no transaction with government could be carried on without bribery, in which many of the officials farmed and traded openly, and the colonists generally became discontented.

From the earliest days of the settlement the government had claimed and exercised the right of sending out of the country persons of bad character, especially those of idle and dissolute habits. During the forty years from 1738 to 1778 thirty-three individuals were thus deported, without a trial before a court of justice. In some instances the burgher councillors or the heemraden requested that a vagabond of some kind should be removed, in other instances notorious offenders were thus summarily disposed of. Governor Tulbagh, during the twenty years that he was head of the colony, had sent away ten. Governor Van Plettenberg in less than eight years sent away eighteen.

The fiscal was detested as few men in South Africa have been, and instead of being a check upon the governor, he was held to be the worse of the two. His control of trade with foreigners opened a door to extensive bribery. The system of paying higher prices at the Company's stores for produce sent to India than for that sent to Europe led also to serious abuses.

The American revolution had commenced, and tidings came over the sea of other colonists resisting rulers who oppressed them. In distant farmhouses and in dwellings in Cape Town the question of rights and liberties was discussed as it had never been before. By some of the least educated very wild views were enunciated, views subversive of all government; but the great majority of the people favoured a strong administration, provided it was honest. Party feeling began to run very high. The junior officials were mostly either colonists by birth or married into colonial families, so that the existing system had its defenders. There was a large party loyal to the Netherlands, but desirous of a change from a bad to a good government, and there was a small party ready to plunge into anarchy, without understanding what they were advocating.

Matters were in this state when the fiercest passions of the burghers were roused by an act of the government as imprudent as it was tyrannical. A man named Carel Hendrik Buitendag, who had been living in the Land of Waveren, had recently come to reside in the town. This man was addicted to intemperance, and when partly intoxicated was very violent in his conduct. He was married into a respectable colonial family, but his treatment of his wife and of his Hottentot servants was at times so brutal that when he was residing at Waveren the landdrost and heemraden of Stellenbosch and Drakenstein petitioned the council of policy for his forcible removal. No action was taken upon this petition, nor was any immediate notice taken of an application to the fiscal by his wife to be separated from him, made during one of his outbursts of intemperance.

Twenty days later, however,—20th of January 1779,—when he was conducting himself properly and the domestic quarrel had been forgotten, he was seized in his own house by order of the fiscal, dragged hurriedly through the streets by the lowest menials of the law, and sent on board the *Honkoop*, a vessel lying in the bay and bound to Batavia. His wife and children followed to the beach, crying and imploring help, but there was not time to effect a rescue. The persons employed by the fiscal to arrest Buitendag and convey him to the ship's boat were the black scavengers of the town, who were used to take drunken slaves to prison. Hardly any act of oppression could have wounded the burghers so deeply as this, for pride of race was part of their nature.

On his arrival at Batavia, Buitendag complained of his treatment to the council of India, by whom permission was given him to return to the Cape. He therefore embarked in the first ship that left, but died during the passage.

The deportation of Buitendag in the manner here related brought on a crisis. The most respectable burghers consulted together, and came to a determination to send delegates to the Netherlands to endeavour to obtain from the stadtholder and the directors redress of their grievances and guarantees against future misgovernment. Then for the first time in the history of the colony was discussed the right of the people to have representatives in the legislature, and the theory rapidly gained ground that such representation would prove the best safeguard of liberty.

At the sitting of the council of policy on the 30th of March 1779 a letter was read from the three burgher councillors, Cornelis van der Poel, Christiaan George Maasdorp, and Gerrit Hendrik Meyer, and four of the heemraden of Stellenbosch and Drakenstein, Philip Albert Myburgh, Jan de Villiers, Joost Rynhard van As, and Hendrik Louw, stating that they had been requested by between three and four hundred burghers to apply for permission to elect some persons to be sent to Holland to lay before the directors the condition of affairs in this colony, and asking leave to do so. The council refused its consent, but asserted its willingness to consider any complaints made to it and to redress any grievances that could be shown to exist.

The opponents of the government were not satisfied with this decision, because they had no confidence in the men who were at the head of affairs. They made no further applications to the council therefore, but elected the burghers Jacobus van Reenen, Barend Jacob Artois, Tieleman Roos, and Nicholas Godfried Heyns as their representatives to proceed to Europe. These persons drew up a memorial of grievances and proposed remedies, which received the approval of their constituents. It was dated the 7th of May 1779. The four delegates then proceeded to Holland, carrying with them a document authorising them to act for the persons who signed it, four hundred and four in number. The memorial contained thirty-seven clauses. The first part was devoted to accusing the officers of government, and particularly the independent fiscal Willem Cornelis Boers, of fraudulent conduct and oppression. Many of the junior officials were accused of trading so openly that shops were kept and accounts made out in their names. The burghers of the town who lived by commerce, it was asserted, could not compete with these traders, and were consequently being ruined. The whole system of exacting fees by the various officials on almost every business transaction was explained, and the individuals receiving them were charged with corruption. But in this the complainants laboured under the same difficulties that those must always do who are ignorant of the confidential instructions of the heads of a government to subordinates. They supposed that the receipt of fees except in certain well-known cases was unauthorised, whereas in reality the various officials were empowered to charge certain amounts, and could in justice only be accused of corruption when these amounts were exceeded.

The complainants asked that the orders issued in 1706 prohibiting officials from farming or dealing in farm produce should be strictly enforced; that the burghers should be allowed to dispose of the produce of the country to strangers, without first obtaining the consent of the fiscal; that persons banished from the colony should be sent to the Fatherland, not to India; that the burghers should be at liberty to punish their slaves without the necessity of first applying to the fiscal; that the laws of the country should be clearly defined and made known; that seven burgher members should have seats in the council of policy, and that these members should send a report upon the colony yearly to the Assembly of Seventeen; that the high court of justice should consist of equal numbers of officials and burghers; that there should be a right of appeal to the courts of the Fatherland, instead of to the court at Batavia; that the burghers should be allowed to trade with the Netherlands to the extent of one or two ships' cargoes yearly; that they should also be allowed free trade with India and in slaves with Madagascar and the east coast of Africa; that the Company should purchase ordinary wine at 8*l.* a legger, from which nothing should be deducted but 12*s.* government dues; that foreigners should not be allowed to travel about the country; that a smaller rental than 4*l.* 16*s.* should be charged on farms of inferior quality; and that more churches should be provided.

On the 16th of October 1779 the four delegates appeared before the Assembly of Seventeen. They made a verbal statement of the wretched condition of the colony and the unjust acts of the officials, and delivered the memorial with a large number of documents supporting it. In the following week the whole of the papers were referred to a committee of the chambers of Amsterdam and Zeeland to examine, collect evidence, and report upon. A copy of the memorial and its annexures was sent to the Cape for the various officers concerned to reply to. The directors at the same time wrote expressing their great regret that there should be an ill feeling between the colonists and the officials, and hoping that tranquillity would be speedily restored. They expressed a desire for the prosperity of the colonists, and commanded that everything that was possible should be done to allay strife. They would be greatly displeased, they said, if any resentment were shown, directly or indirectly, towards those who had signed the memorial.

Governor Van Plettenberg's reply is dated the 21st of March 1781. He did not think the memorial could be taken to represent the views of the whole body of colonists, as there were nearly three thousand burghers in the country, and the delegates had been chosen by only four hundred and four. It had always been a custom for the government to consult the acting and retired burgher councillors whenever it was requisite to make regulations affecting the colonists, and he had not failed on any occasion to do so. The country presented every appearance of prosperity. There was no difference observable between wealthy and poor people, all showed signs of being in comfortable circumstances. Numbers of the Company's servants, who had the condition of affairs before their eyes, were yearly taking their discharge and becoming colonists, in preference to returning to Europe.

On the frontiers, he stated, the people were less fortunately placed, for they were exposed to depredations from Bushmen and Kosas, and had suffered greatly by recent inroads of the savages. With them money was not plentiful, but following the example of Mr. Tulbagh and others of his predecessors, he had usually taken three young bullocks instead of the 4*l.* 16*s.* yearly rent for each of their farms.

Tho colonists in general, he affirmed, desired to lead an indolent life, merely directing the labour of Hottentots and slaves. They were not disposed to qualify themselves either as mechanics or as schoolmasters, in proof of which there were then nearly two hundred of the Company's soldiers on leave earning their living in these capacities; and more had been applied for, but he had refused to allow a larger number to be temporarily released from duty. The colony furnished no seamen, though many of those who complained of poverty could obtain a living in the fleets. They preferred, however, to depend upon a single industry, the chief profits from which were precarious, being derived from foreign ships. Their right to trade in the products of the country was undisputed. The interests of the officials and the burghers were the same, for with few exceptions they were intermarried, most of the junior officials indeed being members of colonial families.

He objected to the admission of burgher members to the council of policy. The interests of the colony should not be lost sight of by the government, but those of the Company were to be regarded as of greater importance. If there were burgher members in the council, everything that the government did for the colonists would be attributed to them, and the Company would lose favour. There would also be constant strife, owing to the divisions among the burgher population. The request of the complainants that the high court of justice should consist of equal numbers of officials and burghers he recommended should be acceded to. He also favoured their petition that the laws should be clearly defined, and stated that the collection of the placaats for that purpose had already been commenced.

He protested that he had done nothing to draw upon himself the enmity of the colonists. He thought the position of high officials would be greatly improved if the suspicion of corrupt dealing were removed by giving them suitable salaries and depriving them of perquisites. The principal perquisite of the governor and the secunde was 1*l.* 6*s.* 8*d.* for the first and 13*s.* 4*d.* for the second on every legger of wine sold by the burghers to the Company. The seller was obliged to sign a receipt for 8*l.*, whereas he only received 5*l.* 8*s.*, the remaining 12*s.* being the government duty. It could make no difference to the Company, and be much better in appearance, if a receipt for only 5*l.* 8*s.* were demanded. The other perquisites of the governor he thought there could be no objection to. They were, first, the produce of the farm Visser's Hok, which farm had from early times been cultivated at the Company's expense for the express purpose of supplying the governor's household with grain and his stable with forage; second, the contractor for meat was required to supply him with twelve sheep monthly and such other meat as he might require for his household at the same price as was paid by the Company.

In conclusion, he requested to be relieved of his duties.

Party feeling was running very high in the colony, he said, and only an entire stranger could restore concord.

The document containing the comments of the fiscal upon the memorial of the complaining burghers is dated 2nd of February 1781, and is of great length. Mr. Boers was a man with many good qualities. He was hospitable, generous, diligent in his duties, fond of scientific pursuits. But his sympathies were all with the ruling classes of society, and he felt and expressed supreme contempt for the colonists, who were to him simply unlettered peasants.

For more than a century the burgher councillors had been consulted by the government whenever enactments affecting the colonists were in contemplation. They had no taxing powers, but upon their recommendation the council of policy levied rates which they collected and applied to the construction and maintenance of roads and bridges, the employment of watchmen, and other purposes now provided for by divisional and municipal councils. They proposed maximum prices for articles, inspected weights and measures, and performed a great variety of other duties. In numberless instances they had appeared before the authorities as the representatives of the burgher community. Yet Mr. Boers maintained that their sole functions were those of assistant members of the high court of justice when cases in which colonists were concerned were being tried, and in support of his contention he quoted the terms of the appointment of the first burgher councillor by the commissioner Van Goens in 1657. Long usage did not affect the question in his eyes.

He admitted that the right of the farmers to free trade in the produce of their land had been recognised by the supreme authorities. But he pleaded that the circumstances of the country were such that the channel in which the trade should flow must be pointed out by the government. The farmers here, he said, were like those in Europe, always eager to make large profits, and were unwilling to sell to the Company when they could get higher prices from foreigners. If no restraint were put upon them, the country might often be in danger of famine, and the consequences might be very serious, for food could not be imported in time to avert starvation. On this account it had on more than one occasion been found necessary to prohibit for a time the sale of grain and cattle to foreigners. The governors De Chavonnes and Tulbagh had been obliged to do so. For this reason, and also to collect the export duty of 1*l.* and the licensed dealer's dues of 1*l.* on every legger of wine and his own fee of 1*s.* 4*d.* on every hundred pounds of grain or meal supplied to foreigners, he had prohibited the sale of anything without his permission. The burghers talked about the law of free trade, he begged to state that there was also a law prohibiting foreigners from selling anything at the Cape, yet it was never observed.

The colonists prated of their rights. Who were these colonists? he asked. A parcel of people who had been released from the Company's service, and permitted as an act of grace to live in the country, under condition that they could be ordered back into service at the will of the government. He quoted the wording of a certificate of permission to a discharged soldier to reside in the country, and argued that as no one could transmit greater rights than he himself possessed, the descendants of released soldiers were in the same condition as their ancestors. He quite ignored the fact that a very large proportion of the colonists were descendants of immigrants who had never been in the Company's service.

A document of great length was drawn up by Mr. Boers in this strain. The other officials who were accused of wrong-doing also drew up statements, admitting some of the charges, denying some, and endeavouring to explain away the remainder. The transmission of these papers to the Netherlands was delayed, however, for several months by the cessation of the ordinary traffic.

On the 31st of March 1781 the French frigate *Silphide* arrived in Table Bay with a despatch from the Dutch ambassador at Paris, announcing that on the 20th of the preceding December Great Britain had declared war with the United

Provinces, and that the States were in alliance with France. The intelligence was received with alarm by the government, for the mother country no longer occupied the proud position among nations which was hers a century earlier, and it was certain that England was casting longing eyes upon the Cape, as the key of the Indian seas.

The colony was almost defenceless. Its revenue was between 15,000*l.* and 16,000*l.* a year. For a long time the balance of expenditure over revenue had averaged 25,000*l.* a year, and the Company, which was declining in wealth and power, could not afford to maintain a large garrison. There were five hundred and thirty soldiers of all arms on the books, but to save expense, more than one-fourth of these had been allowed to take service with farmers, and it was pretty certain that many would never return to their colours. There were further some six hundred and fifty individuals in the Company's pay, including the civil servants, the mechanics at the workshops, the boating establishment, and convalescent sailors. Next there was a corps of free blacks, which had been in existence for many years, and which was usually drilled for a few days in the month of October. From these sources combined about eleven hundred combatants could be counted upon, of whom only one half were well drilled.

At the head of the military forces proper was Captain Gordon, who in February 1780 had succeeded Lieutenant-Colonel Van Prehn as commandant of the garrison. He was a man of unblemished character, an enthusiast in the study of natural history, and an ardent explorer, but with no special qualifications as a leader in war. Next to him in rank was Captain Carel Matthys Willem de Lille, who had been in the colony since December 1773. The seamen and mechanics were under command of the old skipper Staring, as brave a man as ever sailed the sea, but so deeply implicated in the prevailing peculations that he was greatly disliked by the colonists.

The Company relied chiefly upon the burghers to protect the country, but the South African militia, though nearly three thousand strong on paper, could not furnish a fourth of that number of men for the defence of Cape Town. These three thousand burghers were scattered over an immense area, covering not less than ninety or a hundred thousand square miles. Along the frontier, east and north, they were constantly in arms to hold their own against Kosas and Bushmen, to whom their flocks and herds presented an irresistible temptation to plunder.

The struggle between the farmers along the northern border and the Bushmen had become almost incessant. The two races could not live side by side. Occasionally white men, obliged to defend themselves without aid of soldiers or police, committed acts almost equalling in cruelty those of their savage opponents. Yet without violence the country could not be held. All the philanthropic efforts of the present century, supported by a strong police, have not succeeded in establishing a single Bushman community in a civilised mode of life.

The method of conducting warfare against these savages needed no knowledge of complicated military movements. There were probably many contests between farmers and Bushmen of which the government never heard. Those that are recorded, however, give very plain pictures of what was taking place.

In May 1772 a letter was received from the landdrost of Stellenbosch, giving information that a party of Bushmen on the border of the Roggeveld had murdered a burgher named Hendrik Teutman, his wife and daughter, and a servant of Adriaan Louw; and that they had driven off the cattle from several farms. The field corporal Willem van Wyk raised a commando, followed the marauders to a mountain, and besieged a cave in which they took shelter, but was unable to capture it. He then wrote to the landdrost for help. The council of policy resolved to send a corporal and five grenadiers, with a supply of hand grenades, to aid him. A party of Hottentots was also engaged to assist, and upon the arrival of these reinforcements the cave was stormed. Six Bushmen were killed, and fifty-eight of both sexes, great and small, were captured. The prisoners were forwarded under escort to the Cape, where they arrived on the 27th of June. After some delay the men were brought to trial before the high court of justice, and on the 31st of December sentence was passed. One was broken alive on a wheel; one was hanged; four were flogged, had the tendons of their heels severed, and were kept to hard labour for life; and three were flogged and kept to hard labour for life. The women and children were distributed as servants for periods varying in duration.

In October of the same year the landdrost of Stellenbosch reported that a party of Bushmen had stolen eighty-eight head of cattle from the burgher Gerrit van Wyk. Thereupon a commando assembled, followed up the robbers, shot thirty-one of them, and recovered thirty-nine of the cattle.

Despite of such punishment, the Bushmen seemed to become constantly bolder, and at length they did not fear to attack farmhouses in open day. Horned cattle, sheep, and goats were driven off in hundreds together, the herdsmen were murdered, and from several localities the Europeans were obliged to retire. In May 1774 the council of policy approved of the appointment by the board of militia of Stellenbosch of Godlieb Rudolph Opperman, a burgher of long experience and recognised ability, as field commandant of the whole northern border from Piketberg to Sneeuwberg, and operations were planned with a view of punishing the marauders and restoring the farmers to the places from which they had been driven.

The Hottentots and halfbreeds were just as anxious as the colonists to chastise the Bushmen, for they had suffered equally from their attacks. The Hottentots indeed were more embittered than the others, for many of them had lost all their cattle and had besides to lament friends and relatives put to death by torture. Some of the Hottentots were living in reserves, under captains recognised by the Cape government, and were not subject to colonial courts of law except in cases affecting white people. The tract of land called Lily Fontein, in the Kamiesberg, where an important Wesleyan mission was founded in the early years of the present century, for instance, was a reserve secured to the Hottentot captain Wildschut and his people by Governor Van Plettenberg in 1772. Others of this race were living with the colonists, either in charge of herds of cattle or as domestic servants. As many as were needed joined the burghers on the expedition against the common enemy, and were provided with firearms and ammunition.

At the beginning of summer three parties of mixed burghers, halfbreeds, and Hottentots, acting in concert, took the field under Commandant Opperman and the field corporals Nicholas van der Merwe and Gerrit van Wyk. The base of operations was more than three hundred miles in length. The country along the great mountain range of South Africa was scoured, and all the Bushmen found who would not surrender were shot. According to the reports furnished to the government, five hundred and three were killed and two hundred and thirty-nine taken prisoners. Some of these were afterwards released, and others were apprenticed to the farmers for a term of years. Only one European was killed during the operations. From the leader of one party of Bushmen a promise was obtained to keep the peace and abstain from robbery, and to him presents were made as proofs of a desire for friendship. The instance, however, was a solitary one.

It was hoped that the punishment inflicted by the expedition would deter the Bushmen from continuing hostilities, but it had no such effect. They became even more troublesome than before, and year after year it was necessary to call out commandos against them. Thus it often happened that the farmers were unable to attend the musters for drill, which took place at the drostdies yearly in October. They had come to regard these musters as vexatious taxes upon their time, and military drill as useless in their circumstances. The men of the northern border considered their first duty to be the protection of their families against savages, and hardly gave a thought to the Company's interests at the remote seat of government.

On the eastern border matters were in a similar condition.

The colonists there had to deal with the advanced clans of the Kosa tribe, a people who might be called civilised when compared with Bushmen, but who were almost as expert stocklifters.

In 1779 the Imidange under the chief Mahuta, the Amambala under the chief Langa, and some other clans of less note crossed the Fish river and spread themselves over the present districts of Somerset East and Albany. Some persons asserted that the Europeans had provoked the Kosas to invade the colony. There was a story in circulation that old Willem Prinsloo, of the Boschberg, had exasperated the Imidange by shooting one of them whom he caught in the act of stealing a sheep, and by seizing some of their cattle to make good his losses. There was another story that Marthinus Prinsloo, a son of the former, had gone across the Keiskama with a party trading for cattle in defiance of the prohibitions of the government, and had there in a quarrel killed one of Rarabe's immediate retainers. It was stated also that a petty chief named Koba, who was one of those that agreed to the Fish river being the boundary, having crossed over to the colonial side, was driven back again by the colonists with unnecessary violence. It is impossible now to say whether these reports were true or not. They were put in circulation by men who were certainly biassed in favour of the Kaffirs, and the explanations of the Prinsloos, if any were ever given, are not to be found.

The official reports were to the effect that the first parties who crossed the Fish river said they did not want to quarrel with the Europeans, but they had a feud with the Gunukwebe clan, and these, having taken shelter behind the colonists on the Bushman's river, sent out parties to lift their cattle. To prove the truth of their assertions, they murdered a number of Hottentots and took their cattle, without molesting the colonists. But shortly they began to drive off the herds of the white people also, and on the 27th of September 1779 the field corporal Jan Hermanus Potgieter sent a report that the farmers of the Zuurveld or the present districts of Albany and Bathurst, together with those along the right bank of the Bushman's river, had been obliged to withdraw to a place of greater safety.

The same tactics that have been practised by the Kosas in every subsequent struggle with the colony were used in this, the first Kaffir war. Rarabe sent a message to the nearest European outpost, to the effect that the clans committing the depredations were rebels, and that he would be glad to receive assistance against them. The colonists, as yet without experience of Bantu duplicity, believed Rarabe's statement, though some of his immediate followers were among the plunderers.

During the summer of 1779–80 two commandos took the field for the purpose of expelling the intruders. One, composed of the farmers from both sides of Bruintjes Hoogte, was under command of Josua Joubert. The refugees from the Zuurveld and their friends west of the Bushman's river formed the other, which was commanded by Pieter Hendrik Ferreira. The Imidange were attacked and defeated on several occasions, when a considerable number of their cattle were taken; but they were not entirely driven to their own side of the Fish river.

During the winter those who had been apparently subdued crossed again into the colony, accompanied by many others, and it became evident that a grand effort must be made to expel them. On the 24th of October 1780 the council of policy, at the request of the district courts, appointed Adriaan van Jaarsveld field commandant of the eastern frontier, and gave him military authority over the whole of the border farmers. There was no man in the country better qualified for the post than he. Accustomed from his earliest boyhood to warfare with savages, compelled to be ever ready to defend his family and his flocks from marauders, he knew exactly how to act in an emergency of this kind. He had retired to Bruintjes Hoogte from the Sneeuwberg in 1776 to be free of depredations by Bushmen, and he was resolved not to move again if he could by any means hold his own.

On the 14th of November the council of policy resolved that as the Kaffirs had not kept their agreement with the governor to respect the Fish river as the boundary, the commandant should be authorised to expel them by force. On the 5th of December instructions were issued for his guidance, in which he was directed to endeavour to come to an amicable arrangement with the intruders, on the basis of their retirement across the Fish river and a mutual restoration of all cattle captured. If they would consent to this proposal, the commandant was to take care that no European molested them or thereafter entered their country for any purpose, and he was not to interfere in the feuds between the clans. But if they declined, he was to assemble an armed force and drive them over the river.

Early in the summer the old chief Langa, brother of Rarabe and head of the Amambala clan, moved to the west bank of the Bushman's river. As a peace offering he sent to the nearest European camp a small herd of cattle and a few horses taken from farmers in the Zuurveld, with a message that he wished to remain for a short time where he was. He was still there when Commandant Van Jaarsveld offered him the choice of retreating to his own country or being attacked. Langa elected to retire, and did so at once. He was consequently not molested, but of all the chiefs who had invaded the colony he was the only one willing to retreat.

The several divisions of the Imidange, the Amagwali under the chief Titi, the Amantinde under the chief Cika, and a number of other clans of less note declined to move. The commandant therefore collected all the European and Hottentot families of the frontier in a couple of lagers or camps formed by drawing up waggons in a circle and filling the spaces between the wheels with thorn trees. Leaving a few men to defend the lagers, with ninety-two burghers and forty Hottentots, all mounted and well armed, he fell upon the Kosas and smote them hip and thigh. The commando was in the field from the 23rd of May to the 19th of July 1781, and was only disbanded when the last of the intruders was again beyond the Fish river, and the first Kaffir war was over.

The spoil—five thousand three hundred head of horned cattle, among which, however, were many recently taken from the farmers—was divided by the commandant among the members of his force. On the 9th of October the matter was discussed by the council of policy, when it was resolved that the cattle which were taken from the Kaffirs and divided among the men of the commando might be retained on this occasion, but that this decision was not to form a precedent, much less was it to serve as a basis for the colonists to seek a quarrel with the Kaffirs and to rob them of anything that belonged to them.

While these events were taking place, it was too much to expect that the farmers of the eastern districts would leave their families and property exposed, and proceed to Cape Town, four or five hundred miles distant, to keep watch against a foreign foe.

As soon, however, as intelligence was received that the mother country was at war, the burghers within the old settled districts declared their readiness to do all in their power for the defence of the colony. Their disaffection to the government of Mr. Van Plettenberg did not interfere with their loyalty to the Netherlands. A call was made upon the burghers of Stellenbosch to come to the assistance of the garrison, and on the 2nd of April a detachment arrived at the castle. It was arranged that half of the Stellenbosch militia should remain under arms in Cape Town for a month, and then be relieved by the other half, who would remain for the same period.

There were several richly laden ships, homeward bound, lying in Table Bay, and their officers as well as the Cape council considered it injudicious for them to proceed upon their voyage until they could sail under the protection of a fleet of war. But as the winter was approaching they could not be kept in Table Bay, and in Simon's Bay there were no means of defending them in the event of an attack by an English fleet. Under these circumstances it was resolved to protect the entrance to Hout Bay by constructing a battery upon the western point and mounting twenty cannon upon it. Within the next few weeks the ships *Batavia*, *Amsterdam*, *Morgenster*, and *Indiaan* were sent there for safety.

But Hout Bay is too small to contain more than four or five ships of heavy burden, and it was therefore resolved to send any others that might arrive to Saldanha Bay, which was considered less liable than Simon's Bay to be visited. On the 13th of May the homeward bound ships *Hoogkarspel*, *Honkoop*, *Middelburg*, *Paarl*, and *Dankbaarheid* were sent there, and with them was sent the *Held Woltemaade*, an outward bound Indiaman, that she might undergo some necessary repairs and refresh her crew before proceeding to Ceylon. Gerrit Harmeyer, skipper of the *Hoogkarspel*, was appointed commodore of the squadron. He was directed to anchor in a sheltered position and then unbend all the sails of the ships, which he was to stow away in the packets *Zon* and *Snelheid*, which were now useless owing to the war. These vessels were to be sent some distance up the bay, so that they could be easily destroyed in case of necessity. The commodore was enjoined to make the best possible preparations for defence, but no means could be provided by the government beyond the ordinary armaments of the Indiamen.

The day after intelligence was received that the United Provinces were at war, the English brig *Betsy*—a packet used by the government of St. Helena—came into Table Bay and dropped her anchors without suspicion of danger. Some French cruisers were lying in the bay, and as soon as the *Betsy's* yards were lowered they sent their boats and took possession of her without resistance. The French also seized a vessel under Tuscan colours lying in the bay, and retained her as a prize on the ground that she was really English property.

The *Betsy* was transferred by her captors to Governor Van Plettenberg, by whom she was renamed the *Postiljon*. François Duminy, an old French skipper who had been living at the Cape for some time, was placed in command of her, and she was sent with all speed to Ceylon with intelligence of the war. The Company's packet *Herstelder* was ready to sail with a cargo of wheat for Europe. Her destination was altered, and within twenty-four hours she was on her way to Batavia with despatches.

There were several English visitors at the Cape, passengers by Dutch Indiamen to Europe, and others. These, with the officers of the *Betsy*, were sent to one of the Company's outposts, to prevent them from communicating with their countrymen. The English sailors were distributed among the Dutch ships.

Seven weeks of suspense and anxiety passed away without any further knowledge of what was transpiring in the outer world. At length, on the 20th of May, the French frigate *Serapis* dropped anchor in Simon's Bay, and her captain reported that a French fleet with a strong body of troops might shortly be expected to protect the Cape.

The intelligence was correct. As soon as war was proclaimed with the Netherlands, the English government commenced to fit out an expedition to seize this colony. Every particular concerning it, however, was made known to the French court by a spy named De la Motte, who was resident in London, and who was detected, tried for high treason, and condemned to death a few months later. At this time a French fleet was being prepared to assist in the operations against Sir Edward Hughes in the East Indies. Its equipment was therefore hurried on with the utmost expedition, and some transports were added to it for the purpose of conveying land forces to South Africa. It was seen to be a trial of speed, in which the possession of the Cape was to be the prize of the winner.

On the 13th of March 1781 the English fleet sailed from Spithead. It consisted of the *Romney*, of 50 guns, carrying the flag of Commodore George Johnstone, commander-in-chief of the expedition, the *Hero*, 74, *Monmouth*, 64, *Jupiter*, 50, *Isis*, 50, *Apollo*, 38, *Jason*, 36, *Active*, 32, *Diana*, 28, *Infernal*, fireship, *Terror*, bomb, seven light armed cruisers, two cutters and a sloop as despatch vessels, four transports, eight storeships and victuallers, and thirteen Indiamen, in all forty-six sail. Three thousand troops, under General Meadows, were on board. On the fourth day after sailing, a Dutch merchantman was chased by the *Rattlesnake* cutter, and captured after a sharp action.

All went well until the arrival of the fleet at St. Jago, where the commodore intended to take in a supply of fresh water, for which purpose he came to anchor in Porto Praya roads. He had no suspicion of danger, as he did not consider it possible that his destination was known to the enemy. No precautions were therefore taken against surprise, but, on the contrary, the decks of the ships of war were encumbered with casks and lumber of various kinds, and the best of the seamen were sent ashore to bring water to the boats. While in this condition, on the 16th of April some strange ships with no colours flying were observed from the *Isis* to be standing in under all sail, and immediately the intelligence was conveyed by signal to the rest of the fleet. There was hardly time to clear the guns before the strangers were abreast of the outermost English ships, and dropping anchor within cable's length of the *Isis*, the leading vessel poured a broadside into that frigate and then ran the French flag to her mizen peak.

The fleet which made the attack was under command of Pierre André de Suffren, vice admiral of France, and consisted of the *Heros*, 74, *Hannibal*, 74, *Vengeur*, 64, *Artisan*, 64, and *Sphinx*, 64. A corvette and eight transports with troops on board remained in the offing and took no part in the engagement.

Suffren sailed from Brest on the 2nd of March, hoping to reach the Cape before Johnstone. When off St. Jago the *Artisan*, which was in advance, observed the English fleet, and Captain De Cardaillac, her commander, at once put about and informed the admiral. It seemed as if fortune had specially favoured them with an opportunity to destroy their rivals. Suffren instantly prepared to attack. Captain De Cardaillac hailed him, and inquired what was to be done if fire should be opened upon them from a fort on land, as the Portuguese—the owners of the island—were neutral in the war. 'Open fire in return' replied the admiral.

The English fleet was taken at a tremendous disadvantage. The commodore's ship, moored inside the Indiamen, could take little or no part in the defence. The smaller men-of-war were almost useless against such formidable assailants, and the transports, victuallers, and merchantmen were in even a worse condition. The five French ships of the line were anchored to windward, and were pouring in broadsides as fast as their guns could be loaded. As the smoke rolled over the English fleet the enemy could not be clearly distinguished, and some of the transports in the confusion fired into the Indiamen.

But the English seamen were neither idle nor dismayed. Soon after the *Isis* received the broadside of the *Heros* they were answering shot for shot, and in ten minutes from the commencement of the action a cheer arose from the outermost ship and was echoed throughout the fleet as the French admiral's mizen topmast and ensign were carried away. One worthy scion of the seakings, Captain Ward of the *Hero*, was not content with mere defence, but resolved to become the assailant. Having got hands from the nearest ships to assist in working his guns, he boarded the *Artisan* with some of his own crew, and though he did not succeed in capturing that vessel, after a desperate fight in which Captain De Cardaillac was killed, he actually took twenty-five prisoners and brought them away with him. From these prisoners the English officers and sailors first learnt that their destination was the Cape of Good Hope, for the fleet was sailing under sealed orders, no one except the commodore himself being acquainted with the object of the expedition.

After cannonading each other at cable's length for nearly two hours it was still doubtful which side would be victorious, when the *Hannibal's* fire slackened, her mizen mast was seen to fall, and almost immediately afterwards her main and fore masts tottered and went over. Cheer after cheer now went up in the English fleet, and hundreds of men stood ready for the order to spring into the boats and board the wreck. Suffren hailed the *Hannibal*, and asked after the condition of the crew. The captain had been killed and nearly two hundred men were lying dead or wounded on the decks, was the reply. There was not a moment therefore to lose, so the cables of the French ships were cut, the *Hannibal* was taken in tow by the *Heros*, and Suffren stood out to sea. He took with him the *Hinchinbroke* and *Fortitude*, Indiamen, the *Infernal*, fireship, and the *Edward*, victualler, which had been cut out and placed in charge of prize crews.

Johnstone at once gave orders for the ships of war under his command to follow the enemy. But some of them were quite unprepared for sea, and it was only after three hours delay that they assembled outside. The *Isis* was then found to be crippled by the loss of a topmast and several yards, besides having her sails and rigging cut to pieces, and two or three others had sustained injuries which needed prompt attention. Meanwhile the French fleet was increasing its distance, and as night was setting in the commodore judged it expedient to abandon pursuit.

In the action at Porto Praya the English loss was only forty-two killed and one hundred and forty-one wounded, that of the French was somewhat heavier. Both suffered more in material comparatively than in men. Several of the Indiamen were badly cut up. The *Terror*, bomb, lost her bowsprit and foremast; she then caught fire, and her cable parting she drifted out to sea, but managed to get back in the night. The *Hinchinbroke*, *Fortitude*, *Edward*, and *Infernal* were made prizes, but none of them remained under the French flag. The first three were so shattered that the prize crews abandoned them, and they were all recovered within a few days. The *Infernal* was retaken by her own crew while the captors were off their guard. Twenty-one Englishmen, however, had been removed from this vessel and remained prisoners in the *Heros*, against whom, on the other side, must be counted the twenty-five Frenchmen carried off by Captain Ward from the *Artisan*.

Suffren, after the action, made the best of his way to the Cape. Jury masts were fitted up in the *Hannibal,* and as the wind was generally fair, a quick passage, under the circumstances, was made. On the 21st of June the *Heros* arrived in Simon's Bay in advance of the rest of the squadron. It was feared that the English fleet was close at hand, so the signal guns which had been placed on prominent hills were fired, and in response a large body of burghers hastened from all parts of the country within two hundred miles to aid in the defence of Cape Town.

After a few days the French transports arrived, when a company of artillery, part of the infantry regiment of Austrasie, and the regiment of Pondicherry—the last commanded by Colonel Conway, an Irishman in the French service—were landed. These troops marched overland to Cape Town, where they arrived on the 3rd of July. The Austrasie regiment was not intended to remain here long. It was quartered in a large warehouse adjoining the Lutheran church, until it could be sent to Mauritius. The regiment of Pondicherry, which was to remain here during the war, was quartered in a wing of the new hospital. This building was not yet completed, though eighty to a hundred men had been working upon it for nearly nine years. In June 1779 a portion of it was first used as a hospital. One large ward was employed as a grain and another as a wine magazine. And now for the first time, owing to there being no other accommodation available, the right wing was turned into a barrack.

The demand for provisions for the French fleet and troops caused a sudden and great increase in prices. The governor and council considered this circumstance unfair to those who had come to save the colony from conquest, and they therefore invited the acting and retired burgher councillors to form a committee with two government officers to draw up a scale of prices which should be adhered to while the war lasted.

The committee proposed as a maximum: wheat to strangers not higher than twelve shillings a muid, meal fourteen shillings and eight pence farthing the hundred pounds, wine nine pounds a legger (of which one pound was to be paid to the licensed dealer), beef two pence a pound, and mutton a penny a pound. To this scale the council of policy agreed, and all persons were prohibited under heavy penalties from selling at a dearer rate.

To prevent intelligence being conveyed to the English, two Danish Indiamen, homeward bound, that put into Simon's Bay for supplies, were detained there, as it was feared that they might either touch at St. Helena or meet with strangers at sea. The *Held Woltemaade*, however, having completed her repairs, was permitted to sail for Ceylon.

On the morning of the 22nd of July a report reached Cape Town that a fleet of thirty-three sail was in sight off Saldanha Bay. The burgher lieutenant Van Reenen was thereupon hurried off with a troop of mounted men to ascertain particulars, and a messenger was despatched to Hout Bay with orders to the skippers of the vessels there to return at once to Table Bay, to keep close in shore on the passage, and if attacked to run their ships aground and destroy them. Lieutenant Van Reenen had not proceeded far when he met a company of sailors who informed him that an English fleet was in possession of Saldanha Bay.

As soon as Johnstone could refit his ships after the action at Porto Praya, he had sailed for the Cape, which he still had some hope of reaching before Suffren, as he thought it likely that the French admiral would be compelled to put into a Brazilian port to repair his damages. This being doubtful, however, when near his destination he sent the *Active* on ahead, for the purpose of reconnoitring Table Bay.

Soon after parting from the fleet, a strange sail standing to the southward was observed by the *Active's* lookout, upon which Captain Mackenzie hoisted French colours and ran towards her. It was the *Held Woltemaade*, just out of Saldanha Bay. Being hailed in French, the officers of the Indiaman were unsuspicious of danger, and they gave full information concerning the arrival of Suffren and the condition of the five ships they had recently parted from. Captain Mackenzie then hauled down the French flag and demanded the surrender of the *Woltemaade* under pain of instantly sinking her. She was given up without a blow. On taking possession, the captors found in addition to a valuable cargo a sum of money equal to forty thousand pounds sterling, which was intended to aid the government of Ceylon. The *Active* immediately returned with her prize and reported to the commodore, who, upon learning that the Cape was now too strong to be attacked, resolved to make himself master of the five Indiamen.

At half past nine on the morning of the 21st of July, a signal was made from the look-out station at Saldanha Bay that a large fleet under French colours was in sight and standing straight in. An hour later the leading ships were within the entrance, when they hauled down the French and hoisted English colours.

According to their instructions, the Dutch officers should now have destroyed their ships, seeing that defence and escape were alike impossible. But Skipper Van Gennep of the *Middelburg* was the only one of the five who had taken the precaution to have a quantity of inflammable materials in readiness for such an occasion, and the consequence was that although all the ships were hastily set on fire and abandoned, the English sailors got possession of the *Hoogkarspel*, *Honkoop*, *Paarl*, and *Dankbaarheid*, in time to extinguish the flames before any material injury was done.

Three fires were kindled in the hold of the *Middelburg* by her chief officer, Abraham de Smidt, ancestor of the colonial family of this name. He with the steward and one seaman had remained behind for that purpose when the remainder of the crew left, and they did not make their escape until the English were within cannon shot. In a moment the flames were pouring through the lower hatchways, and shortly they reached the magazine, when an explosion took place which hurled chests of tea and bales of cotton goods together with fragments of timber high into the air. What was left of the hull sank to the bottom, but as the water was shallow the remains of the cargo were easily recovered some years later.

The *Zon* and *Snelheid* were abandoned without any effort to destroy them, and thus the captors obtained possession of all the equipage of their prizes. At Saldanha Bay two Indian princes were found, who had been banished by the Batavian government from Ternate and Tidor for political offences. These exiles were released from captivity, and were received as guests on board one of the men-of-war. In two days the Indiamen were got ready for sea, and on the 24th the fleet sailed, leaving nothing afloat but the two empty packets *Zon* and *Snelheid*, which were so old and decayed as not to be worth taking away.

The main object of the expedition having been frustrated, Commodore Johnstone resolved to send the troops on to India and to take a portion of the fleet back to Europe. He therefore placed Captain Alms in command of the convoy, for the protection of which he left five of his best ships of war; and with the *Romney*, *Jupiter*, *Diana*, *Jason*, *Terror*, *Infernal*, one light cruiser, three victuallers, and the Dutch prizes, he stood away for England.

As there was now no danger of an immediate attack, in August the burghers were permitted to return to their homes. The governor reported to the directors that their alacrity to serve had surprised him, and Colonel Conway expressed great satisfaction with their conduct. The defence of the Cape was left to the regiment of Pondicherry and the Dutch troops, together with a small corps of halfbreeds and Hottentots which was raised in the country and stationed in Cape Town. The armaments on the forts were very defective, but in November forty cannon and a large supply of ammunition arrived from Mauritius.

The necessities of the government were pressing and the treasury was empty. No money could be expected from the mother country during the continuance of the war. In these straits, on the 6th of November 1781 the council of policy resolved to borrow from the colonists as much as was urgently needed, to pay interest monthly for the loan at the rate of half per cent, and to promise to repay the principal upon the arrival of the first outward bound fleet. Sufficient money was not to be obtained in this way, however, and after the 30th of April 1782 expenditure was met by notes, which in a short time were issued to the amount of 185,044*l.* This was the introduction of a system of equalising revenue and expenditure that for nearly half a century caused great confusion in commercial transactions.

A few years later notes to the amount of 165,180*l.* were redeemed, either in specie or by bills on Holland, but further issues were afterwards made. In 1795 the amount of such paper outstanding, with no security except the promise of the government to pay when it could, was 122,782*l.* The notes offered great temptation to unprincipled persons to defraud the uneducated farmers of the interior. They were easily forged, and in this way many persons became the victims of swindlers.

In May 1782 the garrison was strengthened by the arrival of a body of troops termed the regiment of Luxemburg, raised in France, but in the pay of the Dutch East India Company. This regiment remained until February 1783, when it was sent to Ceylon. Just before it left the Cape, the regiment of Meuron, a strong body of Swiss troops in the pay of the Dutch Company, arrived to replace it. In February 1783 the French regiment of Waldener, also in the Company's pay, arrived and formed a camp under canvas at Diep River. In April of the same year this regiment left for Batavia. The regiment of Pondicherry, which was sent to assist the Dutch, but was not in the pay of the Company, remained at the Cape until some time after the conclusion of peace, as it was not until April 1784 that it embarked for Mauritius. In 1785 the troops that remained consisted of the Swiss regiment of Meuron, some five hundred Dutch infantry under Gordon, who had been advanced to the rank of colonel, and a few engineers under Major Philip Herman Gilquin, who since June 1779 had been director of fortifications in Table Valley.

Owing to the war with England there was no communication between South Africa and the Netherlands for more than a year, and it was not until the 1st of April 1782 that the replies of the officers of the Cape government to the charges made against them by the burghers could be sent away. When these documents reached the Netherlands they were referred by the directors to the committee which had the case under examination. One of them attracted special attention. This was the statement of the fiscal, the tone of which convinced the directors that Mr. Boers was not an officer who could safely be left in power. They therefore agreed without hesitation to his request to resign his duties, but required him to furnish bail to the amount of a little over 1,000*l.* if he should leave the colony for Europe before the charges against him were decided. He retired from office in April 1783. Mr. Jan Jacob Serrurier was instructed by the council to act as fiscal, and in November 1784 he received from the prince of Orange the permanent appointment.

The principles of Mr. Boers have been commented upon, but another instance of the manner in which he put them in practice may be given. During the war there was such a scarcity of blankets and rough cloth in the colony that the slaves were almost naked. Thereupon several enterprising persons formed the idea of manufacturing blankets and cloth at the Cape, and a company was got together prepared to risk the necessary capital. There was coarse wool to be had in plenty, and a burgher named Frederik Heyneman, who was living in the village of Stellenbosch, and who had been a weaver before he came to this country, was engaged to commence the work. All was in readiness, and only permission was needed from the government. The company—Messrs. Tobias Christiaan Ronnekamp, Jan Frederik Kirsten, Olof Godlieb de Wet, and Gerrit Hendrik Cruywagen, all in the government service, and the burghers Jan Meyndert Cruywagen, Jan Serrurier, Jan Bottiger, and Gerrit Hendrik Meyer—applied to the council for the necessary leave. All the members were willing, except Mr. Boers, who denounced the project of establishing manufactures in a colony as little short of treason, and succeeded in thwarting the plan.

The old skipper Staring, head of the naval establishment, left South Africa before the fiscal. In January 1782 the

Danish ship *Castle of Dansburg* put into Table Bay, where an embargo was laid upon her. Staring and Captain De Lille went on board to communicate the decision of the council, when the Danish skipper ordered sail to be set and tried to get away. Fire was then opened upon the ship from the forts, upon which the skipper obliged Staring to stand in the most dangerous position. He did so with the utmost composure, although the shot was flying thick around him. In a few minutes the Dane was obliged to surrender. But Staring, brave in front of cannon balls, feared the result of the inquiry that was being made into his alleged peculations, and within a week of this event he requested the council of policy to allow him to take his discharge. This was granted, much to the dissatisfaction of the directors when they were informed of it, and he left for Europe in a neutral ship. He was succeeded as head of the naval establishment by Justinus van Gennep, recently skipper of the *Middelburg*.

While the statements of the officials were on the way to Europe, the Assembly of Seventeen met. The delegate Roos had died, but Messrs. Van Reenen, Artois, and Heyns were still in Amsterdam. They delivered to the directors another memorial containing further charges against the Cape officials, supported by numerous documents. The memorial and its annexures were referred to the committee of investigation. The directors resolved to instruct the government at the Cape to do everything in its power, consistently with the Company's interests, to smooth over matters and to allay the discontent of the burghers. But they did not explain how that was to be effected without making concessions or amending the system under which their officers were paid, so that such instructions were practically of no value.

It was not until towards the close of 1783, four years after the matter had been placed in their hands, that the committee of investigation sent in a report. They had come to the conclusion that the complainants could not be held to represent the whole body of burghers at the Cape, and that the charges against the officials had not been proved. They recommended that no changes in the regulations regarding commerce should be made until a general European peace, and that consequently the colonists should not be granted liberty to trade on their own account with Europe and India. They objected to allowing an appeal direct from the high court of justice at the Cape to the supreme court of the Netherlands instead of to the court at Batavia, as that would practically remove the Cape from the jurisdiction of the Company; but they approved of reconstituting the high court of justice, so as to make it consist of six servants of the Company beside the president and six burghers, instead of nine servants of the Company and three burghers as formerly. They were in favour of allowing the Company's servants to have gardens for their own use, but not to sell produce from them. They left to the fiscal his perquisites, including the fee of one shilling and four pence on every muid of corn or meal sold to foreigners; but they proposed to restrict to 40*l.* his power of compounding cases instead of bringing them into court.

On the 3rd of December 1783 this report was adopted by the Assembly of Seventeen, and was communicated to the Cape government by the next ships that sailed. At the same time the directors resolved not to prohibit the banishment of useless persons from the colony, but to instruct the governor and council of policy to use this power sparingly and with discretion, and to give the person deported the choice of removal to Europe or India.

This result of their complaints gave great dissatisfaction to the colonists. Since 1779 the condition of affairs had greatly altered, as there had never before been such a demand for produce as that created by the large garrison and the French forces in the East. A French commissariat officer, M. Percheron, resided at the Cape, and purchased large quantities of provisions at high prices. Other nationalities also had agents here for the same purpose, though their requirements were not nearly so great. Next to the French in commercial dealings in South Africa at this time were the Danes, whose agent in Cape Town was the burgher

Hendrik Justinus de Wet. Many new trading houses had been established by burghers. In Cape Town there was a display of prosperity which astonished strangers. European and Indian wares in the greatest variety and of the most costly description were introduced in large quantities by Danish ships; and though the prices asked were exorbitant, they commanded a ready sale. The defective means of communication with the interior attracted greater attention than at any previous period, and the council of policy was desired to adopt measures for making good roads, that the inhabitants might more easily exchange the productions of the country and obtain foreign wares. The subject of a free coasting trade came also into prominence, and a memorial upon it was addressed to the government.

But the burghers of South Africa, though keenly alive to the advantages of material prosperity, have at every period of their history shown a firmer attachment to what they hold to be their political rights and liberties. There have indeed been times when considerable parties of men have wavered between money and freedom from misrule, but the women have never hesitated in rejecting prosperity at the price of oppression or disdainful treatment. And perhaps nowhere else in the world have women the influence that they have on South African farms. On this occasion neither men nor women were disposed to let the question rest. The government resorted to various petty persecutions, but the party opposed to it increased in strength, and resolved now to appeal to the States General of the Netherlands.

With this object, in December 1784 two memorials, signed by M. Bergh, C. Maasdorp, G. H. Meyer, J. P. Warnecke, J. Myburgh, J. D. de Villiers, J. B. Groeneveld, P. Myburgh, H. Louw, and J. Roos, who had been chosen as representatives by the Cape burghers, were forwarded to the delegates who were still in Holland. In these memorials complaints were made of iniquitous and imperious government, of maladministration of justice, and of the scanty attention paid by the directors of the East India Company to the representations of the colonists.

In the mean time, however, the directors had come to the conclusion that changes were necessary in the government of the Cape, though they could not bring themselves so far as to grant to the colonists liberty of foreign commerce. They had narrowly escaped losing the country altogether, and they were now aware that the burghers were not in a position to defend it from foreign attacks. Governor Van Plettenberg, who had been surprised at the alacrity shown by the farmers to aid the garrison in time of danger, had tried to get a company of burghers stationed in the town, to be relieved monthly by others, but the duty to be permanent. In this he had not succeeded. Early in 1783 the preliminaries of a treaty of peace had been arranged with Great Britain; but it was admitted on all sides that a garrison of at least two thousand men was required to secure the Cape against surprise in the event of another war, and that additional fortifications must be built.

The directors therefore resolved to send out as governor a military officer of rank and experience, to station here a large body of troops as a depôt for India, and to employ these troops in the construction of necessary works. In concurrence with the States General, they selected as governor Lieutenant-Colonel Cornelis Jacob van de Graaff, an engineer officer, who was then controller general of the fortifications in Holland, and who enjoyed the confidence of the stadtholder. Colonel Van de Graaff with his family arrived in South Africa on the 22nd of January 1785, and he took over the administration on the 14th of February. On the 10th of April Mr. Van Plettenberg left for Europe as admiral of the homeward-bound fleet of the year.

During the war with England the Company's trade had been almost annihilated. Its fleets were laid up in harbours or were swept from the seas. It was compelled to employ ships under neutral flags to convey cargoes to and from India, and to prevent the utter ruin of its dependencies was obliged to allow any one who chose to buy and sell freely in its foreign possessions. There was hardly a nation in Europe that did not furnish adventurers to take advantage of this condition of things. The list of ships that put into the two open ports of South Africa during the four years 1781–1784 shows this very clearly.

	Table Bay				Simon's Bay			
	1781	1782	1783	1784	1781	1782	1783	1784
Dutch	29	13	14	38	2	2	7	10
English	2	—	18	18	—	—	—	5
French	19	18	42	40	16	38	8	5
Danish	10	18	20	14	5	5	7	5
Swedish	3	3	8	8	1	1	2	3
Austrian	1	8	27	12	—	—	2	1
Portuguese	1	2	3	2	—	—	—	—
Italian	1	—	1	—	—	—	—	—
Prussian	—	1	8	4	—	—	4	1
Hamburg	—	—	1	—	—	—	—	—
Russian	—	—	2	1	—	—	—	—
Spanish	—	—	—	1	—	—	—	—
American	—	—	—	1	—	—	—	—

Thus out of an average yearly number of 135 ships, only 29 were Dutch, and many of these were owned by individuals or were men-of-war belonging to the national government. In September 1783 peace was concluded, but the old order of things could not at once be restored.

During these years it was not possible to send much produce to Europe, though a considerable quantity of provisions was forwarded to the Company's establishments in India, for the use of the garrisons there. Three or four hundred casks of beef and pork salted at the Cape formed part of these shipments. The years 1783 and 1784 were marked by severe drought in the western parts of the colony, and the grain crops were very poor; but abundance of rain fell in the east, and meat and butter were plentiful and cheap.

While Mr. Van Plettenberg was governor, the colony was visited by distinguished travellers of various nationalities, who have left impressions of what they saw in several interesting volumes. First among these ranks the Swedish naturalist Sparrman. Dr. Thunberg, also a Swede, Captain Stavorinus, a Zeelander, Lieutenant Paterson, an Englishman, and M. Le Vaillant, a Frenchman, gave accounts of the country of greater or less value.

The English explorer Captain Cook touched at Table Bay with the *Resolution* and *Adventure* on his outward passage in November 1772, and when returning homeward in March 1775. He was here again when outward bound on his last voyage with the *Resolution* and *Discovery* in October 1776.

The French explorer Captain Kerguelen when proceeding to visit the South Polar Sea put into Simon's Bay with the *Rolland* and *Oiseau* in May 1773. Just a year later he put into the same port again when returning to Brest.

During this period the following shipping disasters took place on the South African coast:

Contrary to the instructions of the directors, there were five Indiamen in Table Bay on the 1st of June 1773, when a gale from the north-west set in. A little after dawn, one of them—the outward-bound ship *Jonge Thomas*—was driven from her anchors and cast on the beach beyond the mouth of Salt River. It was seen that the wreck could not hold together long, but for some time nothing was done to save the crew. In the course of the morning, however, a dairyman named Wolraad Woltemaade visited the scene of the disaster. Woltemaade, who was mounted on a powerful horse, dashed into the breakers and reached the ship's side. With two men holding to the horse's tail he returned to the shore, and this feat he repeated until he had saved fourteen of the crew. In the next venture he was swept under a breaker and was drowned. Shortly after this the wreck broke up, when one hundred and thirty-eight men lost their lives and fifty-three reached the land, making sixty-seven saved in all. The directors caused the exploit of the brave dairyman to be pictured on the stern of the next ship built for them, which they named the *Held* (or Hero) *Woltemaade.*

On the 31st of January 1776 the Company's homeward-bound ship *Nieuw Rhoon* when attempting to enter Table

Bay was driven by a violent southeaster upon a reef at Robben Island, and was badly damaged. She was got off, and was brought up to the anchorage; but it was found necessary to beach her by the jetty to save her cargo.

On the 15th of October of the same year the French ship *Ceres*, homeward-bound from Pondicherry, in a gale from the north-west parted her cables and went ashore near the mouth of Salt River. The ship broke up quickly, and very little cargo was saved; but no lives were lost.

On the 25th of August 1778 the English East India Company's outward bound ship *Colebrooke* when entering False Bay ran on a concealed reef, and was so much damaged that it was necessary to beach her near Cape Hangklip to save the crew. She went to pieces almost at once, and all the cargo was lost; but the crew, with the exception of two men, were saved by boats sent from ships in Simon's Bay.

In January 1778 the Company's ship *Venus* left Batavia to return to Europe. In July she put into Delagoa Bay with her rudder loose, and only eighteen men able to work. Fifty-five sailors had died of scurvy. One English and two Austrian vessels were found in Delagoa Bay, and with these intelligence of the condition of the *Venus* was sent to Ceylon, whence it reached the Cape. In June 1779 a packet from Table Bay found the ship with forty-five living men on board, out of the original crew of one hundred and twenty-nine. A fresh crew and provisions were sent from the Cape, the damages were repaired, and the *Venus* resumed her voyage.

On the 5th of January 1780 the Company's homeward-bound ship *Mentor* went down in a great gale off the southern coast. On the 9th two of her crew were picked up by the French ship *Salomon*. They had been drifting about on a fragment of the poop, and were the only ones saved.

On the 24th of September 1782 the French corvette *Victor*, having anchored in the night too close to the breakers, was driven ashore in a north-west gale beyond the mouth of Salt River, and went to pieces. Nearly all of her crew were saved.

On the 11th of July 1783 the Danish outward-bound ship

Nicobar ran ashore on the coast a little to the eastward of Cape Agulhas, and became a total wreck. Only eleven of her crew managed to get to land.

On the 27th of January 1784 the French 64-gun ship *Sevère* when trying to beat up to the anchorage in Table Bay missed stays, and ran ashore on the Blueberg beach. She became a total wreck, but her crew got away safely in boats.

On the 7th of July following the Company's ship *Hoop* ran ashore in the night close to Mouille Point, and became a wreck. Only one of her crew was lost.

More noteworthy than any of the above was the wreck of the English East India Company's ship *Grosvenor*, which was lost on the coast a few miles north of the Umzimvubu river in August 1782. This wreck has been a favourite theme for poets and romance writers, and to the present day speculations are frequently put forward as to the fate of the lady passengers. The *Grosvenor* sailed from Trincomalee on the 13th of June, having on board one hundred and fifty souls, passengers and crew all told. Among the passengers were several officers of position in the English East India Company's service, viz. Colonel James, Mr. Hosea, Captain Adair, and Messrs. Williams, Taylor, and Newman. Colonel James was accompanied by his wife, and Mr. Hosea by his wife and three children. The other passengers were Captain Talbot, of the royal navy, Colonel D'Espinette and Captain Olivier, French exchanged prisoners of war, Mrs. Logie, wife of the chief officer of the ship, and several children proceeding to England to be educated.

The ship was believed to be still a day's sail from the African coast, when at half past four in the morning of the 4th of August some seamen aloft saw land ahead. The fact was reported to the officer of the watch, who would not believe it. Presently the land was seen from the deck, though it was not yet daylight, and as the officer was still incredulous, a quartermaster ran below to the captain's cabin and begged him to hasten up. Captain Coxon instantly gave orders to wear ship, but before that could be done the *Grosvenor* was in the breakers and struck heavily.

A raft was made, but it broke adrift and was dashed to pieces. Two lascars then swam ashore with a lead line, by which means a hawser was stretched between the ship and the beach, and a number of men went safely along it. The wreck soon broke up, when a portion of the poop and quarter, upon which the passengers had crowded, drifted ashore. One hundred and thirty-six persons now found themselves on dry land, the remaining fourteen had been drowned. Some provisions were washed on the beach, and having collected these, on the third day after the disaster the whole party, except two men who preferred to remain where they were, set out in hope of being able to make their way to the Cape. They had sufficient food to last eight or nine days, and were provided with five or six cutlasses. A great many natives made their appearance, but instead of helping the distressed people, they robbed the lady passengers of their trinkets, and carried off all the iron they could find.

Shortly after setting out, a quarrel arose with some natives, but it ended in a skirmish without a serious battle. Then the crew broke up into several parties, and the sturdiest pushed on ahead. One hundred and sixteen days after the wreck, six sailors, who had suffered very severe hardships from want of food, reached a farm on the Zwartkops river, where they were treated with the utmost kindness. Five of them were sent on to Swellendam, where they arrived on the 4th of December. By order of the governor and council, a relief expedition, consisting of one hundred Europeans and three hundred Hottentots, was at once organised, with which two of the sailors returned to the Kaffir country. Before reaching the Fish river, three more sailors and a lascar were met. Captain Hillegard Mulder, who was in command of the expedition, left the waggons at the Kei, and pushed on with a party on horseback, but was obliged to turn back by the hostile attitude of the Tembus. In the Kaffir country six lascars and two black women who had been servants to the lady passengers were found. These stated that to the best of their belief all the other shipwrecked people had either been killed by the Kaffirs or had perished of want and fatigue.

They had been eye witnesses of the death of many, but as they had left parties still struggling on behind, the fate of the others is involved in mystery. Two white men lived for some years near the scene of the wreck, but whether they were the same who remained behind, or others who turned back, is doubtful. One of them formed a connection with a native woman, and left a son who in 1824 was in the service of Mr. F. G. Farewell at Natal. This man informed Mr. Farewell that two women had also lived near the wreck for a time, but that upon an invasion by a tribe from the westward, they had hid in a forest, and were there starved to death. Who these women were cannot be ascertained, but it is nearly certain that they were not wrecked in the *Grosvenor*.

The lady passengers—Mrs. James, Mrs. Hosea, and Mrs. Logie—were with their husbands and Captain Coxon when they were last seen by those who were rescued. Three girls —Misses Dennis, Wilmot, and Hosea—were also with this party. No trace of any of these has ever since been found, and there can hardly be a doubt that they all perished of hunger and fatigue.

In 1790-1 an expedition under the leadership of Mr. Jacob van Reenen proceeded from the colony to the scene of the wreck in search of survivors, but found none, and heard no tidings of any. Mr. Van Reenen's party visited a village in which they met three aged white women, survivors of a wreck which must have taken place on the coast about 1730 or 1740. They could not speak any European language, nor did they know to what nationality their parents belonged, though from one of them being called Bessie it was concluded that they were English. No information was obtainable from them. They had been married to natives, and had a numerous offspring, whose descendants are still living in the Pondo country.

There was an almost entire change in the clerical staff during this period.

The church in Cape Town continued to be ministered to by three clergymen until December 1778, when Mr. Kroonenburg retired on pension, owing to age and ill health. He died in June following. It had been understood that upon the first death or retirement a successor would not be appointed; but the directors now annulled their former decision, and sent out the Rev. Christiaan Fleck, who was inducted as third clergyman of the Cape in January 1781. In July 1784 the number was again reduced to two by the death of Mr. Bode.

At Stellenbosch the death of Mr. Appeldoorn in September 1772 left the congregation without other ministrations than those of a consulent. The post remained vacant until April 1777, when the Rev. Philip Kuys arrived from Holland, and was appointed resident minister of Stellenbosch. Mr. Kuys died in February 1785, when the church was again for a time attended to by the clergyman of Drakenstein acting as consulent.

The church at Drakenstein was an arena of strife during the early years of this period. The election in January 1772 of Thomas Arnoldus Theron as an elder was objected to by a considerable section of the congregation, on the ground that he was not properly qualified, and the controversy soon became violent. Four of the opposite faction were excommunicated by the consistory. By 1775 the strife was so great that many persons refused to attend the services, and the disaffected party sent Messrs. Pieter Marais and Jan Roos to Holland, to bring their case before the directors and the classis of Amsterdam. Mr. Marais died soon after reaching the Netherlands. The directors declined to interfere in the matter, but the classis investigated the dispute, and tried to conciliate the opposing factions. The dissension in the congregation was continued, however, until March 1781, when Mr. Van der Spuy was obliged to retire on pension, owing to age and bodily infirmities. In April 1784 he was succeeded by the Rev. Robert Nicholas Aling, who was sent out by the directors.

In June 1774 the congregation of Waveren was left without a clergyman by the failure of Mr. Harders' health, and his consequent retirement on a pension. In April 1777 the Rev. Johannes Abraham Kuys arrived from the Netherlands, and was stationed there.

The church at Zwartland was without a clergyman until April 1774, when the Rev. Daniel Goldbach arrived from the Netherlands, and was appointed to that charge. Mr. Goldbach died in March 1783, and the church was then for a time left to the care of a consulent.

Before 1780 no other public worship than that of the Dutch Reformed church was tolerated in the colony; but the Lutherans, who were numerous in Cape Town, now obtained permission to have a resident clergyman of their own denomination. They had been striving for this privilege during more than half a century. It was at last granted by the directors, on condition that they should pay the minister's salary and all other expenses, without assistance from the Company. The Lutheran church in Amsterdam was requested to select a clergyman, with the sole reservation that he should be a Netherlander by birth. The choice fell upon the Rev. Andreas Kolver, who arrived in South Africa on the 22nd of November 1780, and on the 10th of December held service here for the first time. The church in Strand street had previously been erected and presented to the congregation by a wealthy burgher named Martin Melk.

In the staff of officers in the country districts the following changes had taken place:

In August 1773 Landdrost Faber, of Stellenbosch and Drakenstein, died. The secretary of the district—Abraham Faure—acted until October, when Marthinus Adriaan Bergh was appointed landdrost. In December 1778 Mr. Bergh retired at his own request. His term of office had been marked by violent altercations with the burghers, and it had become impossible for him to hold the situation longer. He was succeeded by Olof Godlieb de Wet. In February 1782 Mr. De Wet was promoted to be master of the warehouses, and was succeeded as landdrost by Daniel van Ryneveld.

During Mr. Van Ryneveld's tenure of office the council

of policy authorised the landdrost and heemraden to divide the old churchyard into building lots, and dispose of them for the benefit of the church and district. The site of the old church was alone reserved. It was enclosed by a wall built upon the foundations, which had not been disturbed since the fire that had destroyed the building. The alienation of the cemetery was repugnant to the feelings of many of the inhabitants, who threw the blame of the transaction entirely upon the landdrost. Even after his death several years later the matter was not allowed to be forgotten, and for a couple of generations children in the village heard from their elders tales of a spectral landdrost doomed at dead of every night to bewail the desecration he had committed.

In February 1776 Landdrost Mentz, of Swellendam, retired from the service at his own request, and Sergeant Pieter Diederik Boonaker was appointed by the council to succeed him. But upon this appointment being reported to the directors, they expressed their disapproval of it, on the ground that a new landdrost should have been chosen from the civil—not from the military—branch of their service. Sergeant Boonaker was therefore replaced in May 1777 by Daniel van Ryneveld. In February 1782 Mr. Van Ryneveld was transferred to Stellenbosch, and Constantyn van Nuld Onkruydt succeeded as landdrost of Swellendam.

In May 1774 Mr. Kirsten, the resident at Simon's Town, was promoted, and the bookkeeper Christoffel Brand was appointed to succeed him.

The outposts at Saldanha Bay, Groenkloof, Klapmuts, Zonder End, and Buffeljagts River were still maintained. In July 1777 another was formed at Zwart River, in Outeniqualand, between the present villages of George and Knysna. A few soldiers were sent there, but the object was not so much to establish a military station as to assist a party of woodcutters who were employed in felling and preparing timber for the Company's use.

CHAPTER XXV.

CORNELIS JACOB VAN DE GRAAFF, GOVERNOR, INSTALLED 14 FEBRUARY 1785; LEFT SOUTH AFRICA 24 JUNE 1791.

JOHAN ISAAC RHENIUS, SECUNDE, ACTING HEAD OF THE GOVERNMENT, 24 JUNE 1791 TO 3 JULY 1792.

Character of the new governor—Decision of the directors concerning the complaints of the colonists—Changes in the administration at the Cape—Long drought—Mossel Bay opened to trade—Timber shipped at Plettenberg's Bay—Erection of fortifications in Table Valley—Troops in garrison at the Cape—Formation of the district of Graaff Reinet—Site of the drostdy—Pursuits of the frontier farmers—Struggle with Bushmen—Dealings with Kaffirs—Condition of the Kosa tribe—Invasion of the colony by Kosa clans—Measures of defence adopted by the colonists—Humiliating arrangement made by the government—Grievances of the frontier colonists—Condition of the people in the districts of Graaff Reinet, Swellendam, Stellenbosch and Drakenstein, and in Cape Town—Reckless waste of the Company's effects by the governor—Public expenditure—The colonial revenue—Insolvency of the East India Company—Reduction of the garrison at the Cape—Very extensive retrenchment—Quarrels among the principal officers of government—Petty conduct of the governor—Political changes in the Netherlands—Recall of Governor Van de Graaff—Flight of the fiscal Van Lynden through fear of incensed burghers—Condition of the fortifications in Table Valley—Cost of the new hospital—Census returns of 1791—Commerce in European wares thrown open to private individuals—Belief in the existence of gold in Great Namaqualand—Journey of exploration undertaken by Mr. Willem van Reenen—First authentic information concerning the Ovaherero or Damaras—Condition of those people—Their subjugation by the Namaquas—First meeting of Europeans with the degraded race known as Berg Damaras—Meeting with the Hottentot clan now called the Red Nation—Statistics of shipping—Wrecks on the coast—Changes in the staff of clergymen—Formation of a consistory at Graaff Reinet—Arrangement of a dispute concerning baptism between the Dutch Reformed and Lutheran consistories at the Cape—Desire for the establishment of better schools in the colony—Investigation of the East India Company's affairs by the States General of the Netherlands—Appointment of a board with very extensive powers to carry out reforms and suppress abuses—Instructions concerning the Cape Colony given to Messrs. Nederburgh and Frykenius, two members of this board—Arrival of Messrs. Nederburgh and Frykenius at the Cape, and their assumption of the government as Commissioners General.

Colonel Van de Graaff had the reputation of being an able military officer, but his qualifications were small for such a situation as that of governor of the Cape colony. He was arbitrary and headstrong in disposition, violent in temper, and utterly careless in business matters. In addition to the salary and perquisites of his predecessor, which amounted to about 3,650*l.*, he had a special allowance of 1,500*l.* a year. He had the official residence in the castle, the house in the gardens, and the country seat at Newlands. He was provided with carriages and horses, and had the produce of the farm Visser's Hok, besides the established table allowances.

On the 10th of May 1785 the last memorial sent from the Cape was laid by the delegates of the burghers before the States General of the Netherlands. By that body it was referred for report to the chamber of Zeeland. An informal conference of the leading members of the legislature and of the directorate of the Company was held, the result of which was that on the 28th of July the Assembly of Seventeen announced its resolution to make several changes in the system of government.

The members of the council of policy were all to rank as senior merchants, and the secretary, who was not to have a voice in the proceedings, was to rank as a merchant. The high court of justice was to be presided over by the secunde, and was to consist besides of six servants of the Company and six burghers, all of whom were to rank as merchants. Its secretary was to rank as a junior merchant. Only members of the Dutch Reformed church could sit in either the council of policy or the high court of justice; but Lutherans could be appointed to any other offices.

The Company would purchase and send to Europe all grain, wine, and other produce of the colony that could not be sold to foreigners, after the wants of the Cape and India had been supplied. The prices were to be fixed yearly by a board to be appointed by the council of policy from the members of the high court of justice, and to consist of three servants of the Company and three burghers. This board was also to propose to the council of policy the method and amount of taxation; it was to have the care of roads, bridges, and other colonial works; it was to let the public mills, to employ watchmen for the town, and to perform various municipal duties.

The council was directed to report upon the likelihood of obtaining produce at various bays, pending the receipt of which report no decision would be arrived at concerning a coasting trade.

The request of the frontier colonists to have a landdrost and a clergyman stationed among them was to be complied with, and a new district was to be created, with a board of heemraden similar to those of Stellenbosch and Swellendam.

All the governing bodies in the Netherlands were agreed that the system thus introduced should have a fair trial, so no further redress was to be had from the States General.

The change in the high court of justice was made in March 1786. One of the three councillors under the old system retired at that time, and out of eight names presented by the court, the council selected Christiaan George Maasdorp, Gerrit Hendrik Meyer, Jan Coenraad Gie, and Hendrik Justinus de Wet to make the number of burghers up to six.

The board that was to fix prices and perform so many other duties was established at the same time. It consisted of six members of the high court of justice, three of whom—Gerrit Hendrik Kruywagen, Salomon van Echten, and Jan Marthinus Horak—were servants of the Company; the other three—Jan Smuts, Andries van Sittert, and Christiaan George Maasdorp—being burghers. This board was a failure from the very first. The officials and burghers could not work amicably together, and everything proposed by one party was objected to by the other. As for fixing prices of produce, it had no opportunity of making trial of its ability. The harvest of 1785 entirely failed, owing to protracted drought, and when in 1786 the ship *Negotie* arrived from Amsterdam to take in a cargo of wheat and wine, there was not a muid of grain to be had, and the government was obliged to send her to Batavia in ballast. The directors were thus disappointed, and the plan was never again brought forward.

In its stead, in October 1789 the directors gave the colonists permission to export wine to Holland on their own account, provided it was sent in the Company's vessels, and 1*l*. 13*s*. 4*d*.—shortly afterwards increased to 2*l*. 13*s*. 4*d*.—a legger freight paid upon it.

There being a large profit to be made on wheat, the Company endeavoured to procure as much of that article as possible for the European market. In 1786 it was necessary to import large quantities of flour from Europe and rice from Java to ward off actual famine; but in that year the long drought broke up, and in 1787 and later there was a considerable surplus of grain in the colony.

To encourage its growth in the district of Swellendam, a magazine was built at Mossel Bay, where the grain was received, so that the long overland journey to the Cape was saved to the farmers. The first cargo shipped at that port was in July 1788, when the Company's yacht *Johanna Jacoba* was laden with wheat for Batavia. It was purchased by the officer stationed there at 9*s*. 7½*d*. a muid clear to the producer, after the tithe was deducted, which was the price given at the Cape. But after 1789 the price at Mossel Bay was reduced to 7*s*. 2¾*d*. a muid, after the deduction of the tithe, the difference between that and the price given at the Cape being set against the cost of sending vessels specially for it.

In the same year a magazine for storage of timber was opened at Plettenberg's Bay, the post at Zwart River having been broken up and the men removed to the forest nearest the bay. Mr. Jan Frederik Meding was placed in charge of the magazine. The first cargo of timber was shipped in August 1788, when the Cape packet *Meermin*, of which François Duminy was master, was laden with waggon wood and material for gun carriages.

When Governor Van de Graaff arrived in South Africa, the construction of the Amsterdam battery was so far advanced that he was unable to alter the design, though he considered it faulty. He therefore completed it, and in February 1787 the guns were mounted. On the 23rd of that month the first trial of the armament was made, when one of the cannon burst, and two men were killed and five badly wounded. The governor, who was standing close by, was also slightly hurt.

A battery was then built in Rogge Bay, and after its completion some additions to the old battery Chavonnes were commenced. The remaining forts in Table Valley were repaired. The earthen embankment thrown up by the French troops in 1781 between Fort Knokke and the Devil's Peak—commonly called the French lines—was strengthened, as was also the line between the castle and Fort Knokke.

In the summer of 1787–8 the regiment of Wurtemburg—a body of mercenary troops two thousand strong—arrived at the Cape to relieve the Swiss regiment of Meuron, which proceeded to Colombo. The garrison included also the national battalion, as it was called, under Colonel Gordon, about six hundred strong, and four hundred engineers and artillerymen.

As landdrost of the new district, to the formation of which the directors had consented, on the 13th of December 1785 the council of policy selected an old burgher resident in the village of Stellenbosch, named Maurits Herman Otto Woeke, who was believed to be a man of sound judgment. He was directed to make a tour along the border, to select a site for his court, and to report fully to the council. The district at the same time had the name Graaff Reinet given to it, in honour of the governor and his lady. It was decided that it should be bounded on the west by the Gamka river from its source to the Zwartberg, that range of mountains to the Gamtoos river, and thence the Gamtoos to the sea; on the east by the Great Fish river; and on the south by the ocean. On the north the boundary was undefined, the only fixed point being the beacon that had been placed by Governor Van Plettenberg on the bank of the Zeekoe river.

As the best site for the public offices, Mr. Woeke selected two farms near the source of the Sunday river, then in occupation of a burgher named Dirk Coetsee, who agreed to dispose of the buildings on them for about 530*l.*, and to accept land of equal extent elsewhere. This arrangement was ratified by the council. In July 1786 a board of six heemraden was appointed, two of whom were thereafter to retire every year, and to be succeeded by others selected by the council of policy from a double nomination. The first members were Adriaan van Jaarsveld, David de Villiers, David Schalk van der Merwe, Andries Pieter Burger, Josua Joubert, and Jacobus Gustaf Triegard. In October the landdrost opened his court for the first time.

In the new district, cattle breeding was almost the only pursuit of the Europeans. Until building sites were given out in the village of Graaff Reinet, there was not a rood of ground held under any other tenure than that of yearly lease. Once in a twelvemonth each family who could do so sent a waggon laden with butter and soap to Cape Town to procure household requisites; but the people, without feeling it a hardship, managed to live with very few imported articles. From long warfare with savages, their habits of self-reliance were highly developed, and they were exceedingly averse to restraint.

It was intended by the government that the district should be nearly self-supporting, that is, it was to cost the Company very little for defence or maintenance. Funds for local purposes were to be raised, as in Stellenbosch and Swellendam, by a yearly tax of one shilling and four pence for every hundred sheep and one penny for every head of horned cattle, besides special rates when necessary.

The struggle for existence carried on with the Bushmen in the new district was constant, and on neither side was any quarter shown or indeed possible. The reports of murders of Europeans and farm servants, of depredations and reprisals, are wearisome to read, and it would need volumes to repeat them all, without any clearer idea being given of the nature of the warfare than can be conveyed in a few sentences. No European dared venture an hour's ride from his homestead without arms in his hand. From four farms adjoining the drostdy the cattle were swept off within a few weeks after the arrival of the landdrost. The Hottentots suffered even more severely than the Europeans, whole clans being ruined, and numerous individuals being tortured to death by Bushmen. On the other hand, commandos of Europeans and Hottentots were almost constantly engaged hunting the marauders in the mountains, and shooting down all who would not surrender. The government provided ammunition, but nothing else. Captive women and children were distributed among the farmers in the vain hope of compelling them to live by industry, but they invariably made their escape after a short detention, and returned to their predatory habits. This was the normal condition of things throughout the district of Graaff Reinet and along the northern border of the district of Stellenbosch.

Mr. Woeke was instructed by the council to visit the principal Kaffir chiefs in the neighbourhood of the colony, to assure them of the friendship of the government, and to make them presents of brass wire, beads, and other articles of small value which they were known to prize highly. He was ordered to take great care that the Fish river was observed as the boundary, and that no Europeans crossed it or molested the Kaffirs in any way. The bartering of cattle by the colonists was strictly forbidden.

The condition of the Kosa tribe at this time was such that it was difficult to make any satisfactory arrangements. Since the first Kaffir war, the chief Rarabe had been killed in an engagement with a Tembu army. His great son, Umlawu by name, had died before him, and had left a lad of tender years as heir to the dignity of principal ruler of all the clans west of the Kei. Upon Rarabe's death, his councillors selected his son Ndlambe as regent during the minority of Gaika (correct Kaffir spelling: Ngqika), heir of Umlawu. This was in accordance with custom, and there was no other person who could be appointed; but the clans that had crossed the Kei before Rarabe maintained that with his death their vassalage had ceased, except to Galeka, the paramount head of the whole tribe. There was thus a great deal of jealousy and discontent among the chiefs.

Mr. Woeke had a meeting with Ndlambe, who expressed

himself desirous of living in peace and friendship with the white people, and presents were exchanged between them. The landdrost reported, however, that a rupture between the two races could easily take place. There were Kaffirs in service with farmers all over the country, even to within two days' journey of the village of Swellendam, and the colonists were unwilling to part with them. A single case of ill treatment might at any moment bring on hostilities. Not a few lawless individuals also were engaged in the forbidden cattle trade with the Kaffirs, and as they were not accustomed to restraint, mere placaats had no terrors for them. With fifty or sixty soldiers stationed in posts along the Fish river, it would be possible to maintain order; but without physical force to support the law, the irregularities complained of would continue.

The condition of suspense described by the landdrost lasted until March 1789, when a large body of Kaffirs, headed by the chiefs Langa, Cungwa, and others of less note, suddenly crossed the Fish river, and spread over the Zuurveld. The farmers fled before the invaders, but were unable to save the whole of their cattle. The landdrost immediately instructed the burgher captain Daniel Willem Kuhne to take measures for the defence of the district, and despatched an express to Cape Town with a report that war was unavoidable and a request that the council would send a hundred soldiers to his assistance.

Mr. Woeke's letter reached Cape Town on the 20th of March. The council at once met, and came to a decision that war with the Kaffirs must be avoided at any price. The landdrost was censured for giving instructions to call out a commando for defence, as a collision might be the result. The secretary of the district—Jan Jacob Wagener by name—had tendered his resignation some time previously, and the council now appointed a clerk named Honoratus Christiaan Maynier to succeed him. Mr. Wagener was a professor of the belief that simplicity and innocence were virtues of savage life, and Mr. Maynier, who on all occasions studied his own pocket more than anything else, professed whatever principles his superiors for the time being held, so that he could be depended upon to carry out the views of the government. The council appointed these two men to form with the landdrost a commission to arrange matters with the Kaffirs who had overrun the Zuurveld, and they were plainly instructed to buy the enemy off with goods supplied to them for the purpose.

In the meantime Captain Kuhne had raised a commando, which was no sooner in the field than the invaders, without waiting to be attacked, fell back to the Fish river, which they found in flood, so that they were unable to cross. They were lying on the bank, and the burgher commando was approaching, when the instructions of the council were received by the landdrost. He put on record his opinion that a mistake fatal to the future tranquillity of the country was being made, and forwarded to the council a letter to that effect; but he carried out his orders with as much zeal as if they had been in accordance with his own views. The commando was at once discharged. Not a shot had been fired in retaliation for the losses sustained by the invasion, nor a single head of cattle recovered, so the burghers were indignant and almost mutinous when they were required to disband.

As soon as the new secretary Maynier arrived at Graaff Reinet with the goods provided by the government, the members of the commission made ready to visit the Zuurveld and seek an interview with the Kaffir chiefs. On the 7th of June they left the village, accompanied by the heemraden Josua Joubert and Jacobus Gustaf Triegard, the militia captains Jan du Plessis and Andries Burger, the militia adjutant Barend Lindeque, and the burghers Pieter Lindeque and Roelof Kampher, all men well known for their friendly disposition towards the Kaffirs in former years. Upon arriving at the Kowie river, they found the stream swollen by heavy rains which had recently fallen, so they encamped on its bank, and sent some Hottentots to request the Gunukwebe chief Tshaka to pay them a visit.

On the 21st of June the Hottentots returned with several

petty Kaffir captains, who informed the landdrost that Tshaka and his son Cungwa were unable to travel, on account of sickness in their families; but they had been sent to hear what the white men had to say. With this characteristic Kaffir address, they presented two oxen in the name of the chief Tshaka. The landdrost asked why they had invaded the colony. They replied that they did not regard their action as an invasion, because they considered the country between the Fish river and the Kowie belonged to them, they having purchased it some years before from a Hottentot named Ruiter.

The landdrost asked them if they were not aware that after the war of 1781 the Amambala chief Langa, the Imidange chief Mahuta, the Amantinde chief Cika, and the Amagwali chief Koba—the same people who were now with the Gunukwebe clan in the colony—had consented to the Fish river being the boundary between the two races. They did not deny that it was so, but said they were willing to pay as much tribute to the government for the district between the Fish river and the Kowie as the farmers had paid rent. And in language that bore but one meaning they declined to give up possession of it. The commission sent large presents of copper plates, brass wire, knives, &c., to the chiefs, but could not induce them to retire to their own country.

Finding their efforts useless, Messrs. Woeke and Maynier with the burghers returned to Graaff Reinet, leaving Mr. Wagener to arrange matters as best he could. Just at this time a rumour reached the Kaffirs that the farmers away towards Swellendam were going into lager, and remembering the prelude to Van Jaarsveld's campaign of 1781, they were seized with a sudden panic. Not only did they retire in haste beyond the Fish river, but many of them fled far beyond it, and concealed themselves in the thickets of the Amatola mountains.

This was the condition of things when Mr. Wagener, attended by an escort of twelve armed men, on the 18th of July met the chief Cungwa and a party of Kaffirs at a ford of the Fish river. Cungwa pressed his claim to the ground as far as the Kowie, basing his pretensions upon its purchase from the Hottentot captain Ruiter, who was little better than a freebooter, and whose only right to sell was derived from a brief occupation. Mr. Wagener declined to admit that Ruiter's sale was binding upon the Europeans, but to remove the grievance, he offered to refund to the Kaffirs as much as they had paid for the district. Cungwa would not agree to this proposal. Mr. Wagener then consented to the return of the Kaffirs and to their occupation of the land between the Fish river and the Kowie during the pleasure of the government, without prejudice to the ownership of the Europeans. With his report to this effect to the board of landdrost and heemraden of Graaff Reinet on the 3rd of August 1789, ends the official account of the second Kaffir invasion of the colony and of its disastrous consequences to the farmers.

In documents issued by the government the arrangement made by Mr. Wagener was henceforth termed a restoration of peace and quietness; but the burghers of Graaff Reinet chose to call it by a very different name. Almost any other people in the world would have abandoned a district in which they were exposed to such ruinous losses as those sustained by the hardy and persevering frontier colonists at this period. But they were determined to hold their own. In the neighbourhood of the Kaffirs they guarded their herds with arms in their hands, while along the great mountain range they were continually struggling with the Bushmen.

The wild, free, healthy life which they led had many charms for people of adventurous disposition, and several travellers contrasted it favourably with the dull routine of the farmers' existence in European countries. Comfortable and well-furnished houses were not to be found on the frontier, for no one cared to build or to buy what might be destroyed the next day; but there was no lack of food or of other first necessaries of life.

The burghers were constantly complaining that they

received from the Company nothing in return for the rents which they paid and the tithes of such produce as they sent to Cape Town. They had another grievance in the paper money. The butchers at the Cape were in the habit of sending out agents to purchase slaughter cattle, and these had always given in payment notes of hand of their employers. The farmers who now took these notes to Cape Town received only paper money, which was by law a legal tender. In the interior the paper was almost worthless, for, in addition to its not being redeemable at pleasure, so many forged notes were in existence that people were afraid of it.

After 1789 there was very little respect paid to the government authorities in the district of Graaff Reinet. Mr. Woeke became addicted to drunkenness, and allowed a violent temper to become his master. On several occasions he poured torrents of abuse upon the heemraden and militia officers, which they were not slow to resent. He and the secretary Maynier were also continually quarrelling, and the latter, being a favourite with the government, did not scruple to irritate his superior officer. The condition of the district was thus very little removed from anarchy.

In the district of Swellendam matters were almost as bad. Many of the farmers had fallen in arrear with their land rents, which, in fact, some of them took little trouble to pay, though the government was willing to receive cattle instead of money. The landdrost Onkruydt, after getting the district accounts into inextricable confusion and allowing the public buildings to fall into ruin, resigned and returned to the Netherlands, when the secretary of Stellenbosch and Drakenstein—Anthony Alexander Faure—was appointed to succeed him, 21st of April 1789. Mr. Faure did his utmost to restore order in his office, but was unable to do so. The people of this district were, however, comparatively free from robberies by Bushmen and Kaffirs, and were therefore in more comfortable circumstances than their friends on the border.

The district of Stellenbosch and Drakenstein was more populous than either of the others. Along its northern border, warfare with Bushmen was constant, and the colonists were in the same condition as those of Graaff Reinet. But in the long-settled parts of the district the people were living in comfort and ease. Many of the substantial dwelling houses erected before and during this period remained until our own times, as did also the oaks and other trees with which the homesteads were beautified. The life led by the owners of the largest of these establishments was that of country gentlemen all over the civilised world, a healthy, enjoyable, useful life. The rough labour of the farms was performed by African slaves under the direction of European overseers; the mechanical work, such as that of the carpenter, mason, and cooper, was chiefly executed by natives of the Indian islands, either free or slave. In August 1785, upon the death of Mr. Van Ryneveld, Hendrik Lodewyk Bletterman was appointed landdrost of the district.

Cape Town at this period was a very different place from what it had been in earlier times. With the arrival of the French troops in 1781 an expensive fashion of living had set in, and every one was now striving to become possessed of a handsome house filled with costly furniture and a retinue of useless slaves. All kinds of European wares were introduced in Danish ships, and were sold at enormous profits. The directors at Amsterdam became alarmed when they ascertained what large amounts were due in Holland for house furniture alone purchased on credit, and complained that the Cape was becoming known to travellers as 'Little Paris.' Money seemed plentiful, and every one forgot that the apparent prosperity was based upon the insecure foundation of military expenditure.

The governor, Colonel Van de Graaff, lived in the most extravagant manner at the expense of the Company. The stables, which in Van Plettenberg's time contained sixty-six horses, were now provided with double that number; and equipages, from a state coach and a travelling waggon to a light two-wheeled fly, were multiplied to an unreasonable number. The governor's son, Captain Sebastiaan Willem van de Graaff, was appointed master of the stables, and was left to do almost as he pleased. Everything else was in the same style, reckless waste of the Company's effects being entirely disregarded.

The public expenditure, or the money paid out of the Company's chest for all purposes at the Cape, now reached a sum of rather over 120,000*l*. a year.

The revenue had gone on steadily increasing from 17,274*l*. in 1781 to 28,912*l*. in 1791, the increase being due chiefly to the larger sums paid for the right to sell wines and spirits and to a different manner of collecting the tithes of grain. In former years the farmers were required to make statements as to the quantity of grain gathered by them, and upon these statements the tithes were charged. The standard of truth with regard to such returns was very low, just as it is to-day in the matter of returns for municipal taxation. For instance, there were years when the quantity of wheat exported was considerably in excess of the quantity grown according to the census rolls. But recently a system had been introduced of collecting actual tithes either in money or in kind upon all grain passing the barrier into town, and it was found to give a much larger revenue to government, although the whole quantity consumed in the country districts became exempt from taxation. The total revenue received from the 1st of July 1781 to the 1st of July 1791 was 221,075*l*., or at the rate of 22,107*l*. 10*s*. yearly. It was made up of the following items:

Licenses to sell wines and spirits, sold yearly by public auction, and the export duty on sales of wines and spirits to foreigners, also farmed out	£105,227
Rent of 4*l*. 16*s*. each on ordinary cattle farms	42,784
Tax of 12*s*. on each legger of wine brought to town	26,265
Transfer dues on sales of land, at 10 per cent on the purchase amount when the property had been held for less than 3 years, 5 per cent when it had been held from 3 to 10 years, and 2½ per cent when it had been held over 10 years; also since July 1790 2½ per cent on sales of improvements on leaseholds	21,835
Stamps	12,521
Tithes of grain	9,519
Rent of 4*l*. 16*s*. each on cattle farms held in connection with freeholds under Van Imhof's tenure	1,814
Freight and insurance from Mossel Bay	855
Rent of garden plots at 2*s*. a morgen	265
Total revenue during ten years	£221,075

The profits on the sale of goods out of the Company's stores were on an average about 6,200*l.* There was thus a deficiency to be made good of nearly 92,000*l.* a year, and the Company was at this time almost hopelessly insolvent. Its debt in 1785 was nearly seven million pounds sterling, and the states provincial of Holland and Zeeland were obliged to come to its rescue, or it would have sunk under the burden. These provinces became security for heavy loans, besides raising by a special tax a sum of about two and a half millions sterling, which money was lent upon low interest to the Company, in order that it might have a chance of recovering itself. Its condition was commonly attributed to losses during the war with England, but there were many men in the Netherlands as well as in the Indies who knew that the corruption of its own officers had quite as much to do with its decline.

From sheer inability to raise more money, in 1790 the Company was obliged to reduce its expenditure very greatly. On the 10th of October of that year the directors issued orders that the regiment of Wurtemburg was to be sent to Java immediately, and that all work upon fortifications was to be stopped. They admitted that the remaining troops were insufficient for the defence of the Cape in the event of war, but they were helpless in the matter. A few days later they gave instructions that the military outposts in the country districts should be abandoned and the stations be sold, that the country seat used by the governor at Newlands should be sold, that their slaves should be reduced in number to four hundred and fifty, that all the mechanics and sailors who could be spared should be sent to Batavia, and that the horses and vehicles of all kinds in their stables should at once be disposed of and the proceeds be paid into the treasury.

The governor had never given them satisfaction. They complained that he kept them in ignorance of everything that it was important they should know, while forwarding despatches covering hundreds of pages of foolscap and containing nothing that could not be told in a few sentences.

This complaint was thoroughly well founded. After the governor's departure, the council informed the directors that he had kept the whole staff of clerks in the secretary's office engaged in writing and copying these worse than useless letters. They were also greatly displeased with his extravagance, though they were still ignorant of the full cost of his administration. His quarrelsome disposition was another cause of complaint, and his arbitrary conduct in issuing orders and incurring expense without consulting the council was strongly disapproved of.

And certainly the directors had cause to complain, for the government of the colony had never before sunk so low in the estimation of those who came in contact with it. In August 1786 Mr. Hacker had retired at his own request, and had been succeeded as secunde by Johan Isaac Rhenius, a member of an old South African family, but whose life had been passed chiefly in the Company's service in India. The fiscal Serrurier had died in May 1785, and in February 1789 Jan Nicholas van Lynden arrived from the Netherlands and assumed the duty. Both of these men were quarrelsome by disposition. To the colonists the government appeared corrupt almost beyond power of expression, and the bickerings of the principal officers called forth contempt as well as hatred. During the debates in the council, violent scenes often took place. On one occasion the governor in a passion drew his sword and would have wounded the dispenser Le Sueur, if the latter had not warded off the blow with his cane. The proceedings, as recorded, contain protests and counter protests in great profusion.

Out of the council, these wretched disputes affected all classes of the community, and discord prevailed everywhere. Whole reams of paper are filled with records of petty quarrels of no interest to any one now. A single instance of the depth to which the representative of the Company descended will be sufficient as an illustration. In a sermon upon Jezebel the Rev. Mr. Serrurier gave offence to the governor, who maintained that his lady was pointedly alluded to. Shortly afterwards a committee of the high court of justice was appointed to name the new streets and squares of the town, when Berg street—now St. George's—upon which the parsonage fronted, was changed to Venus street, and the signboard was nailed above the clergyman's door. Mr. Serrurier protested, but without avail, and it was only after the governor left the colony that the old name of Berg street was restored.

The directors were desirous of dismissing the governor, but the stadtholder, with whom he was a favourite, would not consent, and at that time the stadtholder's power as governor-general of the East India Company was greater than it had ever been before, owing to the political revolution which had recently taken place in the Netherlands. The inhabitants of that country were divided into two parties, one of which was in favour of democratic government and alliance with France, the other in favour of the government of the stadtholder and alliance with England. The first of these was supreme in 1785, and in November of that year a treaty of close alliance with France was concluded. The arrest of the princess of Orange, who was a sister of the king of Prussia, on her attempting to enter the Hague in June 1787, brought into the country a Prussian army, which was welcomed by the conservative faction, and the government of the stadtholder was restored. In April 1788 a treaty of mutual defence was entered into between the Government of England and the States General, and in the same year a triple alliance was concluded between Great Britain, Prussia, and the Netherlands.

The stadtholder, as governor-general of the East India Company, would only agree to the recall of Van de Graaff under pretence of his being required at home to give information upon the colony. To this effect a despatch, written by the directors on the 14th of October 1790, arrived here on the 10th of the following February, in which the governor was instructed to leave for Europe within three months after its receipt, and to transfer the administration during his absence to the secunde Rhenius. The three months expired, and the governor was still in Cape Town.

The secunde and his party in the council protested against this disobedience of the orders of the directors and the detention of a first-class Indiaman in Table Bay during the winter season; but the governor took his own time. When he was ready, on the 24th of June 1791, he issued instructions to Mr. Rhenius how to act during his absence, and embarked in the *Beverwyk*.

Colonel Van de Graaff returned to Holland, where he retained the title of governor of the Cape colony and received his salary as such, although early in 1793 he resumed his duty in the national army. In 1794 he was promoted to the rank of major-general, and appointed director of fortifications from the Waal to the Zuiderzee, when he resigned his situation in the Company's service. The revolution a few months later deprived him of employment, on account of his adherence to the stadtholder's cause, and he retired to Germany, where he died in 1812.

The fiscal Van Lynden returned to Europe in the same ship with the governor, without leave from either the directors or the Cape council. On his arrival in the Netherlands, he stated that he dared not remain in South Africa after Van de Graaff's departure, as there would certainly be an insurrection, when his life—or his limbs at least—would be in danger. He went on board the *Beverwyk* during the night, leaving his family at the Cape. The governor's son—Captain Sebastiaan Willem van de Graaff—was married to his daughter, and this family connection had enabled him to act in such a manner as to draw down the intense hatred of the colonists. On one occasion Van Lynden had put a white man to torture, who, to be relieved of pain, confessed himself guilty of a crime of which he was afterwards proved to be innocent, but for which he suffered punishment. In October 1789 the directors had issued instructions that a duty of five per cent upon the value of all articles imported or exported, except by themselves, should be levied for the benefit of the Company; but these instructions were not carried out, because the fiscal had previously imposed the same charges for his own benefit, and continued to collect and keep the money, under the plea that it was a legitimate perquisite of his office.

Upon Van Lynden's flight, the council appointed Mr. Jacob Pieter de Nys to act as fiscal until the pleasure of the directors could be made known.

The instructions concerning the breaking up of the military posts in the interior were carried out, and the stations were sold by public auction to the highest bidders. The horses and all the varied contents of the Company's stables in Cape Town were disposed of in the same manner. The country seat at Newlands, which had been the favourite residence of Father Tulbagh and had been used by both the succeeding governors, was purchased by Mr. Hendrik Vos for 4,400*l.* The country seat of Rustenburg, at Rondebosch, was retained. It had been occasionally used by the secunde in Tulbagh's time, and constantly ever since; but two-thirds of the wine made from its vineyards had been claimed by the governors as a perquisite, the remaining third being left to the secunde. From its extensive gardens, cultivated by the Company's slaves, both the governor and the secunde had drawn all the vegetables needed in their establishments, after which whatever was left was sent to the hospital.

When the work on the fortifications was stopped, the enlargements of the battery Chavonnes, designed by Governor Van de Graaff, were not quite completed. A battery which he had planned between the castle and the Devil's Peak, and which had been named the Coehoorn, was only a little advanced beyond the foundations. The battery Gordon, built in 1781–2 at the upper end of the line of earthworks between Fort Knokke and the Devil's Peak, was greatly out of repair. The remaining fortifications in Table Valley were in good order. The new hospital was not yet finished, though it had cost the Company nearly 52,000*l.*, exclusive of slave labour.

The census returns of 1791 show the population of the colony as consisting of 3,613 European burghers, with 2,460 married women, and 6,955 children; 39 European men servants; 456 European men—exclusive of soldiers—in the Company's service, with 291 married women, and 760 children; and 11,026 men slaves, 3,687 women slaves, and 2,683 slave children, belonging to the Company and to private individuals. The small number of slave children is chiefly due to emancipation. No mention is made of free blacks or of Hottentots in the returns.

Another great change was notified by the directors in March 1791. They had abandoned the exportation of all European wares on their own account, except to China and Japan, and had thrown that trade open to private individuals upon payment of customs duties. Foreigners, however, were not to be allowed to take part in it. From the Cape, wine could be exported by private individuals, and in February 1791 permission to send a cargo of wheat to Europe was accorded by the council to the burgher Tieleman Roos, of Drakenstein.

For several years there had been an impression among certain burghers that gold was to be found in large quantities in the desert region north of the Orange river and bordering on the Atlantic. It was currently reported and believed that the English traveller Paterson had discovered rich ore there, though he had not made his discovery known. Mr. Sebastiaan Valentyn van Reenen, who had accompanied Lieutenant Paterson on one of his excursions, had really become possessed of a piece of ore or rock from which a chemist had extracted some grains of gold, though the place where the substance had been found was unknown.

Fired with the idea of making a discovery that would enrich himself and benefit his native country, Mr. Willem van Reenen, of the farm Zeekoe Vlei, on the Elephant river, with the permission of the council fitted out an exploring expedition at his own expense, and on the 17th of September 1791 set out for the north. He had with him as companions Messrs. Pieter Brand, Adriaan Louw, Barend Freyn, and Frederik Wysman, besides several half-breeds and a large party of Hottentots.

On the 30th of October he crossed the Great river, and on the 18th of November rested at the furthest point reached by Captain Hop's expedition in 1761. The country was parched by heat and drought, Bushmen and lions were very troublesome, and the oxen were beginning to die; but Van Reenen and his companions still pushed on. On the 23rd of January 1792 they reached a mountain, where was a spring of very hot water, from which the flow was so great that several morgen of ground might be irrigated. Copper ore was found there.

During the night after their arrival they were attacked by a party of Namaquas, who killed two of their Hottentots and wounded a slave; but next morning the chief of the attacking party sent to say that the assault had been made by mistake, and presented three oxen and four sheep as a peace offering. The name of the chief is not given, but his people are called the Godousies. It is not possible to connect that title with any clan now living in the country. The mountain had until recently been in possession of the Ovaherero or Damaras, but the Namaquas were then masters of it. Mr. Van Reenen named it Mount Rhenius. At this place a camp was formed, while the country around was explored. In the diary of the expedition there are no indications by which the locality can be identified, except those here given; but from an observation in another document, it is found to have been within easy reach of Walfish Bay.

Pieter Brand with a party of Hottentots pushed on fifteen days' journey further, and made himself well acquainted with the condition of the Damaras, who belong to the Bantu family, and of the Namaquas, who are Hottentots. The Damaras had been conquered by the Namaquas, and had been deprived of their horned cattle, goats, and sheep. They informed Mr. Brand that he would yet have to travel nine days before he would find Damaras in possession of cattle. They had been able to hold their own, they said, until the Namaquas obtained iron in large quantities from the south, when they had been subjugated. Copper rings of their own manufacture were plentiful with them.

Mr. Brand also met with black people living like Bushmen on nothing but game and roots, but speaking a dialect of the Hottentot language. This is the earliest notice of the people now commonly called Berg Damaras, whose condition is a mystery to travellers. No subsequent inquirer has learnt more than Pieter Brand has put on record: that they are Bantu by blood, Hottentots by language, and Bushmen by habit. On the 14th of March the party moved from Mount Rhenius to a place close by, which they named Modder Fontein. Here they remained until the 23rd of April. There was abundance of game in the neighbourhood, and they had plenty of food. Of rhinoceroses alone they killed sixty-five, and of giraffes six. Having laden the waggons with ore which they believed contained gold, but which on their arrival at the Cape was proved to be copper, they turned homeward. On the way they visited a clan of Namaquas called in the diary the Keykous, who can be identified with the people now known as the red nation. The name of the chief is given by Mr. Van Reenen as Nonbelo, but the colonial Hottentots called him Roode Mos. He was very friendly, bringing four oxen as a present, and offering to assist the Europeans to punish the Godousies for attacking the party on its arrival at Mount Rhenius. The offer was declined. On the 20th of June 1792 the expedition reached Mr. Van Reenen's farm Zeekoe Vlei, having been absent nine months, and having lost by drought and Bushmen one hundred and forty oxen.

From these travellers was received the first authentic account of the condition of the Damara clans, and of the feud between them and the Namaquas, a feud which has continued with scarcely an intermission down to our own day.

During the five years 1785–9, the average number of ships that put into Table Bay was 139, and that put into Simon's Bay 25. Of the whole number, 334 were Dutch, 212 French, 84 English, 70 Danish, 62 American, 29 Portuguese, 10 Austrian, 8 Spanish, 7 Swedish, 4 Prussian, and 1 was Italian. After 1789 it is impossible to give statistics of shipping, as several of the journals and outgoing despatch books are missing from the archives.

The following vessels were wrecked on our coast during these years:

In the night between the 3rd and 4th of May 1785 the Company's homeward-bound ship *Brederode* struck on a reef off Cape Agulhas, and went to pieces. Most of the crew got away in boats, but twelve lives were lost. None of her cargo was saved.

On the 3rd of May 1786 the wreck of a small French schooner, with a cargo of wine from Bordeaux, was found on the coast a little to the eastward of Cape Hangklip. Two dead bodies were found close by, but no further particulars could be ascertained.

In the evening of the 11th of May 1786 the Dutch national frigate *Holland*, one of a fleet of ships of war bound to Java, when entering False Bay struck on a reef and became a total wreck. Eight lives were lost.

On the 19th of August 1786 the wreck of a French brig named the *Rozette* was found close to Cape Point, and it was ascertained that she was from Bordeaux bound to Mauritius. There was no living person on board. Some days later six seamen were found under suspicious circumstances at the Cape, and were arrested, when it was discovered that they had murdered the officers and other sailors of the *Rozette*, and had then run the vessel ashore. They were tried and executed for the crime.

On the 7th of October 1786 the Company's schooner *Catwyk aan Rhyn* was driven ashore in Simon's Bay in a violent gale, and became a wreck, but no lives were lost.

In the night between the 16th and 17th of May 1788 the Company's ship *Avenhoorn* was driven from her anchors in Table Bay by a gale from the north-west, and was lost. She was about to proceed to Mossel Bay to take in wheat for Batavia, and had no cargo on board. All hands were saved.

In August 1788 the Company's ship *Maria*, homeward-bound from Ceylon, was met off Plettenberg's Bay by the Cape packet *Meermin*, and found to be in a condition of distress. Her crew had been attacked by scurvy, and only the skipper and four men were able to walk. By the help of the *Meermin's* crew, the *Maria* was taken into Plettenberg's Bay, where she was brought to anchor; but a few days later in a gale from the south-east she was driven ashore and became a total wreck. No lives were lost.

In the night between the 16th and 17th of October 1788 the French frigate *Penelope*, when trying to enter Simon's Bay, ran ashore on Muizenburg beach and went to pieces. There were 430 men on board, most of whom got safely to land.

On the 16th of May 1789 the Dutch ship *Drietal Handelaars*, homeward-bound from Ceylon under charter by the Company, was driven from her anchors off Zwartklip in False Bay, and went to pieces on the rocks. No lives were lost.

On the 12th of April 1790 a fleet of ships—mostly under foreign flags—was at anchor in Table Bay. The weather was stormy, with the wind from the north-north-west, accompanied by heavy showers of rain. In the morning a French ship parted her cables and went ashore near the mouth of Salt River, where she was joined shortly afterwards by the Genoese barque *Maria*. In the afternoon a French brigantine, an American barque, an English whaling ship, the Danish Company's fine ship *Erfprins van Augustenburgh*, and the Cape packet *Helena Louisa* went ashore. Towards evening the wind abated, or the number of wrecks would have increased, as other vessels had parted one of their cables. No lives were lost on this occasion. The *Helena Louisa* was got afloat again, and her damages were repaired.

Owing to this disaster, in January 1794 the directors issued orders that their ships were thereafter to make use of Simon's Bay from the 10th of April to the 1st of October, instead of from the 15th of May to the 15th of August, as previously.

In November 1787 an English fleet, to which considerable interest attaches, put into Table Bay for supplies. It was the fleet that conveyed the first convicts, male and female, to Botany Bay, to found the colony of New South Wales.

In November 1789 the British transport *Guardian*, under command of Lieutenant E. Riou, put into Table Bay, and took on board large supplies of grain and live stock, intended for the use of the settlement at Botany Bay. On the 24th of December, when about twelve hundred miles from the Cape of Good Hope, the *Guardian* struck upon an iceberg, and was so much injured that next day it was feared she would sink. Lieutenant Riou would not leave the ship himself, but he ordered the four boats to be got out, and with his approval as many of the crew as they could contain embarked in them and set sail for the African coast. The launch fell in with a French ship on the 4th of January 1790, and her crew of fifteen were taken on board and brought to the Cape. Those in the other boats must have perished. Contrary to expectation, the *Guardian*, though waterlogged, did not go down, and several days after the disaster a Dutch vessel homeward-bound from Batavia fell in with her. Assistance in men and materials was rendered, and she was brought back to Table Bay, the Dutch vessel keeping by her until she was safe in port.

Since the arrival of Governor Van de Graaff there had not been many changes in the staff of clergymen. In May 1785 the Rev. Meent Borcherds, who had recently arrived from Holland, was appointed third clergyman of the Cape. In September of the following year the Rev. Helperus Ritzema van Lier arrived from Holland, when Mr. Borcherds, at his own request, was transferred to the vacant church of Stellenbosch, and Mr. Van Lier succeeded him as third minister of the Cape. In April 1786 the Rev. Petrus van der Spuy, junior, who had completed his studies in the Netherlands, returned to South Africa, and was appointed to the vacant church of Zwartland.

Graaff Reinet, like Swellendam, had as yet only a sick comforter, who was also schoolmaster. In September 1791 the directors engaged the Rev. Jan Hendrik Manger to minister to the people of Graaff Reinet; but when he arrived in South Africa no instructions had been received concerning him, and the council therefore resolved to keep him at the Cape until advices should come to hand. He was still doing duty instead of Mr. Van Lier, who was ill, in July 1792.

Steps were, however, taken in anticipation to establish a consistory at Graaff Reinet, and on the 13th of March 1792 the council approved of Marthinus Wessel Pretorius and Jan Jacobsen as elders, and selected from a double nomination Andries Pretorius and Barend Burger as deacons of the newly-formed congregation.

There had been a little friction between the Dutch Reformed and Lutheran consistories at the Cape on the subject of baptism of children whose parents did not both belong to the same church. The directors settled the matter to the satisfaction of all but a few who held extreme opinions, by issuing instructions that boys should be baptized in the church to which their father belonged, and girls in the church to which their mother belonged, all persons to be free at eighteen years of age to leave one communion and join the other, if they wished to do so.

There was at this time a strong desire expressed by the leading colonists for better means of educating their children. More than half a century earlier there had been a high school in Cape Town; but it had not been sufficiently supported, and had therefore been discontinued. All who could afford it employed private tutors, but in the country districts the men who were engaged as teachers were usually unfit for their calling, through want of education and character. In and near the town a better class of persons could be obtained, and a few of the wealthiest colonists sent their sons to Europe to complete their studies. In 1791 a movement was commenced for the establishment of a good school at each church and seat of magistracy in the country, and of a high school in Cape Town, in which the Latin and French languages should be taught. A committee was appointed, and after long discussion a plan was prepared, which was submitted to the council and approved of in March 1792. It depended chiefly upon voluntary subscriptions to commence with, and payment of school fees thereafter. A sum of money was collected for the Latin school in Cape Town, and a building in Graaffe—now Grave—street was purchased from Skipper François Duminy for 1,000*l.* In September 1793 Cornelis

Josias van Baak was engaged as preceptor, and the institution was opened; but the course of political events shortly afterwards caused it to be closed, and with that the whole plan fell through.

In consequence of the helplessness to which the East India Company was now reduced, the States General appointed a commission of four members to examine minutely into its affairs and to check further abuses. These gentlemen—the baron Van der Does, the lord of Marquette, Mr. P. H. van de Waal, and Mr. H. van Straalen—sent in preliminary reports in February and July 1791, one result of which was that a board with very great powers was constituted to examine into abuses in India and rectify them.

The individuals selected to form this board were Mr. Sebastiaan Cornelis Nederburgh, chief advocate of the East India Company, Captain Simon Hendrik Frykenius, of the national navy, Mr. Willem Arnold Alting, governor-general, and Mr. Hendrik van Stokkum, director-general of Netherlands India. On the 19th of August 1791 a commission was issued by the stadtholder and the directors, empowering the members of this board, who could act separately anywhere but at Batavia, to investigate all matters connected with the Company's affairs, to bring to light abuses and malpractices, to make necessary reforms, to dismiss corrupt officials of every grade and either send them to Holland or cause them to be tried by a court of justice, to fill all vacant offices with trustworthy men, and generally to do as they should judge best, for which purpose the same power was given to them as was held by those who signed the document.

It will not be necessary to enter into the instructions given to the board regarding the dependencies in India, where fraudulent practices throughout the administration, carelessness for the Company's interests, and insubordination among all classes of officials, were pointed out as the chief evils to be checked. Only two members could visit the Cape, and to them special instructions were given by the stadtholder and the directors, acting with the concurrence of the commission appointed by the States General.

Messrs. Nederburgh and Frykenius were directed on their arrival to see that the stoppage of public works resolved upon in the previous year was carried into effect. They were to establish the administration in the simplest and least expensive manner, and endeavour to increase the revenue. They could grant the colonists liberty to carry on a trade in slaves with Madagascar and the east coast of Africa, to establish whale fisheries, and to convey farm produce to any of the Dutch possessions in India and dispose of it there to the best account, provided that the vessels employed were owned in the colony or the Netherlands, were manned by crews consisting of at least half Cape colonists, and did not go beyond prescribed limits. They could allow private individuals to export wheat from Mossel Bay and timber from Plettenberg's Bay. They were to impose import and export duties, and farm them out to the highest bidder. They were to investigate the causes of the continued dissatisfaction of the colonists, to rectify abuses, to settle complaints, and to take with them to Batavia a full statement of such matters as they could not summarily dispose of, in order that, conjointly with the other members of the board, they could come to a decision there and afterwards make it known at the Cape.

Messrs. Nederburgh and Frykenius embarked in the national ship of war *Amazoon*, which cast anchor in Simon's Bay on the 18th of June 1792. On the 23rd there was a special meeting of the council at two o'clock in the afternoon, when they were present and delivered an address; but they were not formally installed until the 3rd of July, when with as much state as was possible they assumed supreme control of the administration.

CHAPTER XXVI.

SEBASTIAAN CORNELIS NEDERBURGH AND SIMON HENDRIK FRYKENIUS, COMMISSIONERS GENERAL, 3 JULY 1792 TO 2 SEPTEMBER 1793.

Discontent of the burghers—Struggle of the burgher councillors for the maintenance of their privileges—Addresses by the commissioners general—Reduction of public expenditure—Additional taxes—Resistance of the colonists to the imposition of auction duty—Amount of revenue and expenditure—Price of wheat—Liberty granted to the colonists to export produce to the Netherlands and India, and to carry on whale fishing under certain restrictions—Prohibition of trade with foreigners—Effects of these measures—Establishment of a loan bank, and further issue of paper money—Proposed overland expedition to Great Namaqualand in search of gold mines—Expedition by sea—Possession on behalf of the East India Company taken of Thomson's Island, Angra Pequena, and Walfish Bay—Account of the inhabitants of the coast at those places—Exploration of the country east of Walfish Bay—Continuation of the war with the Bushmen—Conduct of the Namaqua captain Afrikaner—Dismissal of the landdrost Woeke, and appointment of Honoratus Maynier as his successor—Unpopularity of Mr. Maynier—Condition of the western Kosa clans—The second Kaffir war—Humiliating terms of peace—Partial report of Mr. Maynier upon the causes of the war—Fear of an insurrection of Hottentots in Swellendam—Arrest and confinement of the Hottentot captain Kees—Efforts made by several colonists to improve the breed of cattle in the colony—Establishment of a mission to the Hottentots by the Moravian Society—Appointment of wardmasters in Cape Town—Promotion of various officers—Changes in the staff of clergymen—Declaration of war between France and the Netherlands—Stagnation of trade at the Cape—Formation of a pennist corps and pandour company—Appointment and installation of Abraham Josias Sluysken as commissioner general and head of the Cape government.

The commissioners were not many hours in the colony before they became aware that their task in South Africa would not be an easy one. They had been instructed to increase the revenue, and the first thing they heard upon reaching Simon's Bay was that the council had been obliged by the attitude of the burghers to withdraw a proclamation imposing a succession duty, or tax upon inheritances, which the directors had ordered to be levied. On the 25th of June the burgher councillors—Messrs J. Smuts, G. H. Meyer, H. J. de Wet, A. Fleck, H. A. Truter, and H. P. Warnecke—requested an interview for the purpose of presenting a memorial on the condition of the country, which they desired to deliver in the name and on behalf of the whole body of colonists. The commissioners declined to receive them as representatives of the people, and asserted that they would only recognise the legally constituted committee of the high court of justice, which consisted of three servants of the Company and three burghers. They offered, however, to listen to the complaints contained in the memorial, if the councillors would appear as private individuals. Two days in every week, they stated, would be set aside purposely to hear complaints and to investigate grievances.

The burgher councillors withdrew dissatisfied. They maintained that from the earliest days of the colony to the recent establishment of the committee of the high court of justice, their predecessors in office had been regarded as representatives of the burgher population, and they were determined to make a resolute stand for the maintenance of the privilege. Immediately, public meetings began to be held all over the country, and addresses were signed, which were forwarded to them for presentation to the commissioners. In these addresses the principle was kept in view that the colonists could not in justice be required to assist the Company out of its difficulties, as they had in no way contributed to its losses, and that as the expenditure for purely colonial purposes was less than the revenue, the taxes should be reduced, instead of being increased. The farmers desired that the tithes should be abolished, and a tax substituted of five per cent upon the value of produce sold. The commissioners learned that the supply of wheat in Cape Town was only sufficient for eighteen days consumption, and that the country people would not bring in more until their grievances were heard.

On the 9th of July the burgher councillors presented themselves again with numerous memorials, and were again informed that they could not be recognised as representatives of the people. But it soon became evident to the commissioners that on this point concession must be made. Much as the people talked about taxation, they talked more about their rights; and this matter of being represented by burghers alone, instead of by a mixed body of Company's servants and burghers, was the right that just then they made most of. The commissioners therefore at length gave way, and while still retaining the committee of the high court of justice for the management of municipal affairs, consented to receive the six burgher councillors as representatives or advocates of the colonists.

Messrs. Nederburgh and Frykenius now issued addresses appealing to the people to aid the government in its distress and to desist from further opposition. They exhorted the citizens of the town to return to the simple style of living of their forefathers, as by so doing large incomes would not be needed. That was the course the Company had determined to adopt, they stated, and it was the only practicable means of overcoming the difficulties under which all were labouring. These moral injunctions had little or no effect, though the commissioners flattered themselves that a good impression had been made by them. The people denied that they were disloyal to the States General, and maintained that their opposition was confined to the corrupt administration of the East India Company. But the East India Company is the machinery provided by the States General for your government, said the commissioners, and they thought that by this assertion all objections ought to be removed.

After a rigid examination of the records and practices of each department, Messrs. Nederburgh and Frykenius came to the conclusion that it would be possible to reduce the expenditure at the Cape to about 66,000*l.* a year. They struck off nearly all the perquisites of the officers of government, and allowed them small, but suitable, salaries instead. The officers were permitted, however, to retain the fees which they derived from various sources. The Company's gardens in Cape Town and the country seat of Rustenburg, used by the secunde, were leased by public tender, and a great number and variety of other charges upon the Company were summarily cut off.

To increase the revenue they imposed the following taxes:—

(*a*) A duty of 2*l*. upon every slave imported, and of five per cent upon the value of all articles imported or exported, except by the Company.

(*b*) An increase of transfer dues on sales of land held over ten years, from two and a half to four per cent.

(*c*) A charge upon carriages and vehicles kept for pleasure, varying from 12*s*. to 2*l*. a year, according to the class.

(*d*) A charge of 2*l*. on every vessel not belonging to the Company anchoring in either of the bays.

(*e*) The farming out of the saltpans.

(*f*) A duty of 12*s*. on each legger of brandy brought to town, similar to the former duty on wine.

(*g*) A charge of five per cent upon the effects of all persons above the rank of junior merchants leaving the colony, unless they returned within three years.

(*h*) An increase of the stamp duty. Under this heading came also auction duty, at the rate of three and a half per cent on the value of movable and one and three quarters per cent on the value of landed property, this tax being made payable by means of stamps on the vendu rolls or lists of articles sold, which the auctioneer was required to make oath to.

The last-named was a most unpopular tax. From the earliest times goods of all kinds were constantly being disposed of by auction in the town, and periodical sales were held in the several country districts. Every three months, upon the celebration of the communion, the farmers were in the habit of attending the different churches. Many of them travelled seven or eight days for that purpose, and usually arranged to remain at the church place from the Thursday or Friday preceding to the Tuesday following. Those who had goods or cattle to dispose of took advantage of these opportunities, and it seldom happened that auction sales were not held. The clergy set their faces against the practice, but the circumstances of the country were such that the sales went on in spite of their denunciations. A tax upon auctions was therefore a tax that affected the pockets of every one.

The burgher councillors, after using all the arguments they could command, protested against the levying of this tax, but to no purpose. The heemraden of Stellenbosch and Drakenstein, attended by between three and four hundred farmers of that district, came to town, and remonstrated against it, but also to no effect. Then at public meetings it was resolved to purchase nothing at auctions until the obnoxious tax was withdrawn. The commissioners went to Stellenbosch, where the opposition was strongest, and endeavoured to appease the people; but though they were listened to patiently and treated with the greatest respect, they were unsuccessful. During the month of May 1793 not a single sale by auction took place in the colony, the few who were disposed to purchase being intimidated by the attitude of the great majority of the burghers.

The commissioners informed the directors, however, that it was only a question of time, as without such sales the business of the colony would cease, so that sooner or later the people would be obliged to submit. And it happened as they foresaw. A sale by auction was announced to take place at the Paarl, where the church of Drakenstein was situated; and Mr. Willem Stephanus van Ryneveld, secretary of the high court of justice, was sent to try and induce people to bid. For some time the auctioneer could get no offer for anything. But at length an old woman was persuaded by Mr. Van Ryneveld to make a trifling bid for a slave, and this being accepted and the slave pronounced sold, others could not resist the temptation to try to make like bargains. The bidding soon became spirited, and the sale was successful. In Cape Town the people held out a little longer, but were at length compelled to submit.

The several measures adopted to increase the revenue and reduce the expenditure were productive of the following results, as shown by the Company's books for the three years preceding the 31st of August 1794, the latest date to which the accounts were audited. The total expenditure at the Cape during those three years was 203,070*l*., or on an average 67,690*l*. a year. The total revenue was 91,752*l*., or on an average 30,584*l*. a year. And the amount derived from selling and leasing property belonging to the Company, including profit on East Indian produce, was 30,796*l*., or 10,265*l*. a year. Thus the yearly outlay was reduced to within 27,000*l*. of the income, instead of 92,000*l*. as previously.

The commissioners claimed that the benefits which they conferred upon the colonists greatly outweighed the burdens imposed by the increased taxation.

In the first place, they raised the price paid by the Company for wheat to 11*s*. 4*d*. a muid, from which, however, the tithe—either in money or in kind—was to be deducted. At this price, the Company was to retain the right of demanding as much wheat as it needed. The farmers could dispose of the surplus as they pleased, or could export it to India or the Netherlands, provided it was sent in Dutch ships.

For several years the coast of South Africa had been frequented by English and American whalers, to such an extent that on one occasion over twenty were engaged in St. Helena Bay alone. In September 1792 the commissioners threw this industry open to the colonists, on condition that the vessels employed should be built and equipped in the Netherlands, that ships engaged to take oil to Europe should be chartered through the agency of the Company, and that the oil should be sent only to the Netherlands. Whale fishing by means of open boats only was restricted to Table and False bays, in order that no establishments requiring protection might be formed at other places.

Next, in November 1792 liberty was given to the colonists to send the produce of the country to any part of Netherlands India for sale, provided that the ships employed were built in Holland; but return cargoes could only be purchased from the Company. The ports of Table Bay, Mossel Bay, and Plettenberg's Bay were declared open for this trade. The ships engaged were not to go beyond certain limits, which were laid down. A trade in slaves with Madagascar and the east coast of Africa was also permitted.

At the same time the commissioners strictly prohibited the importation of any goods in foreign vessels. Trade with strangers was restricted to the sale of provisions for money, unless special permission was first obtained from the government.

The privileges, as the commissioners termed them, gave little satisfaction to the colonists. The prohibition of trade with foreigners, they protested, would ruin them. For more than a century the Cape had been a place where persons coming from Europe could buy Indian wares, and those from India European wares, a large proportion of which was obtained from foreigners. The trade was illegal, but was nevertheless conducted openly. Nearly the whole of the gold and silver in the colony was derived from the English, French, and Danes who visited the ports. The Indian trade, fenced in by such restrictions as those imposed by the commissioners, would be of no benefit. The liberty to establish whale fisheries would be of advantage to a few persons, but could be of little aid to the colony at large.

Distress, consequent upon the reduction of the garrison and an almost total cessation of trade, was at this time general. Men were unable to pay debts less than one-tenth of the nominal value of fixed property in their possession, and judgments of court in some cases could not be satisfied, as purchasers were not to be found for land at any price. To relieve this distress, and at the same time to increase the revenue, in March 1793 the commissioners established a loan bank. A quantity of paper was stamped to represent different sums, was declared a legal tender, and was issued through this bank to applicants offering sufficient security for the loan. In the town an advance was made to the amount of one-half the value of the property mortgaged, and in the country to the amount of two-thirds; but as additional security two persons of means were required to pledge themselves for the repayment of the loan. This issue of paper, or cartoon money as it was called, amounted to 135,473*l.*, upon which interest at the rate of five per cent was payable by the borrowers yearly. By this means relief from pressure of debt was obtained by many landed proprietors; but the effect of issuing such a quantity of inconvertible cartoon money was greatly to increase the general distress.

The belief in the existence of gold in Great Namaqualand had not yet died out. Mr. Sebastiaan Valentyn van Reenen, who was a man of means and an enthusiast in this matter, addressed the commissioners on the subject, and an arrangement for another exploring expedition was made. The commissioners, on behalf of the Company, intended to take formal possession of all the bays on the coast of Namaqualand that were likely to be frequented by whalers, and it was therefore planned that the packet *Meermin* should be sent northward for that purpose, that Mr. Van Reenen with his party should have a passage in her to a bay where a train of waggons which he was to send overland should meet him, and that Skipper Duminy should render every possible assistance.

When the expedition under Willem van Reenen was in Namaqualand, one of the party—Barend Freyn—had heard of a Hottentot chief named Ynemand, who was said to reside at a bay about twelve or fourteen days' journey north of the mouth of the great river, and who was reported to be friendly to strangers and to know where the gold mines were situated. Mr. Sebastiaan van Reenen now engaged Barend Freyn to proceed with a train of waggons to the kraal of Ynemand, and make the acquaintance of that chief. He undertook to be there not later than the 1st of January 1793, and to wait until the arrival of Mr. Van Reenen.

On the 3rd of January 1793 the *Meermin* sailed from Table Bay. She had as passengers the brothers Sebastiaan Valentyn and Dirk Gysbert van Reenen, Pieter Pienaar, a European servant, eight Hottentots, and two slaves. Five days after sailing she reached an island close to the coast in latitude 27° S., where some Englishmen and Americans were found killing seals for their oil and skins. Pienaar went ashore on the main land, and came across some Hottentots, but could obtain no intelligence concerning Freyn and the waggons. The only white man that the Hottentots knew of as being in the country was one Gideon Visagie, who led a wandering life among the savages. Some stone beacons had been brought from the Cape, with the arms of the States engraved on one side and the mark of the East India Company on the other. On the 12th of January one of these was taken ashore on the island, and erected at a spot which was set down in the diary as latitude 27° S., longitude 32° 45′ east of Teneriffe. The sealhunters called the place Thomson's Island, but in South Africa it has been known ever since this date as Possession. The sheet of water between it and the mainland was named by Skipper Duminy Elizabeth Bay. A chart was made, which is now in the archives of the colony.

On the 13th the *Meermin* sailed. She cast anchor next in latitude 26° 21′ S., and parties went ashore and explored the country around Angra Pequena, without finding any trace of Ynemand or Barend Freyn. On the 20th possession was formally taken, and a beacon was erected at a point marked in the chart—which is now in the colonial archives—as latitude 26° 30′ 26″ S., longitude 15° 57′ 9″ east of London. The longitude is incorrect, as in nearly all the calculations of that time. The variation of the compass is set down as 23° 31′ W. The island now called Halifax was named by Skipper Duminy Meermin Island, the sheet of water between it and Pedestal Point he named Daniel's Bay, the recess between Pedestal Point and the point farther eastward on which he erected his beacon he named Rhenius Bay, and Angra Pequena itself he renamed Beschermer Haven.

Sailing again, on the 23rd of January the *Meermin* cast anchor in Walvisch or Whale Bay, latitude as given 22° 56′ S. Skipper Duminy had been there two years before, when he had seen about a hundred head of horned cattle in possession of a kraal of Hottentots. On the 25th the brothers Van Reenen went ashore and found the Hottentots, who appeared highly delighted at the sight of strangers. Presents were made to them, and two cows, a calf, five sheep, and some copper ornaments were obtained in barter. These Hottentots knew of Captain Ynemand, and pointed to the south-east as the direction in which he lived. They declined, however, to furnish guides, though tempting offers were made. They stated that the copper mine, from which they procured the metal which they had in abundance, was not very far away. After a short acquaintance, they were found to be persistent beggars and inveterate thieves.

On the 29th of January Pieter Pienaar and the Hottentots brought from the Cape left to explore the country to the eastward. They returned on the 20th of February, when Pienaar reported that the day after leaving he met two Damaras who acted as guides, and conducted him for twelve days up the valley of a river. Beyond this valley on each side the country was burnt up, as he was informed no rain whatever had fallen for five years. In the valley he found fine large trees growing, and in some places rich grass in flats three quarters of an hour's walk from one side to the other. Water was obtained by digging in places known to the natives, though none was flowing above the surface. He passed five Damara kraals in the valley, and procured some copper from the people residing in them. They informed him that there were no clans with cattle to the north, but many to the south and south-east. They knew of Willem van Reenen's expedition; but could give no information about the Captain Ynemand or any other metal than copper. Game was very abundant in the valley. Pienaar had seen elephants, rhinoceroses, gemsboks, buffaloes, gnus, springboks, and lions. With some of the savages, the men were fat and strong, owing to their being able to get game, but the women and children were wretchedly thin and seemingly starving. They had offered to sell some children, and Pienaar had bought two about eight or nine years of age, little better than skeletons.

It was now evident that Freyn was not in Namaqualand, and Mr. Van Reenen came to the conclusion that he had been prevented by the drought from penetrating the country, which was afterwards found to be correct. No information whatever concerning gold was to be obtained, nor was it possible to reach Ynemand wherever he might be. Further exploration was therefore reluctantly abandoned.

On the 26th of February a beacon was erected by Skipper Duminy as a mark of possession, but the old name of Walvisch—or as now written Walfish—Bay was not changed. On the 3rd of March the *Meermin* sailed, and on the 10th of April cast anchor again in Table Bay.

Owing to advantages gained by the Bushmen in the war along the interior mountain range, and the abandonment of about a hundred farms by the colonists, the government directed the landdrosts of Graaff Reinet, Swellendam, and Stellenbosch, with the heemraden of those districts, to hold a combined meeting in Cape Town on the 1st of July 1792, under presidency of Colonel Gordon, for the purpose of arranging a plan of military operations. On the day appointed, Mr. Woeke did not appear, so on the 2nd of July the council suspended him from duty, and called upon him to answer for his conduct. A military officer—Captain Bernard Cornelis van Baalen—was directed to proceed to Graaff Reinet as soon as arrangements could be made, and to act there as landdrost until further orders. The old secretary Wagener and Mr. Jan Gysbert van Reenen, the latter of whom was a man of experience in frontier matters, were requested to aid the combined landdrosts and heemraden with their advice.

On the 13th of July Colonel Gordon laid before the council of policy the report that had been agreed upon. It recommended that a commando of at least a hundred burghers should be called out in the district of Swellendam, and another of equal strength in the district of Stellenbosch and Drakenstein, that these commandos should be provided for a campaign of three months, and should meet at the farm of Jan Adam Raubenheimer at the Zwartberg, on the 31st of August. Mr. Jan Pieter van der Walt, of the Cold Bokkeveld, was named as a competent man for the chief command,

and his brother—Tjaart van der Walt—as the person best qualified for the second place. It was proposed that Captain Van Baalen, when on his way to Graaff Reinet, should call upon Mr. J. P. van der Walt, and arrange a plan of action; that he should then assemble as many of his burghers as could be got together, and act in concert with the other forces in the field.

The council adopted the report, and issued the necessary instructions to have it carried into effect. The usual injunctions to act with humanity were added, and as an inducement to the burghers to take prisoners rather than shoot their opponents, a reward of 3*l.* was offered for every individual of Bushman race, big or little, male or female, delivered at the Cape. The council determined that such prisoners should be sent to Robben Island as convicts for life.

Before these arrangements could be carried into effect, a robbery of unusual magnitude took place, followed by punishment of terrible severity. On the 11th of June two hordes of Bushmen, under leaders to whom the colonists had given the names Flamink and Couragie, attacked at the Leeuwen river the drovers in charge of some cattle belonging to the contractor for the supply of meat to the Company, killed a European, wounded a slave, and captured 11,000 slaughter sheep and 256 oxen. The burgher lieutenant Nicholas Smit, of Graaff Reinet, assisted by Tjaart van der Walt and Philip Botha, got together thirty-three burghers of Swellendam, and followed up the robbers. On the 24th of July this commando fell in with Flamink's horde, and shot about three hundred individuals of all ages, including the leader. Fifteen children were taken alive, and eight hundred and sixty sheep, fifty-three oxen, four horses, and eight muskets were recovered.

On the 1st of September the commandant-general Van der Walt left Raubenheimer's farm with a force of sixty Europeans and forty half-breeds to search for Couragie's horde. The country about the source of the Zak river was scoured, and over two hundred Bushmen were killed. Seven hundred and twenty-five sheep and fifteen oxen were recovered. On the 24th of November the Europeans and half-breeds, divided into three parties, went out again from the camp; but did not succeed in falling in with the marauders.

The burghers of Graaff Reinet took no part in these operations. Captain Van Baalen did not arrive at the drostdy until the 12th of September, when he found that the secretary Maynier had issued notices to the farmers to assemble on the 24th, too late to act in concert with the other forces.

The Europeans had an active ally in the Namaqua captain Afrikaner, a man whose name in later years was made famous by missionary journals. Afrikaner with his clan scoured the country further down the Zak river while Commandant Van der Walt was engaged at its sources, killed one hundred and thirteen Bushmen, and took twenty prisoners. He then applied to the landdrost of Stellenbosch for a supply of ammunition to enable him to proceed with the work of clearing the country of robbers. The landdrost forwarded the application to government, and on the 20th of November the council resolved to comply with the request. A farmer named Pienaar, who lived on the border, was known to have a large stock of powder and lead on hand. The landdrost was instructed to procure advances from Pienaar, which the council would gladly repay, and at the same time he was to convey to Afrikaner the particular satisfaction of the government with his conduct.

The Namaqua captain did not use the ammunition for the purpose for which it was granted. There was a band of half-breed and Hottentot marauders living on the northern bank of the great river, under the leadership of a European renegade. With this band Afrikaner's clan had a feud, and an opportunity so favourable for an attack was not allowed to pass by. The result was several killed and wounded on both sides, the loss by Afrikaner of the staff of office supplied by the government, and his driving his opponents from the field of action and making prize of six of their guns. With the spoil he proceeded to Cape Town, where on the 7th of August 1793 he delivered the guns to the government, and obtained another staff of office.

Towards the close of 1792 the commandos operating against the Bushmen were disbanded, and the burghers of Stellenbosch and Swellendam returned to their homes. Two farms in the Nieuwveld were given free of rent to Mr. J. P. van der Walt, on condition of his occupying them; and power was conferred upon him to call out commandos whenever he might find it necessary, without previous reference to any of the landdrosts.

Immediately after the suspension of Landdrost Woeke, of Graaff Reinet, complaints of his domineering conduct were made by the secretary Maynier, the sick comforter De Vries, the former heemraad Van Jaarsveld, and others, all of which he was called upon to reply to. Instead of defending himself, he accused his opponents of various kinds of improper conduct, so that between the two sets of papers and those which followed, whatever evil deeds had been committed in the district were brought to light. Acts of violence were very rare, considering the condition in which the people were living. One monstrous deed, of which the tradition is still preserved by the Imidange clan, was brought home to Adriaan van Jaarsveld. In the campaign of 1781 he had caused a volley to be fired into a party of Kaffirs who were scrambling for bits of tobacco he had thrown to them. The atrocity of the act was pointed out, as it was done in cold blood, and could not be considered proper in war, although the commandant had previously given notice to the Kaffirs that they would be shot if they did not cross the Fish river.

With regard to his not attending the combined meeting of landdrosts and heemraden in Cape Town, Mr. Woeke gave a satisfactory explanation. Communications between the seat of government and the drostdy of Graaff Reinet were frequently from three to four months in passing. On this occasion, he only received the order on the 20th of June, and it was therefore impossible to obey it. The commissioners general, however, considering that he had not repelled the charges against him and that he had certainly lost the confidence of the people of the district, dismissed him from the Company's service, and provisionally appointed the secretary Maynier landdrost in his stead.

It was one of the most injudicious appointments ever made in South Africa, for no one could have been more out of sympathy with the colonists than Maynier was. A historian needs to be very careful in describing the character of one who is dead, especially if he has left no descendants or partisans to vindicate his acts, if they can be vindicated; but apart from the accusations of his contemporaries and the hatred with which this man's memory is still regarded on the frontier, he can be judged by his correspondence with the government. He possessed in perfection a kind of ability which enabled him to ascertain exactly what his superiors desired and to win their favour and confidence. The motive of all his acts was self-interest, and he did not scruple to pervert truth to gain his ends. He was a near relative of the secunde Rhenius, but he does not seem to have owed his appointment to the influence of that officer so much as to his own address. The frank, outspoken, generous, though rough colonists of the frontier were no match in argument for one so full of subtlety and meanness as he was; they felt their helplessness against his misrepresentations, and detested him accordingly. At the very first meeting of the court under his presidency, 6th of May 1793, the majority of the district officers expressed their dissatisfaction, and were with difficulty induced not to resign their appointments.

It was a trying period on the frontier. A long and intensely severe drought had prevented the cultivation of the ground, all the reserve grain had been consumed by the Kaffirs, and those in the Zuurveld had lost most of their cattle. The regent Ndlambe was at open war with the chiefs on this side of the Fish river, and three white men —Coenraad du Buis, Christoffel Botha, and Coenraad Bezuidenhout—were taking part in the strife, nominally in his favour, really for the sake of spoil.[1] The old chief Langa

[1] My relation of the cause of the feuds between the different Kaffir clans

had been made prisoner, and was detained at Ndlambe's kraal. Coenraad du Buis had not scrupled to take a girl just married to the captive chief, and keep her as his concubine, thus exasperating the Amambala clan. Far and wide within the colony the Kaffirs were stealing the farmers' cattle, and parties of them even sent word to the drostdy that they would continue to do so until the three white men with Ndlambe ceased to molest them.

When intelligence of Maynier's appointment was received in the district, some of the farmers, in utter despair, took the law into their own hands. Several large cattle robberies had just taken place, so the burgher Barend Lindeque raised a commando without reference to the landdrost, got assistance from Ndlambe, and on the 18th of May surrounded a kraal and took eight hundred head of cattle from it by way of reprisal. Half of this spoil was sent to Ndlambe, the remainder was restored to the farmers from whom the cattle had been stolen.

A few days after this occurrence, a great horde of Kaffirs crossed the Fish river to the assistance of those on this side, and an attack was made upon the colonists. There were one hundred and twenty farms occupied between the rivers Kowie and Zwartkops, and one hundred and sixteen of these were laid waste. The Europeans and Hottentots fled westward for their lives. Some parties were overtaken, when the men were tortured in a shocking manner and then murdered, but the women and children were permitted to proceed. Pieter Vivier, Jan Grobbelaar, Frederik Jordaan, Juriaan Potgieter, and Stephanus Cloete were thus murdered, and Frederik Buys was left in such a condition that he died some time afterwards of his wounds. A lad about

varies slightly from the official records and contemporary accounts. More than a quarter of a century ago I commenced gathering native traditions with a view of getting the Kaffir version of what had occurred in bygone times, and obtained very complete information upon the regency of Ndlambe and the dealings of that chief with the heads of the clans in the Zuurveld. It is from this source that I am able to explain a few circumstances that seemed obscure to the actors in 1793, unacquainted as they were with the intricacies of Kaffir history.

sixteen years of age, named Stroebel, was taken away, and his fate could never be ascertained. About forty Hottentots also were overtaken and put to death. According to returns afterwards sent in, 65,327 head of horned cattle, 11,000 sheep, and 200 horses were swept off in this raid.

Upon a report of the outbreak reaching Swellendam, the burgher lieutenant Pieter Hendrik Ferreira, with twenty-six white men and fourteen Hottentots, set out with the utmost speed to the assistance of the fugitives, and on the 22nd of June met some fifty families at the Zwartkops. It was at once arranged to make use of that river as a line of defence, and to guard it until assistance could reach them. It was estimated that there were six thousand Kaffir warriors in the field, so that offensive operations were not to be thought of.

On the 18th of June Mr. Maynier, accompanied by the secretary Stanhoffius and the heemraden Stephanus Naude and Hendrik Meintjes van den Berg, left Graaff Reinet to try to restore concord by means of presents to the chiefs. He first opened up communication with Ndlambe, and arranged with him that the Kaffirs in the colony might return unmolested to their own side of the Fish river. Most of them had in fact already done so, with the object of placing their spoil in safety. Many of Ndlambe's own followers had taken part in the raid, and the colonists were convinced that a reconciliation of the clans had taken place and that all were united against them.

Mr. Maynier, who professed to believe that the Kaffirs were incapable of acting with duplicity, next sent a Hottentot named Willem Hasebek to the chiefs who had led the raiders, to propose peace on condition of their restoring the captured cattle and respecting the Fish river as the boundary. They replied, agreeing to the boundary of the Fish river, but declining to give up the cattle. Mr. Maynier then returned to Graaff Reinet, where tidings reached him that large numbers of Kaffirs were again on the colonial side of the river, that they were plundering farms in distant parts of the district, and that on the 30th of July a son of Theunis Botha and a Hottentot had been murdered.

Meantime the government had sent instructions to the landdrost of Swellendam to call out a strong commando and proceed to the devastated district. He was to compel the Kaffirs to cross the Fish river and to restore the captured cattle or make compensation; but was not to inflict further punishment, and upon these conditions being complied with, he was to make peace. The military ensign Hans Abue was sent to the frontier to aid the landdrost with his advice.

When this intelligence reached Graaff Reinet, Mr. Maynier, fancying that a slight had been put upon him, resolved to take the field at once. He called out the burghers, and convened a meeting of the heemraden and militia officers on the 19th of August. The distrust felt towards him was, however, so general that no one would consent to act as commandant under his direction. There were only two heemraden—S. Naude and H. M. van den Berg—to say a word in his favour, and the result of the meeting was therefore that the landdrost took command himself, and appointed these two his assistants. On the 27th of August he left Graaff Reinet, at the head of 117 mounted burghers.

On the 8th of September the Swellendam commando commenced its march. It consisted of about four hundred burghers—including many fugitives from the Zuurveld—and one hundred Hottentots, under the militia captain Laurens de Jager, accompanied by the landdrost Faure. At the devastated farm of Cornelis van Rooyen, not far from the site of the present city of Graham's Town, this commando joined the one under Maynier.

A strong party of the Graaff Reinet burghers, having as spokesmen Carel Jan Triegard, Jan Botha, and Cornelis Faber, now agitated for the appointment of De Jager as commandant-general. Mr. Maynier and his two partisans objected, and as he quoted law which could not be disputed, his opponents were obliged to give way. It was then resolved that as the Kaffirs had again gone over to the eastern side of the Fish river, a large division of the force, under command of Maynier, should follow them up, while the remaining division, under De Jager and Faure, should guard the camp on this side.

On the 14th of September Maynier with a small flying column appeared at the Koonap, near its junction with the Fish, where the captain Cika of the Amantinde clan was lurking, and recovered about 1,300 head of cattle. On the 26th of the same month he made another quick march to the same place, but on this occasion only obtained 200 cattle. The Kaffirs lost some ten men killed and wounded by these two expeditions.

The column next took another direction, and crossed the Fish river at a place where a Hottentot captain named Trompetter formerly had a kraal, from which circumstance the ford was known as Trompetter's drift. On the 1st and 2nd of October about 2,500 head of cattle were recovered, but very few Kaffirs were killed. A certain petty captain, called Hans by the colonists, now joined the commando with a few followers. This man was the head of the division or clan of the old Gonaqua tribe which had least mixed with the Kaffirs, and he was almost a pure Hottentot in appearance. Cungwa, the principal chief of the tribe, was one of the most active enemies of the colonists; but Hans professed to be friendly. Every day his following increased in number, and some of them, being quite black, stated that they were adherents of Ndlambe. From the time of their arrival no cattle could be found, and the burghers, who observed that these strangers always made large fires at night, became suspicious of them and desired leave to drive them away. Mr. Maynier would not consent to this, and professed to believe that Hans and his followers were truthful and harmless.

Eight or ten days were now occupied in searching for a ford in the upper waters of the Keiskama, and as one could not be found, the column marched to the mouth of that river and waded across the bar. The bulk of the farmers' cattle had in the meantime been driven far beyond reach, and had been placed in care of Kawuta, the head of the Galeka branch and paramount chief of the whole Kosa tribe. The warriors of the hostile clans had doubled upon the commando, had crossed the Fish river between Trompetter's drift and the sea, and were again in occupation of the Zuurveld. Hans and his party being left behind in the rapid march of the burgher horsemen, on the 14th of October the commando was able to surprise a strong body of the enemy on the Buffalo river, when in a hot skirmish about forty Kaffirs were killed and seven thousand head of cattle were captured. One hundred and twenty women and children and a couple of men were made prisoners.

A dreadful crime was perpetrated after the action was over. One of the women and the adult male prisoners were shot in cold blood by relatives of some of those burghers who had been murdered in the Zuurveld. The ferocious deed was spoken of with horror by one of those present who placed the circumstance on record, but no punishment was inflicted upon the perpetrators. It is not referred to in Maynier's despatches. After a very short detention, all the other prisoners were released unharmed.

As the horses were worn out and there was no grass in the parched-up country, the commando was now obliged to fall back. On reaching the Keiskama a friendly visit was paid to Ndlambe, who repeated the promises he had before made, and accepted such presents as were offered to him. He accounted for the cattle with colonial marks seen in his possession by the assurance that they had been taken by his people from the clans at war with the colonists, who were his enemies also; and he promised Mr. Maynier to restore them to the white people if time were allowed him to collect them together. The landdrost considered this very satisfactory, and parted with Ndlambe on the best of terms.

In the march from the Keiskama, many of the cattle taken on the Buffalo had to be abandoned, and upon approaching the Fish river the scouts reported that the ford was occupied by a strong body of Kaffirs. By means of some Hottentots, communication was opened with the Swellendam commando, then in camp on the farm of Lucas Meyer three hours' march from the river, and a relief party was sent out. On its approach the Kaffirs retired from the ford, and the Graaff Reinet burghers crossed without molestation.

An attempt was now made to drive the enemy out of the Zuurveld. The Kaffirs were too wary to risk an encounter in the open field, and did not even make a stand in natural strongholds. The few who were encountered by chance professed to be friendly, and, upon a mere promise to go across the Fish river, were left unmolested by order of Maynier. After two or three weeks' marching backward and forward from one forest to another, only to learn that each place was occupied again as soon as they left it, the burghers found themselves with horses and oxen quite worn out, very little food of any kind to be had, and no prospect of better fortune in the future. They had recovered a few cattle, all with colonial brands, and in a couple of slight skirmishes had taken prisoners sixty women and children and four Hottentots who had joined the enemy. That was all that had been done.

It was evident to every one that there were only two methods of bringing the war to a close. One was the plan adopted by Adriaan van Jaarsveld twelve years before: no quarter, let every man of the invaders leave the colony or be shot. The other was for the Europeans to submit to the best terms obtainable. The war council, consisting of the landdrosts Maynier and Faure, the military ensign Hans Abue, the Graaff Reinet burgher officers Stephanus Naude and Hendrik Meintjes van den Berg, and the Swellendam burgher officers Laurens de Jager and Hillegard Mulder, took the latter course.

The women and children who had been made prisoners were released and sent with presents to invite the hostile chiefs to a conference. After six days' absence, some of the women returned with a message that the chiefs were willing to make peace, but were afraid to visit the camp—then at Assagai Bush—and therefore requested the landdrosts to meet them at a place five hours' journey distant. The landdrosts went unarmed to the spot indicated, and had a conference with two sons of Langa, one of whom—Tuli by name—returned with them to the camp. The chiefs stated their willingness to desist from hostilities, but protested that they were unable to restore the cattle taken from the colonists. All had been killed and eaten, they declared; and such of their own cattle as had not been seized by Ndlambe had perished in the drought.

While Tuli was in the camp, word was brought that the burgher Hendrik van Rensburg had raised a separate commando, and was preparing to attack some of the clans. The landdrosts hastened to meet him, and persuaded him to desist. They then had a meeting with the chiefs of the Amambala, Amagwali, Imidange, and Amantinde clans, when it was agreed that there should be peace. The chiefs promised to surrender any horses and horned cattle that were still alive, as also several Hottentots who had aided them.

With these terms the members of the war council expressed themselves obliged to be content, as no better conditions were obtainable. In their report, they state that in their opinion it was quite enough to have the Bushmen to contend with, and that any terms of peace with the Kaffirs were therefore preferable to continuing the war. But the great majority of the burghers were of a very different mind, and were indignant at what was taking place. They wanted some one in command in whom they could have confidence, and the war to be prosecuted until the colony was cleared of invaders. They also scouted the assertion of Maynier that Ndlambe's friendship could be relied upon, and insisted that his people had taken part in the raid into the colony and that he was harbouring their cattle. They dispersed in a spirit which needed very little provocation to induce an open revolt against the East India Company and its officers.

It was on the 27th of November 1793 that the burghers left Assagai Bush, those who had homes to return to them, the others to form new homes where best they could. Just before the landdrost Maynier took his departure, messengers from the Gunukwebe chief Cungwa arrived to propose that his clan should be included in the peace. Cungwa was then occupying the banks of the Bushman's river. The landdrost went to see him, and made the same terms as with the others.

The arrangement gave to the Kaffirs all the fruits of victory. And so far was it from putting an end to hostilities by them, that the burgher Abel Erasmus was murdered near the Zwartkops river and all his cattle were carried off before the Swellendam commando reached home. The forces were hardly disbanded when a farmer named Strydom was murdered, another named Schoeman was badly wounded, and even a white woman was murdered by Kaffirs a considerable distance from the Zuurveld.

Upon receiving presents to a much greater value, Ndlambe sent in some 400 head of cattle, and about 12,500 had been recovered since the beginning of the war. Many of these had been slaughtered for the use of the commandos, others had been abandoned in Kaffirland, and others had died, so that only 4,000 head remained. These were divided, in proportion to their losses, among the farmers who had been obliged to retire from the Zuurveld.

The landdrost Maynier was afterwards instructed by the government to investigate the causes of the war. In his report he expressed an opinion that the farmers had been sufficiently remunerated for their losses. He pointed out that the individuals who claimed to have had 65,327 head of horned cattle taken from them had returned their stock for taxation purposes just before the outbreak at 8,004 head. As has been stated already, the standard of truth with regard to returns for taxation purposes was in general very low indeed; but the discrepancy here shown was not entirely due to that cause. At the birth of a child it was customary with the farmers to mark a certain number of heifers as its property, and the increase of these belonged to the child, so that when grown up a son or a daughter might have something to commence the world with. Such cattle were by a kind of tacit understanding exempted from the tax of a penny a year on each head levied for district purposes. Then there were the young cattle still growing, which the landdrost and the government knew it had been customary to exempt. Still, the discrepancy really exhibits the proneness of the people to escape taxation at the cost of truth.

The report of Mr. Maynier, which was evidently prepared to meet the views of the government, attributed the origin of the war chiefly to the outrageous conduct of Coenraad du Buis and the commando of Barend Lindeque, but gave as secondary causes the occupation of ground east of the Fish river by twenty-eight families of colonists, wrongs to which the Kaffirs had been subjected by cattle barterers, cruelties practised towards Kaffirs in service with farmers, and the conduct of a Hottentot to whom the late landdrost Woeke had given a gun. The Kaffirs are described in it as a quiet and peaceably-disposed people. This report, which exhibits in every paragraph a strong desire to put the Kaffir case in the best light and to throw as much blame as possible on the burghers, entirely ignores the chief cause of the war as shown in subsequent struggles between the two races. Outrages perpetrated by farmers are brought to light, but nothing is said of offences against them. In addition to those already mentioned, this paper records an act of violence committed by Frederik Jordaan—one of those overtaken and murdered in the raid. He had knocked some teeth out of a Kaffir servant with a bullet mould. Read to-day, the report has the opposite effect from what the writer intended to produce. Any impartial person, observing the spirit that pervades it, will be surprised at the small amount of crime that existed, considering the circumstances under which the people lived.

An order was now issued by the landdrost, and confirmed by the government, that three or four families should always live close together, for mutual protection. In point of fact, such an order was superfluous, for there was no other way of existing in the greater part of the district of Graaff Reinet than by combining in lagers. Proclamations were renewed, forbidding Europeans under very severe penalties from crossing the Fish river or carrying on cattle barter or intercourse of any kind with the Kaffirs. The landdrost was instructed to conciliate those in the Zuurveld with presents, and to induce them in a friendly manner to return to their own country. The burghers who were foremost in advocating a renewal of the war were threatened with dire punishment, and Coenraad du Buis was summoned to Cape Town to answer to the crimes laid to his charge. He declined to obey the order, and it was not possible to have him arrested.

The conduct of Mr. Maynier during these transactions was so much in accordance with the views of the government that in March 1794 he was confirmed in the appointment of landdrost.

In August 1793, while the greater part of the colony was in a disturbed condition, the people of Swellendam became apprehensive of an attempt by the Hottentots either to murder them or to drive them out of the country. In October 1788 a Hottentot captain named Kees had drawn suspicion upon himself by unfriendly and insolent demeanour, and at this time there was strong circumstantial evidence of his implication in the murder of two burghers named Labuscagne and Van Wyk and the wife of a third named Jan Oosthuizen. These murders had taken place under circumstances of peculiar atrocity, and as the perpetrators had not been discovered, the people of the district were in a state of great alarm. Kees and the principal men of his clan were arrested and sent to Cape Town. Kees's son Klaas admitted that there was a design to rise against the Europeans, but no other direct evidence could be obtained. After a time most of the Hottentots were set at liberty, but Kees and a few others were kept in permanent confinement as political prisoners.

It is a relief to turn from these scenes of contention and disorder, to notice the efforts that were made at this time by several colonists to improve the domestic animals of the colony. In 1792 Mr. Jan Frederik Kirsten imported from England eight horses and three bulls for breeding purposes. So little encouragement did the government give to the enterprise that he was obliged to pay a duty of five per cent upon their value. In the same year Mr. Jacobus Arnoldus Kirsten imported five horses from Boston. Some skippers of American vessels, finding others disposed to imitate the Kirstens, made arrangements to bring over cattle of good quality, and in 1793 quite a number of horses, mares, bulls, and cows arrived from the New England States.

An association, of which Mr. Sebastiaan Valentyn van Reenen was principal director, made an effort to introduce merino sheep. They tried first to obtain Dassen Island as a run where stock could be kept pure, but the government being unwilling to allow them the use of the island, in 1793 they imported a few Spanish rams, which were placed with common ewes at Groen Kloof. Six hundred half-breed lambs were cast. Mr. Jan Gysbert van Reenen removed his share, 200 in number, to the Hantam, where they were found to thrive remarkably well. Some other flocks also did well, and though the experiment failed from causes hereafter to be related, it was proved that wool of fair quality could easily be produced.

A ton of hair of the common sheep was sent by Mr. Abraham de Smidt to Holland, to ascertain whether it was of any value there, when it was proved not to be worth the cost of transport.

Since the return to Europe of George Schmit, the Moravian Society had frequently requested the Assembly of Seventeen to permit missionaries to be sent to the Hottentots, but hitherto without success. At this time the required leave was granted. In a despatch, dated 22nd of December 1791, the directors informed the Cape government that they had given the United Brethren permission to send two or three missionaries to South Africa and to administer the sacraments to any converts they might make, the only restriction being that they were not to occupy ground where Christian churches were already established. The government was instructed to give them such assistance as they might need.

In November 1792 three missionaries—by name Heinrich

Marsveld, Daniel Schwinn, and Johan Christiaan Keuhnel—arrived from Holland in the *Duifje*. After looking about for a suitable site for a station, they selected Baviaans Kloof, where George Schmit had laboured, and on the 18th of December the council, on their application, granted them the use of as much land there as they might require. Mr. Marthinus Theunissen, superintendent of a cattle station that had not yet been sold, was directed to provide transport for their effects, and to see that they obtained whatever they needed on the way.

Upon the arrival of the missionaries, they found an aged Hottentot woman who had been baptized by Schmit, and who still preserved a New Testament which he had given to her. Under an old pear tree, planted by Schmit, they commenced to hold religious services, and soon succeeded in drawing a considerable number of Hottentots together. They laid out gardens, and gave one to each family to be retained during good behaviour. In this manner a village soon grew up. A large extent of ground was brought under cultivation by the personal labour of the missionaries, with such assistance as they could obtain from those who gathered around them. It was not long before a mill for grinding corn was built, and that was followed by the establishment of a small factory for making knives. A school for children was opened at once, and at stated hours that would interfere least with field labour the adults were collected together for instruction and prayer. The necessity of industry and cleanliness was impressed upon the pupils, not only by precept, but by example and the rules of the institution.

Baviaans Kloof henceforth became the home of a number of Hottentot families, some members of which were soldiers in the pandour corps and others in service with colonists. There these people were looked after by the missionaries with the greatest care, and whatever was possible was done for their improvement.

Everything went on well until the first baptisms took place, when a spirit of jealousy was aroused. The consistory of Stellenbosch, maintaining that Baviaans Kloof was within their parish, then came to the council of policy with a request that the Moravians might either be required to remove from their district, or to cease from administering the sacraments and so setting up a rival church. The request, however, was very mildly urged, and the government replied that it could not be acceded to. The missionaries themselves were men of good common sense as well as of great zeal, and from the first commanded the respect of the farmers in their neighbourhood. Political partisanship was studiously avoided, and social equality between European colonists and individuals just emerging from barbarism was not taught. The converts were regarded as children, requiring to be kept constantly under tutelage and moderate restraint. Thus these excellent men with the assistants who soon arrived and their devoted wives firmly laid the foundation of mission work by the Moravian Society, which has been of incalculable benefit to the coloured inhabitants of the colony.

To preserve order in Cape Town, the commissioners-general introduced a new system of police. In December 1792 the town was divided into twenty-three wards, and the gardens at the foot of Table Mountain into two wards, in each of which two burghers of respectability were selected to act as wardmasters. Their duties were to prevent nuisances of all kinds, to enforce cleanliness in the streets and public places, to give directions in case of fire, and generally to maintain order. All persons moving their residence from or into any ward were required to report to the wardmasters, and the arrival and departure of foreigners or strangers were to be reported to them by the lodging-house keepers. They were required to have their names and the word 'wykmeester' posted up in large letters in front of their houses. Instead of a salary, they were exempted from the payment of rates and taxes levied for local purposes. They were subject to the directions of the committee of the high court of justice, to whom they were bound to send in periodical returns upon the state of the town. Every year half of the number were to be relieved of duty, and successors were to be appointed by the council of policy from a list of twice as many names submitted by the whole body of wardmasters and approved by the committee of the high court of justice.

In the staff of the public departments the commissioners-general made several changes. The appointment of the acting fiscal independent, Jacob Pieter de Nys, was confirmed, and he took his seat in the council of policy. He was the last who held that office, for upon his death in December 1793, the system was altered, and the great powers and privileges possessed by the fiscals independent were abrogated. Willem Stephanus van Ryneveld, who had been secretary of the high court of justice since April 1788, was then appointed with the title of fiscal only, and was made subject to the government just as much as the cashier or the issuer of stores, a seat in the council being given to him much lower down the table. Egbertus Bergh, secretary of the council of policy since August 1791, was promoted to be cashier, and a voice in the debates was given to him, but without the right of voting, as he was not a member of the established church. George Frederik Goetz was appointed his successor as secretary. Christoffel Brand, the resident at Simon's Town, had a seat in the council given to him whenever he might be at the castle. Jan Arnold Voltelen was appointed head of the naval establishment, without a seat in the council. Major De Lille was promoted to the rank of lieutenant-colonel.

In October 1792 the Rev. Mr. Manger commenced his duties in Graaff Reinet. In July 1792 the health of the Rev. Mr. Van Lier, third minister of the Cape, broke down, so the commissioners-general permitted him to retire on a pension. The situation remained vacant until May 1794, when the Rev. Mr. Kuys was removed from Waveren to fill it. The only other change in the staff of clergymen for several years to come may be mentioned here. In March 1794 the Rev. Michiel Christiaan Vos, a colonist by birth, arrived from Holland, where he had completed his education, and was appointed to the church at Waveren.

In the Netherlands the antagonism between the democratic and conservative parties continued. The former leaned towards France, the latter towards England, with which kingdom the government of the stadtholder had been in close alliance since 1788. France had become a republic. Events had for some time been tending towards a rupture, when on the 1st of February 1793 the Convention issued from Paris a declaration of war with Great Britain and the United Netherlands.

From this date the ocean commerce past the Cape was greatly diminished. There are no shipping returns in our archives for the years between 1789 and 1796, except for 1794, in which year the number of vessels that put into South African ports was 37 under the Dutch flag, 18 English, 12 American, 11 Danish, 5 Italian, and 3 Portuguese, only 86 in all; but the constant complaints concerning the stagnation of trade, the absence of gold and silver money, and the want of merchandise, show how severely the colonists suffered.

Upon tidings of the commencement of the war reaching the Cape, the commissioners-general were at a loss to know what to do for the defence of the colony. No regular troops could be expected to strengthen the garrison. They formed all the clerks and junior officers in the Company's service into a military company, which they termed the pennist corps, and appointed the member of council Willem Ferdinand van Reede van Oudtshoorn its commandant. Further, they raised a company of half-breeds and Hottentots, put them in uniform, and set them to learn to be soldiers. This corps was termed the pandours. No other means could be devised of strengthening the colony.

Messrs. Nederburgh and Frykenius now prepared to proceed to Java, the only duty left being to appoint some one to carry on the administration. Colonel Van de Graaff still retained the title of governor of the Cape colony, but they were aware that he would never return from Europe. Of the secunde Rhenius they had not formed a high opinion. While they were looking about for a competent person, an old servant of the Company, Abraham Josias Sluysken by name, arrived at the Cape on his way to Europe from Surat, where he had for some years been employed as director of trade. He had resided here once before for a few months, when in 1765 he was taken ill and detained on the way to India. He was now returning home with a view of retirement when, in accordance with a rule of the service, he stopped at the Cape until his accounts could be audited, and while here made the acquaintance of Messrs. Nederburgh and Frykenius. They proposed to confer upon him the same power that they held themselves, and after a little persuasion he consented to undertake the duty of commissioner-general. He had thus more authority than a governor, for he could act in any matter without consulting the council, if he chose to do so. No salary was agreed upon. It was arranged that he should draw at the rate of 240*l.* a month, and leave further remuneration to be settled by the directors.

Mr. Sluysken was raised to the dignity of ordinary councillor of Netherlands India and was formally installed as commissioner-general and head of the Cape government on the 2nd of September 1793, and immediately afterwards Messrs. Nederburgh and Frykenius embarked for Batavia.

CHAPTER XXVII.

ABRAHAM JOSIAS SLUYSKEN, COMMISSIONER GENERAL, FROM 2 SEPTEMBER 1793 TO 16 SEPTEMBER 1795.

Insolvency of the East India Company—Condition of the Cape colony—Erection of forts at Simon's Town and round Hout Bay—Misrepresentations by the landdrost Maynier—Expulsion of Maynier by the burghers of Graaff Reinet—Proceedings of a commission sent to Graaff Reinet—Establishment by the burghers of a practically independent government at Graaff Reinet—Similar proceedings at Swellendam—Character and force of the garrison at the Cape—Negotiations between the British government and the stadtholder—Condition of the Netherlands—Departure of a Dutch merchant fleet from Simon's Bay—Capture of eight of the ships off the island of St. Helena—Arrival in Simon's Bay of an English fleet of war and an army—Invitation to place the colony under the authority of the British government—Negotiations between the British officers and the Cape government—Rejection by the Cape government and people of the proposal of the British officers—Military operations—Feeble defence of the colony—Surrender of the country to the British troops—Terms of the capitulation.

Mr. Sluysken took over the government of the Cape colony under circumstances of great difficulty. The credit of the East India Company was exhausted, and its debt was ten million pounds sterling. In February 1794 it was obliged to declare itself unable to meet the interest on its loans. To maintain a garrison capable of defending the country in case of attack was beyond its power.

In the colony gold and silver coin had disappeared, and in its stead was a quantity of cartoon money resting on no other security than the ability of the Company to redeem it at some future time. Under these circumstances, internal trade, except by means of barter, had almost ceased. Debts could be paid in paper, for it was a legal tender, and therefore no one cared to give credit. The prohibition of trade with foreigners had created such distress that its enforcement had been suspended for three years; but now very few foreigners called. The little merchandise in the country was sold at such excessively dear rates that individuals of moderate means were obliged to dispense with many of the ordinary comforts of life. Fortunately, the seasons from 1786 to 1796 were good, and there was no scarcity of food in the country; but there was hardly any market for the surplus. Nothing worth speaking of could be exported to Europe, and the government had a difficulty in sending to India the wheat, wine, butter, and tallow that could be made use of there. The colonists had not yet been able to organise a foreign trade on their own account.

Along the whole northern border the struggle with the Bushmen was constant. On the eastern frontier war with the Kaffirs was being carried on, with no other assistance from the government than a scanty supply of ammunition. The great majority of the people were incensed with the Company, and, without thoroughly comprehending the question, were freely discussing the rights of man, as proclaimed by the French revolutionists. When they were informed that Messrs. Nederburgh and Frykenius had left South Africa without granting to the colonists any representative rights in the government, and that Mr. Sluysken had been placed with extraordinary powers at the head of affairs, several of them—among whom were Willem de Klerk, Frans Kruger, and Marthinus Prinsloo—openly refused to take the oath of fidelity. They were prepared to swear allegiance to the States General of the Netherlands, they said, and to keep their oath; but the East India Company and its officials they would no longer obey. The government threatened them with punishment, but was unable to put its threats into execution.

Mr. Sluysken's chief attention was directed towards means of defence against the French. He caused two small forts to be built in Simon's Town, chiefly by means of convict and slave labour. The cost was thus trifling, for it was estimated that a slave was maintained for 4*l*. 14*s*. 9*d*. a year. The forts were completed in March 1794, when cannon were mounted on them, and they received the names Boetselaar and Zoutman. In May a garrison of 130 men was stationed in Simon's Town.

Three forts were also built at Hout Bay, so that if necessary ships might be sent there for security. They were named Sluysken, Gordon, and Little Gibraltar. The two first-named had cannon mounted upon them, but as there was no more artillery to spare, Little Gibraltar was left to be armed with the guns of any ships that might take shelter in the bay. A good deal of dependence was placed upon red-hot shot, and appliances for heating cannon balls were attached to all the batteries.

In March 1795 a company of the Stellenbosch burgher militia was required to repair to Cape Town to strengthen the garrison, and was kept at the castle until the 15th of May, when it was supposed that an enemy would not care to enter Table Bay.

During 1794 the complaints of the burghers of Graaff Reinet were unceasing with regard to the paper money, the stagnation of trade, the heavy taxes, the conduct of the landdrost, their being left without assistance to defend themselves against Kaffirs and Bushmen, the conditions of the arrangement with the Kaffirs which the government termed peace, and a few other matters of less import, such as being obliged to pay a toll for a pontoon on the Breede river whether they used it or not, and the necessity of every one about to be married appearing before the matrimonial court in Cape Town. The landdrost took no notice of their complaints, and while the colonists were being plundered and harassed by the Kaffirs in the Zuurveld, in his reports represented everything as in a peaceable and orderly condition. The burghers then sent a deputation to Cape Town, provided with an enormous mass of evidence to show the falsehood of Maynier's representations, and to request that he be recalled and a more honest man appointed in his stead; but Commissioner Sluysken would not even investigate the matter. By this treatment the patience of the colonists was at length entirely exhausted.

On the 4th of February 1795 a party of forty burghers assembled at the village of Graaff Reinet, under the leadership of Adriaan van Jaarsveld and Jan Carel Triegard, who demanded an interview with the landdrost. They postponed pushing matters to an extremity, however, until the 6th, when the heemraden assembled. An altercation then took place, in which Marthinus Prinsloo, Jan Durand, and Pieter Joubert were the chief speakers on the side of the burghers. They required that the landdrost should leave the district. He endeavoured to remonstrate with them, but to no effect, and he was obliged to proceed to Cape Town. Further, they expelled from office the lieutenant of militia Cornelis Coetsee and the heemraden Stephanus Naude and Hendrik Meintjes van den Berg, on account of their being partisans of Maynier; but they made no changes in the form of government of the district. As the Company's officers wore orange cockades, the burghers displayed the tricolour, and called themselves 'Nationals.' They declared that their opposition was not to the States General, but to the corrupt servants of the East India Company.

The landdrost Maynier was charged with another offence, not yet mentioned. His opponents accused him of sheltering runaway servants and criminals to such an extent that at this time he had more than one hundred and twenty Hottentots in his private employment, cultivating his land. Many of these Hottentots, they asserted, were guilty of such serious crimes as housebreaking and robbery; but they could not be brought to justice, owing to the landdrost refusing to receive complaints against them as soon as they entered his service.

Mr. Sluysken then sent a commission consisting of Mr. Olof Godlieb de Wet, president of the high court of justice, and Captain Von Hugel, officer in charge of the depôt for recruits for the Wurtemburg regiment, with Mr. Jan Andries Truter, secretary of the high court of justice, as secretary, to try to pacify the burghers. On the 30th of April the commission met the leaders of the 'Nationals' at Graaff Reinet, and after a short discussion, agreed to relieve the district of Mr. Maynier. Mr. Lambertus Philippus van der Poel, previously a clerk in Cape Town, was installed provisionally as landdrost, with Mr. Hendrik Roselt as secretary. The commission was then requested by the burghers to make a tour along the frontier, and especially along the border of the Zuurveld, in order that an accurate report of the condition of the district might be made to government. But neither Mr. De Wet nor Captain Von Hugel would do this, though they were willing to receive evidence at the drostdy. What the burghers desired was that with their own eyes the members of the commission should see that the Zuurveld was actually in the occupation of the Kaffirs, and that a large portion of the remainder of the district had been devastated; but that was just what the government, whose servants they were, did not want to know or believe. The matter was frequently discussed during the next six weeks; but finding that their wishes would not be complied with, on the 14th of June an armed party compelled the members of the commission to leave the district.

On the 6th of July a meeting of the acting and retired heemraden was held, when six representatives—Marthinus Prinsloo, Barend Bester, Christiaan Botha, Christiaan Lotter, Hendrik Klopper, and Andries Krugel, elected by the people, took their seats at a separate table. The different officials were asked whether they were willing to continue their duties under a burgher administration. The provisional landdrost Van der Poel replied that he was, but he desired leave to visit Cape Town. Thereupon he was appointed landdrost, and leave of absence was granted to him, Mr. Jan Booysen being chosen to act until his return. The secretary Roselt declared himself unwilling, on account of his oath of allegiance to the Company. He was dismissed, and another was appointed. The clergyman Manger consented to acknowledge the new authorities, and to unite in marriage any persons approved by them, without reference to the matrimonial court in Cape Town. After this, the obnoxious auction duty was declared abolished.

As Mr. Van der Poel was not permitted by Commissioner Sluysken to return to Graaff Reinet, on the 27th of August the heemraden and representatives of the people appointed the lieutenant of militia, Carel David Gerotz, provisional landdrost, and confirmed his appointment on the 14th of September. On the 27th of August Adriaan van Jaarsveld was appointed to the highest military office in the district, with the title of president of the council of war.

All these proceedings were reported to Mr. Sluysken and the council of policy, as if they were quite in order, and the letters ended by the representatives of the people trusting that their conduct would meet with approval; but the fact was patent to every one that the district of Graaff Reinet was lost to the East India Company.

In Swellendam the people acted in a similar manner. Landdrost Faure was not detested by the burghers as Maynier was, and there was no complaint concerning his administration of justice; but he was accused of being a zealous agent of the East India Company, and of having permitted himself to be guided by Maynier in the Kaffir war of 1793. One offence only was brought home to him. Before the cattle recovered from the Kaffirs were divided, the militia officers proposed to present him with twelve oxen, and he accepted the present. His friends subsequently declared that the officers were instigated by Maynier, whose object was to have it in his power to get his fellow landdrost into trouble whenever he chose; and this is very likely. At any rate, Mr. Faure took the cattle, and was now charged by the burghers with corruption for having done so.

On the 17th of June 1795 the court of landdrost and heemraden was in session at Swellendam, when a party of nine armed burghers, whose spokesman was Paul Fouche, interrupted the proceedings, and commanded the members not to leave the drostdy. There was a difference of opinion among the inhabitants of the district, a considerable number being still averse to revolutionary measures, but others had combined with the Nationals of Graaff Reinet, and had elected a burgher named Petrus Jacobus Delport as their commandant. This party had determined to expel the officers of the East India Company, for which purpose they had come to the drostdy. In the afternoon a second message was sent to the board: that it was not convenient for the burghers to make known their desires that day, but they would do so on the following morning, and in the meantime no one must leave the place.

On the 18th the landdrost Faure and the heemraden Laurens de Jager, Pieter Pienaar, Hermanus Steyn, Hillegard Mulder, and Pieter du Pré assembled in the courtroom again. A large number of burghers had collected in front of the drostdy. These sent a deputation of four persons—Esaias Meyer, Jacobus Steyn, G. F. Rautenbach, and J. J. Botha—to communicate their orders to the board. The landdrost, secretary, and messenger of the court were commanded to resign their offices and to give over the drostdy, the secretary's house, and all the documents and funds belonging to the district, to Mr. Hermanus Steyn. The heemraad Laurens de Jager, who maintained that he was bound to the Company by his oath of office, was also dismissed. Hermanus Steyn was appointed landdrost, and a representative body, termed a National Assembly, was established. Thus a majority of the inhabitants of the district of Swellendam had thrown off the rule of the East India Company.

In Stellenbosch and in Cape Town itself there were many who sympathised with these movements, and it is certain that a very large proportion of the burghers in these places were only waiting for a favourable opportunity to free themselves from the East India Company's domination.

The troops in the colony consisted of a regiment of infantry mustering twenty-five officers and five hundred and forty-six rank and file, a corps of artillery mustering twenty-seven officers and four hundred and three rank and file, fifty-seven men belonging to the depôts of the regiments Meuron and Wurtemburg, and a corps of pandours two hundred and ten strong. The head of the whole military force was Colonel Robert Jacob Gordon. The infantry regiment was termed the national battalion, though it was composed of soldiers from nearly every country in the north of Europe, and there was hardly a Netherlander in it. It was commanded by Lieutenant-Colonel De Lille. All its officers were staunch adherents of the Orange party, and the rank and file were adherents of the party or nation who paid best. The artillery was in every respect superior. The men were Netherlanders with a small mixture of French and Germans, and were attached to the mother country. If not the whole, at least a large majority of this corps favoured the republican cause in Europe, and would have preferred to fight with the French rather than the English as allies.

With so many elements of weakness, the colony invited invasion. The English government was apprehensive of its falling into the possession of the French, by which the sea route to India would be endangered; and as soon as hostilities with France were certain, had proposed to the stadtholder to strengthen it with British troops. Negotiations to this effect were carried on for some time, but at length fell through, as the stadtholder by consenting would have furnished the democratic party in the Netherlands with an opportunity to assail him.

When the war commenced, England and the government of the stadtholder were in alliance; but a large proportion of the Dutch people favoured the French, and all were doubtful whether they might not soon change sides. An intimation to this effect was made to Commissioner Sluysken in a letter dated the 10th of October 1794, and signed by P. J. Guepin, chief advocate of the East India Company, with the knowledge and approbation of the directors. It was thus informally written that the stadtholder might know nothing about it. Mr. Guepin stated that matters were in a doubtful condition; the French armies were approaching, and had already occupied part of the country; it would therefore be necessary to keep careful watch, so as not to be surprised by any European enemy whatever. This letter was received at the Cape on the 7th of February 1795.

Except a rumour of the fall of Nymegen on the 8th of November, brought by a Swedish ship, nothing more was known of the course of events in the Netherlands until the

12th of April 1795, when the national frigate *Medenblik* arrived with two chartered ships in convoy. She had left Texel on the 22nd of December, and Captain Dekker, who commanded her, reported that a French army under General Pichegru was then besieging Breda and threatening to cross the Maas. The *Medenblik* brought no letters or despatches.

There were nine homeward-bound ships at anchor in Table Bay, and as more were expected it was considered advisable to detain them that all might sail together. They were therefore sent to Simon's Bay, where they were soon afterwards joined by seven others. The cargoes of the whole were valued at 835,000*l*. On the 19th of May they sailed under protection of the frigate *Scipio* and the brig of war *Comeet*, two vessels which had been waiting here six months for that purpose. Just after leaving Simon's Bay they scattered, and eight of them were picked up by hostile cruisers lying in wait off the island of St. Helena.

After the arrival of the *Medenblik* no intelligence from Europe was received until the 11th of June 1795, when a report reached the castle from the resident at Simon's Town that at noon several ships of unknown nationality were beating into False Bay. Three hours later this report was followed by one from Muizenburg that the ships had cast anchor, and at ten in the evening a note was received from Simon's Town stating that Captain Dekker of the *Medenblik* had sent a boat with a lieutenant to one of the strangers to ascertain particulars, that the lieutenant was to have waved a flag if they were friendly, but that no such signal had been made, and the boat had not yet returned.

The commissioner hereupon called the council of policy together, and at half past ten as many of the members as were in Cape Town met in the castle. There were present, beside Mr. Sluysken, the secunde Johannes Isaac Rhenius, Colonel Gordon, and Messrs. Jacobus Johannes le Sueur, Willem Ferdinand van Reede van Oudtshoorn, and Willem Stephanus van Ryneveld. They resolved unanimously to cause the signals of alarm to be made, summoning the burghers of the country districts to hasten to Cape Town.

Lieutenant-Colonel De Lille was directed immediately to proceed to Simon's Town with two hundred infantry and one hundred gunners, to strengthen the garrison there, which consisted of only one hundred and fifty men all told. The troops left within an hour, and reached their destination before the following noon.

The council broke up a little after midnight, but the members remained at the castle, and at half past two in the morning of the 12th the commissioner called them together again. He had just received a letter from Mr. Brand, the resident at Simon's Town, informing him that Captain Dekker's boat had returned, bringing a gentleman named Ross with letters from the English admiral Elphinstone and Major-General Craig for the head of the government. Mr. Brand had supplied Mr. Ross with a horse and a guide, and he had arrived at the castle. The letters delivered by him were three complimentary notes from the directors of the English East India Company to Commissioner Sluysken, and an invitation from Admiral Elphinstone to Commissioner Sluysken and Colonel Gordon to visit his ship for the purpose of receiving important information as well as a missive from the stadtholder. Mr. Ross, who was conversant with the Dutch language, was secretary to Major-General Craig. He evaded all questions concerning the state of affairs in Europe or the destination of the fleet.

Lieutenant Van Vegezak, of the *Medenblik*, who had been on board the English admiral's ship, arrived at the castle while the council was still sitting. He stated that he had not been able to obtain any other information than that the fleet consisted of three ships of 74 guns, named the *Monarch*, *Arrogant*, and *Victorious*, three of 64 guns, named the *America*, *Ruby*, and *Stately*, a frigate of 24 guns named the *Sphinx*, and two sloops of war, the *Echo* and *Rattlesnake*, respectively of 18 and 16 guns. The admiral commanding was Sir George Keith Elphinstone, and there were troops on board, how many he could not ascertain, under command of Major-General Sir James Craig.

In reply to the letter of Admiral Elphinstone and General

Craig, the council informed them that it was not possible for either Commissioner Sluysken or Colonel Gordon to leave Cape Town, and invited them to send a trustworthy officer with the information and despatches. The resident at Simon's Town was instructed to permit the English fleet to take in provisions, but not to allow armed men to land.

There was at Muizenburg a signal station, with a couple of mortars in position to command the road from Simon's Town, but no fort. Before daylight the militia captain Pieter de Waal with eighty-four Cape burghers, and thirty gunners with three small field-pieces, were on their way to occupy that post.

The defensive works of Simon's Bay consisted of the batteries Boetselaar and Zoutman, the former provided with six and the latter with four small cannon. They were incapable of offering effectual resistance to a force such as that under the English admiral. On the 13th of June instructions were sent to Lieutenant-Colonel De Lille to leave a small garrison in each of them, and to strengthen the post at Muizenburg with two hundred infantry and one hundred and forty artillerymen.

In the afternoon of the following day there arrived at the castle Lieutenant-Colonel Mackenzie, of the 78th regiment, Captain Hardy, of the *Echo* sloop of war, and Mr. Ross, secretary to General Craig, who handed to Commissioner Sluysken a mandate from the prince of Orange, dated at Kew on the 7th of February 1795, ordering him to admit the troops of the king of England into the forts and elsewhere in the colony, also to admit British ships of war into the ports, and to consider such troops and ships of war as the forces of a friendly power sent to protect the colony against an invasion of the French. They also delivered to the commissioner a letter from Admiral Elphinstone and General Craig, in which an account of the condition of the Netherlands was given. The winter in Europe had been an excessively severe one, he was informed, and towards the close of January the rivers were frozen so hard that the French armies crossed into Utrecht and Gelderland, compelling the English forces to retire into Germany and the Dutch forces to surrender. In a few days the whole country fell into possession of the French without any treaty of capitulation, and the stadtholder was obliged to make his escape in a fishing boat, which conveyed him from Scheveningen to England. Great Britain and her allies, were, however, raising large armies, and they were confident of being able to drive out the French in the next campaign.

The statements made in this letter fell short of giving complete particulars, and, throughout the negotiations which followed, the officials and inhabitants of the colony were studiously kept in ignorance that the democratic party in the Netherlands had given the French an enthusiastic welcome, that the national government had been remodelled, and that the States General had abolished the stadtholderate. No newspapers were supplied, though asked for. The view which the British officers tried to impress was that the Netherlands had been conquered and were being subjected to very rigorous treatment by the French. They did not wish it to be known that a national government was still in existence, and that the majority of the people regarded the French as friends.

The council took the mandate of the prince of Orange and the letter of the English officers into careful consideration. Even if written in the Netherlands, the mandate would not have been officially of any force, as it was signed by the prince of Orange alone; but having been written in a foreign country by a fugitive prince, it could not be held to have any weight whatever. Every member of the council sympathised strongly with the Orange faction, but there was no evading the fact that their allegiance was due to the mother country, and not to a party. Any day intelligence might arrive from the Netherlands, and it was therefore important to gain as much time as possible. With this object in view, the council wrote to Admiral Elphinstone that the fleet would be supplied with provisions, and requested that only small parties of unarmed men might be sent on shore. They were grateful, they said, to the British government for the evidence of its friendship, and in case the colony should be attacked by the French they would ask the British officers in the fleet for assistance, though they were in the fortunate position of being able to resist a hostile power. They desired to be informed what number of troops could be furnished to aid them, if necessary.

An answer was sent that General Craig would proceed to Cape Town and give them further information. In the mean time the burgher forces were beginning to arrive from Stellenbosch, and on the 15th of June two hundred horsemen were sent to strengthen the post at Muizenburg.

On the 18th of June General Craig, attended by three officers and his secretary, arrived in Cape Town and had an interview with the commissioner. On the following day the council of policy met, when the general communicated to the members the object of his mission and the manner in which he had been instructed to carry it out. The fleet and troops, he stated, had been sent by His Britannic Majesty to protect the colony until the restoration of the ancient form of government in the Netherlands, when it would be in His Majesty's power to restore it to its proper owner. No alterations would be made in the laws or the customs of the country without the expressed desire of the inhabitants, nor would any additional taxation be imposed. The people would be required to defray the cost of their government as it then existed, but nothing more. They would be at liberty to trade with England and the English possessions in India. The troops would be paid by England, and would be required to take an oath of allegiance to His Britannic Majesty for the time that he should be in possession of the colony. The civil servants would retain their offices until His Majesty's pleasure should be known.

The council replied in writing, declining to entertain the proposal, and informing the general that they were determined to protect the colony with their own forces against any power that should attack them.

Admiral Elphinstone and General Craig, upon the return of the latter to Simon's Bay, issued a proclamation in which the government and inhabitants were invited and required to place themselves under His Britannic Majesty's protection, as the French would undoubtedly endeavour to obtain possession of the dependencies of the Netherlands.

Three days later the English officers issued an address, in which the offer of protection under the conditions named by General Craig was repeated, and a committee of the inhabitants was invited to come to Simon's Town to confer with them. The address was issued in the Dutch and German languages, and a good many copies were distributed. It put before the colonists the alternative of a French or an English occupation. The former was pictured as a government on jacobin principles, with the tree of liberty and the guillotine, freedom of the slaves accompanied by such horrors as those which had laid waste the rich and beautiful islands of St. Domingo and Guadeloupe, total cessation of intercourse with Europe, annihilation of commerce, and absence of money and the necessaries of life. The latter as protection by the only power in Europe able to assure safety of person and property under the existing laws or others that the inhabitants might desire, free sale of all productions of the country at the best prices obtainable, release from imposts intended for the exclusive benefit of the Dutch East India Company, commerce by sea or land from one part of the colony to another, and better pay for such soldiers as might choose to enter the English service.

In consequence of this proceeding, the council notified a desire to be excused from further communications; still the correspondence was continued. On the 26th the admiral and general wrote a long letter, the keynote of which was that the Netherlands had been absorbed by France, and as the Cape colony if left to itself would be absorbed also, His Britannic Majesty could not allow it to fall into the hands of his enemies. The council replied that there was a great difference between offering assistance against an invader and requiring them to surrender the colony to the British government.

At this stage the further supply of provisions to the fleet was prohibited. The post at Muizenburg was strengthened by another detachment of burgher horsemen, and by the pandours under Commandant Jan Gerhard Cloete. The troops that had garrisoned the battery Boetselaar were also removed to Muizenburg, only one man being left behind to spike the guns in case the English should land.

As soon as the design of the British officers was known, those burghers of the Cape and Stellenbosch who had hitherto been refractory ceased opposing the government, and declared themselves ready to assist in the defence of the colony to the utmost of their power. When the commissioner announced that the country would not be surrendered, he was met with loud huzzas in the streets, and was hailed as Father Sluysken. The great majority of the colonists, being attached to the republican party in Europe, were ready to welcome the French, if they could not be left to themselves. They reminded each other how English visitors had for years been insulting them by boastfully predicting that the colony would one day be subject to Great Britain, and now an attempt was being made under the name of friendship to turn that prediction into reality. English arrogance was spoken and written of as if it was the most prominent feature of the English character.

On the other hand, the high officials, though professing that it was their duty to defend the colony, were at heart lukewarm in the matter. Colonel Gordon stated that he was prepared to admit the English troops if the jacobins should threaten an attack. The English officers believed when they arrived that he would at once join them, probably reckoning upon his being of Scotch descent as well as Orange proclivities, but he was not ready to go as far as that. He did not throw his energy into resisting them, however; neither did Commissioner Sluysken. Most of the officials of lower grade and a few of the burghers of the town were willing to welcome the English troops, and went about singing Orange songs, believing that the object of the British government really was to hold the country in trust for the fugitive stadtholder.

On the 21st of June the *Medenblik* sailed for Batavia,

but unaccompanied by the two ships which had come from Europe under her protection. Captain Dekker was desirous of conveying intelligence to the Indian authorities of events in the Netherlands and at the Cape. The British admiral made no objection to his leaving, but required him to promise on his word of honour not to put into any French port on the passage.

The offer of being taken into the British service with an increase of pay, made to soldiers who were chiefly foreign mercenaries and who had long received nothing but cartoon money, was sufficient to induce some of those of the so-called national battalion at Muizenburg to desert. In less than a fortnight twenty-three of them changed sides, and desertions continued to be common until a few weeks later when two who were caught by a burgher patrol were tried and punished with death. Not a single artilleryman abandoned his colours.

The militia at Muizenburg were living in great discomfort. The soldiers were provided with tents, but there were very few to spare for the burghers, who had to make shelters of bushes and reeds. It was the winter season, and although during June and July the weather was unusually mild and very little rain fell, sleeping in the open air was unpleasant. The burghers were relieved every third day by fresh detachments from the town, so that they were able to keep their horses in good condition. Each man received daily eight shillings in cartoon money, with which to provide for himself and his horse.

The two chartered ships which had come from Europe under protection of the *Medenblik* were still lying in Simon's Bay, and on the 24th of June a homeward-bound ship from Batavia came to anchor there also. Commissioner Sluysken sent their skippers instructions to proceed to Table Bay, but Admiral Elphinstone prohibited their sailing. On the 28th of June two small vessels under the American flag arrived in Simon's Bay. One—the *Columbia*—was from Amsterdam, where she had been chartered to convey despatches to the Cape and Batavia. She was at once placed under guard by the English admiral, and her mails were taken possession of. Instructions were issued that no newspapers should be allowed to reach the shore; but one escaped the vigilance of the sentries, and came into possession of a Cape burgher. It contained a notice by the States General, dated the 4th of March 1795, absolving all persons in the Netherlands and in the Dutch colonies from the oath of allegiance to the prince of Orange. The letters were examined by British officers, and portions of many of them, as also all annexures to despatches, were detained. The residue of the correspondence was then sent by the admiral to Cape Town for delivery. But from the notice in the newspaper and the letters to private individuals, mutilated as they were, it was ascertained that the French were treating with the Netherlands as an independent republic, that the stadtholderate had been abolished by the national will, and that the French were regarded as friends.

With this knowledge, the commissioner and the council asserted that it was simple duty to do their utmost to prevent the English from obtaining possession of the colony. There was a possibility that the fleet might be forced to sail if no provisions could be obtained. There was further a possibility of aid reaching them from Europe if they could hold out long enough. With these objects in view, and perhaps, as the burghers afterwards declared must be the case, because there was nothing to lose in opposing the English provided they did not altogether repel them, and there might be a strong combined French and Dutch fleet on the way out, in which case their heads would be in danger if they made no show of resistance, on the 29th of June the commissioner and the chief of the army, with the concurrence of the remaining members of the council, issued orders for the abandonment of Simon's Town. That night all the provisions in the place were destroyed, the guns in the batteries Boetselaar and Zoutman were spiked, all the ammunition that could not be carried away was thrown into the sea, and the troops and most of the inhabitants retired, leaving behind only the assistant resident—Mr. Jan Hendrik

Brand—with two slaves to serve him, and the widows Auret and Aspeling with their households. Mrs. Auret left a few weeks later, but Mrs. Aspeling preferred to remain and take care of her property. The troops joined the other forces at Muizenburg.

Two English men-of-war were blockading Table Bay, where the Company's packet brig *Star* was at anchor. The council therefore chartered from Messrs. Van Reenen a cutter of theirs which was at anchor in Saldanha Bay, and sent her to Batavia with despatches.

When the signals calling the burghers to the Cape were first made, only seventy men belonging to the district of Swellendam responded to them. The Nationals declined to obey. On the 22nd of June Commissioner Sluysken wrote urging them to do their duty, and on the following day Messrs. A. Horak and N. Linde addressed a strong appeal to them. Still they made no response. On the 7th of July the burgher councillors requested Commissioner Sluysken and the council of policy to offer them an amnesty for the past and reasonable redress of grievances as soon as possible, if they would assist in the defence of the country. This request was complied with, but the offer was not at first well received, as they wished the term 'reasonable redress of grievances' to be clearly defined.

At the instance of a considerable number of burghers, on the 16th of July the five individuals who called themselves the National Assembly—Hermanus Steyn, Anthonie van Vollenhoven, Ernst du Toit, Petrus Jacobus Delport, and Louis Almoro Pisani—met in session, and framed an answer. In language which is only intelligible to those who are acquainted with the circumstances of the country at the time, they stated that they were resolved to shed the last drop of their blood, if necessary, in defence of freedom; but they were willing to treat with the commissioner and to render assistance if he would guarantee to them exemption from direct taxation, free trade, the withdrawal of the cartoon money, permission to retain in perpetual slavery all

Bushmen made prisoners by commandos or individuals, and several other favours of less importance.[1]

The letter was hardly despatched, however, when many of them became suddenly conscious that their claims would certainly be ignored if the English got possession of the country. They therefore resolved, while maintaining their right to self-government to a very large extent, to aid in the defence; and one hundred and sixty-eight mounted men, under the National commandant Delport, left for the Cape. Upon arriving at the farm of the widow Morkel on this side of Hottentots Holland kloof, they sent to ask assurance of safety. Messrs. A. Horak and G. H. Meyer were instructed by Commissioner Sluysken to convey this to them, and on the 26th of July they arrived at the castle. The Swellendam burghers were then formed into three companies, one of ninety-six men under Captain J. J. Botha, one of eighty men under Captain H. Mulder, and one of sixty-two men under Captain L. de Jager.

After Delport left, some forty or forty-five individuals, chiefly discharged soldiers and persons of little standing, elected Pisani to be their commandant, and threatened to confiscate the property of those who were aiding the Company. Pisani was an Italian who had arrived in this country as a soldier. After a while he deserted and wandered over the colony, but returned to his regiment on a promise of pardon. When the garrison was reduced he obtained leave to seek service among the farmers, and finally, in 1792, was discharged and became a burgher. He was married to a daughter of the farmer Jan Crafford, and had three children. Under this man's leadership, the extreme section of the Nationals marched towards the Cape, and on the 10th of August reached Waveren. From this place, Pisani wrote to Commissioner Sluysken, demanding a reply to the letter from the National Assembly, and threat-

[1] This document is printed in Mr. Sluysken's *Verbaal*, and by the insertion of a comma where none should be it is made to show that the slavery of Hottentots also was demanded. This was not the case. The Bushmen were commonly called in the colony Bushmen-Hottentots, and the words should have been printed in this form, not 'Bushmen, Hottentots,' &c.

ening hostilities if a favourable answer were not forwarded within twenty-four hours. The commissioner at once set a price of 200*l.* upon his head, dead or alive. Some of his former associates joined an expedition against him, and on the 13th of August he and two other discharged soldiers were arrested at the house of Marthinus Roux at the Tigerberg. Pisani was committed to prison, from which he only emerged some months later to go into banishment from the colony for life.

From the district of Stellenbosch and Drakenstein six hundred and fifty-eight mounted burghers had arrived. They were in five companies, under the captains Loubser, Myburgh, Van der Byl, Hoffman, and Cloete. The Cape district furnished two hundred and forty-four mounted burghers, formed into two companies under the captains De Waal and Goosen. Thus there were altogether in the field eleven hundred and forty burgher horsemen. About two hundred were constantly at Muizenburg, the others were stationed in Cape Town, with pickets along the road to the camp.

On the 9th of July Admiral Elphinstone took possession of the three Dutch ships in Simon's Bay, stating that he did so to prevent their destruction by their crews. On the 14th four hundred and fifty men of the 78th regiment and three hundred and fifty marines were landed and occupied Simon's Town.

With most people these would certainly be considered acts of war, yet neither the English commanders nor Commissioner Sluysken chose to regard them as such. The commissioner issued orders that no attack was to be made upon the English patrols, nor anything done to provoke them to retaliate or give them an opportunity to throw the blame upon the Dutch of commencing hostilities. On the 4th of August a burgher officer named Jacobus van Reenen with a party of pandours proceeded along the hills above Simon's Town to make observations, and fired towards an English picket, though at too great a distance to do any harm. For this he was reprimanded, because in the commissioner's opinion the English might construe it into an act of war. And in General Craig's despatches it is described as the commencement of hostilities.

Boats from the English ships were allowed to come unmolested and take soundings in front of the camp at Muizenburg. A strong battery had been erected to command the road from Simon's Town, but there were no defences on the side of the sea. The burgher and artillery officers desired that earthworks should be thrown up to protect the camp from the guns of ships, but the commissioner and Colonel Gordon decided that it would be unnecessary labour, as in their opinion no ships could get close enough to the shore to do any damage. And when at last leave was obtained to place two 24-pounders in position to face the sea, no platforms were made for them to rest on, so that they were practically of little use.

The soldiers at Muizenburg had no lack of provisions. There was a year's supply of grain and wine in the magazines at Cape Town, and food in abundance was forwarded without difficulty. So much wine and brandy, indeed, was sent, that there was sufficient for a month's consumption in advance.

On the morning of the 7th of August there were at the camp 200 men of the national battalion, 120 artillerymen, 200 burgher cavalry, and 150 pandours. There was also a small guard at Kalk Bay. About an hour after noon another hundred burgher horsemen arrived as a relief. Just as they reached the camp it was observed that some of the English ships were under sail, but no particular regard was at first paid to their movements, as for several days previously Admiral Elphinstone had caused vessels to cruise round the bay.

In a very few minutes, however, it became evident that the British forces were about to make an attack. For this purpose a column had been formed of soldiers of the 78th regiment, marines, and sailors, in all sixteen hundred men. Major-General Craig was in command, and under him the naval brigades were led by Captains Spranger and Hardy of the *Rattlesnake* and *Echo*, sloops of war. The sea in False

Bay was smooth, but a gentle breeze was blowing from the north-west, sufficient to keep a ship in motion. The *America, Stately, Echo,* and *Rattlesnake,* under command of Commodore Blankett, loosed their sails and stood over to the Muizenburg beach.

Along the margin of False Bay, from Kalk Bay to Muizenburg, a steep mountain rises only a few paces from the water's edge. On the narrow strip of comparatively level ground was the road, then as to-day the only passage by which troops could march from Simon's Town to Cape Town. At Muizenburg the mountain terminates abruptly, and is succeeded by the sandy plain called the Cape flats, extending from False Bay to Table Bay and forming the isthmus that connects the Cape peninsula with the African continent. On these flats, close to the end of the mountain, is a large sheet of shallow water called Sand Vlei, with a brook, which flows only after rain and is known as Keyser's river, emptying into it on the northern side. The Dutch camp was at the foot of the mountain facing False Bay, and eleven pieces of artillery commanded the road.

The English ships fired a few guns at the outpost at Kalk Bay, which caused the picket there to retire over the mountain. Sailing on until abreast of Muizenburg, they opened their broadsides upon the camp; but the first shot was hardly fired when De Lille with the infantry of the national battalion abandoned the post. The main body, led by the colonel, fled hastily through Sand Vlei. One company of fifty men, under Captain Warnecke, retired in better order and more slowly along the base of the Steenberg.

Some of the artillerymen followed, leaving a company under Lieutenant Marnitz to work the two 24-pounders. With these the English fire was answered, but without much effect. The *America* had two men killed and four wounded, and one of her guns was disabled by Lieutenant Marnitz's fire. The *Stately* had one man wounded. A few balls passed quite through both these ships, but only injured them to a trifling extent. The range of the English guns was so high that the shot passed over the camp and struck the mountain above. The Dutch guns, resting on loose soil, required to be got into position after every discharge, and Lieutenant Marnitz was soon convinced that the camp could not be held. He therefore spiked the two cannon, and retired as the English column, which had marched from Simon's Town, but was without artillery, came charging along the road. Nothing was taken from the camp by the retreating troops but five small field-pieces.

It is no stigma upon the burgher cavalry and the pandours that they were swept round the mountain in confusion by the fire from the ships, and did not wait to meet the advancing column. The English followed with cheers; but at the first point out of range of the ships' guns, the artillerymen and burghers made a stand. From this they were driven by a charge of two companies of the 78th under Major Moneypenny. Behind the mountain, however, they again turned upon their pursuers. Captain Kemper, who was retreating with some artillerymen on the other side of Sand Vlei, seeing this, brought a gun to bear upon the English with such effect that they fell back to Muizenburg. The casualties were one English officer, one burgher, two Dutch artillerymen, and one pandour wounded.

De Lille with the infantry could easily have made a stand behind Sand Vlei, at the mouth of the brook, as at that point his front would have been protected and the field-pieces which he had with him would have commanded the road where it leaves the beach at Muizenburg and turns off nearly at a right angle into the sandy plain. Instead of doing so, he continued his flight in the greatest confusion to Lochner's farm at Diep River, some half mile or thereabouts on the western side of the present main road, and between Rathfelder's hotel and Constantia. The colonel arrived there without knowing what had become of the artillerymen and the burghers.

As soon as the signal was made that the English were advancing, five companies of burgher horsemen hastened from Cape Town towards Muizenburg; but on the way they

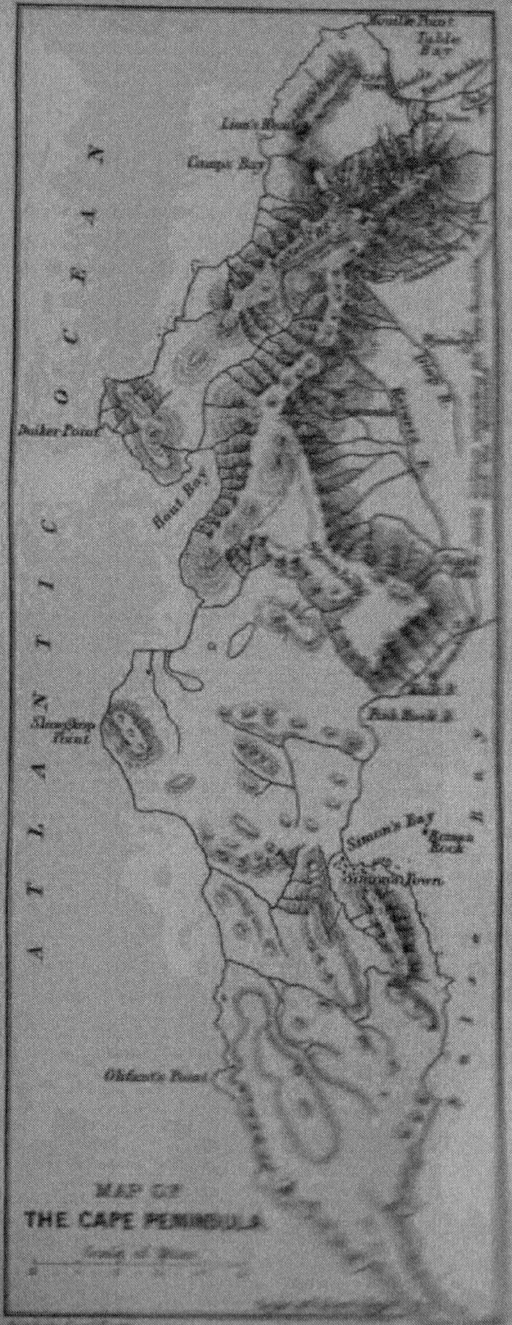
Table Bay
Lion's Head
Camps Bay
ATLANTIC OCEAN
Duiker Point
Hout Bay
Simon's Bay
Roman Rock
Simon's Town
MAP OF
THE CAPE PENINSULA

met the fugitives, and learned that the camp was lost with everything in it. They remained on the flats that night, scattered about in parties of ten and twenty.

Next morning De Lille with some of the infantry returned to the head of Sand Vlei, but fled precipitately upon a column of English seamen and marines advancing to attack him, though they had to wade through the vlei with the water in some places above their waists. The English pursued until they were surprised by finding a party of burghers and pandours emerging from behind some sandhills on their flank. They in their turn then fled, thinking they were being drawn into a trap, and were followed by the burghers and pandours until these were checked by the fire of the cannon which had been abandoned and spiked by Lieutenant Marnitz on the previous day, but which General Craig had caused to be drilled and placed in position at the end of the mountain. In the pursuit of the English De Lille gave no assistance whatever, but, on the contrary, while they were running towards Muizenburg he was running in the opposite direction. That evening he formed a camp at or very near the site of the present military buildings at Wynberg, about a mile from the farm where he had passed the previous night.

The burgher officers Botha, Loubser, De Waal, Van der Byl, Goosen, Hoffman, and Mulder now drew up a document in which Lieutenant-Colonel De Lille was charged with treason, and forwarded it to the commissioner. He was thereupon sent to the castle under arrest, and on the 10th of August Captain Van Baalen was placed in command of the camp at Wynberg. De Lille's conduct was investigated by the fiscal, and he was acquitted of treason. The popular fury against him was, however, so great, that he was kept in confinement to ensure his safety. There is certainly no proof, or even probability, that he deliberately entered into an agreement with the British officers to betray his trust; still his conduct cannot be attributed to either imbecility or cowardice. He was a devoted adherent of the Orange party, and regarded the English as supporters of the Orange cause, so would not fight against them. Successful resistance, in his opinion, would have been equivalent to giving up the country to the Nationals, whom he hated. At the earliest opportunity he entered the British service, and we shall hereafter find him as barrack master in Cape Town, wearing the Orange cockade, professing devotion to the English, and in his revels venting abhorrence of the jacobins, whether in France, or the Netherlands, or South Africa.

As the land forces on board the fleet were inconsiderable, the *Sphinx* had been sent to St. Helena to obtain as many soldiers and cannon as the governor of that island could spare. Three hundred and fifty-two men in the service of the English East India Company, with nine pieces of artillery, were embarked in a transport named the *Arniston*, which arrived in Simon's Bay on the 9th of August.

Three days later Admiral Elphinstone and General Craig wrote again to Commissioner Sluysken, the council, and the inhabitants. They announced that they had received some reinforcements, and expected immediately three thousand more soldiers. They had left England hastily in order to reach the Cape before the French, and only brought with them such land forces as could be accommodated in the men-of-war. But when they sailed, a number of Indiamen were being made ready to bring out troops, and these were now due. They repeated the offer to take the Cape under British protection upon the same terms as those announced ever since their arrival, and they added that their people were becoming exasperated and it might be impossible to restrain their fury if resistance were made much longer.

The commissioner laid this letter before the council of policy, the burgher council, and the burgher militia, with a request for an expression of opinion. In the council of policy, Messrs. Sluysken, Rhenius, Gordon, De Wet, Brand, Van Ryneveld, and Bergh voted not to give up the colony while resistance could be offered. Mr. Le Sueur differed, as he saw no possibility of successful resistance against so powerful an enemy. Mr. Van Reede van Oudtshoorn was absent.

The burgher council, consisting of Messrs J. Smuts, G. H. Meyer, H. J. de Wet, A. Fleck, H. A. Truter, and

H. P. Warnecke, unanimously adopted a resolution that the colony ought to be defended to the very last. The burghers were assembled, and the letter was read to them. They were of the same opinion as the councillors, and the militia officers without an exception signed a document to that effect.

On the 18th of August the commissioner communicated to the British officers the resolution of the people, and announced that the colony would still be defended.

But in spite of these brave words, even if all who used them were in earnest, which is doubtful, the means of resistance were daily becoming less. There were rumours that the Bushmen in the interior were particularly troublesome, and that the Hottentots in the district of Swellendam and the slaves in Stellenbosch and Drakenstein meditated insurrection. Whether these rumours were true or false, many burghers returned home to protect their families. Feelings of patriotism, however strong, were too weak to keep a body of militia together under such circumstances. From eleven hundred and forty men, which the burgher cavalry numbered during July and the first fortnight in August, they fell off to about nine hundred at the beginning of September. The burgher infantry, three hundred and fifty strong, which was composed of residents of the town, remained at its full strength. The government endeavoured to enlist more pandours, and a commission was sent to the country districts to obtain half-breeds and Hottentots for the purpose, but met with no success.

On the morning of the 1st of September the burghers, aided by some of the pandours, attempted to get possession of the English outposts on the Steenberg; but not being supported by the regular troops, nor being allowed the use of the field-pieces which they needed, they were unsuccessful. Among those severely wounded on the English side on this occasion were Major Moneypenny of the 78th and Captain Dentane of the St. Helena regiment. The total loss of the English forces since the arrival of the fleet was brought up to three rank and file killed and four officers and thirty-three rank and file wounded.

On the same day a mutiny broke out in the pandour corps. Commandant Cloete was ill, and the men had little regard for the other officers. One hundred and seventy of them marched with their arms to the castle, declaring they would fight no longer. They complained that some of their families had been ill-treated by colonists during their absence, that their pay was inadequate, that they were subject to abusive remarks, that 40*l.* which had been promised to them as a reward for good conduct had not yet been distributed, and that their rations of spirits were insufficient. Commissioner Sluysken did what he could to pacify them. He promised to raise their pay from eight to twelve shillings a month, to see that they and their families were well treated, and to allow them an increase of spirits and wine. He succeeded in inducing them to return to the camp, but they went back sullen and obstinate, and were thereafter of very little service.

An attack by night upon the English camp at Muizenburg was planned, and was about to be attempted when on the 4th of September a fleet of twelve Indiamen, under convoy of three men-of-war, entered Simon's Bay. They had on board the 84th, 95th, and 98th regiments of the line, and a strong body of engineers and artillerymen, in all three thousand troops, under command of General Sir Alured Clarke. Many of the burgher cavalry now gave up all hope, and left for their homes, so that ten days later there were only five hundred and twenty-one men of this force in the field.

On the 9th of September Admiral Elphinstone and Generals Clarke and Craig issued another address, inviting the inhabitants to submit to the protection of the overwhelming force that must otherwise take possession of the country by violent means. Commissioner Sluysken replied, as before, that his oath required him to defend the colony for its lawful owners.

At nine o'clock in the morning of the 14th of September an English force, between four and five thousand strong, in two columns, marched from Muizenburg towards Cape Town. As soon as the signals were made, all the burgher cavalry, with the exception of one company, were sent to assist the regular troops. Some joined the camp at Wynberg, others attempted to harass the columns on the march, in which they succeeded so far as to kill one sailor and wound seventeen soldiers. In this service a party of the Swellendam Nationals, under Cornet Daniel du Plessis, particularly distinguished themselves. They so won the respect of General Clarke that after the final surrender he invited Du Plessis to dine with him, and highly complimented the sturdy burgher. But the force to which they were opposed was too strong to be checked by any efforts that they could make.

Van Baalen—now promoted by Commissioner Sluysken to the rank of Major—who was in command of the camp at Wynberg, arranged to meet the shock of battle by drawing up his forces in a faulty manner and placing his cannon in such a position that they were practically useless. Some artillery and burgher officers remonstrated, but to no purpose, for as soon as the English were within range, he retreated with the greater part of the national battalion. The burghers cried out that they were being betrayed and sold. It was a scene of confusion. One company of infantry and most of the artillerymen made a stand for a few minutes, and then fell back towards Cape Town, abandoning the camp with everything in it. One burgher and one soldier were killed, and another soldier was wounded. The burgher cavalry, strongly impressed with the idea that Commissioner Sluysken and Colonel Gordon, as well as the officers of the national battalion, were traitors at heart, and considering that if they crossed the lines they would be in a trap and must become prisoners of war, dispersed and returned to their homes.

While this was taking place, a squadron of three British men-of-war and an Indiaman was threatening Cape Town from the side of Table Bay, but did not come within gun-shot.

At six o'clock in the evening of the 14th of September the council of policy met. All the members except Colonel Gordon were present. The position was as follows. A

British army, over four thousand strong and in thorough discipline, was in bivouac at Newlands. The force which still nominally remained at the disposal of the government was composed of 542 men of the national battalion, 403 artillerymen, 57 men of the depôts of the regiments Meuron and Wurtemburg, 71 convalescent sailors, 350 burgher infantry, 95 burgher cavalry, a corps of 125 pennists, a corps of 42 Malays, and a few seamen belonging to the ship *Castor* and brig *Star*, altogether about 1,720 men. Nearly half of these had retreated during the day from the camp at Wynberg, and at dusk were reported to be at Drie Kopjes—now Mowbray. The remainder were distributed among the fortifications in Hout Bay, Camps Bay, and Table Valley. Even supposing them all thoroughly loyal and determined to fight to the last, they could not have held their own for any length of time; but they were without a leader in whom they could have confidence, and a very large proportion of those who were disciplined were not disposed to meet the English in battle.

Under these circumstances further defence seemed impossible; but one member of the council—Mr. Van Reede van Oudtshoorn—still objected to voluntary surrender. He was commandant of the pennists. In that capacity he offered with his corps to be employed in the hottest part of a final battle, and declared that with his consent the colony would never be given up. The remaining members were unanimous that, to save the town from being taken by storm, they ought to capitulate on the best terms obtainable. With this view a messenger with a flag of truce was sent to the English bivouac at Newlands, with letters to the generals and admiral requesting a suspension of hostilities for forty-eight hours, in order to arrange terms. At midnight General Clarke consented to an armistice for twenty-four hours.

In the morning of the 15th Messrs. J. J. le Sueur and W. S. van Ryneveld were sent with the conditions proposed by the council to confer with General Craig, who had come for that purpose to Rustenburg, the garden and country seat of the early Dutch governors at Rondebosch. Some of the articles proposed were agreed to, others were modified, and only one was refused. This one related to a few deserters from the English forces who had joined the Dutch, and for whose safety a promise of pardon was desired. The rejection of this article caused some delay, as Commissioner Sluysken, on being referred to, declined to consent to the capitulation without it. General Craig then, while still refusing to have an article promising pardon inserted in the terms of surrender, gave his word that no notice would be taken of the deserters. The commissioner and council, late in the night of Tuesday, the 15th of September 1795, agreed to the terms as modified by General Craig, and signed them. Early in the morning of the 16th the arrangements for the capitulation were completed by the document being signed by Sir Alured Clarke and Sir George Elphinstone at Rustenburg. At eleven o'clock the council closed its last session by ordering the publication of the articles and official notification of what had occurred to be given to the heads of departments and officers in the country districts.

The terms provided for the surrender of the Dutch troops as prisoners of war, but the officers were to be at liberty either to remain in Cape Town or to return to Europe, upon giving their word of honour not to serve against England during the continuance of hostilities. The colonists were to retain all their privileges, including the existing form of religion. No new taxes were to be levied, but, in consideration of the decay of the colony, the old imposts were to be reduced as much as possible. Everything belonging to the East India Company was to be handed over to the English officers, but all other property was to be respected. The lands and houses belonging to the East India Company were to be held in pledge for the redemption of that portion of the paper money which was not secured by mortgages on private property.

At three o'clock in the afternoon of Wednesday, the 16th of September 1795, twelve hundred British infantry and two hundred artillerymen under General Craig arrived at the castle and drew up on the open ground in front. The Dutch troops marched out with colours flying and drums beating, passed by the English, and laid down their arms, surrendering as prisoners of war. Some of them were in a state of great excitement, and were uttering imprecations upon Commissioner Sluysken and Colonel Gordon for having brought disgrace upon them. One soldier even went so far as to attempt to assault the colonel. It is asserted by Lieutenant Marnitz, in his relation of these events, that the only occasion after the arrival of the English on which the head of the military drew his sword was when he gave the order for the troops he had commanded to lay down their arms.

In the evening General Clarke arrived with two thousand infantry and a train of artillery. The naval brigades and marines were sent back to Simon's Town from Newlands. Unfortunately for the good reputation of the British forces, against whom no charge of breach of discipline or interference with private property had yet been made, some of the marines and blue-jackets on their return march broke loose from control, and pillaged the farm-houses. One party visited Great Constantia, then, and for sixteen years previously, the property of Mr. Hendrik Cloete, who was noted for his hospitality to strangers of all nations. They destroyed a great deal of the furniture, broke open the cellar, and knocked in the heads of a number of kegs of wine. Their propensity to do mischief was only checked by the wine taking effect on them. This was the only kind of violence, however, perpetrated by any men in the British uniform, and even this was limited to a few farms.

Two homeward-bound Dutch Indiamen—the *Vertrouwen* and the *Louisa Antonia*—had recently arrived in Table Bay. The Company's ship *Castor* and the Cape packet *Star* were also lying at anchor in the bay. The British admiral made prizes of them all. The old Cape packet *Meermin*, of which Skipper Gerrit Ewoud Overbeek had taken command upon the retirement of Skipper Duminy, had been chartered by some colonists, and had left for Holland with a cargo of Cape produce before the arrival of the British expedition.

On the 18th an American vessel from Bordeaux reached Table Bay, bringing intelligence that a close treaty of alliance between the republics of France and the Netherlands, in which war with Great Britain was one of the specified objects, had been concluded in the preceding month of May.

Dutch writers, when relating the surrender of the colony, have usually charged Commissioner Sluysken and Colonel Gordon with imbecility or with downright treason. The secret debates and resolutions of the council and the correspondence of the commissioner are now open for public inspection, and as far as language goes they disprove the charge of treason. But the language and the acts of these high officials did not correspond. There was only one way in which a real earnest defence of the colony could have been made, and that was by co-operating heart and soul with the democratic party, which neither the commissioner nor the colonel had any inclination to do. No opposition surely was ever so strong in words, so weak in deeds, as that which ended in the capitulation of the Cape colony to the English troops. Commissioner Sluysken and Colonel Gordon had constantly before their minds another, and to them a more distasteful capitulation: the surrender of the settlement to the National party. By prolonging a nominal defence they could gain time, and something might happen in Europe to put another complexion on affairs. This is the only reasonable explanation of their conduct.

Mr. Sluysken returned to Europe in a cartel ship as soon as the transfer of the effects of the East India Company was completed. Colonel Gordon died by his own hand during the night of the 5th of October, unable, his enemies declared, to bear the reproaches with which he was continually assailed.

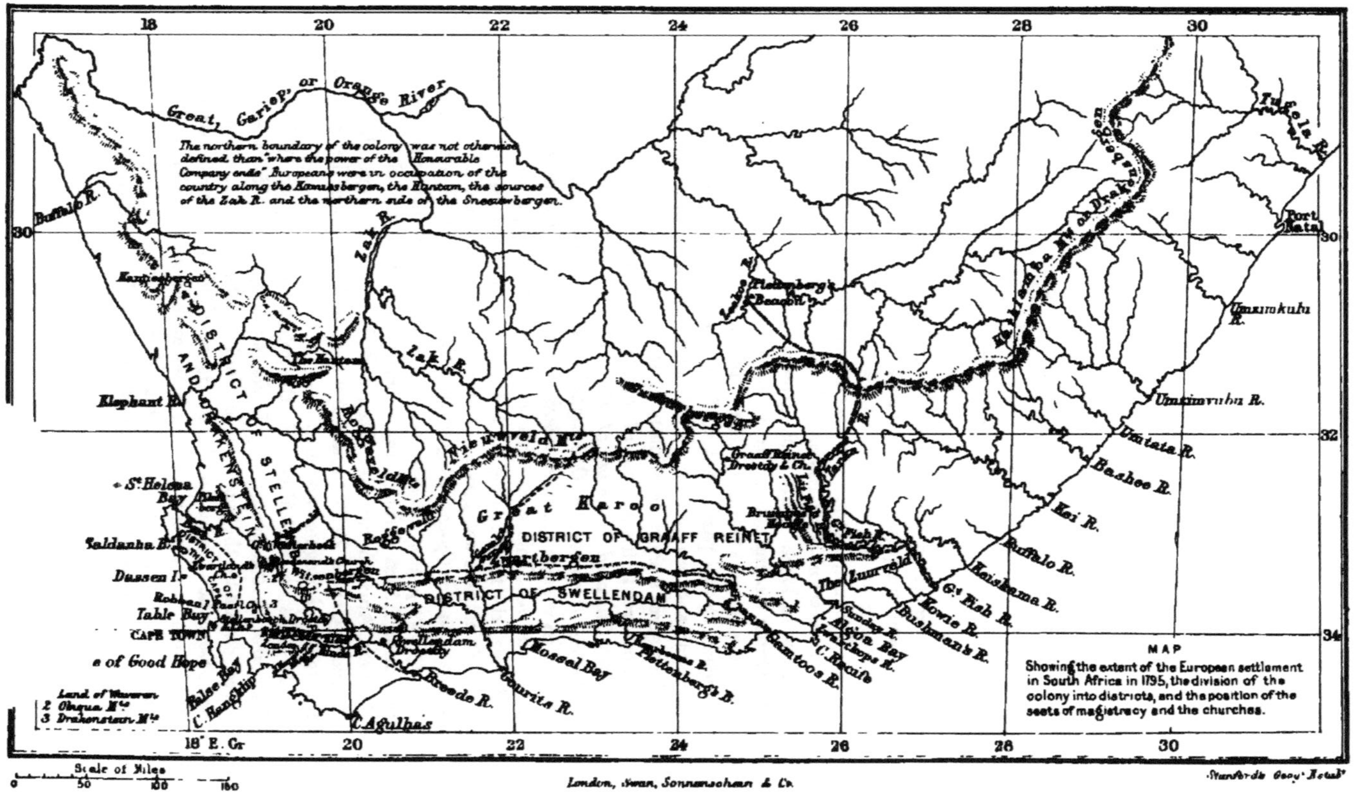
MAP
Showing the extent of the European settlement in South Africa in 1795, the division of the colony into districts, and the position of the seats of magistracy and the churches.
The northern boundary of the colony was not otherwise defined than "where the power of the Honourable Company ends." Europeans were in occupation of the country along the Kamiesbergen, the Hantam, the sources of the Zak R. and the northern side of the Sneeuwbergen.
Great, Gariep, or Orange River
Buffalo R.
Zak R.
Lak R.
Elephant R.
St. Helena Bay
Saldanha B.
Dassen I.
Robben I.
Table Bay
CAPE TOWN
False Bay
C. Hangklip
C. Agulhas
Breede R.
Gourits R.
Mossel Bay
Plettenberg's B.
Gamtoos R.
C. Recife
Algoa Bay
Bushman's R.
Kowie R.
Gt. Fish R.
Keiskama R.
Buffalo R.
Kei R.
Bashee R.
Umtata R.
Umzimvubu R.
Umzimkulu R.
Port Natal
Tugela R.
DISTRICT OF STELLENBOSCH
AND DRAKENSTEIN
DISTRICT OF SWELLENDAM
DISTRICT OF GRAAFF REINET
Great Karoo
Nieuwveld Mts.
Zwartbergen
The Zuurveld
Graaff Reinet Drostdy & Ch.
Plettenberg's Beacon
Land of Waveren
2 Obiqua Mts.
3 Drakenstein Mts.
18° E. Gr.
20
22
24
26
28
30
32
34
Scale of Miles
0
50
100
150
London, Swan, Sonnenschein & Co.
Stanford's Geog. Estab.

APPENDIX.

WHILE preparing this volume, I carefully examined the following books, and compared the information contained in them with that extracted from the manuscript official records of the colony :—

de Bucquoi, Jakob : *Aanmerkelyke Ontmoetingen in de Zestien Jaarige Reize naar de Indien.* A small quarto volume published at Haarlem in 1744. This book gives an account of the formation of the Dutch trading station at Delagoa Bay, with some particulars of that event not found in the Cape archives. De Bucquoi was attached to the party sent to form the station, in the capacity of surveyor and chartmaker. He was at the Cape some years later, and he gives a short description of the town, but the interest of his work centres in his account of what he witnessed at Delagoa Bay.

Het Ontroerd Holland, of Kort Verhaal van de Voornaamste Onlusten, Oproeren, en Oneenigheden die in de Vereenigde Nederlanden in voorige tyden, en allerbyzonderst in deze laatste Jaaren zyn voorgevallen. This work was issued at Harderwyk in three neat volumes, the first volume in 1748, the others subsequently. The author's name is not given. The first volume contains *Een beknopte Historie van de Opschuddingen aan Cabo de Goede Hoop*, which covers twenty-two pages. It is an account of the disturbances which arose in South Africa through the rapacity and tyranny of Governor Wilhem Adriaan van der Stel, and is compiled from the *Korte Deductie*, *Contra Deductie*, and *Neutrale Gedachten*, together with the testimony of Bogaert and Kolbe.

de la Caille, M. l'Abbé : In the volume for the year 1751 of the *Mémoires de l'Académie Royale des Sciences*, Paris, 1755, there are three papers by the Abbé de la Caille. The first is entitled *Suite des Observations faites au Cap de Bonne-Espérance pour la parallaxe de la Lune*, the second *Diverses Observations astronomiques et physiques faites au Cap de Bonne-Espérance*, and the third *Relation abrégée du Voyage fait par ordre du Roi au Cap de Bonne-Espérance.*

The first of these papers is of no interest except to astronomers, and the last needs no comment, as the diary of the journey will be referred to under another head. The second paper contains an account of a variety of work performed and observations recorded by the author at the Cape, which can be studied with pleasure and interest by ordinary readers as well as by those who make a special study of astronomy and meteorology. This paper covers fifty-eight pages of the *Mémoires*.

de la Caille, Nicolas Louis (l'Abbé): *Journal Historique du Voyage au Cap de Bonne-Espérance*. This is a small octavo volume of which a considerable portion is occupied with a biography of the Abbé de la Caille, who died in 1762, a year before the publication of his journal. The chapters of this book which were written by him embrace the journal kept during his residence in the colony, 85 pages, remarks upon the customs of the Hottentots and other inhabitants of South Africa, 55 pages, and notes upon Kolbe's work, 41 pages. In point of interest these chapters come very far short of the instructive paper mentioned under another heading, for their author was dealing with subjects outside of his line of work; still they are not without considerable value. Perhaps their chief worth, historically considered, is the exposure given in them to some of Kolbe's errors, though in correcting his descriptions of the Hottentots, De la Caille really made almost as great blunders himself. From this date, at least, Kolbe ceased to be considered a standard author, which was an enormous gain to students of Cape history.

Francken, Jacob: *Rampspoedige Reize van het O. I. Schip De Naarstigheid, in de terugreize van Batavia over Bengale naar Holland*. Haarlem, 1761. This is an illustrated quarto pamphlet of 112 pages, written by the sick comforter of the *Naarstigheid*, a vessel which lay in Delagoa Bay for more than two years in a shattered condition. Francken gives an interesting account of the surrounding country and of the natives at the bay, as well as of the people met by various parties that endeavoured to make their way overland to the Cape but were compelled to return. The last chapter, which is a short one, is devoted to an account of the Cape colony.

Hedendaagsche Historie of Tegenwoordige Staat van Afrika, waarin uitmunt de Beschryving van Barbarie, Senegal, Guinee, de Kaap der Goede Hope, &c. This is one of a collection of works upon contemporary history published by Isaak Tirion at Amsterdam, of which the twelve volumes upon the Netherlands form most perfect pictures of that country in the middle of last century. The volume upon Africa contains 810 pages, and was published in 1763. One the Dutch settlement; of the administration of the government, &c., &c. It contains a great many errors.

Thunberg, Charles Peter, M.D.: *Travels in Europe, Africa, and Asia, performed between the years* 1770 *and* 1779. Originally written in Swedish, but translated into English and published at London in four small octavo volumes in 1795. The portion referring to South Africa occupies nearly the whole of the first and more than half of the second volume. Thunberg travelled as a botanist in the Cape colony from April 1772 to March 1775, under the patronage and in the pay of the Dutch East India Company, in one of whose ships he came from Europe as a surgeon. His style of writing is not attractive, owing to the abrupt manner in which he has thrown together information of various kinds, making his work resemble a series of memoranda rather than a connected narrative. He was also so credulous as to believe and repeat many absurd tales which he heard during his wanderings. Further, his work contains little or nothing of any permanent value that is not to be found in Sparrman's or Le Vaillant's. It must, however, be said in its favour that it contains a great many facts, though irregularly strung together, and that if no other travellers had written books about the Cape at that time, his would be considered one of considerable merit. There are editions of it in French and German as well as in Swedish and English.

Sparrman, Andrew, M.D.: *A Voyage to the Cape of Good Hope, towards the Antarctic Polar Circle, and round the World; but chiefly into the Country of the Hottentots and Kaffirs, from the year* 1772 *to* 1776. Originally written in Swedish, but translated and published in English, French, and German. The second English edition, in two volumes, with map and plates, was published at London in 1786. Sparrman arrived in South Africa in April 1772. In November of the same year he left the Cape in the *Resolution*, having engaged to accompany the English exploring expedition as a naturalist, and sailed with Captain Cook round the world. In March 1775 the *Resolution* reached the Cape again, and Dr. Sparrman at once set out upon a tour through the colony, which occupied him until April 1776. The results of his observations are given in the work under notice, which is the most interesting and most trustworthy account of the Cape colony and the various races of people then residing in it, that was published before the beginning of the present century.

Paterson, William: *A Narrative of four Journeys into the Country of the Hottentots and Caffraria, in the years* 1777, 1778, *and* 1779. London, 1789. A quarto volume containing 135 pages of reading matter in the form of a journal, 24 pages of weather tables, and 10 descriptive of animal and vegetable poisons. It is illustrated with seventeen full page plates, principally of plants, and a large map. In the best copies the plates are coloured. A second English edition was published in 1790, and Dutch, French, and German translations were speedily issued. Lieutenant Paterson, whose chief pursuit was the study of botany, travelled eastward nearly to the Keiskama and northward beyond the Orange river. Unfortunately, his narrative is little more than a record of stages made and of specimens of plants secured. As a description of the country or of the people it is worth nothing, but it contains two or three observations of some historical value.

Stavorinus : *Reizen*. I have not yet been able to procure a copy of this excellent work in the original Dutch, but I have examined French and English translations of it. The last is entitled *Voyages to the East Indies by the late John Splinter Stavorinus, Esq., Rear Admiral in the Service of the States General. Translated from the original Dutch by Samuel Hull Wilcocke. With Notes and Additions by the Translator. The whole comprising a full and accurate Account of all the present and late Possessions of the Dutch in India and at the Cape of Good Hope.* This English translation is in three thick royal octavo volumes, published at London in 1798. At the time of making his voyages to India Stavorinus was a post captain in the national navy. The States were at peace, and as he wished to acquire more experience in matters pertaining to seamanship, he asked for and obtained permission to take command of an Indiaman. In that capacity he visited Table Bay in 1768, 1771, and 1778, and Simon's Bay in 1774. Altogether he spent about fifteen weeks in South Africa. One hundred and thirty pages of his work are devoted to subjects connected with this country, and in addition nineteen pages of the appendix are occupied with an abstract of Oldenland's catalogue of plants. In these chapters the author gives an account of Cape Town and its inhabitants, a description of the government, an account of an excursion to Klapmuts and Stellenbosch, particulars of the commerce of the colony, &c. He draws a broad line of distinction between the inhabitants of the town and those of the country, and institutes a comparison greatly in favour of the farmers. He denounces the rapacity of the public servants and the arbitrary nature of the government, and recommends the suppression of the first and the amelioration of the last. Stavorinus confines his observations to the European settlement, and has nothing to say of the natives. Attached to the work is a chart of the country and coast from Hottentots Holland to Saldanha Bay.

Cook, James (Captain): *A Voyage towards the South Pole and round the World, performed in His Majesty's ships Resolution and Adventure in the years* 1772–1775. The third edition, in two quarto volumes, was published at London in 1779. Captain Cook was at the Cape in November 1772 and in April 1775. He has made a few observations, which are interesting but too brief to be of much value. Some short remarks are also to be found in the account of Captain Cook's last voyage, the third edition of which, in three quarto volumes, was published at London in 1785. This work is entitled *A Voyage to the Pacific Ocean undertaken by the command of His Majesty for making Discoveries in the Northern Hemisphere; performed under the direction of Captains Cook, Clerke, and Gore, in His Majesty's ships the Resolution and Discovery, in the years* 1776–1780. Volumes I and II were written by Captain Cook, volume III by Dr. King. The expedition was at the Cape in November 1776 and in April 1780.

Sonnerat: *Voyage.* I have not yet been so fortunate as to procure an original copy of this work, and must therefore refer to the Dutch translation published in three octavo volumes at Leiden in 1786, and entitled *Reize naar de Oost Indien en China in de Jaaren* 1774–1781, *op last des Konings van Frankryk, gedaan door den Heer Sonnerat.* The French naturalist Sonnerat, having spent five years in travelling in Mauritius, Bourbon, Madagascar, New Guinea, the Moluccas, and the Philippine islands, where he made rich collections of specimens in the animal and vegetable kingdoms, returned to Paris and published a work in quarto illustrated with 120 plates. He was then sent by the king to make further researches in other parts of the East, and was absent from France on this occasion for seven years. He returned in 1781 with a magnificent collection of animals and plants. Sonnerat called at the Cape on several occasions, and in 1781 spent some weeks here. He is mentioned by other travellers of the time, who considered the meeting of a man of such eminence in the study of natural history a noteworthy event. In the volumes here referred to there is but one chapter upon the Cape colony, and it covers only five pages. These are pages of correct information, but the whole is too short to draw attention, were it not for the name of the author.

Raynal, Guillaume Thomas: *Histoire Philosophique et Politique des Etablissemens et du Commerce des Européens dans les deux Indes.* This is one of the great histories produced in the eighteenth century, and its writer holds in French literature a position similar to that occupied by Hume and Gibbon among English authors. There are many editions of the work. One of the best is in ten octavo volumes with large quarto atlas, published at Geneva in 1782. In this edition sixteen pages are devoted to the establishment of the Cape colony. With all the industry, regard for truth, and power of patient research of the Abbé Raynal, he has failed to give a correct account of this event. One reason is that the archives of the East India Company were closed to him, and he had only printed works upon South Africa to refer to. Another is that the Cape colony, in relation to many other countries of which he was writing, was considered so unimportant that only a certain amount of time as well as of space could be devoted to it.

le Vaillant, François : *Voyage dans l'Intérieur de l'Afrique, par le Cap de Bonne-Espérance, dans les années* 1780, '81, *et* '82. Paris, 1790. The two volumes of M. Le Vaillant's work, in which an account is given of his journey to Kaffirland, contain a large amount of interesting matter, though the author's vivid imagination caused him to colour some of his descriptions too highly. Le Vaillant came to South Africa in the *Held Woltemaade*, the Dutch Indiaman which was captured by Commodore Johnstone's fleet soon after she sailed from Saldanha Bay. He reached the Fish river towards the close of 1781. There are admirable translations of this work in Dutch and English.

Dalrymple, Alexander : *An Account of the Loss of the Grosvenor Indiaman, commanded by Capt. John Coxon, on the 4th of August*, 1782, *with a Relation of the Events which befel those Survivors who have reached England, viz. Robert Price, Thomas Lewis, John Warmington, and Barney Larey, being the Report given in to the East India Company*. This is an octavo pamphlet of fifty-eight pages, published with the approbation of the Court of Directors, at London (second edition), in 1785. An appendix of thirty-eight pages contains the report of William Hubberley, another of the survivors. In this little work the particulars of the wreck are given briefly, the greater portion being taken up with an account of the wanderings and sufferings of the narrators. A list of the names of those who were left behind is given.

Carter, George : *A Narrative of the Loss of the Grosvenor East Indiaman, which was unfortunately wrecked upon the Coast of Caffraria on the 4th of August* 1782. *Compiled from the Examination of John Hynes, one of the unfortunate survivors*. London, 1791. This work is an illustrated volume of 174 pages, and contains an account of the wreck, of Hynes' journey until he reached the residence of a colonist, and lists of names of those saved, left behind, and known to have perished.

L'Afrique Hollandaise; ou Tableau Historique et Politique de l'Etat originaire de la Colonie du Cap de Bonne-Espérance comparé avec l'Etat actuel de cette Colonie. Publié sur le manuscrit d'un Observateur instruit. An octavo volume of 322 pages, published in Holland (no city mentioned) in 1783. The writer's name is not given, but it is evident that he was a Cape burgher. This work was published at a time when the colonists of South Africa were divided into two factions, and party feeling was running extremely high. The writer was a special pleader of one of the factions, and therefore anything like an impartial account of the colony is not to be expected from his pen. His account of the early days of the settlement is almost fabulous in its inaccuracy. Thus Van Riebeek is represented as a kind of hero, and his immediate successors as tyrants who destroyed the liberal form of government which he introduced. He is said to have wrested the country from the Portuguese, and to have brought out a body of planters with him. A large portion of the book is taken up with a refutation of the defence of the fiscal Boers. The value of the work consists in the fact that it gives a picture of the administration of the East India Company, at the time it was written, from the point of view of a large section of the colonists of South Africa.

James, Silas: *A Narrative of a Voyage to Arabia, India, &c. containing, amidst a variety of information, a Description of Saldanha Bay, &c., &c.* An octavo volume of 232 pages, published at London in 1797. The author of this work was a seaman on board a ship in the fleet of Commodore Johnstone, and was present in the engagement with the French at Porto Praya on the 16th of April 1781, of which event he gives some particulars not found in the official reports of either the English or the French commanders. He describes also the capture of the *Held Woltemaade*, and the seizure of the Dutch Indiamen in Saldanha Bay. His account must be compared with official documents, however, as it is not strictly accurate. On the return passage James was in Saldanha and Table bays from September 1783 to March 1784, but his account of that visit contains nothing of interest.

Kaapsche Geschillen. Four bluebooks, containing in all 1146 large quarto pages, printed in Holland in 1785. They contain the principal documents concerning the complaints of the burghers from the 1st of March 1779 to the 28th of July 1785, with the replies of the officers at the Cape.

le Vaillant, François: *Second Voyage dans l'Intérieur de l'Afrique, par le Cap de Bonne-Espérance, dans les années* 1783, 1784, *et* 1785. Paris, l'An 3 de la République une et indivisible. This work is in three octavo volumes, in which Le Vaillant gives an account of his journey from the Cape to Namaqualand. It has the same faults as the account of his journey to Kaffraria, and would have been greatly improved by the omission of many of the adventures described with wearisome minuteness as well as such tales as that of his bursting into tears and throwing himself into the arms of a savage. The great defects in this book of Le Vaillant have caused some of his critics to express an opinion that he never really crossed the Orange river into Great Namaqualand, but drew upon his imagination for the account he has given. This view is incorrect, and there can be no reasonable doubt that he went as far as he states that he did. His account of the lower portion of Great Namaqualand and its people will be found fairly correct, if separated from his own exploits. His troubles south of the Orange, the suffering from thirst, the loss of his cattle, and the abandonment of his waggons until he procured aid from a Hottentot clan, coincide with the experiences of many other travellers. When ultimately he reached the great river, he found himself compelled to leave his waggons on the southern bank, and to push forward with horses and pack oxen. He states that he had formed a design to traverse the continent from south to north, and only abandoned it when it was proved to be absolutely hopeless. The work is illustrated, but is not divided into chapters.

Degrandpré, L. (Officier de la Marine française): *Voyage à la Côte Occidentale d'Afrique, fait dans les années* 1786 *et* 1787; *suivi d'un Voyage fait au Cap de Bonne-Espérance, contenant la description militaire de cette colonie.* Two volumes octavo, Paris, 1801. Nearly the whole of the second volume is devoted to the Cape colony. The author was a man of keen observation and of extensive reading. His work is therefore valuable as well as interesting. His description of the Cape is of a period just before the first English conquest of the colony, though it was written after that event. Of the country beyond the isthmus Degrandpré says but little, as his furthest journey inland was only along the Berg river to its mouth. He treats very fully of the navigation and winds at Table Bay, and describes Robben Island, Cape Town, and Table Mountain at great length. Into military matters he enters largely, as stated in the title of his work. Speculative remarks upon the formation of Table Mountain and upon the circumnavigation of Africa by the ancients also occupy a good deal of space. This author is very severe upon the colonists, to whom he attributes the destruction of the Hottentot race. He speaks in the highest terms of Sparrman's work, and exposes many romances in that of his own countryman Le Vaillant, to whose ability, industry, and extensive researches in natural history, however, he testifies. It produces a smile to find Degrandpré in his preface indignantly denouncing Damberger as an impostor, and seriously pointing out errors that this African Munchausen had fallen into. A good chart of the coast from Saldanha Bay to False Cape and a plan of the Cape castle are attached to the work.

Huysers, Ary : *Beknopte Beschryving der Oost Indische Etablissementen.* Utrecht, 1789. Only four pages of this volume are devoted to the Cape colony, and those chiefly to its finances, but there is some interesting matter in the appendix.

Riou, Capt. Edward : *A Journal of a Journey from the Cape of Good Hope, undertaken in* 1790 *and* 1791 *by Jacob van Reenen and others of his countrymen, in search of the wreck of the Honourable the East India Company's ship The Grosvenor, to discover if there remained alive any of the unfortunate sufferers. With additional Notes and a Map.* A quarto pamphlet of 51 pages published at London in 1792. It is a literal translation of the journal of an expedition that travelled through Kaffirland to about the mouth of the Umzimkulu. The map added by Captain Riou is a curiosity. In it Natal and even St. Lucia River are placed a long way south of the Umzimvubu. With a knowledge of Kaffir proper names and a good modern map of South Africa, there is not the slightest difficulty in following the course of Van Reenen's party from the journal, but Captain Riou believed that it nearly reached Delagoa Bay. There are Dutch and French editions of the work.

Staat der Generale Nederlandsche Oost Indische Compagnie, behelzende Rapporten van de Heeren Haar Ed. Groot Mog. Gecommitteerden G. J. Doys, Baron van der Does, Heer van Noordwyk, Mr. P. H. van de Wall, Mr. J. Rendorp, Heer van Marquette, en Mr. H. van Straalen, als mede Nader Rapport van gemelde heeren gecommitteerden, en Bylaagen. Two volumes. Amsterdam, 1792. These volumes contain a large amount of statistical and other valuable information concerning the Cape colony.

de Jong, Cornelius: *Reizen naar de Kaap de Goede Hoop, Ierland, en Noorwegen, in de Jaren* 1791 *tot* 1797. Three octavo volumes, published at Haarlem in 1802. The author of this work was captain of the Dutch frigate *Scipio*. His ship lay at anchor in Table or Simon's Bay from the 27th of March 1792 to the 31st of May 1793. In the following year Captain De Jong returned from Europe to the Cape, and remained on this occasion rather longer than six months. His official position, combined with his being an intimate friend of the commissioner Sluysken, gave him a thorough knowledge of the events then taking place in the colony. Several short tours afforded him opportunities of observing the country and people, and his marriage with a Cape lady must have added to the interest which he took in the colony. In the form of a series of well-written and lively letters to a friend, Captain De Jong has placed on record his observations. In point of value to a student of Cape history, this work ranks high. It is ornamented with a view of Simon's Town and harbour, and with two large pictures of Table Mountain and Bay, one of which is from the pencil of the celebrated Kobell.

Nederburgh, S. C.: *Verhandeling over de Vragen of, en in hoe verre, het nuttig en noodzakelijk zijn zoude, de Oost Indische Bezittingen van deezen Staat, ofte sommigen derzelven, te brengen op den voet der West Indische Volkplantingen; en of, en in hoe verre, het voordeeliger voor dit Gemeenebest, en desselfs Ingezeetenen, zijn zoude, den Handel op voormelde Bezittingen bij aanhoudendheid door eene uitsluitende Compagnie te drijven, dan wel die voor allen 's Land's Ingezeetenen open te stellen; en in dit laatste geval: op welke voorwaarden, en onder welke bepalingen.* An octavo volume of 252 pages, published at the Hague in 1802. The author of this work, Mr. Sebastian Cornelis Nederburgh, had been commissioner-general of the whole of Netherlands India and the Cape of Good Hope. There are only a few pages of the book devoted to this colony. These contain little beyond some severe comments upon the burghers and some remarks upon the introduction of Spanish rams and the production of merino wool.

Nederburgh, S. C.: *Echte Stukken betreffende het volbragt onderzoek der verrichtingen van de General Commissie in den jare* 1791 *benoemd geweest over de O. I. Bezittingen van den Staat en de Kaab de Goede Hoop, benevens den Finalen Uitslag van hetzelve.* An octavo volume of 156 pages published at the Hague in 1803. The items in this work of greatest interest to a student of Cape history are some official documents connected with the arrival of Admiral Elphinstone's fleet in Simon's Bay in 1795, and to the subsequent intercourse between the English and Dutch officers.

Some important papers are to be found in the *Annual Register or View of History, Politics, and Literature*, published at London. Thus the volume for 1758 contains an account of the wreck of the *Doddington*; the volume for 1790 contains a narrative of the disaster to the *Guardian*; and the volume for 1795 contains despatches, copied from the *London Gazette*, concerning the conquest of the colony, from the officers commanding the English forces.

van Hogendorp, Gysbert Karel : *Verhandelingen over den Oost Indischen Handel.* Three octavo volumes, Amsterdam, 1801. The second volume, of 388 pages, is devoted to the Cape colony.

van Ryneveld, W. S. : *Aanmerkingen over de Verbetering van het Vee aan de Kaap de Goede Hoop, inzonderheid over de Conversie der Kaapsche in Spaansche of Wolgeevende Schapen.* A pamphlet of 104 pages, printed at Cape Town in 1804. Some information concerning the attempts made to improve the breed of cattle at the Cape is to be found in this little work.

Sluysken, A. J. : *Verbaal gehouden by den Commissaris van de Caap de Goede Hoop.* An octavo volume of 330 pages, published at the Hague in 1797. This is Mr. Sluysken's account of events from the 10th of June to the 16th of September 1795, and contains the whole of the correspondence between the officers commanding the English forces and himself. A large portion of it has been copied from the secret resolutions of the council of policy preserved in the Cape archives.

Campagne, H. D. : *Memorie en Byzonderheden wegens Overgave der Kaap de Goede Hoop*, 1795. *Als mede Relaas gegeven door den 's lands kapitein Dekker wegens het voorgevallen tusschen denzelve, den Engelsche Admiraal Generaal Sir George Keith Elphinstone, en den Commissaris Sluysken aan Kabo de Goede Hoop.* Manuscript in the archives of the Netherlands, a copy of which has been obtained by the Cape government for preservation with its records. This is a very graphic and complete account of events from June to September 1795, by an eye-witness. The writer belonged to the corps of pennists, but his sympathies were with the democratic party. In an appendix a well-written account of the Kaffir war of 1793 is given, the writer having been engaged in it.

Marnitz, Philip Wilhelm : *Verhaal van de Overgaave van de Kaap de Goede Hoop aan de Engelschen. Door een vriend der waarheid aldaar. In't tweede jaar der Batavische vryheid.* This work is in manuscript in the archives of the Netherlands, and a copy has been procured for preservation with the Cape records. Its author was an eye-witness of what he relates. He gives a version of occurrences from the arrival of the British fleet to the surrender of the colony, from the standpoint of an artillery officer attached to the democratic party in Europe. He is very severe upon Commissioner Sluysken and Colonel Gordon.

Drakenstein Baptismal Register.

The following is a copy of the 'Liure de Register des Enfans qu'on a Baptize dans notre Eglise françoise dedrakestein.' It includes every entry made in the French language. The original register was kept by Paul Roux. The first baptism is dated 29th of August 1694, and until the 27th of November 1701 the entries are frequent. A few months after this date the Rev. Mr. Simond was succeeded by the Rev. Hendrik Bek, who kept the register himself in Dutch. Twelve entries were subsequently made in French by Paul Roux, on occasions when different clergymen visited Drakenstein and baptized children. At the end of this is the register complete to the close of 1710. The spelling of every name is just as in the original, but I have arranged the families in alphabetical order.

Date	Name	Parents	Witnesses
21 octobre 1696	—	jacobus Vanas	—
15 mars 1699	Francjna	françois bastians marie Anne	jan Eskeppein jaapis Wellems
29 auril 1699	Pierre	piter beerne blom Caterina blom	piter Rassemus et la mere de lanfant
11 nouembre 1701	Sara	jean de bus Sara jacob	françois dutoit Anne Retif
22 septembre 1709	Jean	jean de buz Sara jacob	daniel jacob Marthe le feure
22 septembre 1709	Jean	dauid dubuisson glaudine Lombart	Jaan Elberst Sophia hapel
8 julliet 1701	Ellaina	beerne beurger Marthe Eskal	françois du toit Susanne Seugnet
25 nouembre 1696	Hendrik	Conra klout	Monsieur jaque de Sauoye
14 juin 1699	Jacobus	konra geer klout Marthe	beerne Beurger marthe Wellems
26 octobre 1698	Philippe	Louis Cordie françoise Martinet	Monsieur pierre Simond Mademoiselle Anne de beureau
11 nouembre 1697	Geertru	Corneillis Corpènant	geert jaanse marie Heelms
27 nouembre 1701	Anne	paul Couuret Anne Walleté	jean Taillefer Elizabet Couuret
4 octobre 1699	—	Jacque de porté Sara Vitout	— —
8 decembre 1697	Anna Ellizabet	Monsieur Araam dimmes	—
14 decembre 1695	—	Cobus Vandray	—
21 septembre 1698	Erassemus	piter Rassemus Marie Elizabet	beerne piter blom Caterina blom
25 octobre 1699	Marie hanna	pierre Rassemus marie Elizabet	pierre Christiaans de jaager Iremena de jaager Wal
10 may 1700	Jean	Christoffle Extreux	

[illegible]	[illegible]	Parents	Witnesses
[illegible] may [illegible]	Jean	la femme du defunt charle marais	Etienne marais Elizabet Villiers
[illegible] aoust [illegible]	Pierre	pierre Marceuene Elizabet de pres	pierre dumas Sisijlia depres
[illegible] aoust [illegible]	Helena	Eskal Willems Van den merue Hanna prenot	—
[illegible] aoust [illegible]	Hendrik Willems	Eskal Willems Van de Meruuen Anne prenot	piter Roobeers une fille de Willems Eskal
30 decembre [illegible]	Charle	Eskaal Wellems Anne prevot	Wellems Eskaal Van den Merue Elsijs jacob
12 fevrier [illegible]	Jacob	Escalk Wellems Anne preuost	piter Roobres et sa famme
[illegible] octobre 1701	Willems	Eskal Willems Anne preuot	beerne beurger Marthe Escalk
28 may 1698	—	beaufils de Wellem Escalk Van den Meruen	—
28 juin 1699	Cornelllija	handrik Norman	—
1696	Jenne	daniel nortie marie Vitout	jean Nortie susanne lanoy
18 septembre 1697	Jean	daniel Nortie marie Vitou	Ercules de pre marie Le feure
14 decembre 1698	—	louis peront	—
[illegible] aoust 1699	Marthe	jacque pinar marthe le feue	gabriel le rous barbara le feue
14 juin 1699	Marie	phillippe de pres Elizabet preuost	pierre Dumond marie Le feue
10 avril 1701	Hercules	phillippe de pret Elizabet preuost	Hercules de pret Sysillia de pre
8 mars 1718	Hanna	jan pretorijs marie Rousseau	pierra Rousseau geertru dutoit
17 may 1711	Elizabet	abraam preuost hanna Marceuene	piter Janoe Van Marceuene Elizabet de pre
10 aoust 1698	Johannes	Classe Raas marie Van Staden	marthe Van Staden Caterina Wellems

4 juillet 1700	Christian	Classe Raas marie Van Staden	Marthines Van Staden gasparde Van Staden
22 septembre 1709	Susanne	Louis le riche Susanne fauche	françois dutoit Susanne Seugnet
14 octobre 1696	Ellizabet	pierre Rousseau hanna Retif	françois Retif marie hanna
27 julliet 1698	Marthe	pierre Rousseau hanne Retif	Monsr pierre Simond Mademoiselle hanna de beureau
3 maij 1700	Pierre	pierre Rousseau Anne Retif	gabriel le rous marie Elizabet taillefer
14 aoust 1701	Gabriel	pierre Rousseau Anne Retif	pierre Villiers Susanne Seugnet
25 decembre 1694	Anne roux	paul roux glaudine Seugneté	françois du toijt Anna Retif
14 octobre 1696	Joseph	paul roux glaudine Seugnet	pierre benezet marie grillion
1 septembre 1697	Jeremie roux	paul roux glaudine Seugnet	pierre jourdan de Cabriere marie aVis
22 auril 1699	Jean	paul roux glaudine Seugnet	Charle marais Hanne de Ruel
29 aoust 1694	Philippe Rodolf	monsieur jacque de Sauoye madame le clair	Rodolf passemant et sa famme
5 mars 1713	Marie	koenraad Sckeper Marie bota	jacobus bota Catherina bota
21 septembre 1709	Abraam	josue Selliet Elizabet Couuret	abraam Villiers Ester Roux
2 januier 1701	Josue	josue Sellie Elizabet Couuret	Claude marais Caterine Tabourdeux
16 octobre 1695	Dauid	dauid Senecal Madelaine dupuit	daniel de Ruel anna dupuit
6 octobre 1697	Salomon	dauid Senecal Madelaine dupuit	Salomon Gournay Susanne Seugnet
27 januier 1700	Jean	Dauid Senecal Anne Medelaine dupuit	le pere et la mere de lanfant
14 aoust 1701	Anne Madelaine	dauid Senecal Anne madelaine du puit	le pere et Susanne Dupuit
25 aoust 1697	Lidie	Monsieur pierre Simond Mademoiselle Hanna de beurau	jsac Taillefer marie Elizabet

Date	Name	Parents	Witnesses
22 julliet 1695	Cristina	christoffle senaymant Marguerite Sauoye	jacobus Vanas Laina basson
1 aoust 1697	Elsij	Christoffle Seniman marguerite Sauoye	Hercules de pret Elsij jacob
25 octobre 1699	Janne	christoffle Senaymant Marguerite Sauoije	Christians de bacre marie de lanoy
24 julliet 1701	Philippe	Christoffle Senaimau Marguerite Sauoye	philippe Rodolf allета Sauoye
23 juin 1695	Marie	daniel Terrier Sara jacob	jean debuze marie janne de pret
10 januier 1697	Susanne	daniel Terrier Sara jacob	Salomon gounay Susanne lanoy
4 octobre 1699	Pierre	Daniel Terrie Sara jacob	Louis barret Susanne Seugnet
24 aoust 1698	Marie	jacque Teront Marie janne	Hercules de pret jaquemine de pres
22 aoust 1700	Jacque	jacque Teron marie janne de pret	jean Maniet Elizabet de prest
22 septembre 1709	Pierre	jacque Teron marie janne de pre	françois dutoit Corneillia Villion
8 maj 1695	Laina	françois dutoij Susanne Seugnet	pierre Sabatie Sara Leclair
24 mars 1697	Pierre	françois dutoij Susanne Seugnet	guillaume dutoij Sara Le clair
28 juin 1699	François	françois dutoij Susanne Seugnet	Jedeon le grand lena dutoit
4 nouembre 1701	Marthe	françois dutoit Susanne Seugnet	beerne beurger marthe Escalk
21 septembre 1709	Marie	françois dutoit Susanne Seugnet	pierre Rousseau marie janne de pret
24 nouembre 1697	Susanne	abraam de Villiers Susanne gardiol	Jean gardiol Susanne taillefer
20 septembre 1699	Jean	abraam Villiers Susanne Gardiol	jacob Villiers Marguerite gardiol
4 nouembre 1695	Marie Elizabet	jacob Villiers marguerite gardiol	jean gardiol marie Ellizabet taillefert

6 octobre 1697	Janne	jacob Villiers Marguerita gardiol	Arahaam de Villiers Mademoiselle Le feure
14 septembre 1699	Jacobus	jacob Villiers marguerite gardiol	Abraam Villiers jsabeau Richar
26 decembre 1695	Pierre	pierre Villiers marie Elizabet Taillefert	jacob Villiers Susanne gardiol
28 juin 1699	Jean	pierre Villiers marie Elizabet taillefer	jean Taillefer geertru dutoy
7 aoust 1701	Marie	pierre Villiers Elizabet Taillefer	pierre Taillefer Elizabet de Villiers
25 aoust 1697	Elizabet	Etienne Viret Marguerite rous	Etienne niel marie Elizabet
14 septembre 1699	Etienne	etienne Viret Marguerite rous	— —
12 feurier 1698	Elizabet	abraam Viuiet Jaqueminne de pree.	Le pere et Elizabet de pree
22 aoust 1700	Marie	abraam Viuiet Jaquemine de pret	jocob Viuiet marie janne depret
22 auril 1695	Anna Caterina	Hernes frederik Waltré Caterina	hansel Verbat Marie la noy

The following entries are in the Dutch language:—

10 September 1702	Elsje	Jacobus Van As Helena Willemse	Schalk Willemse Alletta Willemse
25 November 1703	Willem	Jacobus Van As Helena Willemse	Angela Basson Christoffel Snijman
12 Junij 1707	Fijtie	Jacobus Van As Helena van der Merve	Pieter Robberts Fytie Van der Merve
13 April 1704	—	Francois Bastiaan Anne Marie Pieters	Gerrit Jans Jacobus Schal
24 December 1702	Helena	Pieter Becker Jannetie de klerk	Jacobus Van As Helena Schalk
1 Junij 1710	Helena	Mattys de Beer Elsje Semet	Jean Roux de Blois Jeanne Mouij
12 Augustus 1702	Jacobus	Jacobus van den Berge Jacomina Kaarteniers	Jan Hermense Maarsebroek Wiena Fransina van Jk
13 April 1704	Jacobus	Barent Burger Marrijtie Willemse	Martinus Van Staden Aaltie Willemse

Date	Name	Parents	Witnesses
4 October 1704	Marie	Jan Bus Sara Jacobs	Nicolaas Lanoij Anna Valaite
12 Julij 1704	Catherina	Cornelis Corses Derkje Helmes	— —
11 Julij 1706	Geertruyt	Cornelis Corsel derkje Elmes	Marie Pieters
29 November 1705	Susanna	Paul Couvret Anna Vallette	Mons[r] le grand Susanne Taillefer
1 Junij 1710	Marie	Pierre Cronje Susanna Taillefer	Estienne Croignee Susanna Taillefer, veuve
30 November 1702	Isaac	Jaques del Porte Sara Vitoe	Charles Marais Lysbet Nortie
20 Maart 1707	Susanne	Jacques del Porte Sara Vitout	Estienne Cronje
22 Junij 1704	Laureus	Pieter Rasmus Marije	Pieter Jager Marie Pieterse blom
24 Januarij 1706	Catharina	Pieter Erasmus Maria Elisabeth Joosten	— —
6 Februarij 1707	Larius	Pieter Erasmus Maria Elisabeth	hermanus Buijs Harmina Carelss
25 Maart 1703	Marrijtie	Ary Henderikse van Eck Johanna Haester	— —
8 October 1707	Derk	Ary Derkse van Neck Anna Ester	Frederik Coenraad Armina Coenraad
15 Junij 1710	Willem	Ary Derkse van Nek Anna Ester	Jean le Long Marie Coche
29 November 1705	Sara	Louis Fourij Susanna Cordier	Pierre Lombart Claudine Lombart
1 Junij 1710	Jacques	Louis Flourij Susanna Cordier	Jacob Cordier Geertruyt du Toit
9 October 1707	—	Matthieu Fraschas Jeanne Cordier	Paul Couvret Anna Vallette
2 October 1707	Johanna	Jacob Hasselaar Maria Elisabet	— —
18 October 1705	Daniel	Daniel Hugot Anne Rousseau	Pierre Rousseau Anne Rotiff

15 Junij 1710	Pierre	Daniel Hugot Anna Rousseau	Gabriel Rousseau Marie Rousseau
14 October 1703	Pieter	Daniel Jacob Louise Cordier	Nicolaas Lanoij Sara Jacob
8 Februarij 1705	—	daniel Jacob Louise Cordier	Paul Couvret Marie Griljon
16 October 1706	Daniel	Daniel Jacob Louise Cordier	Gideon le grand Susanna Cordier
28 November 1706	—	Pierre Jaubert Elisabeth Richar	Francois Rey Francoise Meille
27 October 1710	—	Pierre Jaubert Elisabeth Richar	— —
23 Augustus 1705	Marie	Pierre Jourdan Anne Fauche	Josue Seillier Marie Couteau
2 October 1707	Margarete	Mattijs Krugel Elisabet van Staden	Maarten van Staden Catherina van Staden
28 Junij 1705	Christina	Arnoldus Cruysman Martha	derk Bronkhorst Susanna Cordier
18 October 1705	Maria	Johannes Laurens Anna Elisabeth	Matthis Miechiels Catherina
27 October 1710	Hans	Jan Laurens Anna Elizabeth	Antoine Nortie Elisabet Nortie
27 October 1710	Pierre	Guillaume Lauret Elisabeth Jaubert	Pierre Jaubert Anna Vermeulen
12 November 1702	Jacob	Guilliam le Lievre Maria	Francois du Toit Marie le Lievre
16 November 1704	—	Guillaume le lievre Marie	Paul Couvret Anna Vallete
15 Maij 1707	Catherina	Jacques Mallan Elisabeth Long	Pierre Jaubert Claudius Lombard
31 December 1702	Gideon	Gideon Malherbe Marie Grillon	Gideon le Grand Susanne Cordier
28 Junij 1705	Magdalena	Gideon Malherbe Maria Grillion	Charle Marais Marianne Claudine Lombart
16 December 1703	Estienne	Charles Marais Anne de Ruel	Estienne Niel Marie Marais
4 October 1705	Debora	Charles Marais Anne de Ruel	Vader en Moeder

Date	Name	Parents	Witnesses
29 April 1703	Maria	Schalk Willemse Anna Prevoo	Jan Schepping Jacomijntie
18 April 1706	Sophia	Schalk Willemse Anna Prevoos	—
2 October 1707	David	Schalk Willemse Anna Prevoos	Philippe des Pres Elisabet Prevoos
7 October 1703	—	Jacques Mouton Francoise Bevernage	Pierre du Mont Marie Grignon
21 Januarij 1703	—	Estienne Niel Magdelena Marais	Claude Marais Anna Retif
8 Februarij 1705	Estienne	Estienne Niel Marie Marais	Charles Marais Anne de Ruel
10 Julij 1707	Rachel	Estienne Niel Marie Marais	—
26 Junij 1707	Michiel	Jan Neman Margareta Putters	—
27 April 1703	Gerardus	Johannes Oosthuysen Johanna Martens van Griptkerke	—
29 November 1705	Anna	Jan Oosthuijsen Janne Marques	—
13 Julij 1704	Anna Christina	Hendrik Oossel Christina Bastiaans	Francois Bastiaans met syn Vrou
5 Augustus 1706	—	Andries Orselke Christina Bastiaanz	Francois Bastiaans Anne Marie
30 October 1706	Ester	Jaques Pinard Martha le febre	Pierre Rousseau Marie Catherine le Fevre
3 April 1707	Johanna	Jan Harmens Potgieter Clara Garst	—
4 Maij 1704	Cecilia	Hercules des Pres Cornelia Viljon	—
4 April 1705	Philippe	Philippe des Pres Elizabeth Prevos	Schalk Willems Anna Prevos
2 October 1707	Hercules	Francis des Pres Marie Cordier	Hercules des Pres Cicilia Datijs
31 Maij 1710	Hendrik	Claas Princelo Pitronelle van Staden	Mattijs Krugel Elisabet van Staden

4 Februarij 1703	Maria	Claas Ras Marie Van Staden	Maurits Van Staden Elisabeth Van Staden
28 Junij 1705	Leendert	Claas Ras Maria Van Staden	Claude Marais Petronella van Staden
2 October 1707	Nicolaas	Claas Ras Maria Van Staden	Willem van Staden Pietronella van Staden
10 September 1702	Maria	Francois Retiff Marie Mooi	Pieter Mooi Anna Retieff
30 November 1704	—	Francois Retiff Marie Moije	Anne Rousseau
16 October 1706	Jacque	Francois Retiff Marie Mouij	Pierre Rousseau Jeanne Mouij
2 September 1703	Pierre	Pierre Rousseau Anne Retieff	Pierre du Mont Cornelia Villjon
26 Julij 1705	Hester	Pierre Rousseau Anne Retiff	Claude Marais Marie Mouij
9 October 1707	Daniel	Pierre Rousseau Anna Retiff	Claas Elbers Geertruyt du Toit
12 Augustus 1702	Maria Magdalena	Gabriel le Roux Maria Catharina le Febre	Marta le Febre
30 October 1706	Daniel	Gabriel le Roux Marie le Febre	Daniel Hugot Anne Retiff
18 October 1704	Marie	Jean le Roux Jeanne Mouij	Gabriel le Rous Jeanne Mouij
12 December 1706	Pierre	Jean le Rous Jeanne Mouij	Pierre Mouij Marie Catherine le Fevre
4 April 1705	Teunis	Derk Schalkwijk Martha Olivier	Altie van Wyk
14 November 1706	Ocker	Derk Schalkwijk Marie Olivier	— —
10 November 1703	Pierre	Josue Sellier Elizabeth Couvret	Pierre Taillefert Marie Marais
26 Julij 1705	Elisabeth	Josua Seillier Elisabeth Couvret	Jaques Mallan Elisabet Long
30 October 1706	Francoise	Josue Seille Elizabet Couvret	Guillaume Lauret de dogter van Pierre Jaubert
10 Julij 1707	Susanne	David Senecal Anne Magdelaine du Puij	Jean Durand en syn Huysvrou

Date	Name	Parents	Witnesses
[illegible] 1703	Maria	Schalk Willemse / Anna Prevoo	Jan Schepping / Jacomijntie
[illegible]	Sophia	Schalk Willemse / Anna Prevoos	—
21 Maart 170[illegible]	[illegible]id	Schalk Willemse / Anna Prevoos	Philippe des Pres / Elisabet Prevoos
27 Junij 170[illegible]	[illegible]	Jacques Mouton / Francoise Bevernage	Pierre du Mont / Marie Grignon
9 Augustus 170[illegible]	[illegible]	Estienne Niel / [illegible]agdelena Marais	Claude Marais / Anna Retif
9 Augustus 1705	Elisabeth	[illegible] Niel / [illegible]	Charles Marais / Anne de Ruel
24 Maart 1703	Magdalena	[illegible]	—
2 October 1707	Susanna	H[illegible] / Mar[illegible]	—
29 April 1703	Jacob	Jacob[illegible] / Margarie[illegible]	—
9 Augustus 1705	Margarite	Jacob Villi[illegible] / Margarite Ga[illegible]	—
2 October 1707	Abraham	Jacob Villiers / Margareta Gardiol	—
18 October 1705	Anne	Pierre Villiers / Elisabeth Taillefer	[illegible]ans
19 Junij 1702	Jean Viret	Estienne Viret / Margarita Roux	
15 April 1703	Cicilia	Abraham Vivie / Jakemijn des Pré	
2 November 1704	Isaac	Abraham Vivie / Jaquemine des Prez	
9 December 1703	Gideon	Willem van Zeijl / Christina Van Loveren	
12 December 1706	Pieter	Willem van Zeyl / Christina van Loveren	
28 November 1706	een kind van	een Swartin Chaterina	Catherina Clase
31 Julij 1703	Guillaume	Willem van / Trijn Arme	david Senecal / Magdalena du P[illegible]

'oung he was depraved, and defiled one of
ughter of Dibi—to the just scandal of
'ealed to, did nothing beyond calling
sa, with even a less show of proper
.'ed to Ndlambe attacking Hintsa,
father into the country that
.is b maqiya, and there pitched his
.e nativ f Butterworth. This must
nd to ascert ry, as it was many years
nce resided so fa ir as the Bashee. The
.atter to the resident after Hintsa arrived,
est in such researches, of the Bomvanas,
, dated 9th February, 1888 arranged between
.stituted inquiries with a view to of the eastern
ed by the Tembu tribe in about the
invited the chief Dalindyebo to send to s, and Daba
.est and most intelligent of his men. Four of their terri-
e 7th instant, and after resting from the fatigue of and the
rneys—two of them travelled about seventy miles,— ata."
to furnish a good deal of interesting information. The eldest of
four and the principal spokesman was Nanitwa, who was born
the same year as Gubencuka, the great-grandfather of the present
chief. Another was Radeba, son of Kosiansi, who was regent during
the minority of Gubencuka. The two others were approved elders
possessed of great historical lore.

"After I had explained the object for which I had sought the interview, Nanitwa remarked sententiously 'Ah! history is a great inheritance,' and with that we settled to work.

"There was no such chief as Tzeba, but Daba, the father of Gubencuka, must have been Tembu chief at the time mentioned in the Hon. the Sec. for Native Affairs letter (1752). The clan of the Amaqiya then occupied the country as far as the Kei, the Amagcina lived between the Tsomo and the Kei, and the Amatshatshu between the White and Zwart Keis. No Xosas had then any land to the east of the Kei. Gcaleka and his tribe were living in that part now known as Komgha and Kabusi, and indeed in all the country between the Zwart Kei and the sea, the Great Kei forming their eastern boundary. The Amaqiya clan occupied what are now known as the Butterworth and Kentani districts, and their chief in the days of Daba was Ngxoxo, but although Daba was the paramount, Ngxoxo was in reality of the senior stock, and his branch is now represented

Date	Name	Parents	Witnesses
28 October 1703	Susanna	Christoffel Snijman Margareta de Savoije	Ancelaar van Bengale
21 Maart 1706	Elisabeth	Christoffel Snijman Margarite de Savoije	Jacobus Van As Helena van der Merwe
27 Junij 1706	Marthe	Martinus van Staden Alletta Schalk	Maarten van Staden en syn huysvrou
9 Augustus 1705	Elisabeth	Jacques Teron Marie Jeanne	Philippe des Pres Elisabeth Prevos
9 Augustus 1705	Elisabeth	Francois du Toit Susanna Seugnet	Abraham Blusel Elisabet van Staden
24 Maart 1703	Magdalena	Hercules Verdeau Caterina Hucebos	— —
2 October 1707	Susanna	Hercules Verdeau Marie Catherina	Pierre Jourdan Susanna Taillefer
29 April 1703	Jacob	Jacob Villier Margariet Gardiol	Estienne Viret Elisabet Villiers
9 Augustus 1705	Margarite	Jacob Villiers Margarite Gardiol	Jean Gardiol Elizabet Villiers
2 October 1707	Abraham	Jacob Villiers Margareta Gardiol	Abraham Villiers Susanne Taillefer
18 October 1705	Anne	Pierre Villiers Elisabeth Taillefer	Claude Marais Anne Rousseau
19 Junij 1702	Jean Viret	Estienne Viret Margarita Roux	Abraham de Villiers Margareta Gardiol
15 April 1703	Cicilia	Abraham Vivie Jakemijn des Pré	Hercules des Pré Cornelia Viljon
2 November 1704	Isaac	Abraham Vivie Jaquemine des Prez	Philippe des Prez Anna Marsevene
9 December 1703	Gideon	Willem van Zeijl Christina Van Loveren	— —
12 December 1706	Pieter	Willem van Zeyl Christina van Loveren	— —
28 November 1706	een kind van	een Swartin Chaterina	Catherina Clase
31 Julij 1703	Guillaume	Willem van Trijn Arme	david Senecal Magdalena du Puis

Position of the Tembu tribe in 1752.

In the diary of the exploring expedition of 1752 it is stated that the Tembu tribe occupied the country on the eastern bank of the Kei. See chapter 22. This being contrary to the generally received opinion, the head of the native department requested the chief magistrate of Tembuland to ascertain if there were any traditions of that tribe having once resided so far westward. The chief magistrate referred the matter to the resident magistrate of Umtata, who takes great interest in such researches, and who forwarded the following report, dated 9th February, 1888 :—

"I have instituted inquiries with a view to discovering the position occupied by the Tembu tribe in about the year 1750, and to that end I invited the chief Dalindyebo to send to my office some of the oldest and most intelligent of his men. Four of them arrived on the 7th instant, and after resting from the fatigue of their long journeys—two of them travelled about seventy miles,—I got them to furnish a good deal of interesting information. The eldest of the four and the principal spokesman was Nanitwa, who was born in the same year as Gubencuka, the great-grandfather of the present chief. Another was Radeba, son of Kosiansi, who was regent during the minority of Gubencuka. The two others were approved elders possessed of great historical lore.

"After I had explained the object for which I had sought the interview, Nanitwa remarked sententiously 'Ah! history is a great inheritance,' and with that we settled to work.

"There was no such chief as Tzeba, but Daba, the father of Gubencuka, must have been Tembu chief at the time mentioned in the Hon. the Sec. for Native Affairs letter (1752). The clan of the Amaqiya then occupied the country as far as the Kei, the Amagcina lived between the Tsomo and the Kei, and the Amatshatshu between the White and Zwart Keis. No Xosas had then any land to the east of the Kei. Gcaleka and his tribe were living in that part now known as Komgha and Kabusi, and indeed in all the country between the Zwart Kei and the sea, the Great Kei forming their eastern boundary. The Amaqiya clan occupied what are now known as the Butterworth and Kentani districts, and their chief in the days of Daba was Ngxoxo, but although Daba was the paramount, Ngxoxo was in reality of the senior stock, and his branch is now represented by Sipendu, son of Bacela, who lives in the Mqanduli district, and is still subordinate. The history of the subversion of the lineal descent is interesting, though of no moment here.

"The hostility existing at the time of the explorers' narrative between Gcaleka's people and the Tembus arose out of an ill-advised attack made by Daba on one of his own clans, the Dungwanas. Daba, who was a bad-tempered, quarrelsome man, always seeking some occasion of offence, proposed to eat up the Dungwanas on account of an alleged incivility about milk. They, however, had an able, and as it proved a willing friend, in Rarabe, the brother of Gcaleka, who had married their chief's sister; and their appeal to him brought them such sturdy assistance that all Daba's cattle were taken, and he was induced to sue for peace, and to go as far as Izeli, near King William's Town, where Gcaleka allowed him to build a kraal whilst he came to terms with Rarabe, who was on the other side of the Buffalo river.

"Whilst occupying this humiliating position, a wife of his was one day basking in the sun outside her hut door when one of the captured oxen that Daba had managed to wheedle out of Rarabe ran up to her and licked her. A clearer case of witchcraft could not have been wished for, and Rarabe resolved to decoy Daba still further into the country, and then put an end to him and the malign influence that brought cattle to make such demonstrations. To this end he sent messengers to Daba, who said on his behalf: 'Oh brother, come over into my ground and I will give you a better place for a kraal, between two rivers where the grass is good, and there we can talk over this matter and come to a settlement.' But his scheme had got wind, and a Tembu reported it to Daba, who fled incontinently, leaving behind him even the stock that had been returned. After this Daba entertained feelings of animosity towards all the Xosas, and frequent raids and much ill-feeling were the result, but before the days of Daba the Xosas and the Tembus had been friendly.

"After Daba's death there was a long regency, as Gubencuka was very young. Kosiansi before mentioned was the regent, and during his term a terrible scourge of small-pox decimated the Amaqiya and Amagcina, and left the country almost desert for a time. The Amaxosa under Kawuta quarrelled, as Ndlambe, the son of Rarabe, had a grave cause of complaint against Ngqika, his nephew and heir to the house of Rarabe.

"Whilst still young, Ngqika lived at Kawuta's kraal to learn the way of chiefs, but though young he was depraved, and defiled one of Ndlambe's wives—Tutula, daughter of Dibi—to the just scandal of his uncle. Kawuta, when appealed to, did nothing beyond calling the delinquent names, and Hintsa, with even a less show of proper feeling, espoused his cause. This led to Ndlambe attacking Hintsa, who being worsted moved with his father into the country that small-pox had swept of the Tembu Amaqiya, and there pitched his kraal, somewhere near the present site of Butterworth. This must have been in the early part of this century, as it was many years before Tshaka's armies found their way as far as the Bashee. The remnants of the Amaqiya crossed the Bashee after Hintsa arrived, and settled where they now are, to the north of the Bomvanas, whose introduction from Pondoland had been arranged between Hintsa and Gubencuka.

"This account seems to bear out the occupation of the eastern bank of the Kei by Tembus, as stated by the explorers, and Daba appears to have been their last great chief, as much of their territory was lost to them during the minority of Gubencuka and the early part of his reign.

(Signed) "T. R. Merriman, res. mag. of Umtata."

The Namaqua Captain Afrikaner.

The account given by me of the Namaqua captain Afrikaner being at variance with a large amount of literature concerning him published in London forty or fifty years ago, I give the following extracts from original documents in the archives of the Dutch East India Company at the Cape :—

Meeting of the Council of Policy.

Dingsdag den 20 November 1792.

's Voormiddags, alle praesent.

Is door den Heere Gezachhebber geproduceerd en vervolgens by resumptie geleezen geworden de hier onder geinsereerde Missive van den Landdrost van Stellenbosch, Hendrik Lodewÿk Bletterman, waarvan den inhoude op den 12 deeser dadelyk op den ontfangst bereids voorloopig aan de respective Heeren Leeden des Raads gecommuniceert is geweest. Uit welke Missive gezien zijnde hoe dat den Hottentotten Capitain Africaner en de zynen heeft mogen gelukken in de Streeken door hun bewoond werdende een Hoop Bosjesmans-Hottentotten door dewelke zij te vooren aangevallen en beroofd waaren geworden derwijze te verslaan dat van dezelve Een hondert en derthien Stuks gesneuveld en twintig anderen zyn gevangen genoomen, en dat den gemelde Capitain Africaner, om de evengedagte Roovers nog verder Langs de Zak rivier te kunnen vervolgen alleen begeerd door den Burger Pienaar met eenig kruijt en Lood te moogen werden geadsisteerd.

Zo is vermits uit den verderen inhoude van gemelde Missive blijkt dat den voornoemde Pienaar het gevraagde Pulver en Lood aan handen komt te hebben, en er te bevordering van de veijligheid onzer verre Landwaards in woonende opgezeetenen ten hoogsten aan is geleegen dat die woedende Natie door dewelke zij zints eenigen tijd zo deerlijk ontrust, gekweld, en beroofd zyn geworden, nu eenmaal getemd en tot Stilstand werde gebragt, mitsdien dan ook beslooten den gem : Landdrost dadelijk in antwoord op zijne voorschreeven Missive te doen aanschrijven dat den Raade zeer gaarne wil defereeren aan het verzoek van den Capitain Africaner; weshalven hij Landdrost den voornoemde Pienaar daartoe, hoe eer zoo liever, de noodige qualificatie zal moeten doen toekoomen, met belofte en toezegging, naamens dezen Raade, dat het geen hij Pienaar aan gedagte Capitain Africaner aan kruijt en Lood zal koomen bij te zetten hem 's E. Compagnies weegen zal werden gerestitueerd, waar bij egter zo wel denzelven Pienaar als den Wagtmeester van dat District zullen moeten gelast en aangerecommandeerd werden behoorlijk toe te zien en te zorgen dat door meermelde Capitain Africaner van het alzo aan hem aftelangene kruijt en Lood geen ander dan het hiervooren beschreeven gebruijk worde gemaakt, terwijl deezen Raade voorts gereedelijk toestaat dat de gevangen genoomene Bosjesmans-Hottentotten zullen moogen werden Caabwaards gebragt, en eijndelijk begeert dat door voormelde Landdrost ofte den geenen die hij daartoe zal goedvinden te qualificeeren aan den zo dikwijls geciteerden Capitain Africaner en de zijnen 's Raads byzonder genoegen over hunne Conduites in deezen gehouden zal worden betuijgd.

Aldus Geresolveerd ende Gearresteerd in 't Casteel de Goede Hoop ten dage en jaare voorsz.

J. I. Rhenius,
J. J. le Sueur,
O. G. de Wet,
W. F. van Reede van Oudtshoorn.

Mij praesent :
E. Bergh, Pl. Secret.

Extracts from the proceedings of the council of policy, under date 7th of August 1793 :—

De voormelde Landdrost aan den Heere Gezachhebber sub dato 23 der maand July geschreeven hebbende de volgende Missive :

Aan den Wel Edelen Achtb: Heere Johannes Isaac Rhenius, Gezachhebber des Gouvernements van Cabo de Goede Hoop, en den Ressortte van dien, &c., &c., &c.

WEL EDELE ACHTBAARE HEER,

De Hottentotten Capitain Africaander aan my ses snaphaanen hebbende overgeleevert, met berigt dat hy dezelve van de bastaart Hottentotten welke by Continuatie niet alleen het Vhee de Namacqua Hottentotten komen te rooven, maar zelfs zig onder de Bosjesmans-Hottentotten begeeven, had afgenoomen, en dat hy op zyn retour omstreeks de verblyfplaats van den Burger Guilliam Visagie Aryszoon geleegen aan de overzyde der groote Rivier met zyne zoo genaamde Soldaaten gekoomen zynde, denzelven neevens zyn zoon mitsgaders de aldaar zig ophoudende by my zeer wel bekende zwervende bastaart Hottentotten Donderbos, Pokkebaas, Viool, Siewent, en Cupido, op hem en zyne Soldaten hadden ingeschooten zoo dat er vier ter needer geschooten zynde, hy Africaander twee gekwetste had meede gebragt en hy zelvs neevens zyne overige Manschappen defendeerender wyze gelukkig ontkoomen was, en by die geleegendheid zyn Capiteins stok heeft verlooren, zoo heb ik van myn pligt geagt te zyn U Wel Edele Agtbaare hiervan pligtschuldige kennisse te geeven, zoo wel als dat 't dezelve Africaner is die in den gepasseerden Jaare een meenigte Bosjesmans-Hottentotten heeft doodgeschooten, terwyl ik hem ter overbrenging der voorsz: ses snaphaanen op heeden Caabwaards heb gezonden ten eynde U. Wel Edele Agtb: des gelievende, de voorsz: ses snaphaanen ten gebruyke der aan de Caab dienstdoende Hottentotten op de Wapenkamer zou kunnen laten repareeren dan wel ten voordeele der E. Comp: te verkoopen, met needrig verzoek aan voorsz: Africaander een nieuwe Stok en nodige pas tot zyne terugreyze te willen laten toekomen.

Terwyl voor 't overige de Vryheid neeme met de meeste Eerbied my te noemen,

Wel Edele Achtbaare Heer,

U Wel Edele Achtbaare Ootmoedige Dienaar,

H. L. BLETTERMAN.

Stellenbosch, den 23 July 1793.

Zoo is unanime besloofen den Landdrost Bletterman te injungeeren en te gelasten na 't geen door de zwervende Hottentotten Donderbos, Pokkebaas, Viool, Siewent, en Cupido mogt weezen bedreeven een prompt en allernaauwkeurigst onderzoek te doen, terwyl de 6 Snaphaanen door de Hottentots Capitein Africaner van gemelde zwervende Hottentotten afgenoomen zo by de Negotie boeken deezes Gouvernements als by de Wapenkamer zullen moeten worden ingenoomen en verantwoord.

J. I. Rhenius,
J. J. le Sueur,
O. G. de Wet,
W. F. van Reede van Oudtshoorn,
E. Bergh.

My present,
G. F. Goetz, Secret[s].

INDEX.

clergyman of the Drakenstein congregation in April 1731, 102; dies in June 1736, 102

Hats: are first made at the Cape by Isaac Taillefer, 72

Heads of the Cape government, succession of: Simon van der Stel, governor, from 1 June 1691 to 11 February 1699; Wilhem Adriaan van der Stel, governor, from 11 February 1699 to 3 June 1707; Johan Cornelis d'Ableing, secunde acting as governor, from 3 June 1707 to 1 February 1708; Louis van Assenburgh, governor, from 1 February 1708 to 27 December 1711; Willem Helot, secunde acting as governor, from 28 December 1711 to 28 March 1714; Maurits Pasques de Chavonnes, governor, from 28 March 1714 to 8 September 1724; Jan de la Fontaine, secunde acting as governor, from 8 September 1724 to 25 February 1727; Pieter Gysbert Noodt, governor, from 25 February 1727 to 23 April 1729; Jan de la Fontaine, secunde acting as governor, from 24 April 1729 to 8 March 1730, governor, from 8 March 1730 to 31 August 1737; Adriaan van Kervel, governor, from 31 August 1737 to 19 September 1737; Daniel van den Henghel, fiscal independent acting as governor, from 20 September 1737 to 14 April 1739; Hendrik Swellengrebel, governor, from 14 April 1739 to 27 February 1751; Ryk Tulbagh, from 27 February 1751 to 11 August 1771; Joachim van Plettenberg, secunde acting as governor, from 12 August 1771 to 18 May 1774, governor, from 18 May 1774 to 14 February 1785; Cornelis Jacob van de Graaff, governor, from 14 February 1785 to 24 June 1791; Johan Isaac Rhenius, secunde acting as governor, from 24 June 1791 to 3 July 1792; Sebastiaan Cornelis Nederburgh and Simon Hendrik Frykenius, commissioners-general, from 3 July 1792 to 2 September 1793; Abraham Josias Sluysken, commissioner-general, from 2 September 1793 to 16 September 1795.

Helot, Willem: in 1710 assumes duty as secunde, 53; in December 1711, on the death of Mr. Van Assenburgh, is chosen to act provisionally as head of the government, 56; in May 1714 is suspended from duty, 65, and is dismissed from the Company's service, 65

Hemmy, Otto Luder: in April 1774 assumes duty as secunde, 221; dies in January 1777, 226

van den Henghel, Daniel: is appointed fiscal independent, 94; assumes duty in March 1731, 108; upon the death of Mr. van Kervel is chosen by lot to act provisionally as head of the government, 109; is required by the directors to confine himself to the duty of fiscal independent, 109; returns to Europe in 1741, 109

High court of justice: is remodelled in 1786, 273

Holland, Dutch ship: is wrecked in False Bay, 293

van Hoorn, Joan, recently governor-general of Netherlands India: in 1710 visits the Cape as commissioner, 52

Hop, Hendrik, captain of burgher militia: in 1761 leads an exploring expedition into Great Namaqualand, 164

Hop: experiment in the cultivation of, 7

Horak, J. A.: in April 1749 is appointed landdrost of Swellendam, 144; in 1766 leaves the Company's service and becomes a burgher, 169

Horses: are first exported from South Africa in 1769, 175

Lightning Source UK Ltd.
Milton Keynes UK
UKHW021451080720
366217UK00009B/1109

9 780341 878629